Burning Center, Porous Borders

Burning Center, Porous Borders

The Church in a Globalized World

ELEAZAR S. FERNANDEZ

WIPF & STOCK · Eugene, Oregon

BURNING CENTER, POROUS BORDERS
The Church in a Globalized World

Wipf & Stock
An Imprint of Wipf and Stock Publishers
199 W. 8th Ave., Suite 3
Eugene, OR 97401
www.wipfandstock.com

ISBN 13:978-1-61097-426-4

Manufactured in the U.S.A.

Contents

Acknowledgments

JOURNEY, COMPANION, AND CONSPIRACY (breathing together) are some of the metaphors that pervade the pages of this work. My journey has been blessed by companions, some of whom are no longer with us, the living. During my writing of this book, I lost two significant persons in my life: my father (Florentino Fernandez) and father-in-law (Jesus Aberia). As is often the case, only in hindsight did I realize how they have influenced my thoughts. Because of the duration that it took to write this book and the many places I visited and the people I encountered, my list of companions is long as well as widely spread. Given this, I may not be able to give due recognition to all. I trust, however, that I will be forgiven for this limitation.

Journeying with my family has been full of challenges and blessings. I am deeply grateful to my wife Jo and to my daughters Zarine and Joelle for bearing with me as I struggled to give shape to this project. As always, there is the challenge of balancing between family responsibility and scholarly work, which I am not sure I have done well. If there is one thing I can be sure of, it is that I have experienced the prodigal grace, kindness, and forgiveness of my family. This experience, I venture to say, has taught me the difficult lesson of learning to forgive myself for failing to accomplish self-imposed deadlines. I hope I can be forgiving of others as well.

My journey-companions in giving birth to this project, without a doubt, extend beyond my immediate family. As ideas continued to come and crowd my head, often faster than I could write, there were times when I wished I had someone who could arrange my thoughts on the page. I did not have one, but I could not imagine arriving at this point without people who helped me in the writing process. I would like to thank Pamela Wynn, for her copy editing skills, and to Karen Hering, Gage Church, and Zoe Kuester for helping me clean-up and improve my writing. Dale Dobias and Penny Truax provided significant assistance in locating library resources. I also need to mention

Adam Pfuhl and Deb Olsen for technical support and to Bradford Bates, Douglas Abbott, and Joseph Agpaoa for their aide in checking my sources.

I have been blessed with scholars, friends, colleagues, and students who engaged with me in some of the issues raised here and who read whole or parts of the manuscript, such as Peter Monkres, Lester Ruiz, Jayakiran Sebastian, Liberato Bautista, Bradford Bates, Daniel Arvidson-Hicks, Tom Liddle, Gary Kwong, and Don Christensen. I would like to mention as well my colleagues at United Theological Seminary of the Twin Cities who engaged me in a lively conversation that focused on one of the chapters of this book as part of my sabbatical report. I am thankful in particular to our dean, Richard Weis, for his understanding and support throughout the years. Also noteworthy of my appreciation are my students both within and outside the United States who have been my interlocutors and resource of ideas. They will recognize themselves in the pages of this book.

It would be difficult to imagine having arrived at this point if my teaching and speaking engagements did not feed my writing. These are true of my courses at United Theological Seminary of the Twin Cities, particularly Global Encounters at our Doorsteps as well as Reimagining the Church in a Globalized World. I had, likewise, an opportunity to hone some of my ideas for this book when I taught a course (Reimagining the Church in a Globalized World) at the Theological School, Drew University. My deep appreciation goes to Elizabeth Tapia of the Center for Christianities in Global Context for the invitation and generous hospitality. A similar opportunity to test ideas came when I taught an intersession course that dealt with diaspora and empire at Pacific School of Religion. My appreciation belongs to Fumitaka Matsuoka and Deborah Lee of PANA/Pacific School of Religion for the invitation and to the generous hospitality of Jeffery Acido, Israel Alvaran, and Wilson de Ocera. My teaching experience at the Universite Protestante D'Africque Centrale, Faculte De Theologie Protestante De Yaoundé (Yaoundé, Cameroon) provided a similar opportunity to test and develop ideas.

In addition, several speaking engagements aided me in articulating the ideas in this book. My early articulations on globalization and the church began with an address on globalization and its terror delivered at United Theological Seminary in the wake of the September 11, 2001 terrorist attack in the U. S. This was followed by several speaking engagements as the years progressed: a keynote address at the Joining Hands Against Hunger event in Tacoma (Washington); a lecture on globalization and terrorism in San Pedro Sula (Honduras); a series of lectures on the church and our globalized world at the Center for Progressive Christianity (Plymouth Congregational Church, Minnesota); a lecture on Filipino diaspora for the National Association of Filipino American United Methodist (NAFAUM) in Virginia; a couple of lectures on the church and ministry in the era of globalization at the United Church of Christ in the Philippines' General Assembly (Digos City, Philippines); a lecture on globalization and hunger (at a RELUFA event in Yaoundé, Cameroon); globalization and the changing demographics (Synod of Lakes and Prairies of the Presbyterian Church, USA); church and global partnership (Wisconsin Conference, United Church of Christ, USA); and global migration and the church in Reichenbach, Germany, to name a few.

The gestation and articulation of my thoughts took longer than I expected. All of the events and other encounters, too lengthy to mention, did not happen without individuals who helped me in various ways. I would like to express my gratitude to Lynn Connette, Christi Boyd, Valéry Nodem, Timothée Bouba Mbima, Emmanuel Anya Anyambod, Sally Narr, Susan (Elli) Elliott, Bruce and Linda Hanson, Luis Caballero, Aquilino 'Pong' Javier, Zuriel Tiempo, Miguel Udtohan, Marma Urbano, Mark Yackel-Juleen, Mark Molina, and David Moyer. Further, I am indebted to those individuals who helped me during my research travel to Italy and the Netherlands: Noel Tintero, Wennie Flores, Fr. Teody Holgado, Fr. Aris Dospueblos, Eric and Bethe Aquino, Cesar Taguba, and Grace Punongbayan. Christian Amondson of Wipf & Stock also deserves my gratitude for working with me in the publication process.

As the going got rough, I am fortunate to have friends to share stories and laughter over meals. Members of the Philippine Study Group of Minnesota, Dan and Kaelene Arvidson-Hicks, and Peter Monkres continue to rekindle my commitment to the land of my birth—the Philippines. When I needed inspiration and had to re-assure myself that writing makes a difference, Hans and Sannah (son and daughter of Dan and Kaelene) introduced me to the children's story *Frederick*, by Leo Lionni. Lionni's story of a family of mice that survived the long and severe winter because of the nourishing stories of Frederick the mouse has been a source of inspiration in the long writing process. It assured me that stories do matter and, in particular, my story.

Thank you all for blessing me with your companionship. May our journeys be a blessing to the wider world—to our contemporaries near and far, to those who have gone before us, and to those who are yet to come.

Eleazar S. Fernandez
303 Liberty St. NE
Fridley, Minnesota
Summer 2010

Introduction

Every generation is confronted with challenges that create a significant impact, for better or for worse, on its self-understanding and ways of living in the world. This seems to be widely recognized to the point that every generation is tempted to think that theirs is the most challenging time in history. What is of paramount importance, however, is not that some historical moments are more challenging than others, but that every generation must face squarely, creatively, and responsibly its own challenges. For those of my generation, I say that what is crucial is for us to embrace the reality that this is *our* time and *our* challenge. *Our* time, to appropriate the enduring lines of Charles Dickens in *A Tale of Two Cities*, can be the "best of times" and the "worst of times."[1] What is decisive is *how* we respond to the challenges of our times. How we respond to the challenges makes a difference as to whether the challenges are turned into opportunities for exploring greater well-being or occasions for fortress building and closing all possible windows of vulnerability.

Responding creatively to the challenges posed by our always-changing context is, no doubt, the preferred response, but the general trend seems to be moving in the opposite direction. Even as there is much hokum about change, everyone is for change. If we study it closely, however, the most common response to new challenges or change is to do business as usual. Individuals and communities may be bustling with activities, but those activities are mostly along the lines of business as usual. It may even be that busyness is an expression of a failure to understand or to face the depth of the challenges. Of course, there are worse responses than business as usual. A common temptation is to cling dogmatically to the "good old days" or the cherished past and oppose anything that questions the past's authority. There is also the temptation to create a fortress of various sorts when one's sense of security is

---

1. Dickens, *A Tale of Two Cities*, 7.

threatened: hearts constrict, imagination shrinks, and walls of fear and division rise. Finally, another common response is finding a scapegoat. An individual or a society avoids facing the real challenge by blaming someone else for the crisis.

Perhaps part of the reason why a creative response is slow in coming is that it is often counter-instinctual. Christian communities can harvest grains of insight from whitewater rafting and rappelling. In whitewater rafting, when one's raft heads toward a big rock, the right move is not to steer away from the rock. Instead, one must lean toward the rock. In doing so, the raft is pushed away from the rock. Similar insight applies to rappelling, although the moves are different. Instead of leaning closer to the rock to avoid being thrown into the deep ravine (the danger), one must lean away from the rock. Whether leaning toward the rock (whitewater rafting) or leaning away from the rock (rappelling), the main point is not to let our false sense of safety and security kill us. To survive as well as thrive, we must embrace the danger and do what may look suicidal. Embracing the danger is, of course, easier to say than to do. In our efforts to avoid danger, our churches are walking on the path of spiritual tragedy: it is the tragedy of failing to live out our calling; it is the tragedy of failing to participate creatively in the mission of the church.

If we are to grow and broaden our horizons, we need to take risks rather than simply remain in the security of our small world. I am reminded of a revelatory event that happened in one of the Philippine immersion trips that I routinely lead to fulfill a global justice course requirement at United Theological Seminary of the Twin Cities. In the house of one of the fisherfolks I noticed an aquarium with very small fish, the size of a toothpick. I asked our hosts what kind of fish they were. The fisherfolks of Laguna de Bay told our group that the fish (*tilapia*) in the wider lake (the siblings of the *tilapia* in the aquarium) already weighed around two pounds. There was a big difference in size between the fish in the aquarium and those that were out in the lake. I turned to my students and explained the parable: just like the fish, if we stay within our aquariums we will not grow; our world will remain small and narrow.[2] On the other hand, if we take the risk and venture

---

2. This happened in Laguna de Bay. The students who were with me were Karen Aitkens, Sally Mann, and Daniel Narr.

into the wider world, we open ourselves to the possibility of making our hearts and our imagination as large as the world.

Porous hearts, imaginative minds, and daring spirits are what we need to face the challenges of our globalized society. My aim for this project is to create a discourse that faces our challenges with creativity, imagination, and commitment to greater well-being. In this project I attempt to articulate a way of responding to our current challenges that is faithful to the heart of the Christian tradition and creatively responsive to our context. More particularly, I seek to articulate a way of being a church that faces its challenges with the creativity of imagination, the faithfulness of saints, the radicalness of love, the boldness of courage, and the tenacity of hope. We know that the church, like other human institutions, has not always embodied creativity and faithfulness when responding to challenges. Nonetheless, in spite of all its failings—particularly at times behaving as a force of reaction—it is also an institution and a community that is open to creative transformation. Its treasure trove is a rich and powerful tradition of radical love and openness, generous hospitality, and the courage to take risks and let go. Guided by the wisdom of the crucified God, it does not measure itself to the conventional wisdom of worldly success. Birthed by and dwelt in by the Spirit (wind) that blows wherever it wills, the church is not imprisoned by the regimes of truth established by the powerful of this world and is free to move at the Spirit's leading. Inspired by the crucified Jesus, it has the courage to take risks even in the face of death for the sake of subverting death-giving ways of thinking, dwelling, and acting. In short, while the church does not always live up to its promise, it has the resources and is poised in the direction of creative, imaginative, and faithful response to the challenges around it. Other ingredients for developing creative imagination are needed, but they are complementary to what I have just articulated.

The presence of this important tradition at the heart of the Christian faith is not, however, a guarantee that everyone will retrieve it in a liberating way. Every act of retrieval of tradition is already an act of interpretation. A common interpretation (retrieval) of tradition is that of a deposit made long ago from which withdrawals are taken from time to time, but the central objective is to keep the principal deposit secure. The main posture here is to safeguard, preserve, or protect the tradition, and to ensure that it is handed down faithfully. Of course faithfully handing down a tradition is not as neutral as it seems. It is always dictated by an agenda. Nonetheless, there is a different way of understanding tradition. Tradition is a living corpus that exists in the present and is a product of continuing interpretation and re-appropriation by succeeding generations. In contrast to the first interpretation, the past is retrieved not simply to be handed to the present, but the past is retrieved as part of the continuing process of interpretation. It is for this reason that it is called a living tradition. Bishop Thomas Roberts's aphorism offers a helpful distinction: "Tradition is the living faith of the dead, traditionalism is the dead faith of the living."[3]

Anthony de Mello's story of "The Guru's Cat" further illuminates the nature of traditionalism. As the story goes, an ashram cat would get in the way and distract worshipers in their evening worships. In response, the guru ordered that the cat be tied during worship. After the guru died the cat continued to be tied during evening worship. When the cat died, another cat was brought to the ashram to be tied during evening worship. As the years passed by, the guru's disciples wrote scholarly treatises about the liturgical importance of tying up a cat during worship.[4]

Traditionalism is an attempt to bring or repeat a critical event of the past into the present so as to cage the present in the past. Ironically, this attempt to bring and repeat the past in the present is one that is disconnected from its roots because it is removed from the soil that birthed it in the first place. Traditionalism is repetition without roots to the founding experience or to the present context. Without roots in the past or the present, it is the "dead faith of the living." Traditionalism does not bring life; on the contrary, it brings death. It brings death to creative appropriation in the present.

We are a part of a living tradition. It is a part of us even if we are not consciously aware of it. We participate in it. We are creatures of tradition. The metaphor of a footpath may be useful. Stephen Bachelor speaks of a path as a "witness to the presence of creatures like ourselves . . . Even if the path is deserted, even if no one has passed by in days, we are reconnected to the human (and animal) community." [5] A footpath witnesses to those who have already walked on it. It means that there were those who have gone before us. We are not alone in our journey:

3. Roberts, cited in Lakeland, *Theology and Critical Theory*, 143.

4. de Mello, *The Song of the Bird*, 63.

5. Bachelor, "The Other Enlightenment Project," 115.

we belonged to a cloud of witnesses long before we took the first steps of our journey. And, to continue the metaphor of a path, "simply by walking along it, we too maintain it for those who will come later. Being on a path implies both indebtedness to those who have preceded us and responsibility for those who will follow."[6]

How do we stand in relation to the tradition of which we are a part? Douglas Ottati offers an answer: "To stand in the living tradition is to participate in a community that is consciously informed by its common memory, actively engaged in the realities of the present, vitally concerned about its future direction, and genuinely responsive to personally creative acts of appropriation."[7] To put it differently, to stand in a living tradition is to participate in the dynamic process of interpretation (*actus tradendi*) of the received or deposited tradition (*traditum*) in light of the realities and challenges of the present.[8]

Generating the process of interpretation of our tradition is a crucial task if we are to re-imagine the church. The common knee-jerk response is to forget tradition because of its association with the past. But the past is not even past; it is very much present. If we are not consciously aware of the past and its formative presence, the more we are shaped or imprisoned by it. We need to be consciously aware and critically engaged with our tradition and not simply sort out what we think is useful and what is not. At a more fundamental level, we cannot even imagine the future and respond creatively to the challenges of the present apart from it. Critical engagement with tradition is necessary for developing roots and wings: roots that draw nourishment from the history of our community as well as wings to soar and imagine new possibilities.[9] Without deep roots, our imagination cannot soar to new heights. Memory and tradition are not against imagination. Only those who remember can imagine new possibilities. This creative relationship of imagination and tradition (memory) can be likened to good poetry. Following Nobel laureate Seamus Heaney, a good poem is one that "allows [us] to have [our] feet on the ground and [our] head in the air simultaneously."[10]

6. Ibid.

7. Ottati, "What it Means to Stand in a Living Tradition," 86.

8. Hodgson, *Winds of the Spirit*, 22.

9. See McDaniel, *With Roots and Wings*, 23.

10. Cited in Sweet, *The Church in Emerging Culture*, 51.

The story of a boy mastmaker illustrates this point. Once upon a time the only son of a family of thread makers was orphaned. He was adopted into the tribe of nomad weavers but, due to hardships, they had to sell him to a family of shipbuilders. The shipbuilders trained the boy in their trade of mastmaking. While on a business voyage for the mastmakers, the same young man—once an orphaned spinner and weaver and now a mastmaker—was shipwrecked on a primitive island. The people on this primitive island were waiting for the fulfill-ment of a promise that God would someday send a foreigner who would help them save their religious treasures from the harsh climate of the island. Faced with a difficult challenge, the young man came to an integrated understanding of his past and his future. Out of his memory as a spinner of thread he made rope. He remembered his life as a weaver, and so he made cloth. He took the memory of his experi-ence as a mastmaker and out of that experience made long, strong poles. And, out of these memories (spinner, weaver, and mastmaker) he gave his vision of a tent a physical reality that saved the religious treasures of the people on this primitive island.[11] Without memory (tradition), imagination is an orphan.

Having dealt with the significant role of tradition (memory) in re-lation to imagination, I now explore another crucial angle for the work of reimagining the church. If imagination cannot fly without tradition, it cannot walk without contextual grounding. Without taking the con-text seriously, the memory of imagination remains nostalgic. It is only in serious engagement with the context that imagination becomes cre-atively responsive. It is only in relation to its context that imagination acquires its power to grab people's attention and serious consideration. By context I do not mean simply the stage (setting) in which our ideas are to be in-acted or the passive receiver of our interpretations and ac-tions. Context also has an active side: it shapes how we see the world.[12] Understanding the dual dynamics of context is critical. Our awareness of the contextual imprint of our thinking, feeling, and acting is criti-cal on various grounds: epistemologically, theologically, and politically. Along with the recognition of the contextual nature of our thinking, we need to affirm the notion of context as the setting in which we need to respond as religious and moral agents, both individually and collec-

11. See Chittister, *Winds of Change*, 35–36.
12. Kammer, *Ethics and Liberation*, 28–30.

tively. The context calls for our response. Specifically, it is the setting in which we render our missiological and ministerial response.

If imagination cannot soar without tradition (memory) and cannot walk without context, it is aimless without another dimension: mission. In *Alice's Adventures in Wonderland* the young Alice asked the cat, "Would you tell me, please, which way I ought to go from here?" The cat answers, "That depends a good deal on where you want to get to."[13] Where do we want to get to as a church? What is the church's mission? Reimagining the church demands not only a critical engagement with its tradition and its context, it also demands a critical engagement and articulation of its mission. Mission, in spite of, or maybe because of, the many volumes of books on ecclesiology, is still easily confused with ministry because mission is commonly associated with what the church does. What the church does cannot be divorced from its mission, but its mission is specifically distinct from what the church does or is doing in the world. Mission is not simply another task that the people of God must do, but it is at the very core of its existence. Mission is the church's self-understanding of who it is and what it is called to be. It is the "orienting horizon" toward which the church struggles and hopes. Whether overseas or within our neighborhood, mission is not so much about what we do as it is about our response to God's loving and saving acts in the world.

While mission suggests looking-forward, direction, and focus, it should not be confused with linear thinking and tunnel-vision-dogged-determination. My use of the term "orienting horizon" signals my way of seeing mission that includes multiple ways of thinking, seeing, and acting. Orienting-horizon suggests having an expansive view as well as what John Paul Lederach calls "serendipitous thinking" (sideways-looking eyesight), which he names as "the single greatest antidote to static politics and tunnel vision." Serendipitous thinking, continues Lederach, is "the wisdom of recognizing and then moving with the energetic flow of the unexpected . . . Serendipity requires peripheral vision, not just forward-looking eyesight."[14]

With mission informed by multiple ways of seeing, I now proceed to link it with ministry. Our understanding of mission impacts our notion of ministry. Or, to put it differently, the church's ministry is defined

13. Caroll, *Alice's Adventures in Wonderland*, 81.

14. Lederach, *The Moral Imagination*, 115.

by our understanding of mission. Ministry flows from our understanding of mission, even as mission is re-articulated in light of our concrete experiences in the various ministries of the church. Ministry, in other words, is the church's concrete embodiment of its participation in God's mission. Mission and ministry must be in congruence if the church is to move in the right direction and if it is to be effective in its ministry. All ministries of the church must be carried out in the spirit of mission and of its mission. Ministry is missional.

In short, our understanding of mission shapes or informs our understanding and practice of the ministry. Without mission, ministry has no direction; conversely, without ministry, mission has no flesh and blood. Moreover, even as mission defines ministry, the practice of ministry clarifies our understanding of mission. But mission and ministry will only make sense in relation to context. We cannot evade the context if we are to understand the mission and ministry of the church. Missional ministries can only embody faithfully and relevantly the salvific message if they are grounded on an accurate reading of their context. A sound reading is a missiological and ministerial demand. It is a practical and theological necessity.

A story from Tanzania, Africa, underscores the crucial importance of understanding the context and the harm that is often done by those with good intentions:

> The rainy season that year had been the strongest ever, and the river had broken its banks. There were floods everywhere, and the animals were running up into the hills. The floods came so fast that many drowned except the lucky monkeys who used their proverbial agility to climb into the treetops. They looked down on the surface of the water where the fish were swimming and gracefully jumping out of the water as if they were the only ones enjoying the devastating flood.
>
> One of the monkeys saw the fish and shouted to his companion: "Look down, my friend, look at those poor creatures. They are going to drown. Do you see how they struggle in the water?" "Yes," said the other monkey. "What a pity! Probably they were late in escaping to the hills because they seem to have no legs. How can we save them?" "I think we must do something. Let's go close to the edge of the flood were the water is not deep enough to cover us, and we can help them to get out."

So the monkeys did just that. They started catching the fish, but not without difficulty. One by one, they brought them out of the water and put them carefully on the dry land. After a short time there was a pile of fish lying on the grass motionless. One of the monkeys said, "Do you see? They were tired, but now they are just sleeping and resting. Had it not been for us, my friend, all these poor people without legs would have drowned."

The other monkey said: "They were trying to escape from us because they could not understand our good intentions. But when they wake up they will be grateful because we have brought them to salvation."[15]

Like the monkeys who wanted to save the fish, Christians are not bereft of good intentions. Our ministries have always been undergirded by good intentions. Good intentions, however, often result in bad actions when we answer questions that are not even asked by the people we are trying to help and, much more so, when we confuse our answers to their questions. Reinhold Niebuhr makes the claim that "there is nothing more irrelevant than the answer to an unasked question."[16] Extending Niebuhr's point, Robert McAfee Brown argues that "confusing the question one has been asked with the question one is prepared to answer is equally irrelevant."[17] Hence, before we offer our answers, let us focus our attention to the questions that are being generated by our contexts.

Relevant to reimagining the church is casting our interpretations of our context in light of a significant phenomenon of our times: globalization. It is not my intention to write another book on globalization. Instead, what I would like to do is re-imagine the church (ecclesiology) in light of its challenges. In other words, this project is primarily about re-imagining ecclesiology. To pursue this project, I critique globalization's overarching narrative and multiple dimensions or expressions as well as name the challenges that they pose for the church. The chapters of this book highlight the challenges and my attempt to articulate what it means to be a church when we take the challenges with seriousness and creativity.

15. Healey and Sybertz, *Towards an African Narrative Theology*, 136–37.

16. Niebuhr, cited in Brown, *Gustavo Gutiérrez*, 85.

17. Brown, Ibid.

Chapter 1—Linking the Global and the Local: Dimensions and Consequences of Globalization—presents in a broad sense my interpretation of the globalization phenomenon and its various dimensions or expressions. Broadly, globalization refers to the reality that the global is lived locally, and the local is lived globally. We live in a globalized world. Globalization is not new, but it has reached a new height with its accompanying challenges and possibilities. Globalization has various dimensions: technology, economics, media, militarization, medicine, migration, ecology, and religion.

One aspect to which I have given separate attention is militarization, war, and global terror. This is the focus of chapter 2—Terrorism: A New Season of Globalization. In this chapter I interpret militarization and the war on terror as part of predatory globalization. Militarization is not merely an instrument of economic interest but is at the heart of the predatory global economy. It is an expression of the economization of war. There are, of course, various contributing factors and dimensions to militarization, terrorism and counterterrorism, and various forms of violence around the world. No doubt religion is in the thick of the conflicts, particularly on terrorism and counterterrorism, even if it is only a part of the larger dynamics.

Chapter 3—The Church in the Midst of Globalization: Reorienting the Church—presents my attempt to re-orient or offer a compass for the church vis-à-vis the temptations and distortions that globalization poses, particularly the global market. We not only live in a "market economy," we live in a "market society" in which "market-based values define the atmosphere in which we live and move and have our being."[18] The church itself is not outside of the influence of the global market even as it continues to claim itself as the "christified" portion of the world. We can discern the influence of the market in many aspects of the church life. Without a clear orientation, the church can easily be gobbled up by the predatory global market and colonized by the values of the market society. Articulating the church's mission or reason for being is the most basic approach to finding its orientation. I adopt this approach and orientate mission in light of the reign of God. Confronted by the worldview, values, and idols of the market society, chapter 3 reminds the church to "strive first for the kingdom of God and his righteousness, and all these things will be given to you as well" (Mt 6:33).

---

18. McDaniel, *Living from the Center*, 41.

After the task of re-orienting the church in light of God's *basileia*, chapter 4—The Church as a Translocal (Glocal) Community: Catholicity and Mission in a Globalized World—takes the challenge of globalization in relation to the catholicity or universality of the church, particularly through the concept known as "glocalization." By "glocalization" I do not mean simply that the global has become local, which is a unidirectional way of seeing. Rather, it is the simultaneous, multidirectional, and multidimensional interweaving of the global and the local.[19] One does not exist apart from the other. Taking this concept seriously, how shall we articulate the catholicity of the church without perpetuating hegemonic and homogenizing practices? How can the church be catholic/universal while honoring the particular? How shall we articulate the relationship between the universal church and local churches? What does the shift of the church's vitality from the global North to the global South mean for our understanding and practice of mission? These are some of the questions that chapter 4 seeks to address.

Chapter 5—The Church as a Community with a Burning Center and Porous Borders: Naming our Globalized Spiritual Crisis—critiques globalization in relation to the spiritual crisis of our times of which the church itself is a part. When global wealth soars to an enormous height while at the same time leaving many to wallow and die of poverty, without a doubt something is terribly amiss. When communication technologies that make it possible for people to communicate and dialogue are used also to disseminate false information and foment hatred, without a doubt we are in the midst of a deep crisis. When nation-states spend more for policing dissent, prison systems, and armaments of hostilities over against education and health care, we are in a deep crisis. This chapter argues that our crisis is at heart a spiritual one. With this premise, it attempts to articulate an ecclesiology that is primarily a spiritual community—a community with a burning center and porous borders.

Following the chapter on the church as a community birthed, nurtured, and empowered by the Spirit (chapter 5) is my account of the church in response, primarily, to the challenges posed by the economy. Chapter 6—The Church as a Household of Life Abundant: Another Economy is Possible—opens with a critique of the economy under the

19. See Van Engen, "The Glocal Church," 159.

era of predatory globalization and its impact on people's lives and the ecosystem, particularly to the most vulnerable. It attempts to articulate an ecclesiology that is a symbol and an embodiment of alternative economics, one that is egalitarian and ecologically healthy. The egalitarian meals that Jesus performed and the eucharist are helpful in giving a picture of alternative economics. I refer to this church that seeks to embody alternative economics as a household of life abundant. This church embodies the alternative *oikonomia* (economics) in the various aspects of its life, empowering in particular the members of the Body of Christ to resist the values of the market, consumerism and classism, and to advocate for a just and ecological economics.

Chapter 7—The Church as a Community of Peacebuilders: Exorcising Globalized Violence and Terror—is my account of the church as a community committed to building peace. Building on my critique of the globalization of war, militarization, and terrorism from chapter 2, I now explore the place of the church in the global conflicts. Where is the church? What is it saying and doing? Amidst the rhetoric of global village, global walls are rising, hearts are constricting, and imagination is shrinking. In many instances, the church has been captive to narrow nationalism or identified with ethnic groups. This situation calls for a new way of being a church. This is the main direction and task of chapter 7. In this chapter, I articulate a way of being a church whose main identity is that of a community of peacebuilders and whose mission is to pursue peace. Along this line, I play with metaphors of the church as a wall-buster, bridge-builder, and peacemaker. Moreover, this chapter pursues peace as a form of spirituality.

Another challenge that globalization poses is the diaspora phenomenon. Diaspora is, of course, not new. The diaspora that I speak of, however, is a massive global phenomenon that is primarily a creation of the predatory global market. The diaspora of people all over the world has intensified at an alarming rate in recent years. The United Nations Department of Economic and Social Affairs reports that in 2005, 3 percent of the world's population (191 million people) lived in a country other than the country in which they were born. One-third of this population moved from the so-called developing countries or the global South to the global North; one-third moved from the global South to other nations of the global South; and another third originated from countries of the global North.[20] Included in the statistics of global diaspora or migration are those categorized by the United Nations as a "population of concern" such as refugees, asylum-seekers, internally displaced persons (IDPs), and stateless persons.[21] The diaspora phenomenon poses some daunting challenges as well as new and creative possibilities. How shall we respond as a world community in general and as communities of faith in particular? How shall we respond as a church to the challenge of the diaspora-strangers in our midst? Articulating a way of being a church in response to the diaspora-stranger in our midst is the main task of chapter 8—The Church as a Community of Radical Hospitality: Diaspora and the Strangers in Our Midst.

Chapter 9—The Church as a Community of the Earth (Green) Spirit: The Challenge of the Ecological Crisis—calls us to take seriously a pressing global challenge of our times: the ecological crisis. The earth is suffering from an ecological crisis of global magnitude, and we are suffering with the earth. This statement should not, however, be naively interpreted to mean that we all have suffered evenly—no, not at all. We should not forget that many of the ecological disasters have long affected the poor neighborhoods. Worse, the marginalized communities have been the target of "environmental terrorism" or "radioactive terrorism" by the elite and powerful nations. With this strong caveat, I insist that the ecological crisis is *our* crisis. Integral to this crisis is a crisis of faith-praxis: failure of theological worldview and Christian practice. If the Christian faith-praxis is part of the problem, it can—and has to—be a part of the solution. For it to be a part of the solution (ecological healing), it must detoxify itself from toxic habits of theologizing related to ecology. Beyond the task of detoxification, Christian faith-praxis must articulate a way of being a church that ushers in the flourishing of the web of life. To accomplish this task, I have used the earth (green) Spirit—the same Spirit that inspired or gave birth to the

20. United Nations, "International Migration and Development."

21. United Nations High Commissioner for Refugees (UNHCR) in its 2006 *Statistical Yearbook* reported 9.9 million refugees. Most of these refugees are from troubled spots of the world such as Afghanistan, Iraq, Sudan, Somalia, Democratic Republic of Congo, and Burundi. Some of the refugees may also fall in the category of stateless persons, but stateless persons are different from refugees. Statelessness may be the direct result of discriminatory practices against certain ethnic groups in the population. In the same document, UNHCR reported 5.8 million as stateless persons.

(red) Pentecost—to articulate the direction and substance of this green ecclesiology and, consequently, earth-wise congregations.

From the ecological challenge I call on the church to respond to another pressing issue, the global health crisis. Chapter 10—The Church as a Community of Mending-Healers: Mending the Sickly State of Global Health—names the global health crisis of our times and locates it in the context of the predatory global market's assault on health. Thousands die every day of preventable diseases and for lack of medical care. What is heart-rending and appalling is that this is happening when our medical and technological capability has reached a certain level of sophistication that is more than adequate to respond to the need. What is heart-rending and appalling is that these deaths are happening when huge pharmaceutical corporations, health insurance companies, and health maintenance organizations (HMOs) are reaping massive profits. In chapter 10, I contend that what we are seeing are only symptoms of a deeper malady—a deeper pathology. Our body politic is sick—terribly sick! A sick body politic undermines the health of its people and makes them sick. Sadly, the church is not an innocent bystander in this context. Christian theologies and practices have contributed to the making and perpetuation of this sick body politic. So, what does it mean to be a church in this context? Responding to this question is the main task of chapter 10. Similar to the previous chapter, I execute a double move: deconstruction (detoxifying unhealthy theological ideas) and construction of a way of being a church that supports holistic health and embodies the mending-healer identity in its ministry.

Another major challenge that the church in a globalized world needs to address creatively and responsibility is the continuing vitality of religion even after the secularist-modernist assault, the significant influence of religion in movements and upheavals around the world, and the increasing encounter of people of various religious faiths. Without negating that life-giving encounters happen between people of different faiths daily (unfortunately they do not become news headlines), religion is in the thick of many worldwide conflicts. As Hans Küng powerfully puts it, there is "[n]o world peace without peace between the religions."[22] The church needs to re-examine itself in relation to the presence and claims of people of other religious faiths. How can

---

22. Küng, *Global Responsibility*, xv.

we be faithful and creatively responsive to the challenge of a religiously plural and politically explosive context? How shall we articulate mission and ministry? Can we be open and passionate with our deep convictions without putting down others? Chapter 11—The Church as a Community of Dialogians of Faith: Living in a Religiously Diverse World—wrestles with and seeks to answer these questions. Here I contend that being open is not a contradiction to being passionate but an expression of a mature faith. Openness is not simply a matter of expediency; it is an expression of our faithfulness and, I venture to say, is the Spirit's call of the moment. The historical moment (*kairos*) is pointing toward dialogue as the shape of God's liberating presence in our polycentric, multicultural, and multi-religious but socio-politically conflictive global context.

I refuse to end this project without a note of hope. I cling to this note of hope not because of my belief in history's inevitable progress, rather, I refuse to accept the alternative: despair, cynicism, and hopelessness. Hence, I wager in hope, or I wager to hope. There is much that could drive us to despair and hopelessness or to shallow optimism, which is more deceiving. We must be vigilant of this bloated optimism because our society, especially the elitist bourgeois world, likes to play footsy and eventually go to bed with it. Optimism has an elitist respectability. Yet it may be more dangerous than we would like to acknowledge; it wears a false smile and it does not deal with the magnitude of our globalized problem. Hope exposes this false smile and makes us deal with the hard facts of life but without letting our precarious present dictate the horizon of the possible. Hope is an expression of a deep Christian faith; it is at the heart of the crucified and resurrected Christ; it is central to the life of the church. If so, then hope must be a distinctive mark of being a church in our globalized world. This is the central message of chapter 12—The Church as a Community of Hope: Facing Global Cynicism and Despair—the final chapter of this book.

So it is with this concluding note on hope that I wager in hope, or I wager to hope. This work is in itself an expression of my wager to hope. At times I have asked how a project like mine—a straw before the wind (Job 21:18)—could offer a ray of hope in what appears to be an insurmountable challenge. Nevertheless, I have decided to wager in hope with my piece of straw (a seemingly worthless straw), for straw is all that I have. May this piece of work—a straw before the wind—help build a hopeful tomorrow for the church and for our world.

1

Linking the Global and the Local

Dimensions and Consequences of Globalization

Taking account of global dynamics in relation to local dynamics is something I have done since my work in the Philippines, but I did not use the term globalization until I started teaching in the U.S. My introduction to the term was through theological education, particularly when theological education started to take seriously the context of globalization. A consultation I attended in Hong Kong (1997) and another one in Suva, Fiji (1999) interwove the themes of theological education and globalization. At United Theological Seminary of the Twin Cities, I was part of a committee that was responsible for making global experience an essential part of the curriculum. In the past few years, I have offered two courses, Philippine Immersion Trip and Global Encounters at Our Doorsteps, with the second primarily designed for students who could not travel abroad for various reasons. This book is not another one on globalization but primarily about an ecclesiology (doctrine of the church) that takes the phenomenon of globalization seriously and uses its major challenges as a launching pad for reimagining the church. Before I can do that, I have to analyze and identify the basic challenges of globalization. Hence, this chapter attempts to take account of our globalized context.

GLOBALIZATION: A DESCRIPTOR OF OUR CONTEMPORARY CONTEXT

At the turn of the nineteenth century, industrialization was the catchword that drew the attention and energies of nations. Industrialization was rapidly changing the face of the planet. The steam engine became

1

the symbol of this period. The steam ship and the steam train made it possible for people to travel long distances and transact business more easily than before. Industrialization was the much-coveted vehicle for development and progress. There were, of course, pockets of resistance, but the global momentum was toward industrialization. Industrialization was the way for the so-called developing nations to catch up with the rest of the developed and industrialized nations.

As non-industrialized nations struggled to catch up with the rest of the industrialized world, a new phenomenon came onto the scene. The countries first on board with industrialization were experiencing what was called "deindustrialization" and were becoming "post-industrial."[1] It was at this juncture, around the middle of the twentieth century, when "modernization" gained ascendancy as the new catchword.[2] Development means modernization. Failure to be on board with modernization means remaining backward and underdeveloped. Ideas, styles, architecture, and products must be modernized if one is to catch up with the rest of the modern world. Religious discourse of the time was not free from its influence. Even Christian theologians from the global South who voiced nationalist sentiments integrated the ideas of modernization into their theological constructs.

A new term has replaced "modernization" and become the descriptor of our contemporary context: globalization. Globalization did not suddenly appear out of nowhere. Its historical roots are deep. This phenomenon had its beginnings even before the arrival of the modern period, although it was in the modern period—the period of discovery, colonization, conquest, and economic expansion—that a significant step toward globalization took place. However, we are once again experiencing a significant and qualitatively different expression of globalization.

Globalization has been defined in many ways, depending on the concerns and perspective of a particular scholar. There is, however, a general agreement that it is about the increasing interconnections of our common life at the global level, which is also to say that our interconnections extend to specific localities. We are globalized to the point that the global is lived locally and the local is lived globally. The global is not simply "out there" but also "in here," wherever our loca-

---

1. Sernau, *Bound*, 1.
2. Ibid., 1–2.

tion is. The slogan "think globally and act locally" is not as simple as it sounds, because the lines criss-cross. Even the terms "Third World" and "First World" are complex, for much of the Third World lives in the First World, and the First World in the Third World. Many scholars today would rather use the term "global South" and "global North."

Even as there are global trends and connections, the global is being played out also in the local in different ways, or, to put it in another way, the global is received by various localities in different ways.[3] As the globalization of the local is happening, so is the localization of the global. It is not surprising that a hybrid term has emerged: "glocalization" (*dochakuka* in Japanese).[4] Important in studying globalization are not only the global dynamics, but also the local impacts of globalization. What are the impacts of the global interactions in our own localities or neighborhoods? How is the global dynamic manifest in specific localities? Conversely, how is the local influencing and affecting the global, that is, the interconnections of the locals?

GLOBALIZATION IN ITS VARIED DIMENSIONS

There are many ways in which the issue of globalization can be approached. I may emphasize one approach, but my main concern here is to highlight the various dimensions of globalization and their interweaving. This seems more useful for my project, which is to imagine and construct ecclesiology or the doctrine of the church. By exploring the many expressions of globalization, I will be able to play with multiple images or metaphors for reimagining the church, its mission and ministry. Thus, what follows is my presentation of the multiple expressions of globalization.

Globalization is multidimensional, covering such aspects, to appropriate Arjun Appadurai's categories for mapping the complex and disjunctive order of the new global cultural economy, as technoscapes, finanscapes, mediascapes, ideoscapes, and ethnoscapes. I would like to add mediascapes as the universal consequences of the HIV/ AIDS (human immunodeficiency virus/acquired immunodeficiency

3. See Hoedemaker, *Secularization and Mission*, especially page 23 in which he talks about the globalization of what is basically a Western problem and its reception in different cultures.

4. See Robertson, "Globalization", 64. Also, Arthur, *The Globalization of Communications*, 11.

syndrome), SARS (severe acute respiratory syndrome), and what is commonly called swine flu (H1N1) epidemic continue to unfold and remind us.[5] Another dimension that needs to be included is ecoscapes as we are being confronted with a serious ecological crisis. Finally, not to be forgotten is religioscapes, especially since encounters among believers of various religions are becoming more common in localities that were once relatively homogenous.

Communication Technologies, Travel, and the Media: Extension and Compression

The interconnections of various localities into a global system have become possible through the advancement in travel, media, and communication technologies. Faster travel and telecommunications networks facilitate transactions between international and domestic borders. Buying and selling products, distance learning, and cross-cultural encounters have become realities through the use of cyberspace. In major cities around the world, there are cybercafes where people can take bites and bytes for their computers. In the global South, where most people cannot afford to have their own computers, the Internet cafes provide convenient access to the world of cyberspace.

We are experiencing the power of technologies to "extend" as well as to "compress." As technologies extend our reach, so they also "compress both our sense of time and our sense of space."[6] While not all localities are hooked up to the most advanced communication technologies, many local centers are now within reach by technological advancements. Technological globalization has also reached and shaped rural areas. With the aid of telecommunications systems, a significant number of North Americans, for example, have chosen to move from cities to towns and rural areas.[7] In Asian countries, the proliferation of mobile phones illustrates the reach of the new technologies that have never been imagined before.

Religious groups are not exempt from the effects of communication technologies. Now it has become fashionable to talk about

---

5. Appadurai, "Disjuncture," 295–310. Also cited by Richmond, *Global Apartheid*, 32–33. Also, see Robertson, "Globalization," 53–68. Robertson argues for the multidimensional aspect of globalization.

6. Schreiter, *The New Catholicity*, 11.

7. Jung et al, *Rural Ministry*, 62.

cyberfaith, cyber Christians, and online churches.[8] I am reminded of a full-page advertisement with an image of Jesus, a computer on the side, and a paraphrased caption of the Lord's Prayer that read, "Our Father who art *On Line*." Theological language and the way we do theology are slowly being shaped by technology. Cyberspace words are now slowly becoming part of our religious metaphors. Technological globalization is posing a theological challenge.[9]

Tied to the rapid advancement in technology is the world of media. Through advancements in media technology, news and entertainment are spread throughout the world instantly. Those with sophisticated communications technologies can watch events that are happening in other parts of the world instantaneously in their living rooms. CNN and BBC offer round-the-clock news and the latest on the stock market. It is also possible to access news from around the world through the Internet. Indeed, through powerful media technologies, one experiences the compression of time and space.

The constant flow of information all over the world is a mixed blessing. We are suffering from what Pierre Babin refers to as the "*pollution* of information."[10] We are bombarded with information and competing images in what Neil Postman calls a "peek-a-boo world" where "now this event, now that, pops into view for a moment, then vanishes again."[11] Our consciousness is being flooded with a fast-moving plethora of images, and what passes as "news" is a "cacophonous presentation of images of genocide commingled with beer commercials and stock market reports and tidbits on the lives of the latest celebrities."[12] The biggest challenge is to sort out the profound from the trivial or the sublime from the ridiculous, which is, of course, shaped by our values and priorities. Failure to discriminate effectively the plethora of news leads into our preoccupation with what George Steiner calls "the pornography of insignificance" and the risk of "descent into vast triviality."[13] Lest we forget, the emphasis on the cacophony of images

8. See Messer, *Calling Church and Seminary*, 113–25.

9. See Lochhead, *Shifting Realities*.

10. Babin, cited in Arthur, *The Globalization of Communications*, 24. Emphasis in the original text.

11. Postman, cited in Arthur, 25.

12. Griffith, *The War on Terrorism*, 39.

13. Cited in Arthur, *The Globalization of Communications*, 26.

should make us aware that "news" can be sanitized, as in the latest war with Iraq and Afghanistan.

Nancy Abelmann and John Lie offer a similar comment but with a different twist. For Abelmann and Lie, something more serious is involved than "the pornography of insignificance" and the risk of "descent into triviality" in the "peek-a-boo world" of global information. In the era of sound bites, they argue, "we suffer not so much from the absence of diverse perspectives but from dearth of sustained syntheses and interpretations." When alternative frameworks are absent, "a dominant frame emerges to 'make sense' of various voices, while muffling other voices and interpretations."[14]

It is critical that we be more discerning as we are bombarded with competing information and images. To be discerning, however, is not enough: one must be creative and resourceful as well. One must not rely totally on the dominant news outlets, such as CNN and Fox News. Public broadcasting is available, and much better still for getting independent or alternative news is Link TV, with excellent programs such as Democracy Now and Mosaic. If news reports are sanitized by the major media industries, the same telecommunications technology can also be used to access other sources of information. It should not be a surprise that even as the major media industries sanitized the war in Iraq and Afghanistan, people obtained news outside of the mainstream media sources. The Internet has become an affordable and easily accessible means by which various individuals and groups can disseminate news and opinions.

Antihegemonic movements are not far behind in using new telecommunications technologies. The EDSA II, a people's movement to oust Philippine President Joseph Estrada, was mobilized with the benefit of e-mails and mobile phones. Zapatista rebels in Chiapas, Mexico, sent communiqués from their jungle hideouts to sympathizers in several places around the world. The new video technology circumvented government-controlled broadcasting that contributed to the fall of Eastern European socialism, according to Lech Walesa.[15] Certainly technology has increased the power to control, but it has also created new opportunities for resistance.

14. Abelmann and Lie, *Blue Dreams*, xi.
15. Sernau, *Bound*, 155.

Finance: A Unified Global Economy

Although it is only one aspect of globalization, the most common way of interpreting globalization, especially from the global South, is through the economic lens.[16] Globalization is the development of an integrated global market economy or a unified global economic system. Globalization seeks to incorporate all nations into a single world unit of production, trade, investment, and consumption. While we continue to hear economists speak of national economies, the unified global market has made it possible for us to speak of world economy. There is no national economy in this world that is not affected by the global capitalist market economy. As Robert Reich notes, "the very idea of an American economy is becoming meaningless, as are the notions of an American corporation, American capital, American products, and American technology."[17]

A major feature of economic globalization is that capital is free to move around wherever it finds a "favorable investment climate." By favorable investment climate I mean fat tax breaks, low wages, no insurance and social security benefits for the workers, no labor unions, and less governmental regulation regarding environmental safety. These are the conditions that invite the flow of capital to a particular country. When these conditions are not met, the capital may move to another location. Wanting to have investors come to their shores, countries compete with each other to offer the most "favorable investment climate."

A distinguishing characteristic of the dominant global economy is the shift from the predominance of what Reich calls "national multinationals" with primary loyalties to their home country, to "pure multinationals" with little commitment to their home country.[18] Peter Dicken defines a pure multinational or what is commonly called transnational corporation (TNC) as "a firm which has the power to co-ordinate and control operations in more than one country, even

---

16. Robertson argues that economics is only one aspect of globalization. To make economics as the sole subject and all others as expressions or consequences is to fall into "economism." See Robertson "Globalization" 53–57.

17. Reich, cited in *Global Village*, 18.

18. Reich, *The Next American Frontier*, 260, 264. Cited in Eisenstein, *Hatreds*, 90–91.

if it does not own them."[19] These TNCs are the key actors in the new global economy. Of the top one hundred economies in the world, fifty-one are TNCs and only forty-nine are countries. One United Nations report cited an increase in the number of TNCs from 7,000 in 1970 to some 44,000 in 1998. In addition to affiliates, TNCs operate through links such as strategic alliances between parent companies and other entities, subcontracts, and licensing agreements.[20]

The power, control, and influence of TNCs would not be complete without institutional mechanisms. For the global market to operate efficiently, some institutional mechanisms and policies have to be in place. In July 1944, the U.N. Monetary and Financial Conference (Bretton Woods, New Hampshire) created three institutions: the World Bank, the International Monetary Fund (IMF), and the General Agreement on Tariffs and Trade (GATT). After successive rounds of GATT, the World Trade Organization (WTO) was established to set and enforce the rules of trade.[21]

The World Bank, IMF, and WTO work closely to coordinate their efforts in making sure that the global market runs according to the logic of the global market. The WTO acts as a world court to settle disputes that relate to international trade, and its decisions are binding to member nations. Any WTO member country can challenge the domestic laws of a member country that put up barriers to free trade or any violation of WTO rules. A panel of "trade experts" will hear the charges behind closed doors. If the country's laws are found to violate the rules of the WTO, the laws must be eliminated or a trade sanction will be imposed.[22]

The World Bank, IMF, and WTO may also adopt other measures to impose compliance among member nations. One is the so-called "structural adjustment program" or what is sometimes referred to as "austerity measures." In response to the debt crisis, the IMF and World Bank launched the structural adjustment program that serves as conditions for new loans. The program includes (1) liberalization—the lowering or removing of tariffs, duties, and the like; (2) deregulation—withdrawal of the state from exercising control and oversight

19. Brubaker, *Globalization at What Price?* 19.

20. Ibid., 20.

21. Ibid., 25.

22. Brecher and Costello, *Global Village*, 59.

over economic and financial transactions, and elimination of government actions such as public subsidies and price controls that could hinder the free functioning of the market; (3) privatization of public enterprises, which allows the private sector a major and critical role in providing types of goods and services to the public; (4) currency devaluation; (5) radical reduction of public-sector spending, usually taking the form of budget cuts for health, education, and welfare; and (6) lowering wages or constraining their rise to make exports more competitive.[23]

What is the result of the structural adjustment program, especially if we look at it from the experience of the people from the global South? The result, argues Mary John Mananzan, "is an export-oriented, import-dependent, foreign-investment-controlled, and debt-ridden economy."[24] An export-oriented economy leads to the production of more export cash crops at the expense of the production of staple foods for local consumption. For example, ricefields are converted into plantation for sugarcane, asparagus, and cut flowers. Consequently, an export-oriented economy leads to mono-cropping over against biodiversity and overdependence on artificial fertilizers and pesticides, which are largely imported or obtained from local subsidiaries of transnational companies. Alongside export-orientation is import-orientation, because the locals have become dependent on foreign goods or products. With the economy geared toward massive production of export goods, requiring massive capital outlay, and the local taste attuned to the global taste, the economy becomes foreign-investment controlled. This means the death of small farms and local industries because they cannot compete with the foreign investors. Added to this is the subsidy that farmers in the global North receive from their governments. Roberto Bissio's comment is pointed: "With European [or U.S.] subsidies it would be possible to send every European cow around the world on a business class ticket."[25] Lastly, the economy becomes debt-ridden, and as a consequence, dependency is further re-enforced.

The excellent repayment record of debtor countries to the World Bank says more about its power and less about the quality of the loans.

---

23. Ibid., 56–57; also Brubaker, *Globalization at What Price?* 29.

24. Mananzan, "Globalization and the Perennial Question," 269.

25. Fort, "Globalization and Health," 2.

Debtor countries dare not default or else they will become international economic pariahs. The bank's imprimatur, along with the IMF, is the guarantee for the next loan. Also, the World Bank and IMF make it possible for borrowers to meet their payment schedules by routinely making new loans to pay for the old ones. Therefore, the debtor nations are all the more buried in debt. Thus, debtor nations have to accept the conditions under the structural adjustment program.

Many governments today face a situation where over half of their country's export earnings must go to pay the interest and fees on debt while the principal, the original amount borrowed, remains untouched. The Indian government, for example, services a debt burden to the tune of $20 million (U.S.) a day as interest payments alone to international financial institutions. Over a course of ten years, Brazil paid more than $200 billion and still owes about $240 billion.[26] Other debtor countries are in a similar plight. Between 1981 and 1997, developing countries paid more than $2.9 trillion (U.S.) in principal and interest, but the debt of these countries remained at $2 trillion.[27]

The new economic globalization thrust has brought enormous wealth that the world has not experienced before. The main beneficiaries of the global market made people believe that the rising tide of economic wealth will translate into economic betterment for the majority. Notwithstanding plaudits and accolades from the evangelists of globalization, there is a painful side to the story. Metaphorically speaking, contrary to the belief that "a rising tide raises all boats," the reality has been that "a rising tide raises all yachts."[28] Worse, the world's poor do not even have boats, and they are drowning in the tsunami of corporate profits. Economic globalization has created and promoted "asymmetries, conflict, and a sense of no alternatives for those not included in the flow of its information, technology, capital, and goods."[29] A study shows that

> [f]rom 1960 to 1991, the ratio of income shares between the richest 20 per cent of the world's population and the poorest 20 per cent went from 30:1 to 61:1. Over this same period, the share of the total global income taken by the richest 20

26. World Council of Churches, *Globalizing Alternatives,* 47.

27. Brubaker, *Globalization at What Price?* 36.

28. Borg, *The Heart of Christianity*, 141.

29. Schreiter, "Contextualization," 82.

per cent grew from 70 per cent to 85 per cent. Meanwhile, the shares of all other four-fifths fell; the share of global income for the world's poorest 20 per cent dropped from 2.3 per cent to 1.4 per cent.

Thus one-fifth of humankind, mostly in the developed countries, controls well over four-fifths of global income. And some one billion people survive on daily cash income equivalent to less than one USA dollar.[30]

While most of those who have fallen by the wayside are still concentrated in the global South, citizens in the affluent North have not been spared. The CEOs of top U.S. companies are earning 212 times what their average worker is earning. And, it is no mere coincidence that as the top CEOs earn more than their average workers, many have been victims of downsizing (euphemistically called "rightsizing"). General Motors earned $34 billion in profits over a fifteen-year period—and eliminated over 240,000 jobs.[31]

Ideology: Market Culture and Antiglobalisms

Globalization happens not only in the realm of technology and economics but also in the realm of culture and ideology. We are now experiencing what is called a "global culture." There are varied expressions of this global culture. One may say that it is a homogenized culture under the McDonald's arch or the McDonaldization of the world. Similarly, others speak of the Coca-colanization of the world. The capitalist global market is its financial underwriter, with Hollywood and the media industry acting as the ministry of culture. From the global North to the global South, globalization is creating a global culture typified, writes Schreiter, "by American cola drinks, athletic and casual clothing, and American movie and television entertainment."[32] This global culture forms distinct values, lifestyles, and tastes that view the local as inferior, backward, outmoded, and traditional in comparison to the shining world that the global media presents. It assumes that people who choose this global culture are superior to those who do not or to those who resist its influence. Market globalization

30. United Nations Human Development Report, 26. Cited in *A Moment to Choose*, 26.

31. Moore, *Downsize This!* 10.

32. Schreiter, "Contextualization," 82.

is also spreading a culture of consumerism, self-centered individual-ism, hedonism, and violence as it continues to undermine local and indigenous cultures.

Market globalization has produced identities that revolve around possession and consumption. An identity that is forged in the crucible of market globalization, according to Peter McLaren, is the "shopping mall self." Possession and consumption define one's subjectivity and identity.[33] Possession and consumption define who one is or how one is perceived and given value by others. What is possessed and consumed is not simply the use value of something but the exchange value. That which is consumed is not simply the thing that is purchased but, more specifically, the image value. Commodities are more than material objects; they are also social signifiers. Image enhancement, not only use value, defines what is of value. In fact, image value supersedes use value and image value is the object of fixation. Everyone is driven to consume and acquire the goods that elevate one's status in society. Designer footgear and work clothes have become the homeboys and homegirls' obsessions of the hip-hop nation.

When a consumer attains a certain level of taste, sophistication, and, of course, financial means, he or she seeks compatible commodi-ties of high social signification, pushing him or her deeper into the consumer trap. But, just as consumers seek compatible commodities, or, just as commodities seek compatibilities, consumers seek subject compatibility or compatible social relations. This means that people who own similar commodities (social signifiers) are more likely to limit their interaction to people who own similar commodities. Thus, commodities (social signifiers) dictate the horizons of relations and interaction that people make.[34]

Even the poor people of the global South are duped into the global consumeristic culture. They know the expensive brand names of shoes, watches, clothing, and so forth. Often they attempt to pro-cure them at the expense of their meals in order to achieve the sta-tus that is derived from owning an expensive brand name. Outward trappings provide the sense of identity that is desperately needed in a class society. While one often hears the lament that people are in economic crisis, shopping malls are crowded and many malls are still

33. McLaren and Gutierrez, *Revolutionary Multiculturalism*, 197.
34. McLaren and Zeus Leonardo, Ibid., 120.

being constructed. There are, of course, other reasons why malls in the global South are crowded: they serve as air-conditioned hangouts. [35] Regardless of other reasons, the poor of the global South keep flocking to shopping malls in great number as consumers.

Consumerism not only involves the consumption of an image value that an individual desperately needs to elevate his or her status, it is also an expression of a deep psychological alienation. Greater conspicuous consumption provides greater psychological compensation for the rote meaninglessness of one's job. The solution to boredom in a consumeristic society is to consume, especially when the communal bond is weak. This statement sounds simplistic, nevertheless, it is true to the experience of common people. If one is bored, one may engage in the act of consumption by watching (consuming) a movie and munching (consuming) something while watching. Or, one of the major ways in which people address boredom is to go shopping (consume).

Among those who have been crushed or marginalized by corporate globalization, we can speak of the spread of a global culture of despair, cynicism, powerlessness, and fatalism. Feeling betrayed by the promises of the global market, many have succumbed to false hope. A growing number of those who have been marginalized have found their hope by buying lottery tickets. For example, in 1994 people in the United States spent an average of $93 million a day on lottery tickets. Every time a person buys a lottery ticket, that person buys a piece of hope.[36] Unable to compete in the global market, the sidelined find hope for a better life in a lottery ticket or anything of that nature.

Overwhelmed by the forces of predatory globalization, a global culture of powerlessness and fatalism can be observed. In my years of work in the parish and in community organizing, it was disheartening to observe the painfully slow growth of people's empowerment. Many of those I encountered would rather have the wealthy and educated make decisions for them. They often express their willingness to volunteer their labor and time but relegate the planning and decisions to the so-called educated and the wealthy. The sense of powerlessness of many has reached the level of fatalism.

---

35. A similar phenomenon is happening in the United States as teenagers, dubbed "mall rats," use malls as hang-outs. See Naylor and Willimon, *Downsizing the U.S.A.*, 59.

36. Woods, *Congregational Megatrends*, 80.

The sense of powerlessness, fatalism, and cynicism may find other expressions such as "badass" behavior and violence. The term "badass" combines two words, "bad" and "ass": the "*bad* indicates deviance from wider social values and *ass* connotes a combination of toughness and meanness." In East Los Angeles, "badass" is shown in the way one walks, often called the "barrio stroll." Ted Peters describes it as "a slow, rhythmic walk with flamboyant arm movement, chesty posture, and head up toward the heavens."[37] While the "badass" posture shows pride, it is more of an expression of powerlessness; it is a form of compensating for one's powerlessness in a society that has pushed the powerless to the margin.

It would be inaccurate, however, to confine one's presentation of the global culture only in terms of homogenization or the globalized culture of escape. The predatory acts of corporate globalization have generated a broad spectrum of counterglobalist movements (from movements of transformation to movements of reaction). On the reaction end of the spectrum, we can see the growth of "antiglobalist" movements. In religion, Schreiter names fundamentalism or revanchism (regaining grounds thought to have been lost) as a possible expression of "antiglobalism." Whatever form it takes, its logic is retreat from the onslaught of globalization altogether.[38] It is significant to note that as the homogenizing globalization spreads, movements of various motivations—ethnic, religious, nationalistic, and cultural—are also rising. The threat of monoculturalism brought by the homogenizing globalization has encountered the assertion of multiculturalism and multi-ethnic identities. "Universalisms, both secular and religious," contends David Lochhead, "have encountered the rise of a stubborn particularism in the guise of resurgent nationalism."[39] As new boundaries are being redefined and artificially imposed divisions of the Cold War politics vanish, ethnic conflicts and culture wars have intensified. In this situation in which people attempt to redraw boundaries that once seemed safe, new forms of "heresies" are likely to be identified.[40]

It may not be fully accurate that this phenomenon be totally attributed to predatory and homogenizing globalization. Nonetheless,

37. Peters, *Sin*, 99. Emphasis from the original.
38. See Schreiter, *The New Catholicity*, 21–23.
39. Lochhead, *Shifting Realities*, 100.
40. Kurtz, *Gods in the Global Village*, 213–14.

one major reaction to the rapacious activities of corporate globalization that has drawn the attention of the world and has shaped geopolitics is the rise of religious fundamentalism and its linkage with international terrorism. To a large extent, the factors that have triggered the violent acts or terrorism are local and particular, as well as diverse for various localities. They are as diverse as the release of nerve gas by members of a Hindu-Buddhist sect (Aum Shinrikyo's group) in Tokyo subways, the bombings in India by Sikh and Kashmiri separatists, the terror unleashed by Tamils and Sinhalese militants in Colombo, the killing of 30 Muslims in the Tomb of the Patriarchs by Baruch Goldstein, the bombings of U.S. embassies in Kenya and Tanzania in 1998, and the violence of right-wing Christian militias in the U.S. However, the frequency and widespread appearance of violence around the world suggests that in some cases global factors are at work.[41]

Predatory corporate globalization is a major triggering factor in many expressions of terrorism around the world. Globalization, as a short hand term that represents not only the economy but also the spread of the Western project (civilization, liberal democracy, and secularism), has surfaced in many fundamentalist militants' rhetoric as a threat that must be stopped by all means and at all costs. Often undergirded by religious motivations, the militants see their acts of terrorism as a religious duty directed against those who represent or against any representation of ungodliness, decadence, or unbridled political and economic greed. Fundamentalist militants feel that the traditional values that they hold dear have been eroded by the global capitalist market, or by Hollywood entertainment industries. After years of seeing their dreams betrayed and cherished cultural-religious values undermined, many individuals and communities have "lost faith" in the Western-secular-democratic project and are turning to religion for vision and empowerment.

Globalization has also generated a global culture of resistance to the homogenizing process. The same technology that has been the vehicle of homogenization has also been used to spread a globalized culture of resistance. This culture of resistance is growing everywhere as various communities experience the undermining of their way of life and as the dehumanizing effect of globalization is widely felt. As a counterforce to globalization that emanates from the top and the

---

41. Juergensmeyer, *Terror*, xii.

powerful, people from around the world have taken the initiative of forging a "globalization from below."[42] Globalization from below is spearheaded by people's movements and various communities that have seen the need to establish international links in order to counter the disastrous effects of globalization. Other movements can be included under this banner: the ecological movement, feminist movement, and various human rights organizations.

Global Migration and Mobility of People

Migration has been a permanent feature in human history in both positive and negative ways. With faster means of travel and communication, this movement of people within and across borders should not be surprising. Although there are still places that are difficult to reach, globalization through communications technology and transportation has made the movement of people within and across borders much easier than before. Recently, however, we have witnessed disturbing patterns in large-scale movements of people that point to a profound new reality of global migration. What is more disturbing than the increasing movement of people because of cross-border transactions and tourism, or even voluntary movement in pursuit of education or for family reasons, is the massive movement of inhabitants from the global South to more-affluent countries, in spite of the tightening of immigration laws and increased surveillance. Particularly alarming is the reality of massive "forced" displacement. The disastrous effects of globalization have triggered this migration.

It is difficult to give accurate data of migration, either within (internal migration) or across (external migration). The common countries of origin of the diaspora population are still from the global South, and the common destinations are the countries of the global North. While this is the dominant pattern, some changes in migration flow are happening. Some Asian nations, including China, Hong Kong, Malaysia, the Republic of Korea, Thailand, and Japan are becoming important countries of destination. The oil rich countries of Western Asia have been a host to 22 million migrants (2005). Within Western Europe, many countries from which migrants departed in

---

42. See Brecher and Costello, *Global Village,* 169–84. Also, Brecher et al., *Globalization from Below.*

large numbers in the past century, including Italy, Ireland, Portugal, and especially Spain are now major destinations.[43]

The figures presented above indicate the different categories that have been used to classify people's movements. My use of these categories may be looser than what is current in international law. A more general and common distinction is between "voluntary" and "forced" forms of migration. While it is difficult to speak of "pure" voluntary movement because there are always factors that push people to move, a significant distinction has been made because of different circumstances such as between immigrants and refugees. Within this general category of immigrants and refugees are more specific categories such as migrant workers and asylum seekers. Asylum seekers, for various reasons, may be classified under the refugee category, though there are disagreements in this regard.[44]

Competing theories or approaches have developed in an attempt to take account of people's migration. These approaches fall under three major headings: (1) neo-classical, (2) historical-structural, and (3) migration systems and networks.[45] I will not offer a critical assessment of these here. In their strengths and weaknesses they help us see dimensions that we need to be attentive to. The best approach is the one that helps us see the complexities and subtleties at various levels: macro, meso, and micro. People migrate for various reasons and their choice of an area of destination is shaped by many factors. The most common factor is economics. Though it is not always the economically desperate people who migrate, they continue to be the most common migrants. When economic conditions make basic survival almost impossible in certain localities, people move or migrate for survival or to attain a better living condition. Internal migration usually flows from the rural areas to the urban centers or to places where jobs are available. External migration follows a similar pattern, with residents from less-developed countries migrating to more economically developed countries. But the movement of people is not only limited to affluent places either within or outside of the country, such as the more affluent countries of the global North. There are also movements of people within the neighboring countries, such as from

43. Ibid.

44. *A Moment to Choose*, 9–10.

45. Castles and Miller, *The Age of Migration*.

Bangladesh to India. The large-scale migration of Muslim population from Bangladesh to Hindu-dominated India since the late 1970s has culminated in a number of conflicts between the newcomers and the receiving population.[46]

Besides economic factors, various forms of political instability, such as human rights violation, persecution, and particularly war have triggered massive migration. The long and bloody war in Southeast Asia, the eventual withdrawal of U.S. forces from Vietnam, and the victory of Communist North Vietnam over South Vietnam in April 1975 led to waves of Vietnamese, Laotian, Cambodian, and Hmong refugees.[47] Many thought that armed conflicts would subside with the end of the Cold War. On the contrary, armed conflicts have increased, mostly within nation-states but also between nation-states as well as between nation-states and non-nation-state entities. Africa is a continent that has experienced the escalation of civil wars (Angola, Mozambique, Sierra Leone, Congo, Liberia, Rwanda, Somalia, etc.). Many of these civil wars are fought not on ideological grounds but for control of economic resources.[48] Without the traditional support of the two former rivals (United States and the Soviet Union), many have turned to natural resources to self-finance civil war. The civil wars on the African continent, the ethnic wars in the Balkan region, the conflict in Sri Lanka, the low-intensity wars in Central America, the Gulf War, and the long conflict in Afghanistan, followed by the most recent U.S. attack, have created a groundswell of refugees.

On top of the economic and political factors that trigger migration is environmental disaster. Deforestation, desertification, declining soil fertility, drought, and floods have forced people to move on a massive scale. But more dramatic and traumatic are industrial disasters, exemplified by the Chernobyl nuclear accident. From the industrial disaster in Bhopal, India, to Moravia in the Czech Republic, and to Love Canal in New York, the United States of America, "the health effects of accidents and toxic wastes have obliged the relocation of people literally to ensure their very survival."[49] The "environmental refugee" now joins the classic "political refugee."[50]

46. *A Moment to Choose*, 45.

47. Phan, *Christianity with an Asian Face*, 228–29.

48. Kobia, "Violence in Africa," 10.

49. *A Moment to Choose*, 44.

50. Castles, *Ethnicity and Globalization*, 129.

The migration of people has created a different demographic, with more homogenous communities experiencing in a massive scale the presence of new faces in their midst. A prime example is rural southwestern Minnesota in the United States Midwest. Southwestern Minnesota towns such as Marshall, Tracy, Worthington, St. James and Mountain Lake, Madelia, Montevideo, and Willmar have become the home of many Hispanics, Hmong, Somalis, Laotians, Vietnamese, Kenyans, Eastern Europeans, and residents of the former Soviet Union.[51] These groups have been drawn to southwestern Minnesota because of the presence of factories and packing plants such as Swift & Company and Campbell Soup. The global South is now present in rural southwestern Minnesota.

When millions of people move from one country to another to resettle and look for jobs, these hordes of newcomers are often considered a threat by the inhabitants of the receiving countries or communities and heighten anti-immigrant sentiments. Around the world we can observe the frightening rise in racist and xenophobic hostilities directed against the newcomers. In the face of perceived threats, society usually finds the weakest of its members to scapegoat. We are familiar with this following sequence: "a man gets chewed out by his boss at work, goes home and yells at his wife, and she scolds her child, and the child kicks the dog."[52]

The rise of racist violence against newcomers or long-time resident minorities in countries like Germany and the United States is too well known to require detailed description. Two years after German unification, neo-Nazi organizations spread and waves of racist-xenophobic violence were on the daily news. From the middle of 1990 to the middle of 1991, about thirty foreigners died from racially motivated attacks. While a higher percentage of these attacks happened in the former German Democratic Republic (GDR), it escalated to West Germany.[53] Xenophobia is rising steadily in the whole of German society.

In the United States, beyond outright racist violence against minorities, conservative groups and their corporate supporters have been successful in passing legislation that rolls back years of affirmative action. Politicians have been able to rally huge support from the

---

51. See Amato, *To Call it Home.*

52. Peters, *Sin,* 183.

53. Castles, *Ethnicity and Globalization,* 155–56.

population by fanning their fears of racial others. When scrutinized carefully, Young Lee Hertig sees California Proposition 209 as no other than violence dressed in the rhetoric of equality and discrimination.[54] Racist violence can be so sophisticated as to hijack the language of the Civil Rights Movement.

Globalization and Ecological Concern

It is not only the human population that suffers from the effects of globalization but also the ecosystem. One of the consequences of rapid global economic activity and increase in consumption is the devastation of the natural environment and the pollution of the earth's ecosystem. Liberalized trade conditions have increased the volume of trade, accelerating the depletion of natural resources and the global destruction of the natural environment. Around the world, forests are being cleared for timber, agriculture, and grazing, and flooded for dams and hydroelectric power. Rivers and lakes have become dumpsites for the booming industries, and the ocean has been overfished to support ever-increasing demands both domestic and international.

Logging for export has been a major culprit in the destruction of forests around the world. It has been a way for many countries of the global South to pay their foreign debts. Brazil, for example, uses the Amazon rain forests to pay for its loans. We encounter similar stories in Indonesia, Philippines, Papua New Guinea, the Solomon Islands, and in other areas as well. Papua New Guinea has one of the world's few surviving jungles, but the logging of its forest is happening at a rate that is an imminent environmental disaster.[55] Japan's use of 12 billion throwaway chopsticks a year has largely contributed to the destruction of hardwood forest in the Philippines and Indonesia. Malaysian-owned logging operations have been the culprits in the massive deforestation of the Solomon Islands and, along with it, the desecration of indigenous peoples' sacred sites and the pollution of water supply and the sea.[56]

Forests have also been destroyed for grazing. Twenty million acres of virgin rain forest are burned each year in Brazil to give way to cattle grazing. In response to the gigantic appetite of North Americans for

54. Hertig, "The Korean Immigrant Church."
55. *A Moment to Choose*, 44.
56. Verán, "Resisting Exploitation," 24.

hamburger, virgin forests in the Amazon and in Costa Rica have been cleared to give way to pasture lands. The result is the hamburgerization of Brazil and Costa Rica's rain forests. What is economic "growth" for transnational corporations (e.g., hamburgers for McDonald's and Burger King) is resource depletion for Brazil and Costa Rica: degraded land, washed away topsoil, denuded forests, and so on.[57]

The construction of hydroelectric dams and thermal plants has been destructive to the world's forests, too. In response to the need for a reliable power supply for transnational corporations and irrigation to support huge agricultural farms, the World Bank and the IMF released loans for the construction of hydroelectric and irrigation dams and thermal power plants to many countries in the global South. One of the consequences of these projects has been the destruction of the forest, including various forms of plants and animals, and the displacement of the indigenous people in the areas affected. The damming of rivers has submerged human settlements and the habitat of various species.

The destruction of the world's forest is imminently alarming. Seventeen million hectares of forest—an area the size of Austria—are destroyed each year.[58] Within the past 50 years 65 million hectares of productive land turned into desert in sub-Saharan Africa alone. The deterioration of Europe's forests from air pollution causes economic losses of $35 billion a year.[59] If the current rate of deforestation continues, some studies predict that "the tropical rain forests will have disappeared well before the middle of the next century."[60]

We can also see the continuing destruction of lakes and ocean and the depletion of various forms of marine life. The world's lakes and seas are overfished to respond to the ever-increasing demand of the global market. Like the rain forest, commercial fishing in countries of the global South has been used to pay foreign debt. And, as in the case of the small-time farmers and indigenous people, the small-time fisherfolks are at a disadvantage against the huge fishing companies with their destructive fish trawlers. Open-sea fishing is usually dominated by "distant water fishing nations" that travel thousands of miles

57. See Surendra, "Global Solidarity for the Future," 23.
58. Cited in Edwards, *Jesus the Wisdom of God*, 4.
59. *A Moment to Choose*, 41.
60. Edwards, *Jesus the Wisdom of God*, 5.

in order to locate the best fishing grounds. Not only the ocean but also the ecosystems that produce the fish, including mangrove swamps and marshes, have been destroyed as a result of overfishing.

Industrial growth has contributed to the overall pollution of the ecosystem through discharge of toxic effluent, dangerous fibers, poisonous fumes, dusts, and particles. Emission from automobiles (rapid increase from less than 50 million in 1959 to 400 hundred million automobiles in 1989) is a major contributor to the overall pollution. Our rapidly growing globalized and industrialized world has produced 70,000 kinds of chemicals. Many of these are now part of the earth's global circulation.[61]

The tourism industry, one of the main sources of income for many countries, has done serious damage to our ecosystem. What happened to Boracay, an island in the Philippines, provides an example of ecological destruction due to tourism. Boracay has been a tourist magnet because of its magnificent beach. But this pursuit for hefty profits was not balanced by environmental concern. Ground water in the island has been overdrawn causing saltwater seepage and contaminated drinking water. Government officials and business owners have considered putting in safe water facilities to respond to tourist needs. But for environmental activist and artist Perry Argel, head of the Center for Art, Creativity and Consciousness, "[t]he cost of water is not the issue. The big issue here is the destruction of Boracay's environment."[62]

Whether in the Cold War era or in the new wave of globalization, militarism in support of economic globalization has created environmental disasters of immense consequences. During the Cold War era, the Pacific Ocean was not peaceful. It became the testing site of the deadliest nuclear bombs by the United States, France, and the former Soviet Union. The Marshall Islands suffered the most. The United States conducted 67 tests there from June 30, 1946, to August 18, 1958. In 1954, the United States detonated what it dubbed Bravo bomb, which was 750 times more powerful than the atomic bomb dropped on Hiroshima. The result has been nuclear fallout on some of the islands and atolls. We can see the effects in what are called "jellyfish babies." The only reason we know that they are human babies, says one Marshallese parent, is

61. Rayan, "Theological Perspectives on the Environmental Crisis," 223.
62. See Lujan, "Boracay on the Brink," 35.

their brain. This callous disregard for human life and for all forms of habitat in the region is part of the U.S. legacy.[63]

We can observe militarization's toxic legacy around the world, not only by the United States but also by other nations. The Subic Naval Base and Clark Air Force Base in the Philippines and the naval bombing site in Vieques, Puerto Rico, testify to militarism's toxic legacies. Some parts of countries in Asia (e.g., Cambodia) are not fit for human habitation after years of carpet bombings and landmine planting. After 12 years of war, Cambodia is the most heavily mined country in the world with one landmine for every two persons. One in every 236 Cambodians is an amputee because of a landmine explosion.[64] The United Nations estimates that 105 million unexploded landmines are buried in 62 countries.[65] The toxic legacies due to militarization are also present in the Balkan region and other countries.

While the global ecosystem is in danger, it has been in the poor neighborhoods and in the countries of the global South that ecological destruction is more acutely felt. Powerful nations have dumped, clandestinely or for some consideration of money and pressure, hazardous and toxic wastes on the poor. Even in the midst of the Cold War, West Germany continued to send its toxic wastes to the East German government that was desperate for foreign exchange. This was a well-kept secret until it was exposed after the collapse of the Berlin Wall.[66] A Norwegian ship dumped fifteen thousand tons of toxic incinerator ash from the United States on Kassa Island off the coast of Guinea in West Africa. Another scandal happened near the port town of Koko, Nigeria, when the dumping of 150 tons of PCBs (polychlorinated biphenyls) shipped from Italy was discovered and exposed.[67] The islands and waters of the South Pacific have also become dumping sites for toxic wastes by powerful nations, with disastrous consequences to the health of the Pacific islanders.[68] Global South, indigenous people around the world, and poor communities have been

63. A Pronouncement on a United Church of Christ Ministry and Witness with Micronesians. Also see my essay, "Colonial Legacies," 30–31.

64. *A Moment to Choose*, 24.

65. *Hunger*, 35.

66. Center for Investigative Reporting and Bill Moyers, *Global Dumping Ground*, 96–100.

67. Meyer and Meyer, *Earth-Keepers*, 59.

68. Rayan, "Theological Perspective on the Environmental Crisis," 225.

the target of "environmental terrorism" or "radioactive terrorism" by the elite and powerful nations. Eighty to ninety percent of uranium mining and milling in the United States, for example, has taken place in or adjacent to American Indian reservations with serious consequences to the health of American Indians.[69] "As long as there are . . . minority areas to dump on," argues Leon White, "corporate America won't be serious about finding alternatives to the way toxic materials are produced and managed."[70] The struggling racial communities have discovered that there is a functional relationship between racism and the industry's assault on the environment.

The United States and some European nations also export their toxic products to other parts of the world. Some pesticides that are banned in the United States are exported to countries of the global South by a network of multinational chemical corporations. Some of these pesticides include DDT, benzene hexachloride, lindane, dieldrin, and heptachlor.[71] Nevertheless, these toxic products come back to U.S. dining tables through imported foods with heavy pesticide residues. In the effort to poison the pests and weeds, the cycle of poisoning continues as the groundwater, the workers, the agricultural produce, and, finally, the consumers are also poisoned.

Ecological destruction is being felt everywhere. With the destruction of the rain forests, various ecological disasters, too, have come. The consequences of deforestation are numerous and enormously destructive: soil erosion, flashflood, global warming, greenhouse effect, desertification, and extinction of many species. People who live near the ocean have not failed to notice the rise of the sea level, which now threatens the populace. Emissions from automobiles and industrial toxic wastes have reached a level that is destructive to humans, animals, and plants. Pollution from industrial wastes has reached lakes and oceans, destroying the habitat of various forms of marine life and ending up as meals at our tables. Globalization has become a globalization of ecological disasters.

69. Thorpe, "Our Homes are Not Dumps," 47.

70. Cited in Lee, "Evidence of Environmental Racism," 25. Also, see *Toxic Wastes and Race*.

71. Meyer, *Earthkeepers*, 56.

Globalization, Health, Politics of Medicine, and Pandemic Diseases

Health is another dimension that has made us aware of the globalization phenomenon. The focus of standard medical diagnosis on the biological-psychological pathology often fails to take account of the pathological body politic that is causing massive epidemic and deaths. Socio-political inequality and massive poverty are the roots of common diseases that a majority of the world's people are suffering and dying from. It does not require meticulous research to see the correlation between socio-economic condition and diseases, life expectancy, and overall health. The widening economic gap caused by predatory globalization has sharply exacerbated this correlation. In recent years we have seen the resurgence of diseases that our global society had thought were a thing of the past, such as tuberculosis, typhoid, maternal mortality, infant death, and so forth. There is also the resurgence of malaria and other diseases carried by mosquitoes, which points to the unsanitary living conditions of most of the world's poor people. No amount of medical intervention can solve the global health problem unless we address our sick body politic.

Another aspect of globalization that relates to medicine is the mobility of various pathogens. If globalization means easy mobility of people and things, it also means fast and easy mobility of pathogens and vectors from one corner of the world to another. Just as people can move easily, so microbes can spread from one corner of the world to another wherever ships and jetliners go. One of the basic health concepts in our globalized world is the traversing of "geobiological boundaries." Health scholars and epidemiologists explain this phenomenon as the "process of leaving one specific biological environment (with its own climate, temperature, pathogens, and vectors), for which a certain degree of adaptation exists, and the movement to other locations where the traveler is exposed to different biological characteristics."[72] The crossing of these "geobiological boundaries" or "epidemiological boundaries" has increased the circulation of pathogens and vectors worldwide and, consequently, increased exposure of the newcomers and the receiving population to these pathogens and vectors.

The movement from one place to another itself has significant consequences to the health of the traveler or the settler. It means in-

72. "Special Article: Migrant Health."

creasing exposure to new health stresses. Moving implies changes in one's lifestyle, food habits, daily routine, relationships, and exercise; it imposes psychological and other forms of emotional stress and a certain degree of isolation. The stress of the individual migrant or permanent settler is compounded with the stress that other members of the family are experiencing. Each of these factors can affect the health and well-being of the traveler or settler and can have potential consequences on his or her physical and mental health.[73]

Epidemiologists have long worried of a deadly viruses that can spread quickly throughout the world as a result of our highly mobile life. This is particularly so with regard to the rise and rapid dispersal of deadly viruses, such as HIV/AIDS, SARS, and swine flu. The HIV/AIDS virus has spread at an alarming rate and has claimed the lives of many, especially in southern Africa. The World Health Organization estimated that by mid-1994 the number of persons with HIV infection was about 17 million. Of this figure, 10 million were in sub-Saharan Africa, 2 million in Latin America and the Caribbean, and 2.5 million in Asia, which has experienced the fastest increase.[74]

The globalization of trade in human beings for the sex industry has contributed to the rapid spread of HIV/AIDS virus. Fifty to eighty percent of prostituted women in Thailand are infected.[75] A study makes a claim that from the mid-1980s between 70 and 80 percent of male tourists who traveled from the United States, Australia, Japan, and Western Europe to Asia did so solely for the purpose of sexual pleasure.[76] It is a common practice to blame the prostituted women or the government for lack of health regulation. But there are economic, social, and cultural factors involved that need to be exposed in combating prostitution and, consequently, the rapid spread of HIV/AIDS infection.[77]

Meanwhile the drugs that may be used to combat HIV/AIDS are slow in coming to those who need them, and they are becoming less affordable, especially in the countries of the global South. The WTO has made it difficult for other nations to manufacture generic drugs. A recent report by Oxfam, a British aid agency, shows that as the WTO

73. Ibid., 2.
74. *Facing AIDS*, 9.
75. See Brock et al., *Casting Stones*, 144.
76. Ryan and Hall, *Sex Tourism*, 136.
77. See *Facing AIDS*, 16.

rules go into effect, drug prices in the global South will increase by 200 to 300 percent. The United States has already used WTO rules to intimidate countries that either make their own generic versions of HIV drugs or else import such drugs. The Bush Administration filed a WTO complaint against Brazil for breaking WTO rules by producing its own drugs. U.S. trade officials filed a similar complaint against Argentina in 2000.[78]

Even as the world struggles with HIV/AIDS, a new virus—SARS—has spread like wildfire. The globe was gripped in fear especially in the early stage of the outbreak. With fewer than 300 confirmed SARS' deaths to date, the global toll is small in number compared with the 3 million who died of AIDS in 2002. The number is also very minute compared with the more than 20 million who died of the Spanish flu (1918–1919). Though the number is small, the overall death rate of SARS is about 6 percent.[79] And, more recently, we are dealing with the outbreak of another pandemic, the H1N1 (popularly called swine flu). While hundreds of thousands of people die of seasonal epidemics, what is critical about H1N1 is that it is caused by a new virus for which most people have little or no immunity. As of July 21, 2009, the World Health Organization reported more than 700 deaths due to H1N1 flu.[80]

Globalization: Encounters of People of Various Religious Faiths

If the Enlightenment thinkers expected that religion would wither away once reason became capable of securing a universal peace, many in the twentieth century were inclined to think that religion would become superfluous once the market could decide all crucial questions of value and meaning. These assumptions have been proven wrong. We are living in the most religious and spiritual time in the history of the globe. After years of assault by the forces of secularism, religious resurgence is happening in various locations.

Globalization facilitates the spread not only of viruses but also of various religious beliefs. Whether we speak of urban or rural areas, increasing religious plurality is now a common sight. Residents are not only from various ethnic backgrounds, but they also come with

78. Statement by Global Exchange, "The Free Trade Area."
79. Lemonick and Park, "The Truth About SARS," 50.
80. Jordans (Associated Press), "WHO: Global Death Toll."

their distinctive religions. When Harvey Cox published *The Secular City* (1965), readers of his work may have thought that he was predicting the demise of religion.[81] Forty years later, Cox admits: "I concede now that I seem to have been mistaken about the 'decline of religion'!"[82] To the surprise of many, today's cities are dotted with churches, synagogues, temples, and mosques. Diana Eck notes that along New Hampshire Avenue, just beyond the beltway of Washington, D.C., there is a stretch of road a few miles long that passes the new Cambodian Buddhist temple, the Ukrainian Orthodox Church, the Muslim Community Center with its new copper-domed mosque, and the new Gujarati Hindu Temple as well as new dimensions of America's Christian landscape: Hispanic Pentecostal, Vietnamese Catholic, and Korean evangelical congregations sharing facilities with more traditional English-speaking "mainline" churches.[83]

So, there has been much talk about religious pluralism being a "newly discovered" reality. Let us be aware, however, that when we speak of religious pluralism as a newly discovered and experienced reality, we are viewing reality from the Westerners' location. Stanley Samartha points out that for people of Asia and Africa religious pluralism is not a discovery as much as a "recovery." It is a recovery of a more religiously pluralistic context that has characterized Asia and Africa, which Christian colonizers and evangelists attempted to silence. Speaking in particular of India, Samartha asserts, "Thus to talk about the 'emergence' or the 'discovery' of religious pluralism in India is like taking a beehive to a sugar[cane] plantation."[84] What globalization has done, in many respects, is create a tense situation of the encounter between believers of different religions. This is true in Indonesia, India, the Philippines, and the Balkan countries.

More than a decade has passed since the end of the Cold War, and the world has been awakened from its slumber to witness that religious beliefs can seem woefully linked to terrible acts of violence. In Asia, Africa, the Pacific Islands, the Middle East, and the United States, we have seen the disastrous consequences of a close linkage between strong religious beliefs and violence. It took the magnitude

81. Cox, *The Secular City*.

82. See Harvey Cox's back cover endorsement to Robinson's *Honest to God*.

83. Eck, *A New Religious America*, 187.

84. Samartha, *One Christ-Many Religions*, 8.

of the September 11, 2001 tragedy for the general public in the United States to admit the potent but dangerous side of religious beliefs. The tragedy has led many to study religion. Since Islam is the faith that has been linked to the tragedy, it is not surprising that many have shown interest in the religion itself. Likewise, it is not surprising that the stereotypical charge against Islam as a violent religion is also on the rise, even as many Muslim leaders have called the terrorist attack a violation of the true Islamic faith.[85]

Western liberal Christians may be undergoing a religious crisis, but this is generally and pervasively not the case with believers of other religious faiths, particularly Islam. Secularism or the privatizing of religious faith among Westerners has led to tolerant but non-engaging niceness with "religious others." Many of those who take pride in our religiously plural context know little about the religious beliefs of others. Liberal Christians tip their hats to it and then walk away. This non-engaging tolerance has made us ignorant about the religious beliefs of even our next-door neighbors, which contributes to our vulnerability. While most fundamentalist people are seeking to lead a peaceful religious life, there are violent forms of fundamentalism of which we remain ignorant at our peril. With the September 11 tragedy, I can only hope M. Douglas Meeks is correct in saying that "[w]e are learning that our secularity is making us vulnerable."[86]

The spread of violence in the name of religion in our globalized world must lead us to consider religion as an important force in the twenty-first century, for the world cannot be fully understood otherwise; however, the recognition of it as an important force is not enough. The escalation of religiously motivated violence around the world must impel believers of different faiths to work together for understanding and harmony. I hope we have come to the understanding that there is no peace in the world without peace and dialogue among believers of various faiths.

85. Armour, *Islam*, 178.
86. Meeks, "What Can We Hope for Now," 258.

2

Terrorism

A New Season of Globalization

ACTS OF TERRORISM HAVE been committed throughout history. Living under a state of terror has been the plight of many; however, it was not until September 11, 2001, that it became a global issue. Before then, it was somebody else's problem, somewhere else. After September 11, it became a global problem. It became my problem, my issue. The images of planes heading toward the Twin Towers and, a few minutes later, the collapse of the once-imposing edifice and the mayhem that followed, still give me an eerie feeling. Like the rest of the general public, I was in a state of shock. It was difficult to believe that what I was seeing was real. In particular, it was difficult for me to believe that it was happening in the United States of America, considered the most powerful nation-state on earth. Suspended in the air of incredulity, the event shattered the myth of security that I was living in; it shattered the miasma of lies beclouding my world. Deep in my heart I was vexed. If the United States is not totally safe, there is no safe place in the world. If this is the case, then I cannot continue to pretend that terrorism is somebody else's problem. We are all embroiled in this global problem, and we must respond creatively or we will be swimming in a burning cauldron of violence. The church, an important institution in society, cannot wish terrorism away. Hence, though it is a difficult topic to address, and though it may lead me to make comments that can easily be construed as unpatriotic, I must take the risk, because it is a crucial issue for the church and the wider society.

GLOBAL VILLAGE, GLOBAL NIGHTMARE

With globalization extending, compressing, and linking the many and different worlds, the notion of a global village is no longer mere rhetoric. Thanks to fast modes of transportation and communication and efficient technology, the global village has become a reality. With an affordable MTN SIM phone card, it was easy to stay in touch with my family while I was teaching in Yaoundé, Cameroon, in January 2007. BBC and CNN kept me abreast of events around the world, and the Internet kept me in touch with friends. No doubt globalization has brought many laudable achievements: technology, transportation, communication, medical discoveries and products, infrastructure, and global trade. Even those who are critical of globalization recognize these outstanding achievements. Many inhabitants of my hometown in the Philippines would readily laud the blessings that globalization, particularly overseas employment, has done for their families. On a stroll through the village of my childhood in the past year, I was surprised to encounter more affluent residential homes, beautiful beach houses, and comfortable hotels, mostly owned by Filipinas married to foreign nationals.

While we can celebrate some of the achievements of globalization, it has also become a juggernaut. It can be read easily as the new form of hegemony: a neocolonization and homogenization. It remains a form of Western domination, an expression of secularism through the market. More than the economic havoc that it brings, it undermines traditional beliefs and community life. For those marginalized and crushed, globalization is not moving to the desired global village but to "global pillage." Instead of the dreamed global village, many have experienced globalization as a nightmare. The march toward progress preached by globalization evangelists has left many victims littering its path. This is not new but has been part of the history of globalization.

GLOBALIZATION AND ITS DISCONTENTS: THE RISE OF COUNTERGLOBALIST SENTIMENTS

We cannot proceed to talk about the globalization of discontent without taking account of the voices of protest against it. With globalization perceived and experienced as gobbling the many, homogenizing and imposing destructive culture, fragmenting communities, violating national sovereignty, secularizing and desecrating the sacred, and undermining deeply held moral and religious values, it is not surprising that we have witnessed the rise of counterglobalist sentiments of various stripes. I use "counterglobalist" as a broader term that includes alternative visions to predatory globalization and to what others particularly refer to as "antiglobalist," with its own competing and, sometimes, conflicting variants.[1] On one end of the spectrum of counterglobalism are the secular and religious groups that articulate an alternative vision. Globalization is resisted for its neoliberal economic agenda, exploitative and oppressive ways, homogenizing project, secularizing assault against religion and deeply held values, consumerist individualism, and assault against the earth, but it is not totally rejected. In this form of counterglobalism, the global civil society takes an active role in making the global market and national governments more accountable to the common good. The World Social Forum (WSF), which stands in contrast to the World Economic Forum, may represent this end of the spectrum. Even as its members and participants have differences, they are united in condemning the evils of corporate globalization and in their affirmation that another world is possible (*otro mundo es posible*).

Many bodies representing various religions have been involved in this form of counterglobalism. Pope John Paul II delivered a homily during his visit to Cuba in 1998 in which he gave a prophetic warning on the "resurgence of a certain *capitalist neoliberalism* which subordinates the human person to *blind market forces* and conditions the development of those people on those forces."[2] The pronouncements of the World Council of Churches (WCC) echo similar concerns. The official report of the WCC assembly in Harare, Zimbabwe (1998), names globalization as a serious threat: it offers a "competing vision to the Christian commitment to *oikomene*" and it is headed to produce a "graceless system that renders people surplus and abandons them if they cannot compete with the powerful few."[3] Globalization has been

1. See Schreiter, *The New Catholicity*, 21–23. Schreiter uses "antiglobalism" to refer to two of its expressions in theology, namely, revanchism and fundamentalism. Juergensmeyer uses antiglobalism to refer to fundamentalist and militant opposition to globalization. See his essay, "Religious Antiglobalism," 135–48.

2. Lechner, "Religious Rejections of Globalization," citing Pope John Paul II (emphasis in the original speech), 122.

3. Ibid., 124.

a common theme of the WCC after Harare. In spite of their strong prophetic content, the pronouncement by the Pope and the WCC do not constitute total rejection of globalization.

Other religions have been involved in a similar form of counterglobalization as well. Sulak Sivaraksa, a Thai activist, recipient of the Right Livelihood award (1995) and prominent articulator of engaged Buddhism, is in concert with other activists in exposing capitalist globalization of its destructive acts in pursuit of profit. Human communities and the ecosystem are sacrificed in global capitalism's pursuit of profit. This leads, he argues, not only to the poverty of the many, but also to the alienation of human beings from each other, the wider community, and their spiritual selves. Beyond exposing the ills of predatory globalization, Sivaraksa brings to our attention the Buddhist teaching of the Four Wheels. As a cart moves steadily on four wheels, so development, he argues, must move with four *dhammas*, namely, sharing (*dana*), pleasant speech (*piyavaca*), constructive action (*atthacariya*), and equality (*samanattata*).[4] This view of development offers an alternative to predatory globalism.

Muslims, especially the moderates and liberals, are no less involved in a similar form of counterglobalization. They have worked with the secular left and other religious groups in resisting the excesses of predatory globalization and in articulating an alternative social vision. Though critical of the sinister side of globalization, moderate and more liberal Muslims adopt and adapt some of what they identify as admirable tenets of modernity. Even Mohammad Khatami, who, according to well-respected scholar John Esposito, does not hold back punches against U.S.-led globalization, is open to a dialogue of civilizations and to learning from the West. Esposito mentions Muslim figures such as Anwar Ibrahim and Abdurrahman Wahid, who are ready to defend Islamic ideals but equally open to the "perpetual interpretation" (*ijtihad*) of the Koran and the Islamic tradition in conversation with the challenges of the modern world. These Muslims are advocating a way beyond the two prescribed paths that lead to the quagmire of global destruction: militant-fundamentalist-jihadist approach and uncritical dependence on the West, or what is called "westoxification."[5]

4. Sivaraksa, "Alternatives to Consumerism," 287–91.
5. Esposito, *Unholy War*, 133–41.

While the above Islamic expressions of counterglobalization have many things in common with the progressive secular and religious left, critiques by Muslims, both lay and religious scholars (*ulama*), are more religiously nuanced. This is not to say that Christian accounts, for example, are not religiously nuanced, but their accounts do not have the gravity that Muslim communities feel with regard to Islam. While Christians articulate their position informed by their Christian faith, they do not see globalization's assault as an assault on Christianity itself to the degree that many Muslims do on their faith. Perhaps Christians, like fish, have become more at home in the waters of globalization and westernization. Or, to put it in a more negative way, they have become overly westoxified. In spite of their serious criticisms of the marriage between Western imperialism and Christianity, Christians have generally come to equate Christianity with Western civilization. There is, however, a pronounced difference among Muslims in general. Though many would not consider globalization and Western civilization as incompatible or in opposition to Islam, there is a pervasive feeling among Muslims that the Islamic faith *itself* is under assault. As with their progressive Christian counterparts, there are "widespread Muslim misgivings about globalization," but, as some writers argue, they "have less to do with 'an expression of opposition to global capitalism' and more with a 'cry of desperation' about the perceived effects of Western dominance on Muslim societies." In short, "Islam is its main victim."[6]

It may be true that while the majority of the Muslim population, though critical of globalization, still falls within the theoretical ambit or circumference of humanizing globalization, there is a growing number who have chosen to pitch their tent on the other extreme of the counterglobalist spectrum, which is classified here as antiglobalism. Robert Schreiter names antiglobalism as "an *attempt* to retreat from the onslaught of globalization forces *altogether*."[7] I emphasize as well as link "attempt" and "altogether" because, as I argued earlier, one cannot be completely outside of the globalization phenomenon. Or, as Schreiter puts it, "The retreat is not a complete withdrawal . . . ; it is a retreat on modern terms (as an exercise of choice) and usually relies

---

6. Cited in Lechner, "Religious Rejections," 125.

7. Schreiter, *The New Catholicity*, 21.

on modern means to achieve it (such as communications technologies or modern weaponry in acts of terrorism)."[8]

Schreiter identifies two manifestations of antiglobalism, particularly in theology. The first is revanchism. Revanchism is not a wholesale rejection of modernity (as in fundamentalism) but an attempt to reclaim what is thought of as lost ground. An example of revanchism is Pope John Paul II's appointments of those who are unswervingly loyal to the Vatican and actions against those who espouse liberation theologies. The second manifestation is fundamentalism, which Schreiter sees as an act of resistance against modernity and globalization. Fundamentalism is marked by certain signifiers that contradict modernist-secularist globalization.[9] Even if Schreiter's definition is generic and limited, he prods me on the right track to explore further the concept of fundamentalism.

Fundamentalism has common markers even if fundamentalist groups respond differently to circumstances. Richard Antoun identifies some of these markers: a quest for purity in a world perceived as impure; the affirmation of the necessity of certainty in the face of perceived uncertainties; making the sacred scriptures speak directly to present-day issues; sharp engagement with the reigning establishment; taking religion into all facets of life; selective modernization and acculturation; and understanding the world as the locus of struggle between good and evil.[10] Gabriel Almond, R. Scott Appleby, and Emmanuel Sivan offer a more in-depth and comprehensive account of fundamentalism's markers. They identify nine characteristics of fundamentalism—five ideological and four organizational. The five ideological markers are reactivity to the marginalization of religion, selectivity, moral Manichaeanism, absolutism and inerrancy, millennialism and messianism. The four organizational markers are elect (chosen membership), sharp boundaries, authoritarian organization, and behavioral requirements.[11]

While I am not going to offer an in-depth examination of these markers, naming them does give us a general sense of the nature of fundamentalism. Looking at this list of markers, it appears that no

---

8. Ibid.

9. Ibid., 21–22.

10. Antoun, *Understanding Fundamentalism*, 164.

11. Almond et al., *Strong Religion*, 92–98.

single marker can stand by itself. We find many of them present in various communities and organizations. Selective appropriations of tradition and sacred texts as well as engagement with modernity are present in various movements we do not normally label as fundamentalist. Further, an additive understanding of all these markers does not constitute fundamentalism. These markers are not a simple checklist. What we call fundamentalism is constituted by the dynamic interaction of the various markers, with some markers constituting the organizing center and others providing the energy. Fundamentalism is a functional system. Almond, Appleby, and Sivan name millennialism and messianism as powerful catalysts; selectivity as the way a community pares down the essentials in the face of the threats; and boundary as the way a community defines identity vis-à-vis the outsiders. The overall impulse of fundamentalism, however, is reactivity or reaction to perceived threats.[12]

The most dominant and pervasive form of fundamentalism is primarily a reaction to the perceived threats of modernity, particularly its secularizing thrust and its perceived attendant evils (individualism, sexual permissiveness, high rates of divorce, out-of-wedlock births, alcoholism, drugs, pornography, etc.). Whoever or whatever is the perceived bearer of secularization or responsible for diluting the purity of the faith is considered an enemy. A religious establishment may be identified as an enemy by fundamentalists if that religious establishment is perceived as "liberal." Fundamentalism may be intertwined with cultural and ethno-nationalist components in which case its reaction could be directed against another ethnic group. Another target of fundamentalists' reaction is the secularizing state, particularly when a state supports such agendas as secular education, divorce, legalized abortion, gay marriages, and empowerment of women. Fundamentalist reaction to the state intensifies when the leaders are perceived as corrupt and as corruptors of the minds of the people. Various forms of fundamentalism, contend Almond, Appleby, and Sivan, "share this family resemblance: across the board they identify three antagonists—the tepid or corrupt religious establishment, the secular state, and secularized civil society—as objects of sustained opposition by true believers."[13]

12. Ibid., 99.
13. Ibid., 101.

With fundamentalist groups seeing the world as a battlefield between good and evil, the surrounding environment as a threat to their purity, and various groups as enemies that must be stopped at whatever cost, fundamentalism can easily slide into the slippery slope of violent extremism. By no means is fundamentalism equivalent to violent extremism. There is no direct correlation between fundamentalism and violent extremism. Some fundamentalist groups would rather withdraw into seclusion. But when the right mixture of fundamentalist markers and context come into play, fundamentalism can find expression in violent extremism. Examples abound of fundamentalism providing the ideological motivation for violent extremism. Terrorism, which itself assumes many forms and tactics (such as suicide attack, proxy bombing, piracy, kidnapping, assassination, aircraft hijacking, narco-terrorism, nuclear terrorism, bioterrorism, agro-terrorism, etc.), is one such vehicle of violent fundamentalist extremism. I shall now focus on this topic.

TERRORISM: DEFINING AN ELUSIVE TERM

If "fundamentalism" is an elusive term that is difficult to define, the term "terrorism" confronts us with a similar challenge. Terrorism has become a popular word in the wake of the September 11, 2001, attacks. It comes from the Latin *terrere*, which means "to cause to tremble" or "to terrify." It came into common use in the political sense during the Reign of Terror in the French Revolution at the end of the eighteenth century, and it was understood as an assault on civil order.[14] Since then, it has been used in varied ways making it difficult to pin down to a single definition. A survey of 109 definitions of terrorism found that 22 elements were present in these definitions, but only three elements were cited by a majority. The three elements were: (1) terrorism involves the use of violence or force, (2) the violence is meant to accomplish political goals, (3) and the violence is unleashed in order to generate fear. Even then, these definitions are not without contestation. Lee Griffith, author of *The War on Terrorism and the Terror of God*, notes how these definitions ignore religious motivations. In the annals of terroristic acts, past and present, religious and political motivations have freely mixed.[15]

14. Juergensmeyer, *Terror*, 5.
15. Griffith, *The War on Terrorism*, 7.

It is not surprising to find words with multiple meanings, but what makes terrorism difficult to define is that it has been intimately woven into the intricacies of power contestation. In other words, it has become part of a discourse that is politically loaded and explosive. What are defined as acts of terror, as the rest of the chapter will show, reveal not only the various meanings of the word but also the power position of individuals who utter it. The old saying "One person's terrorist is another person's freedom fighter" has some truth to it. The term terrorism is as much a subjective judgment about the legitimacy of certain violent acts as it is a descriptive statement about them. Mark Juergensmeyer thinks that the use of the term is dependent to a large extent on one's worldview.[16] If the world is viewed as peaceful, acts of violence appear as terrorism. On the other hand, if the world is thought to be at war, acts of violence may be considered legitimate defensive tactics or as preemptive strikes. A leader in India's Sikh separatist movement would prefer to be called a "militant" than a terrorist. For this militant leader, the term "terrorist" has replaced the term "witch" as an excuse to destroy whom one strongly dislikes. Activists on neither side of the struggle in Belfast, for example, would appreciate being called terrorists. Likewise, leaders of the Hamas movement do not call their violent acts terrorism but defensive maneuvers against existing violence.[17]

An account in Augustine's *The City of God* illuminates the point I am making. Augustine of Hippo retells a tale from Cicero. The story, perhaps apocryphal, recounts a confrontation between Alexander the Great and a captured pirate. The emperor asked the pirate: "What is your idea, in infesting the sea?" With impetuous insolence, the pirate answered: "The same as yours, in infesting the earth! But because I do it with a tiny craft, I'm called a pirate: because you have a mighty navy, you're called an emperor."[18]

The history of terrorism discourse has been controlled by the powerful and guardians of any status quo. Given these power dynamics and power differentials, most acts labeled as terrorist are identified with the extremism of a few individuals such as Timothy McVeigh, Aum Shinrikyo, and Osama bin Laden and his network. Russia, for

16. Juergensmeyer, *Terror*, 9.
17. Ibid.
18. Cited in Griffith, *The War on Terrorism*, 20.

example, wanted the world to label the rebellion in Chechnya as an expression of international terrorism, partly inspired by persons like Osama bin Laden. In a similar manner, the Peoples Republic of China wanted the world, particularly the United States, to accept that it has every reason to stamp out Muslim separatists and "terrorist" groups in the western region of Xinjiang. Also, the Spanish government wanted the ETA—a separatist group wanting an independent Basque state—to be listed as a terrorist group. The Philippines, following the war on terror, successfully convinced the Council of the European Union (EU) to put on the terrorist watch list José Maria Sison and the Communist Party of the Philippines (CPP) along with Abu Sayyaf.

In addition to the terrorism discussed thus far, another form of terrorism exists, one which the world often remains silent about unless it affects or is at odds with the interests of powerful groups or nations—state-sponsored terrorism. With the United States taking the lead in defining terrorism, especially following September 11, 2001, if state-sponsored terrorism is mentioned at all, the references are likely directed against countries like Iran and North Korea but not to the so-called "friendly nations." In the past it was directed against a host of nation-states including Hussein's Iraq, Castro's Cuba, and Qaddafi's Libya. This is not surprising since most of the so-called "experts" on terrorism are affiliated with the U.S. federal government (the CIA, Pentagon, or State Department). What about the "state-sponsored terrorism" of Botha in South Africa, Pinochet in Chile, Montt in Guatemala, D'Aubuisson in El Salvador?[19] What about the terrorism of Marcos in the Philippines?

Indeed, it is difficult to define such a politically contested word as terrorism. There are those who suggest that we define terrorism from those on the receiving end—the terrorized populace. What better experts to define terrorism, they contend, than the victims themselves. The terrorized populace recognizes terrorism when it happens. There is no need for a litany of arguments. The identity of the perpetrators (whether individual or state), the nature of the motivation, and the class of the weaponry employed is of no matter. It is terrorism.[20]

The globalization of terrorism has made it a widely shared experience. The tit-for-tat discourse on terrorism reveals that it is not

19. Ibid., 7.
20. Ibid., 8.

a monopoly of one ethnic group, nation, or religious community. It is present not only among members of the so-called Abrahamic faiths (Judaism, Christianity, and Islam), but also in Buddhism and Hinduism, as in the conflict between Sinhalese Buddhists and Hindu Tamils in Sri Lanka and the violence that Hindus committed against Muslims and Christians in India. In Judaism we have, for example, the fundamentalism of Baruch Goldstein and Rabbi Meir Kahane. On February 25, 1994, Goldstein, a follower of Rabbi Kahane, opened fire with an automatic weapon on Muslim worshippers in the mosque at the Shrine of the Patriarchs in Hebron. More than 50 Palestinians were killed, and more than 150 were wounded.[21] Likewise, Christians have committed terroristic acts. Fundamentalist Christians, such as those identified with the Army of God, committed heinous crimes all in the name of obedience to God and faithfulness to what they believe as absolute truth. On March 10, 1993, Michael Griffin shot to death Dr. David Gunn outside an abortion clinic in Pensacola, Florida. A few months later (July 29, 1994), the Rev. Paul Hill killed Dr. John Britton and his companion at the same abortion clinic. These killings were committed based on the firm religious belief that abortion is legalized murder and an abomination to God and must be stopped at all costs.[22]

GLOBALIZATION AND ITS TERRORS

It may help us to see better the rise of terrorism and its various expressions if we cast it in a wider historical-contextual frame. Terrorisms, particularly those with global networks, did not come out of the blue. From its older to its most current expression, the narrative of globalization has been intertwined with global hegemony. The birth of modernity accelerated globalization to new heights and dimensions, with the Western world taking the lead undergirded by a religio-moral mythos. Against the background of the so-called dark ages of human history, modernity presented itself as a welcome relief from the shackles of the past, especially from heteronomous religious powers that controlled heaven and earth. Modernity is a revolt against heteronomous religious powers and everything that represents the incarceration of reason and free spirit. It overturned the locus of authority from external authorities to the experiencing subject-agent and promised

21. Cited in Antoun, *Understanding Fundamentalism*, 102.

22. Kimball, *When Religion Becomes Evil*, 44–45.

the birth of secular democracies. In the field of theology, the rise of the modern period has been interpreted also as freedom from the "house of authority" in which the form of theologizing is basically citation and translation of unchangeable deposits of faith under the guardian-ship of the church hierarchy.[23]

Yet, there is another side to modernity, which can be viewed as its main mythos and narrative. If "every society is founded upon a poem and every civilization upon a myth," this is the case with modernity: it is founded upon the myth of progress and the conquest of superstition.[24] But the much-celebrated age of reason, enlightenment, and progress is also the age of "discovery" and the resultant conquest, colonization, and exploitation of other races by people of European descent. The age of reason has been barbaric and violent; it is an age of globalized slavery and genocide. At its foundation, the modern Enlightenment project is "ethnocentric" hiding under the facade of "universality, fixity of meaning and coherence of the subject."[25] True to its spirit as the age of reason, the barbarism of the modern period has been couched with seemingly noble intentions: civilizing and chris-tianizing the pagans, and spreading democracy and prosperity.

Synonymous with the birth of modernity, which Enrique Dussel locates as early as 1492, is the birth of the European "I."[26] Outside of this European "I" is the faceless other that has to be conquered and civilized. Rene Descartes' "I think, therefore I am" is also the "I con-quer/discover, therefore I am." This "*ego cogito* of Descartes," I argued elsewhere, "is the theoretical foundation of the *ego conquiro*, and the *ego conquiro* is the practical expression of the *ego cogito*. In actual his-tory, the *ego cogito* is not simply the *Homo sapiens* or the *Homo faber* (human being as worker) but the conqueror."[27]

Discovering and conquering are expressions of the European "I" and its extension—the Euro-American "I." Discovering and conquer-ing others, for the colonial masters, was an adjunct and a proof of their existence. The act of "discovering" assures the colonial masters that they, indeed, are "thinking" and "existing" subjects. While it is the self-

23. See Farley, *Ecclesial Reflection*.

24. Westhelle, "Is Europe Christian," 76–77.

25. Featherstone, *Undoing Culture*, 10–11.

26. Dussel, "The Apparition of the Other."

27. Fernandez, *Toward a Theology of Struggle*, 69–70.

hood of the "discoverer" that is parasitic to the "discovered," by curious alchemy it is now the parasite that grants selfhood to the "discovered." The "discoverer" becomes the guarantor as well as the mirror of the existence and selfhood of the "discovered." The existence and identity of the "discovered" is established as derivative of the "discoverer." In effect, the "discoverer" says to the "discovered" and the conquered, "I discovered you, therefore you exist." Or, "I discovered you, therefore you are." It is only at the point of "discovery" that the history of the "discovered" begins to unfold. Before the "discovery," the life of the "discovered" is prehistory. Yet, even as history begins to unfold in the life of those "discovered," their history continues to be viewed from the perspective of the "discoverer" and colonizer. History has begun for the "discovered," but only insofar as it is beneficial to the "discoverer" and colonizer. In effect, what is considered history is not the history of the "discovered" and conquered, but the history of the triumphant. Only the history of the triumphant counts as history, and the "regime of truth," following Michel Foucault, has established it to be so.[28]

Even after the colonizer is long gone physically, its stamp remains. The day-to-day discourse of the once colonized inhabitants continues to mirror that of the colonizer's discourse. The colonizer's classification and "order of things" continue to reign, even as voices of protest are present.[29] People call themselves according to the name given or conferred to them by their conqueror and colonizer. In spite of their resistance, they continue to use the language of the colonizers to refer to themselves and to challenge its hegemony. Many of the binary categories they use to oppose hegemonic discourse often belie their avowed purpose and continue to be sucked into the hegemonic framework.

Modernity and its attendant myth undergirded the spread of globalization. Undergirded by the myth of progress as conquest and "taming" of the "frontier," the globalizing nations tamed the people of other lands (the racial others) through colonization and/or annexation. Colonial powers extended their reach to various parts of the world, partitioned continents, exploited the people and natural

28. The notion of regime of truth helps us to understand that the relationship between truth and power is not simply a relationship of cause and effect respectively. It is not simply that truth is power or that might is right, but truth and power co-produce each other. See Foucault, *The Foucault Reader*, 51–75.

29. Refer to Foucault's *The Order of Things*.

habitat, engaged in slave trade, and committed horrendous acts of genocide. With superior military might, they were able to control and exploit a large segment of the conquered population. But there was more to the military superiority of the colonial forces that rendered the inhabitants subservient. At this juncture, I am reminded of a statue of Miguel Lopez de Legaspi in the Philippines. In his right hand, Legaspi held a sword, and in his left hand, the cross. The sword and the cross symbolize the apparatus of coercion (political-military) and deception (cultural-religious), respectively. While many of the colonized countries have gained independence, the decolonization process is not yet complete, as in the case of the many island nations in the Pacific and the Caribbean.

The church has been complicit in this history of "discovery," conquest, genocide, colonization, and exploitation. The age of modernity and Western expansion is also the age of Christianity's expansion throughout the world. Wherever there was colonization there was Christian mission. Alongside the sword of the conqueror was the Christian crucifix or the Bible. Any account of the history of Christianity must deal with this shameful history. "Today, I cannot speak of the history of the sixteenth century," Justo González puts it, "without taking into account that on May 26, 1521, the same day that the imperial Diet of Worms issued its edict against Luther, Hernán Cortés was laying siege to the imperial city of Tenochtitlán."[30] The day Christ was proclaimed to the native population of the Americas was also the beginning of the worst genocide in human history. From an estimated total population of 80 million (20 percent of the world's population), they were almost decimated to 8 million in the sixteenth century. Cultural violence followed physical violence. By no means was it a cultural encounter, but rather an ethnocide of mammoth proportions.[31]

Pablo Picasso's painting "The Charnel House," which was conceived at the end of World War II, offers a reminder of the other side of modernity's march for progress. In the upper left-hand corner is a comfortable still-life composition of a pitcher and casserole atop a small table. Underneath are corpses ravaged by hunger and neglect,

30. González, "The Changing Geography of Church History," 25.

31. Arias, "Global and Local," 60–61. The genocide in America is unmatched on a world scale. One estimate provides this figure: 112,554,000 indigenous people in the western hemisphere in 1492 and an estimate of 28,554,000 in 1980. See LaDuke, "Traditional Ecological Knowledge," 515.

the unquiet dead of modern, total war. As art critic John Bentley Mays reflects,

> The great art of our time, I believe, will be an art of this paradox and absurdity, of luxury and the quiet horror hidden under the table. Such is a our legacy from the 20th century, and our unique destiny; to have our pleasures, to create, to live out our days here in the peaceable kitchen of capitalist prosperity—to feast and banter and enjoy ourselves round the table beneath which lie the rotting corpses, the heaps of memories, of the modern centuries' innocent dead.[32]

During the Cold War, globalization and hegemonic wars came in the so-called "low-intensity conflicts," and the global South was the location of these conflicts. As a form of proxy war between the United States and the Soviet Union, they may have been considered "low-intensity" conflicts for the two superpowers, but certainly they were "high intensity" for the affected countries of the global South. At a conference in 1994, a Colombian participant raised the question, "Why do you call this war cold? For us in poor countries, who bore the brunt of East and West proxy struggles, this war felt very hot!"[33] It was certainly a very hot war for those who bore the brunt of the "low intensity" conflicts.

Low-intensity conflicts were present in countries in Latin America, Asia, the Pacific, and Africa. Repressive regimes proliferated under the support of the United States to combat nationalist and popular movements. Countries and people's movements that opposed or were critical of capitalist globalization were readily dismissed as communists. People's movements that opposed projects financed by the IMF and World Bank because of their disastrous effects became the target of military reprisal. Community leaders were "salvaged" and communities massacred. Lest we be misled, low-intensity conflicts are not bygone events, though we have stopped thinking of them in Cold War terms.

The demise of the Soviet Union and the end of the Cold War led many to believe that a new era of global peace was coming, that the United Nations would be stronger, and that conflict resolution would be widely practiced by nations. It is my contention that this idea was founded on the assumption that the main problem was the so-called

32. Cited in Leddy, *Radical Gratitude*, 113.
33. Herr and Herr, *Transforming Violence*, 14.

East-West conflict. For those who have always seen the issue through the prism of North-South conflict, however, there was no illusion that global peace would follow the demise of Soviet Union.

Also, sadly, after the Cold War the world has been plunged into a series of bitter conflicts. For years, colonial masters and the Cold War superpowers created and maintained national boundaries that did not respect ethnic lines. When the boundaries were weakened, ethnic and religious conflicts raised their ugly heads. Bitter conflicts such as those in Sri Lanka, Liberia, Ireland, Angola, and India have been going on for years or decades while others, including Tajikistan, Chechnya, Rwanda, Burundi, and some nations in the South Pacific, are relatively recent. But even in the most-recent civil wars, including the conflict between the Hutus and the Tutsis' in Rwanda and between the Serbians and the Bosnian Muslims in the former Yugoslavia, the roots of the conflict are very deep.[34]

Whether directly or indirectly related to predatory globalization, the world is experiencing the globalization of violence in general and of terrorism in particular. While the United States has been the target of the most dramatic attack, other countries or communities have been victims too. Well-coordinated bombings and attacks shook Madrid (March 11, 2004), London (July 7, 2005), and Mumbai (November 26, 2008). On August 17, 2009, 20 people were killed and 100 were injured when a suicide bomber attacked a police station in North Caucasus (Russia). In spite of the Kremlin's claim that the region has stabilized and fighting in Chechnya has ended, Islamic militants continue with their suicide attacks.[35] These are only a few of the recent expressions of violence, particularly in the form of terrorism, occurring around the world, and it is likely that such violence will be with us for the long haul unless we can address their root causes.

SEPTEMBER 11, 2001: TERRORISM AGAINST THE TERRORISM OF PREDATORY GLOBALIZATION

Not all of our evils can be attributed to predatory globalization; nonetheless, it is a major triggering factor in many expressions of terrorism around the world. Globalization, as a shorthand term that represents not just the economy but also the spread of Western project and mo-

34. See Ferris, *Uprooted*, 25–27.
35. Associated Press, "Suicide bomb kills 20."

dernity, has surfaced in many fundamentalist militants' rhetoric as a threat that must be stopped by all means and at all costs. Often undergirded by religious motivations, the militants see their acts of terrorism as a religious duty directed against any representative or against any representation of ungodliness, decadence, or unbridled political and economic greed. Fundamentalist militants believe that the traditional values they hold dear have been eroded by the global capitalist market or Hollywood entertainment industries. After years of seeing their dreams betrayed and their cherished cultural-religious values undermined, many have "lost faith" in Western-secular-democratic project and are turning to religion for vision and empowerment.

Indeed, religion can provide vision and empowerment. Fundamentalist militants see religion as the remaining bastion against the modernist-secularist-imperialist threats, and they see it as articulating an alternative vision. While religion plays a prominent place in fundamentalist militancy and violence, I would like to make a caveat that it is not the sole factor; rather, it is intertwined with other factors such as political and economic. The use of such a term as "religious" violence or terrorism hides the fact that there are other factors that drive some toward terrorist acts. As Amir Hussain reminds us, "Palestinian terrorists do not attack Israelis [I hasten to say not all Israelis are Jews] because they are Jews but because of the political and economic ramifications of the Israeli occupation of Palestine." Also, Hussain continues, it is "understandable that a young Palestinian man who has no hope for a reasonable future in the Occupied Territories, would volunteer to blow himself up if his family would receive financial support from a sponsoring organization."[36]

With the West, especially the United States, viewed as the primary underwriter of global capitalist and Western-modernist-decadent secularism, it is not a surprise that the target of most recent attacks were the symbol of the global market (the World Trade Center) and military might (the Pentagon). For many militants, the United States is the primary or secondary enemy. The U.S. State Department's counterterrorism unit made a report that 40 percent of all acts of terrorism worldwide in the 1990s have been directed against U.S. citizens and its facilities.[37] Why is the United States the enemy? When you

36. Hussain, *Oil and Water*, 136.
37. Juergensmeyer, *Terror*, 178–79.

ask Osama bin Laden and his followers, they respond that the United States is the "biggest terrorist in the world." The lineup of U.S. crimes in bin Laden's list is long: "occupying the lands of Islam in the holiest of places" (Arabian Peninsula), "plundering its riches, dictating its rulers, humiliating its people, terrorizing its neighbors and turning its bases in the peninsula into a spearhead through which to fight the neighboring Muslim peoples."[38]

It is important to note, however, that the enemy of militant and violent Islamic fundamentalism is not only the United States and its European allies. Muslims can themselves become targets of Islamic terrorism if they are perceived to be in connivance with the forces of global westoxification. Before Al-Qaida shifted its focus to the "far enemy" (the United States and other countries) in 1996, it targeted the "near enemy" of Islam, enemies such as Muslim leaders who were more open to Westernization or were cuddling with imperialist Western powers. Armed not only with guns but also with the militant extremist ideas of Sayyid Qutb, Muslims who are cooperating with the governments of unbelievers have become targets.[39] The enemies include, for example, rulers of Saudi Arabia, kings of Jordan, and the rulers of Egypt. Anwar Sadat of Egypt died from bullets fired by his own soldiers who were members of an Islamic jihadist, Jamaat al-Jihad.[40]

Then there came the shocking and terrifying September 11 attack against a powerful nation. On that day, the leader of the globalizing world had its own experience of terrorism, generally viewed as unprecedented in its history, which of course is not quite true from the perspective of victims such as the Native Americans. Terrorism catapulted into the limelight and became the defining global issue. The terrorists (fifteen of the nineteen hijackers were Saudis) not only harbored the hatred of a long trail of terror but were nourished by a growing Islamic fundamentalism. Though morally indefensible, the act of the terrorists is an expression of desperation to proclaim to the world how Western capitalist domination, spearheaded by the United States, is felt in predominantly Islamic countries. It is readily dismissed by many as based on envy of the Western way of life, but to say this, I

38. Cited in Juergensmeyer, Ibid., 179.
39. Antoun, *Understanding Fundamentalism*, 157.
40. Esposito, *Unholy War*, 90.

believe, is a form of refusal to examine the history of the relationship of the West with the global South and, especially, the Islamic world.

WHOSE SEPTEMBER 11 ARE WE TALKING ABOUT?

Shock, disbelief, and anger reigned in the "land of the free and home of the brave" following the September 11 terrorist attack. In a timely fashion, leaders of various religious groups gathered for worship at the National Cathedral, which was broadcast by various television networks. Even as my heart grieved, I felt a discomfort during the reading of the Beatitudes (Mt 5:3–12). Who are the meek? Who are the persecuted? Is it the empire of the United States of America? In fact, that is what was inferred. Claiming itself as the persecuted, as epitomized in the reading of the Beatitudes at the National Cathedral, the United States launched the war on terrorism with a sense of moral righteousness oblivious to its own culpability in the tragedy. In the same National Cathedral where the Beatitudes were read, words of moral indignation and revenge reverberated. An outrageous sacrilege was committed.

There is no doubt that the 11th of September 2001 is a historical turning point in the experience of the people of the United States. What is perturbing, however, is that we have defined global history only in terms of "our" September 11. To remember "our" September 11 and not the September 11 of others is very dangerous and morally outrageous. It is dangerous because it pushes under the rug the suffering of other nations, especially the suffering caused by the involvement of the United States. It is morally outrageous because what counts as suffering is only that of its own citizens. To think only of "our" September 11 is not simply a question of being uninformed; it is part and parcel of selective and organized forgetting designed to support narrow national interests.

What is perturbing is that so few, even among well-educated people in the United States, know or remember what happened on September 11, 1973. What we do not remember (or want to remember) is that, rather than the victim, the United States (a country that unabashedly claims to be on the vanguard of democracy and freedom in the world) engineered an overthrow of the democratically elected government of Chile.[41] It was on that day, September 11, 1973 (Chile's 9/11), that Salvador Allende died defending democracy. Imagine

41. Cobb, "A War Against Terrorism," 3.

Santiago, Chile on that fateful day: "billowing smoke and raging fire, an apocalypse of destruction and terror, airplanes overhead attacking the Moneda, the symbol of Chilean democracy. And after the airplanes and the fire and the destruction came the disappearances and the tortures, the disbelief and the despair, the unspeakable."[42]

What about September 11, 1990—another 9/11? We do not remember what happened on this date because we were not the ones being hurt. The Iraqis, on the other hand, do not forget this date, for on this day, President George H. W. Bush, then President of the United States, delivered a speech to a joint session of Congress announcing his decision to go to war against Iraq.[43] After a few months of war preparation, the Allied forces launched the first attack in January 1991. Through the sanitized CNN coverage, people around the world watched from their TV screens what appeared to be a "clean war" targeting Saddam Hussein's regular army. But this is far from the reality. Tens of thousands of people, soldiers and civilians, were killed from the devastating bombing. It did not stop here. Over the next decade, U.S. and British forces fired thousands of missiles and bombs targeting not only the enemies but also water treatment facilities, farmland, and other infrastructure, leaving 300 tons of depleted uranium. As a result, there has been a fourfold increase in cancer among children in southern Iraq. Still not satisfied with the havoc that it brought on Iraq, the United States spearheaded the imposition of economic sanctions on the nation. According to an estimate, around half a million Iraqi children died as a result of a decade of sanctions.

Moreover, what about September 11, 1922—another 9/11? This is another sad and unforgettable date in Middle East history, particularly for the Palestinians. On this date, ignoring Arab outrage, the British government proclaimed a mandate affirming imperial Britain's 1917 Balfour Declaration, which promised European Zionists "a national home for Jewish people" in the heart of Palestinian land.[44] Adding insult to injury, in 1937 Winston Churchill had this to say:

> I do not agree that the dog in a manger has the final right to
> the manger, even though he may have lain there for a very long
> time. I do not admit that right. I do not admit, for instance, that

42. Berger, "Fragments of a Vision," 112.

43. Cited in Roy, *War Talk*, 63.

44. Cited in Roy, 57.

a great wrong has been done to the Red Indians of America, or the black people of Australia. I do not admit that a wrong has been done to these people by the fact that a stronger race, a higher grade race, a more worldly-wise race, to put it that way, has come in and taken their place.[45]

Is Churchill's voice an isolated one? We might wish that the more contemporary George H.W. Bush would express his thoughts in a more refined manner than Churchill's harsh rhetoric before him. Unfortunately, confronted on the deaths of 290 individuals aboard an Iranian passenger plane that was shot down by U.S. firepower, Bush, with an arrogant demeanor like Churchill's, said, "I will never apologize for the United States of America—I don't care what the facts are."[46]

Like Churchill's, Bush's voice is not an isolated expression of the U.S. mind. His words articulate the thoughts and practices of the U.S. government throughout the years. Since the declaration of the State of Israel, the U.S. government has been its staunch supporter. It provided economic, political, and military support to Israel. The United States has blocked, along with Israel, almost every U.N. resolution that called for peaceful and equitable solution to the conflict. The arrogant empire could care less about world opinion despite overwhelming facts.

EXHUMING THE SKELETONS IN OUR CLOSET

We cannot fully understand "our" September 11 unless we exhume the "skeletons in our closet." The September 11 that we painfully remember follows a "trail of terror" from the founding years of the republic to its history of annexations and colonial expansion. I could give you a long account of this "trail of terror"; instead, I share with you a story from Alex Chasing Hawk, a nationally famous Indian leader from Cheyenne River and a classic storyteller. This is how Vine Deloria puts it:

> It seemed that a white man was introduced to an old chief in New York City. Taking a liking to the old man, the white man invited him to dinner. The old chief hadn't eaten a good steak in a long time and eagerly accepted. He finished one steak in no time and still looked hungry. So the white man offered to buy him another steak.

45. Churchill in Roy, 58, citing "Scurrying Towards Bethlehem," 5.
46. Ibid., 77. Roy citing Apple, "Bush Appears in Trouble," A1.

As they were waiting for the steak, the white man said, "Chief, I sure wish I had your appetite."

"I don't doubt it, white man," the chief said. "You took my land, you took my mountains and streams, you took my salmon and my buffalo. You took everything I had except my appetite and now you want that. Aren't you ever going to be satisfied?" [47]

Intoxicated by power, the young nation arrogated the name of the whole continent (America) to itself and ventured on with the project of colonial expansion (annexation of western frontier). In the 1920s, the name "United States" gave way to "America." The people liked the name America "precisely for its imperial suggestions of an intoxicating and irresistible identity windswept into coherence by the momentum of destiny."[48] In obedience to its "manifest destiny," the United States took the "errand to the wilderness" to spread the blessings of a "settled" life. It annexed western Florida in order to have access to the Gulf *of* Mexico (1810), and by 1853 it was able to acquire by various means Florida, Texas, Arizona, Nevada, Utah, New Mexico, California, and a good portion of Kansas, Colorado, Oklahoma, and Wyoming.[49] Still not satisfied with its acquisitions in the American continent, it sailed overseas to conquer new territories. By 1898, it gained control of Puerto Rico and Cuba. In that same year, it annexed Hawaii against the wishes of the native Hawaiians and imprisoned Princess Lili'uokalani; occupied Guam and Samoa; and conquered the Philippines in a war of genocide only to be repeated on a massive scale in the "killing fields" of Indochina.[50]

From Latin America to the Caribbean islands, the Pacific, Southeast Asia, Southern and Central Asia, to the Middle East and Eastern Europe, the United States undermined governments that stood in its way. This, we have been told, is necessary to safeguard the way of life of its common citizens. In 1953, the United States engineered the overthrow of the nationalistic Mosaddeq in Iran and installed its "guy" (Mohammad Reza Shah Pahlavi), who was later overthrown by the Iranian people under the leadership of Ayatollah Khomeini

47. Deloria, "Indian Humor," 344–45.
48. Welch, *Sweet Dreams*, xvii.
49. González, *Mañana*, 31–32.
50. Wei and Kamel, *Resistance in Paradise*.

(1978 to1979). In 1954, a year after it helped overthrow Mosaddeq, the United States engineered the overthrow of Guatemalan democracy.[51] On April 1, 1964, it supported Brazil's right-wing military in the overthrow of Joao Goulart's government because of its move to expropriate and redistribute privately owned land and nationalize private oil refineries.

Still fresh from the Iran hostage crisis, the United States secretly traded arms with Iran to fund the Contra insurgency against the Sandinistas for a period of nine years (1981 to 1990). How can a country which has pronounced that it would not negotiate with terrorists and had its citizens taken hostage by another country trade arms with that country? This is an outrageous expression of moral flip-flopping to support self-interest. Within the years of the Reagan administration, 150,000 people were killed in the U.S. sponsored war in Latin America. Also, within this period (April 1982), the U.S.-backed Israeli invasion of Lebanon added 20,000 to the list of victims of U.S.-sponsored international terrorism.[52]

Additionally, the United States vetoed the proposal of the U.N. Security Council for Indonesian withdrawal from East Timor. What ensued was genocide in East Timor that spanned two decades.[53] Earlier, in 1958, the CIA had sponsored a failed coup in Indonesia. Then in 1965, the pro-U.S. Suharto carried out a successful coup and slaughtered several hundred thousand people. Once again, Indonesia became open to robbery by powerful nations.[54] The United States propped up the dictatorial regime of Ferdinand Marcos in the Philippines for many years, and later withdrew its support of the dictator only after the overwhelming people's power revolution.

If the suffering that matters is only that of the United States and its citizens—not the suffering that they inflict on others—it is also the United States that defines what counts as terrorism. Like the emperor in the story I cited earlier, the United States has dominated the terrorism discourse. Anyone who blocks its goal of geopolitical and economic domination risks being labeled a terrorist. The United States, however, has been selective in lobbing the term "terrorist," mostly

51. Chomsky, *The Culture of Terrorism*, 28.

52. Ibid., 29.

53. Griffith, *The War on Terrorism*, 45.

54. Chomsky, *The Culture of Terrorism*, 181.

targeted at less-powerful nations that stand in the way of its geopolitical and economic hegemony. When it was pursuing the ouster of the USSR from Afghanistan, Reagan called the Afghan mujahedeen (with whom Osama bin Laden worked closely) "freedom fighters," the moral equivalents of the "Founding Fathers." On the other hand, Nelson Mandela, a prisoner on Robben Island, was on the official watch list of the Pentagon as a "terrorist."[55] It was only in 2008 that he was taken off the list, which included members of the African National Congress (ANC).

During the Iran-Iraq war, the United States was on the side of Iraq. It provided protection for Iraqi shipping through the gulf and supplied intelligence information on the movement of Iranian troops to Saddam Hussein. Iraq used chemical weapons against its opponent, but the United States was mum about it, for at that moment in history, Saddam was its "guy." In an effort to prevent congressional moves to place sanction against Iraq, Bush and Reagan defended Saddam and praised him for his bold stance against terrorism.[56]

Here is a nation whose foreign policy exemplifies doublespeak. We may ask, How can the United States be accused of terrorism when it claims to be the primary underwriter of "the war against terrorism"? Just as some terrorists have assumed the guise of "freedom fighters," it is likewise possible that "terrorism can assume the guise of a war against terrorism."[57] The war against terrorism appears to be merely another moment in the cycle of terrorism and counterterrorism.

TERRORISM AND THE NEW SEASON OF GLOBALIZATION

A new season is under way, which is not an occasion to be jolly for concerned citizens of the globalized world. President George W. Bush did not hesitate to use the September 11 tragedy as an occasion to launch a new season of imperialism and globalization under the guise of war on terrorism. The September 11 tragedy provided a perfect occasion for the administration to launch, with the support of "terrified" citizens of the "home of the brave," what it had been hatching in the planning room. On May 17, 2001, three months before September 11, the White House released the Cheney report on U.S. energy policy. This report, reflecting the outlook of big oil and coal companies,

---

55. Cobb, "A War Against Terror," 3.

56. Griffith, *The War on Terrorism*, 93.

57. Ibid., x.

called for an aggressive campaign to gain access to oil supplies not only in the Persian Gulf but to other areas as well. U.S. policymakers still hope that at some point, with a change of regime, U.S. companies will be able to draw oil from Iraq and Iran (the second and third largest possessors of oil, respectively, after Saudi Arabia). At the same time, there are other areas that need to be secured and maintained: the Caspian Sea basin, the west coast of Africa, Venezuela, Colombia, and Mexico.[58]

When the September 11 tragedy came onto the scene, a perfect storm became a perfect justification to pursue aggressively the energy plan. Osama bin Laden, who was kicked out of Saudi Arabia and found asylum in Afghanistan under the protection of the Taliban, had to be pursued. The Northern Alliance, in cahoots with the United States, launched a military offensive against the Taliban and in pursuit of bin Laden. With a U.S.-friendly regime in place in Afghanistan, an opportunity came that the hungry oil companies and their partners had been waiting for—the construction of a trans-Afghanistan oil pipeline. Also, on November 25, 2001, barely two months after September 11, Chevron Texaco Corporation and others in the Caspian Pipeline Consortium opened a $2.5 billion pipeline stretching 987 miles from Kazakhstan to the Russian port on the Black Sea. Both Russia and the United States support this project. Russia expects to collect more than $20 billion in taxes over the next forty years.[59]

What about the war on terror in Colombia? Who are the terrorists? What is its connection with the new season of terrorism and globalization? Again, Michael Klare sees the connection to oil, especially since the guerrillas are blowing up oil pipelines and oil facilities. The vital oil supply line is at stake. Thus, the United States announced its intention to support the Colombian government in its campaign against the guerrilla movements.[60] From the point of view of the new season of globalization, the nationalist guerilla groups are terrorists.

Oil, however, is only one aspect of the convergence of the war on terrorism and the new season of globalization. There are other natural resources at stake, especially as they are becoming increasingly

58. Slaughter, "An Interview with Michael Klare," 21.

59. Todres, "Chevron pipeline," cited in Kirk-Duggan, "Civil War, Civil Rights," 44.

60. Klare, in Slaughter, 22.

depleted. For example, it is easy to think of water as an inexhaustible resource: this is not the case. Some parts of the world are already in turmoil because of water shortages and distribution problems. We must act soon if the resource wars are not to escalate into world anarchy.[61]

The war on terrorism has become a convenient justification in rewarding "friendly" governments and punishing those that do not toe the line of corporate globalization. "Friendly" governments are vital to the interest of transnational corporations, which would not be able to carry out their rapacious economic pursuits without them. Thomas Friedman wrote in the *New York Times,* "For globalization to succeed, America cannot fear to act like the omnipotent superpower that it is. The hidden hand of the market will never work without a hidden fist. McDonald's cannot flourish without McDonnell Douglas, the designer of the F-15."[62]

Indeed, "the hidden hand of the market will never work without a hidden fist." McDonald's is accompanied by McDonnell Douglas's F-15. The construction of Chico Dam in the Philippines was accompanied by the hidden fist of the market. In like manner, the destructive logging of the Amazon rainforest has been made possible because of the hidden fist of the market. When the disastrous effects of globalization become unbearable, dissenting movements are to be expected. In reaction, the "friendly" governments become more repressive. The war on terrorism has become a convenient tool of the United States, multinational corporations, and the elites of "friendly" nations to quell nationalistic spirit and any form of legitimate dissent. Since the launching of the war against terror, "in country after country, freedoms are being curtailed in the name of protecting freedom, civil liberties are being suspended in the name of protecting democracy. All kinds of dissent are being defined as 'terrorism.'"[63]

DEATH SQUADS AND POLITICAL KILLINGS IN THE PHILIPPINES: A CASE OF STATE-SPONSORED TERRORISM

The Philippines offers a case of the interweaving of predatory globalization, the U.S. global war on terror, and human rights violation that

61. Griffin, "The Need for Global Democracy," 131.

62. Friedman, "What the World Needs Now." Cf. Friedman, *The Lexus and the Olive Tree,* 373.

63. Roy, "Come September," 10.

I know quite well. The United States views the Philippines as a strategic location in its global war on terror. Many documents speak of
the Philippines as a "second front" on the war on terror—second, for
example, to Iraq and Afghanistan. Some would disagree with such a
designation, especially if we think of Pakistan and Indonesia. If, as al-
legedly expressed by some U.S. officials, that Mindanao is a "doormat
for terrorism in the region," then there is warrant to call it a "second
front."[64] I suspect, however, that there are other reasons for considering the Philippines a "second front": it allows the United States to
situate itself strategically in Southeast Asia.

The United States does not have unlimited resources to wage
a global war on terror. It cannot do the war on terror alone, so the
U.S. co-opts other countries such as the Philippines. The United
States considers it a dependable ally. The face of the war on terror
in the Philippines is basically a copy of that in the United States, but
the Gloria Macapagal-Arroyo administration has adapted it to the
Philippine context. At this point, it is necessary to highlight four issues in the U.S.-Philippines alliance: ideology, antiterrorism laws, the
Visiting Forces Agreement (VFA), and military funding.

A study of the ideological rhetoric of the war on terror in the
Philippines demonstrates how much of a copycat it is of the U.S. ideological rhetoric. Macapagal-Arroyo echoes many of the statements of
George W. Bush, when she says things such as, "if you do not fight
terrorism you are a supporter or terrorist lover. If you are a supporter
of terrorism, you are not a Filipino. If you are not a Filipino, who are
you?" In other words, following Bush and his minions, "if you are not
with us, you are against us. You are an enemy."

Along the lines of the U.S. war on terror, the Philippine Congress
adopted an anti-terror law (similar to the U.S. Patriot Act), including
the controversial "extraordinary rendition." The U.S. doctrine of preemptive strike also finds its direct translation in the Philippines. The
Philippines calls its preemptive strike version CPR—Calibrated Preemptive Response. CPR calls for a comprehensive approach, which
is understood as cleaning up the pond that breeds terrorism. It is so
notoriously comprehensive that it does not make a distinction among
legal activist groups, human rights and social justice advocates, and
armed groups, such as the New People's Army.

64. Docena, "When Uncle Sam comes marching in."

Although the Philippine Congress said no to U.S. military presence, U.S. forces are back in the Philippines through the Visiting Forces Agreement (VFA). A few months before the Visiting Forces Agreement was signed, there was a relentless disinformation campaign. Every day, there was news that China was building a military platform in the disputed oil-rich waters west of the Philippines. Immediately after the VFA was signed, news about China's construction of a military platform disappeared from the media. Why? This has led me to suspect the motivation behind the VFA. Is it to stop the spread of terrorists groups such as Jemaah Islamiyah and Abu Sayyaf, or to put the United States strategically in Southeast Asia, or perhaps both?

What will the Philippines get from the Visiting Forces Agreement and the joint military exercises? This leads to the issue of financing the war on terror. It is difficult to get the exact figure, but there is no doubt that the Philippine government relies heavily on U.S. financial support to carry out its campaign to end the long and festering insurgency problem as well as to silence the vocal critics of the government. Politically motivated killings reached an alarming rate in 2005, with one person killed or disappeared every other day. Since Macapagal-Arroyo was installed as president in January 2001 up to November 2006, Karapatan (the Alliance for the Advancement of People's Rights) documented a total of 6,990 cases of human rights violations affecting 396,099 individuals. On December 31, 2006, Karapatan reported 819 victims of extrajudicial killings, while 357 survived attempts on their lives.[65]

These killings are more than random acts; they are well-financed and systematically carried out in the name of the Philippine government's alliance with the U.S. war on terror and the government's counterinsurgency campaign. Taking advantage of the U.S. war on terror, the military aid that comes from U.S. taxpayers, and adopting the rhetoric of counterterrorism, citizens, NGOs, and church bodies that call for the transformation of the Philippine society have been labeled quickly as "terrorists," which serves as a warrant for repression, if not a death warrant. Relentless in its campaign to eliminate "enemies of the state," the Macapagal-Arroyo administration launched what it calls an "integrated approach" under a culture of impunity. Irony of ironies: the government that has proudly proclaimed to the world it has abolished the "death penalty" has replaced it with "death squads." Even

65. Ibid., 35.

after the visit of Philip Alston, the U.N. rapporteur on human rights, the desperate regime pursues its political killings. This regime continues to believe that more extrajudicial executions will instill fear and silence any prophetic voice from the civil society. With the end of the Macapagal-Arroyo administration and a new administration in place, a renewed sense of hope is in the air that Benigno (Noynoy) Aquino III will be true to his campaign promise in taking the perpetrators of extrajudicial killings to the bar of justice. After only a few days in office, however, extrajudicial executions have become news again.

FAUSTIAN BARGAIN: COMBATING GLOBAL TERRORISM AND HOMELAND INSECURITY

There is a twin to the war on terrorism abroad. The war on terrorism abroad has disastrous connections at home: it is also terrorizing the people at home—the U.S. Terrorized by fear of terrorism, the citizens of the "home of the brave" have become vulnerable to various forms of duct-tape security. Terrified and disoriented, they have been more than willing to make a Faustian bargain with their rulers: we surrender some of our civil liberties with the promise that you protect us from the terrorists.[66] There has been a dramatic and continuing erosion of civil and political liberties. This should not be surprising if we are keen readers of history. Edward LeRoy Long Jr., puts it succinctly: "A society that seeks to be completely protected against the danger of terrorism is very likely to undercut its freedoms in ways that adversely affect all its citizens. A fortress society cannot be created without becoming a police state."[67]

Democracy has suffered in several ways in the United States in the aftermath of the September 11 tragedy. The Patriot Act (a counterterrorism law) was passed hastily in October 2002 without serious debate in public, even before many members of Congress had read it. Congress passed it without any demonstration of its necessity except vaguely as a response to the terrorist attack. But is the Patriot Act truly necessary, and will it make the United States more secure? Subsequent revelations of intelligence blunders indicate that what happened on the 11th of September could have been prevented within the powers that law enforcement and intelligence agencies already had. Whether

66. Branfman, "The Need to De-Mystify," 37.

67. Long, *Facing Terrorism*, 60.

the Patriot Act has made the United States more secure is highly questionable, but there is one thing that lawyer Wendy Kaminer considers certain: "[I]t enhanced the power of the executive branch at the expense of the judiciary, mainly by minimizing judicial review of federal law enforcement efforts whether they target terrorism or not."[68]

Voices of dissent, which are an essential part of a truly democratic society, have been viciously attacked. To express dissent is to risk having one's patriotism questioned. To speak or preach about peace is to court being charged as naïve and unpatriotic. Blinded by this narrow patriotism, some church members find it repulsive even to suggest in a sermon that God blesses other countries, such as Iraq, in a similar manner that we say, "God bless America." I encountered these repulsions in some congregations of the United Church of Christ (USA), a denomination in which I currently hold my membership, in my prophetic sermons regarding the war on terror. Critical judgment has been consumed in the idolatrous patriotism of the American public.

Terrorized by fear and consumed in idolatrous patriotism, a large segment of the public is ready to sacrifice health care and education in favor of increasing the budget for the military. It is hard to disagree with Marcus Borg's statement: "It is difficult to avoid the conclusion that fear is a more powerful political motive in our society than compassion."[69] Congress, without much debate, approved the creation of the Department of Homeland Security and increased military spending, even the costly budget to finance the war in Iraq and, with growing intensity, the war in Afghanistan. Elected officials who had been miserly in appropriating money for various forms of "safety net" programs have become more generous in financing the war on terrorism. Even with a new leader (President Barak Obama) who was catapulted into office under the campaign banner of "change," many are seeing more of the same. This seems to be true with the war on terror even if the official rhetoric has changed. The basic assumptions of the war on terror have remained the same, and it gets the lion's share of the budget. This will continue to be the case with Obama's decision to "finish the job" in Afghanistan by sending more troops. It seems that the war on terror will be with us for the long haul.

68. Kaminer, "Freedom," 22.

69. Borg, *The Heart of Christianity*, 143.

This is a sobering and trying time not only in the life of the United States but also of the whole world. We are, indeed, living in scary times, for scary times make scared people surrender their freedom. But this is also a time when we are challenged to live with integrity and speak truth to power. The war on terrorism seems not a "clash of civilizations," as Samuel Huntington puts it, but a clash between anarchy and anarchy.[70] Rather than a clash of civilizations, this looks like a "clash of fundamentalisms" or a "clash of barbarisms."[71] Narrow and self-serving nationalism or patriotism is a sure recipe for global anarchy. If anarchy is not to be our future, global citizens must act together to forge an alternative tomorrow. Civilizations need not clash. Instead, they must dialogue—a dialogue of civilizations. This is an immense challenge for all; this is an immense challenge for the Christian church.

70. Huntington, *The Clash of Civilizations*.
71. Ali, *The Clash of Fundamentalisms*.

3

The Church in the Midst of Globalization

Reorienting the Church

A S THE PREVIOUS CHAPTERS have shown, globalization is a multifaceted and omnipresent phenomenon. The multiple dimensions
of globalization mentioned in chapters 1 and 2 (technology, finance,
ideology, ecology, migration, health, religious plurality, and terrorism)
pervade and affect all aspects of our lives. We can say that globalization has become the ocean in which we all swim—or sink. Or, to use
another metaphor, it has become the air we breathe. Often we do not
notice when the level of air toxicity has reached a deadly height. A
cultural critique of globalization in general and of the global market
in particular can provide clarification of this point.

The global market is more than a mechanism of control or a network of relations driven by profit; it is creating a global culture that
shapes the way we think, dwell, and act. "The architects of McWorld,"
as Tom Sine reminds us, "are not simply trying to increase global free
trade and free enterprise; they are working to redefine what is important and what is of value in people's lives all over the planet, to
sell their wares."[1] We not only live in a "market economy," we live in
a "market society" in which "market-based values define the atmosphere in which we live and move and have our being."[2] If the market
is not only about financial transactions but also about who we are and
what matters to us, then it is embracing the realm of morality and, furthermore, the realm of religion. That is why an economic and political

1. Sine, *Mustard Seed*, 21.
2. McDaniel, *Living from the Center*, 41.

61

critique of globalization, particularly the market, is not adequate. We must do a cultural and religious critique as well.

SEDUCTIVE-EXPLOITATIVE POWER OF THE MARKET: A CULTURAL CRITIQUE

Without a doubt, for those who have suffered under the direct and brutal hands of the agents of neoliberal capitalism, the market's exercise of power can be terribly coercive. The coercive unhidden hand of the market has been experienced by many who have resisted its control. Torture, killings, and disappearances have been the fate of many who simply refused to keep quiet. Transnational corporations have been conduits with host national governments in silencing opposition to their interest; however, the predatory market's pervasive, deceptive, and enduring power lies in its ability to seduce people to think and live in ways consonant with the worldview and ethos of the market society. Seduction more than assault is its main strategy—a strategy more suited with an understanding of power that is less concentrated on an imposing sovereign but is more diffused and dispersed throughout the system. The global culture industries, particularly the various cultural media outlets, are its main instruments of seduction. I agree with Michael Budde that these global culture industries "collectively influence how people relate to the processes and products of economic activity. Movies, television, popular music, advertising—these are the vectors and initiators for ideas regarding the valued, the innovative, the normal, the erotic, and the repulsive."[3]

Advertising and marketing are the two most common ways the global market seduces people to accept life in a market society. We can imagine how many ads flow out of media outlets every day. Wherever we go and whatever we do, such as when we eat, travel, go to school, work and worship, we are inundated with commercials, and our consciousness is streaming with brand names and trademarks. On top of the three-to-four hours of daily television that individuals in the U.S. watch on average, we can add 20 hours per week of exposure to radio, junk mail, telemarketing, outdoor and billboard advertisements, internet, home and personal music entertainment, and so forth.[4] The

3. Budde, *The (Magic) Kingdom of God*, 32.
4. Ibid., 81.

fact that we are not fully conscious of the barrage probably preserves our sanity, but it does not mean that those messages have no effects.[5]

More than an instrument to facilitate buying and selling, what makes the capitalist market advertising and marketing more insidious is that they define subjectivity and agency. The capitalist market advertising is not designed simply to persuade people to buy certain kinds of products but to become a certain kind of subject—a subject as possessor or consumer. Peter McLaren puts it this way: The "endless acts of consumption provoked by the *danse macabre* of capitalism organizes subjectivity in specific ways around the general maxim: I purchase, therefore I am."[6] Possession and consumption define who one is or how one is perceived and given value by others. That which we consume and possess is not, however, limited to the use value of something: we are consumers of image value. When image value becomes the object of fixation, we can say that the individual's desire finds no limit and, consequently, no satisfaction.

Consumerism involves more than the consumption of an image value that an individual desperately needs to elevate his or her status. It is also an expression of a deep psychological alienation, and even more; consumerism is a spiritual matter. I say spiritual because consumer goods and commodities have been spiritualized or equated with the presence of the spirit. The world of capitalist-consumerism considers increased consumption of commodities a sign of the spirit's presence in one's life. At the heart of this claim is a distorted spirituality. This point provides an excellent segue to my religious critique of the global market.

THE RELIGION OF THE MARKET

The global market is not devoid of any religiosity, but it is a religiosity that runs counter to the central tenets of major world religions. Even at the level of semantics there are obvious correlations: both fields regularly employ such words as trust, fidelity, bond, confidence, fiduciary, debt, redemption, saving, security, and so on.[7] The total market operates on what Franz Hinkelammert calls "entrepreneurial

---

5. Ibid.

6. McLaren, *Revolutionary Multiculturalism*, 197.

7. Meeks, *God the Economist*, 29.

metaphysics."[8] Devotees of this metaphysics speak of "commodities, money, marketing, and capital, as the great object of their devotion; a pseudo-divine world towers over human beings, and dictates their laws to them."[9]

Harvey Cox offers a sharp and cogent critique of the religious claim of the global market.[10] Cox argues that the global capitalist market has usurped the traditional attributes of God: omnipotence, omniscience, and omnipresence. Like the omnipotent God of the Hebrew Scripture, it does not tolerate any other divinities and it demands undivided devotion and worship. And, as an omniscient one, it claims to know all and to know best; thus, every intellect in this world must bow down before it. It seems, argues Cox, that the real venue of *sacrificium intellectum* today is not the church but the shopping mall. In the face of the god of the market devoted consumers crucify their intellect and accept the absurd, saying: *Credo quia absurdum est* (I believe because it is absurd).[11]

Moreover, the market-god is omnipresent; it is pervasive and ubiquitous. No one can run away from it or escape its presence. Wherever we go, the market-god is there. How can we flee from its presence? If we ascend to the heavens, the market-god is there. If we make our bed in Sheol, it is there. And "[i]f we take the wings of the morning and dwell in the uttermost part of the sea," even there the hand of the global market is present (Ps 139: 7–10). The global market has become the god in whom "we live and move and have our being" (Acts 17:28). So it claims: "outside of the market there is no salvation" (*extra mercatum nulla salus*). Global capitalism has created an idol—an idol that sucks the blood of people around the world, though unevenly and differently. True to its name, consumerism consumes and capitalist globalism gobbles the consumers and the gobblers. John Cobb Jr. offers a critique of the religious metaphysics of this global market. Economism is the name of this religion, and its god is endless economic growth. Its priests are the economists; its evangelists are the advertisers; and its lay people are the consumers.[12] The shopping mall

8. Hinkelammert, "The Economic Roots of Idolatry," 165–93.
9. Ibid., 166.
10. Cox, "Mammon," 274–83.
11. Ibid., 278–79.
12. Cobb, "Economism or Planetism," 13.

is its cathedral; competitiveness is touted as virtue; and inefficiency is sin. "Shop till you drop" is the only way to salvation. And, if Jesus saves, we want to know where he shops.

Where shall we flee from its presence? If it is everywhere, the church is no exemption from its reach and influence. While the common discourse on the church and globalization puts globalization as a context that the church must respond to, that which the church must respond to is not totally outside of its own life. It is not an outside phenomenon to which the church must respond faithfully and creatively, but a phenomenon that is happening in the life of the church. Globalization is shaping and impacting the church in general and various congregations in particular around the world.

GLOBALIZATION, MISSION, AND COLONIALISM

There is no beginning in which we can say that the church was outside of the sphere of any globalizing force even when the globalizing force was not as extensive as it is today. The existence of the early Christian communities cannot be understood apart from their relationship with the globalizing power of their time, such as the Roman Empire. When Christianity first opened its young mouth, its language was shaped and informed by a globalizing empire. Even when its primary stance was resistance, it was not completely outside of the globalizing-homogenizing power. The so-called Constantinization of the church, while a significant moment, is but a part of an earlier and ongoing connection between church and a globalizing-imperializing power. As Joerg Rieger puts it, "The heritage of the church—in all its orthodox and heterodox forms—has been shaped by the intersections of empire and church since the early days."[13] This point challenges the notion that suddenly the pure church has become infected with an imperial virus. From the very beginning, the church was born in the "messy middle" and had to wrestle with the presence of globalizing-imperializing power in its life.

The interweaving and intermeshing of globalist colonialism and Christian mission is well documented. Volumes of materials point to the alliance of the church and colonization; as a consequence, I do not feel the need to take a full account of that relationship. The history of mission testifies to the fact that wherever there was colonization there

13. Rieger, *Christ and Empire*, 72.

was Christian mission. The presence of the church in various lands cannot be divorced from its complicity in the history of exploration, conquest, and colonization. The cross came along with the sword and cannons of the *conquistadors*, as the Bible along with the guns of modern imperializing nations.

For those steeped in the worldview of the fifteenth and sixteenth century, the alliance between colonialism and mission should not be a surprise. Under a theocratic worldview, it was unthinkable to separate the church from the state, the pope from the king, mission from colonialism. Whether the colonizers were Catholics or Protestants was irrelevant; both were committed to the theocratic ideal. No Roman Catholic or Protestant ruler of the period would imagine that in conquering and acquiring other nations he or she was only advancing his or her political hegemony. It was taken for granted that the conquered and colonized people must be missionized. Mission and colonization were inseparable: to colonize was to missionize, and to missionize was to colonize. The king colonized and the king missionized. Since the sixteenth century, if one said mission, the immediate understanding was colonization.[14]

The advent of the Enlightenment brought some changes in the thinking and practice of mission. Already in the seventeenth century, a shift is detectable when the theocratic ideal (alliance of church and state) was seriously under assault. Unlike the previous era, the modern missionary enterprise is no longer under the direct patronage of the king or emperor. This is particularly true with the rise of Protestant mission when mission work was supported by mission societies. Indeed, in some instances Western Protestant nations refused missionaries in their colonized territories, because they were considered a threat to commercial interest. This changed in the nineteenth century when colonial expansion would again acquire religious overtones.[15] Nevertheless, the Enlightenment made a rift in the church and state relations, which affected the thinking and doing of mission.

Let us not, however, be led into thinking that the entanglement of mission with colonialism weakened or was already absent because of the Enlightenment's rift in church-state relations. Though mission was no longer under the direct patronage of the king or the state, mission

14. Bosch, *Transforming Mission*, 303.
15. Ibid.

and colonialism continued their unholy affair. The collusion took a more covert form under the facade of secularism. Wherever there was colonial presence, there was mission. Mission and colonialism sailed together to the newly "discovered" world. An evidence of their unholy affair is that the identity of the colonizer often matched the missionary body operating in the colonized land. Thus, it was not a surprise for British missionaries to be present in British colonies, German missionaries in German colonies, U.S. missionaries in U.S. colonies, and French missionaries in French colonies. When the well-known French Cardinal Lavigerie (1825–1892) sent out his "White Fathers" to Africa, he spoke these words to them: *"Nous travaillons aussi pour la France"* ("We are working for France [as well as for the kingdom of God]").[16] One of the clearest legacies of the connection between missionary bodies and colonial powers is in the South Pacific. In reading particular materials produced by the South Pacific Association of Theological Schools (SPATS), I came across a telling connection. The dominance of one Christian group on each particular island is reflective of its major colonizing power: United Methodist in Fiji (UK), Roman Catholic in New Caledonia (France), Presbyterian Church in Vanuatu (UK), Congregational Church in American Samoa (U.S.A), United Church of Christ in the Marshall Islands (U.S.A), Anglican in the Solomon Islands (UK), and Free Wesleyan Church of Tonga on the island of Tonga (UK).[17]

Though there were groups both within the church and the wider society that were critical of the unholy alliance between mission and colonialism, the pervasive mood of the time was enthusiastic approval of colonial expansion as an occasion for mission. Missionaries considered the conquest of new lands as "providential" or an opportune moment (*kairos*) for mission. To turn one's back to this precious opportunity was considered "unpatriotic" to the country and "unfaithful" to the gospel of Jesus Christ.[18] The United States, which claims itself as a "nation with the soul of a church," could hardly avoid equating expansion with providence.[19] Even imperialism was viewed in a posi-

16. Ibid., 304. A living example of this phenomenon is in the islands of the South Pacific. See, Forman, *The Island Churches of the South Pacific.*

17. *SPATS Profile: Toward the New Millennium.*

18. Anderson, *Studies in Philippine Church History*, 279–300.

19. Hamilton, *Recovery of the Protestant Adventure*, 43.

tive and religious sense by the expansionists: imperialist expansion was considered an extension of what is best in American Christian civilization. One spokesman of American imperialism claimed that

> American imperialism, in its essence . . . is American valor, American manhood, American sense of justice and right, American conscience, American character at its best, listening to the voice of God, and His command nobly assuming this republic's rightful place in the grand forward movement for civilizing and Christianizing of all continents and all races.[20]

Sailing high with the wind of good intentions, the church participated in the imperial work with much zeal. The imperial motive came along with christianizing and civilizing the colonized people. Senator Albert Beveridge, an advocate of American expansionism, never failed to mention the God-given duty of the United States toward other nations at the same time pushing for economic profits of the expansion.[21] This idea of being God's agent was intertwined with a profit motive when it first laid out its plans for commercial expansion across the Pacific Ocean to the continent of Asia. Statesman Thomas Hart expected that the United States would "compete with England for the rich Asian trade, at the same time offering modern science and 'true religion' to the people of Asia."[22]

If the church saw the colonial expansion as providential, the colonializing state also saw the missionaries as ideal allies. Who would be the best persons to collaborate with the colonial government, if not the missionaries? They lived among the people, knew their language and customs, and had influence among them. Though missionaries were forbidden from holding political office, many served as advisers to indigenous leaders. In the South Pacific, for example, "missionary-influenced kingdoms" appeared in Tahiti, Tonga, Cook Islands, Mangareva, Hawaii, Wallis, Fiji, and the New Hebrides (Vanuatu).[23] John Philip, in spite of his reputation as champion of the oppressed colored people of the British colonies, had astounding words to say about the services of missionaries to the colonial government: "Missionary stations are the most efficient agents which can be employed to promote the internal

---

20. Cited in Handy, *A Christian America*, 126.

21. See Tucker, *The White Conscience*, 149–50.

22. Ibid., 152.

23. Forman, *The Island Churches*, 9.

strength of our colonies, and the cheapest and best military posts that a wise government can employ to defend its frontier against the predatory incursions of savage tribes."[24] The missionary enterprise was a valuable ally in the history of Western colonial expansion. We may recall the "three C's" of colonialism: Christianity, commerce, and civilization. Or in French, the three "M's": *militaires blancs, mercenaires blancs, and missionaires blancs.*[25] Whether they were aware of it or not, the missionaries became pioneers of Western colonial expansion. They were the vanguard and the rearguard of the Western colonial project. T. O. Beidelman states emphatically that

> Christian missions represent the most naive and ethnocentric, and therefore the most thorough-going, facet of colonial life . . . Missionaries invariably aimed at overall changes in the beliefs and actions of native peoples, at colonization of heart and mind as well as body. Pursuing this sustained policy of change, missionaries demonstrated a more radical and morally intense commitment to rule than political administrators or business men.[26]

"Decolonization" withdrew the "protective umbrella" of the missionary enterprise. Without the "protective umbrella," mission work was left to the church and mission bodies or mission societies. With the colonized nations decolonized and "protective umbrella" gone, many were led to believe that, finally, mission is no longer under the control of Western powers. But the issue is more than gaining national independence and autonomy of the then missionized churches. If that were the case, then we could say that the colonialist traits of Western mission are of a bygone era. Neocolonialism, however, does not warrant that understanding, not to mention the long process of decolonization that must take place. Even as many of the colonized countries have experienced decolonization, models of mission, mission programs, and missionary presence continue to perpetuate Western dominance in various forms of relationship, which have evolved into more subtle and sophisticated, if not, perhaps, more vicious ways.[27] Maybe they are more vicious because we have become less perceptive, critical,

24. Philip, cited in Bosch, *Transforming Mission*, 305.
25. Bosch, Ibid., 305.
26. Beidelman, *Colonial Evangelism*, 5–6
27. Bosch, *Transforming Mission*, 312.

and vocal of the neocolonial trappings in which we have been doing global mission/ministries in recent years, even among liberal mainline Protestant denominations. The sophistication of neoliberal global capitalism has made many of us believe that because direct control is over, we are already "outside" of the power of global capital. That is not the case, because there is no "outside" of global capitalism from which we can build relations. This must always be taken into account if we are to disentangle ourselves from the grip of the global market and the dominance of the Western church.

We need to recognize the best efforts of churches to move away from the old and disempowering ways of doing global mission/ministries: efforts such as autonomy and self-reliance, capacity building programs for missionized churches, inculturation projects, and new ways of doing mission understood beyond the notion of outreach to partnership, critical presence, and mission in reverse. At the same time, we need to be constantly vigilant and critical of practices that continue to perpetuate asymmetrical relations. Efforts at indigenization and inculturation are a step in the right direction, yet, they are not sufficient. First, they continue to assume a static-essentialist view of culture and, second, they do not critique power relations. Similarly, this is true of mission as outreach. Mission understood as outreach, in Rieger's incisive critique, continues to perpetuate global North's hegemony. It perpetuates the monological or unilateral approach (even when invited by the partner church), with the outreach mission-sender church shaping the receivers into its neocolonial image and likeness.[28] Mission as outreach still continues to operate from the position of power and privilege. From the position of power and privilege, the question is, "What can we do?" In fact, this is the kind of question that people of power and privilege like to ask, or like to be asked. But this is not the question that challenges the power asymmetry. The right question, suggests Rieger, is "How might we be part of the problem?"[29] We would know that this is the right question by the cold, if not, defensive and dismissive response from mission senders. Mission as outreach may continue to have validity in response to immediate needs, but in many ways, it focuses on the goodness and generosity of the mission sender at the expense of concealing the asymmetrical power relations

28. Rieger, "Theology and Mission," 201–27.
29. Ibid., 214.

that need to be challenged. The more our attention gets skewed in the direction of celebrating the generosity of the mission sender, the more difficult it is to effect change.

Likewise, we need to examine carefully the model of mission as relationship. While mission as relationship seems a more progressive way of understanding and doing mission in our times, it is not radical enough in critiquing and exposing the power dynamics of the partnership. How can there be true relationship when an asymmetrical power relation is present? In this model, Rieger insists, the power, interest, and concerns of the dominant global North continue to dictate the relationship. Under the asymmetrical power relation, the much celebrated "mission in reverse" would simply turn the missionized people into servants for the "enrichment" of the powerful and privileged. Not even the spiritual treasures of the underprivileged partner (e.g., Native American spirituality) would be safe from mission partners who want to make use of them to boost their own quest for spiritual power.

THE CHURCH IN THE REALM OF THE GLOBAL MARKET

If there is no space that is free from the reach of globalization, particularly from the market forces, can the evangelists of the global market say, "outside of the market there is no salvation?" They can argue that there is no outside of the market, thus there is no other way to salvation except through the market. The church may claim itself as the sanctified portion of the world, but this sanctified portion of the world is not outside of the pale of the market. We can discern the influence of the market in many aspects of the church's life. In mundane ways, we can see the influence of the global market in relation to worship, liturgy, theology, formation, ministries, and power dynamics.

The plight of the church has always been impacted by the shape and activity as well as the ebb and flow of the market. At the height of industrial expansion, churches that were strategically located in an area in the midst of a boom experienced growth spurts and tremendous vitality. Similarly, when rural farming communities experienced growth, rural congregations experienced growth as well. When the economic situation and the behavior of the market changed, churches changed or were forced to change. As industries moved to new locations or as the base of the economy shifted to technology and information, many of the once vibrant churches experienced decline in membership and finances. Similarly, the demise of the family farm in the 1980s, particularly in the U.S., led to the decrease in rural population and, consequently, the demise of many rural churches.[30] The story, however, does not end here. As the economy shifts in favor of huge agribusinesses, rural communities in the U.S. are experiencing a demographic change with the coming of agricultural workers, mostly migrants and new refugees from the global South. This is the case of southwestern Minnesota, a place I have used as a site for my global justice immersion course. With the demographic changes brought about by a shifting economy, the shape and face of rural congregations have also changed. Faces of new ethnic groups (such as Latinos, Laos, Hmong, and Vietnamese) are now part of the make-up of rural congregations in the U.S.

The church's day-to-day life and ministries have always been impacted by the behavior of the market. Generally, we take the market for granted when things go well. Only when the market does not meet with our expectations do we become more cognizant of our dependence on it. When the market is bullish and the coffers full, general optimism reigns and church programs boom. Budget and program projections are often set high in consonance with the market returns. Many programs are launched as if the community will always be riding on the cusp of plenty. But when the bullish market turns into bear, the church undergoes a traumatic experience. Personnel and programs are streamlined, if not downsized (euphemistically called rightsizing). Then the focus usually shifts toward maintenance and survival. Just as it often happens in governments and profit-oriented corporations, the first casualties of downsizings in churches are usually programs that support and empower marginalized people. Seminaries and divinity schools are no exception.

Shifting our focus to the context of the global South, the dire economic conditions today has brought a deluge of social challenges that affect the church. With few local resources, many have left the global South and tried their luck abroad working as domestic workers, construction workers, sailors, and entertainers (a euphemism for sex workers). Some have found well paying jobs, but the majority is barely making it. Whatever money they save, they send to their families back home through banks and other money remittance services. Like the

---

30. Jung et al., *Rural Ministry*, 108.

dependent families and the ailing national economies of migrant or immigrant workers' countries of origin, many countries in the global South are heavily dependent on outside financial transfusion to keep themselves alive. Meanwhile, the family separation brought about by migration has generated social problems in which the church needs to respond with new forms of ministry.

Beyond the direct financial impact of the global market, we can see the influence of the global market in the way congregations think of who and what they are about. Although often motivated by good intentions to help the church adapt to the changing context, in many instances they have lost their critical powers in sorting out healthy from non-healthy adaptation and have been slowly sucked into the world of the global market and culture industries. The infiltration and colonization of the market is evident in the churches' habit of adopting a market model to describe who it is and what it is about. Adopting the market mindset and ethos, what we have is a church whose primary identity is one of a business enterprise committed to producing and/ or selling products and services to customers. We can employ other metaphors or images to think of the church, such as a grocery store, gas station, funeral parlor, entertainment center, therapy clinic, hospice, welfare office, fire station, country club, fitness club, and so forth, but the primary identity remains that of a vendor of personal salvation and other services. As a vendor of services, it is generally nice to those who can pay (especially those who can pay big bucks) or to members of the club. If in this kind of church the members have become customers or clients expecting fast, quality, and efficient services, the pastors, in the words of Ben Campbell, "have metamorphosed into a company of shopkeepers . . . They are preoccupied with shopkeeper's concerns—how to keep the customers happy, how to lure customers away from competitors down the street, how to package the goods so that the customers will lay out more money."[31]

Services that respond to the real needs of church members are important, but there is something crucially missing when the church becomes primarily a vendor of services. If the job of the pastor and lay leaders is primarily vending services and making members happy, I agree with Anthony Robinson's pointed remark that what we may have is a pretty good club, but this does not look like a church. The

---

31. Johnson and Dreitcer, *Beyond the Ordinary*, 18.

church, continues Robinson, does not have members, consumers, or clients because it "exists to form and sustain individuals and a people who are followers of Jesus Christ, who are his disciples."[32] The church must serve in the best way possible, but its primary calling is to make a community of disciples. Keith Russell reinforces Robinson's point: "In our desire to attract people we have offered a variety of services or experiences that might please them, but we have not expected much back in return or asked for more than a minimal commitment."[33]

If the main identity of the church has been co-opted or hijacked by the worldview, ethos, and values of the market, then the rest of the church life falls in line. If the customer is the king, then great care is taken to make the church "user-friendly." This could mean that the church, its doctrines and worship must be seen from the users' or buyers' point of view. This could also mean that the consumers determine what is of value, which is normally defined in relation to what caters to their tastes, as in the Burger King slogan, "Have it your way." Every church must strive to be "user-friendly," but it is another matter when norms are twisted and crucial principles are bent to satisfy the consumers. As Robinson warns, instead of "buying into a consumer model of the church, where the customer is king and the church simply meets customers' needs, the church does more; the church redefines our true needs."[34]

In addition, the market-consumer model church has distorted evangelism and worship. Evangelism, if it is done at all, is equated with marketing strategy and technique to draw potential customers. The corruption of worship follows suit when it is used to support this skewed understanding of evangelism. By no means am I suggesting that we completely disregard marketing strategy, for we live in a world in which people are presented with a plethora of choices, including various forms of religiosity and worship.[35] But let us not allow worship to be used as a marketing ploy. The marketing ploy takes the upper hand when worship becomes entertainment rather than a connection to God that transforms worshippers' lives. Worship is entertainment

32. Robinson, *What's Theology got to do with it?* 163.
33. Russell, *In Search of the Church*, 76.
34. Robinson, *What's Theology got to do with it?* 163.
35. Thompson, *Treasures*, 91–97.

when it fails to challenge the worshippers to live differently and to carry out the ministry of the church in the world.

Without a doubt, the gospel also becomes a casualty. One central message of the market-consumer church is the gospel of niceness. If we listen to the typical sermon or homily for adults, it is likely to suggest that God's primary attribute is being nice—or equivalents like being easy to get along with, helpful in crisis, or useful on a daily basis. D. Stephen Long calls us to imagine the extreme makeover this would give to Isaiah's vision of God: "I saw the Lord sitting on a lawn chair, close and friendly; and the emblem of his ballcap said [Minnesota Twins or anything you want to supply] . . . Seraps . . . called to one another and said: 'Nice, nice, nice is the Lord of hosts; the whole earth is full of his niceness'" (Is 6:1–3, altered).[36]

Along with the "gospel of niceness" is the proliferation of the "prosperity gospel." The "prosperity gospel" does not hesitate to make use of Jesus to advance its message: "Jesus wants you to be rich." Laurie Beth Jones's, *Jesus CEO* is one such a glaring example of how the market has colonized and hijacked the gospel of Jesus.[37] Imagine this sacrilegious interpretation for the sake of the god of the global market: "Jesus was such an action-oriented leader that they literally had to nail him down to keep him from doing more." "Not even the crucifixion of Jesus—a political execution conducted by the bloody Roman Empire—is beyond utilization as a source of business booster-ism and can-do thinking," says Budde.[38]

The colonizing presence of predatory globalization, particularly the global market, is a serious threat to our social well-being. It has the logistical and the technical means not only to sell products but to alter our understanding of our selves and what matters. With new tech-nological innovations and enticing television programming, people spend more time in front of television and playing games on the inter-net than attending to other more important matters such as building relationships. Moreover, advertising and marketing have learned to usurp and exploit religious symbols to create a consumer/possessor subject in a consumer society. The various media of the market culture industries are time bandits, invaders of social space, and predators of

36. Long, "God is Not Nice," 41.

37. Jones, *Jesus CEO*, cited in Budde, "God is not Capitalist," 84.

38. Budde, Ibid.

religious symbols.[39] This, continues Budde, poses a serious threat to the church, particularly in the area of Christian formation. How shall we do Christian formation when the culture industries have become the main agents of formation? Our efforts would seem no match to the resources and technical capabilities of the purveyors of the global market culture. What shall we do?

I am certainly of the opinion that we need to understand the global market so we can communicate the Christian gospel creatively and effectively, but it is easy to lose our theological bearings. I am open to using the language of the global market, if it helps revitalize our congregations. Nevertheless, it is easy to get swallowed by the logic and spirit of the market and, often without knowing it, what started out as a means (using market language and strategies) has colonized and defined us—shaping who we are and what we are about as a church. We need to be clear in reading our theological compass so we know when and how to use the language of the market. Carlyle Fielding Stewart III expresses it well: "In order to reach God's people, we must speak the language of culture. In order to transform God's people we must speak the language of Christ and the Holy Spirit."[40] The church needs to be "user-friendly" and must respond to the legitimate needs of the church members, but what the church is must not be primarily or solely defined in terms of value and utility to its consumers. Additionally, I resist thinking of church members as consumers of the church's products and services for the members *are* the church.

DIS-ORIENTATION: SELF-PRESERVATION, IDOLATRY, AND LUKEWARMNESS

The church is the Body of Christ in an earthen vessel. Like any earthen vessel, it is subject to all human predicaments. Situated in a world of competing demands and loyalties, it has been subjected to constant temptation. On the one hand, we can argue that it has been gobblelized by the forces of the global market. The god of mammon has invaded the church's inner life. The structure and dynamics of church relations reflect the influence of mammon. On the other, we can also argue that in spite of its failings, the Spirit has continued to work for its renewal.

39. Budde, *The (Magic) Kingdom of God*, 82–94.

40. Stewart, *The Empowerment Church*, 15. Original italics removed.

The church has remained a sign and a sacrament of God's saving love in a world of destruction and death.

The church, or any institution for that matter, is vulnerable in moments of perceived profound change and crisis. When threatened with sea-change, it seems to be the case that the most common response is to do business as usual. Or, another very common response to a perceived change or crisis is to panic and, consequently, lose track of one's reason for being. In striving to survive, the confused may run faster but without certain direction. Or, in striving to survive, the disoriented confuses that which promotes life with that which promotes death. We may call this dilemma "goal displacement." Goal displacement is about losing our priorities. To use a common expression, it is about the tail wagging the dog. Goal displacement appears in various forms. It confuses self-preservation with life, growth with vitality, marketing strategy with worship, money with stewardship, techniques with sound theology, gimmicks with reflective practice, fellowship with hospitality; it is about reducing sound ecclesiology and pastoral practice with management and therapy and ministry vending services.[41] And it better be that the vending service is fast, or "customers" will go to another service center. Here, religious "fastfoodism" and goal displacement (buying empty calories) are intertwined. This is a critically sad situation because, as Eric Law attests, "We are trying so hard to survive that we have forgotten to be faithful in this changing world."[42]

As any other institution, the church's constant temptation has been self-absorption and self-preservation, especially in the face of perceived threats to its existence. The church can turn into a club of like-minded people, more concerned about addressing its own needs than in carrying out its mission or its reason for being. Instead of nourishing its life, when the church is self-absorbed it is, in reality, suffocating itself to death. On the contrary, as Jesus proclaimed, "If any want to become my followers, let them deny themselves and take up their cross daily and follow me. For those who want to save their life will lose it, and those who lose their life for my sake will save it" (Lk 9:23–24). Self-preservation produces the opposite of what it is intended to achieve: it leads to death. Moreover, it leads to the death of imagination and creativity. It is interesting to note that a church that is

41. See Hunter, *Desert Hearts*, 11.
42. Law, *Sacred Acts*, 19.

pre-occupied with its own preservation is also the kind of church that is committed to maintaining images that may have lost their power. The church puts on the appearance of business as usual, but deep inside is a church that Douglas John Hall describes as "trying very hard to keep Christendom alive—to put that Humpty Dumpty together again."[43] In other words, we have a church that is not willing to face the new challenges and the costs that they incur.

Threatened by declining membership and with no clear options beyond survival, for many of the once mainline churches in the U.S. and Europe, the most pressing concern is the attraction of new members. With survival as the nagging concern, John Wesley's famous dictum "the world is our parish" becomes the "parish is our world."[44] The ministers and the congregation may be busy doing many things, such as preaching, Bible study, worship services, administration, meetings, and pastoral counseling, but the focus is oriented primarily for the maintenance and survival of the church. Some of the churches have been "successful," but the focus is still toward self-care and self-preservation. And theological education seems to support this self-preoccupation. Not to discount the critical importance of pastoral care in congregations, it is nevertheless true that "contemporary theological education has been oriented primarily toward the pastoral care of congregations, not the church's mission to the world."[45]

Worship is one of the most vulnerable aspects of church life with regard to goal displacement, particularly in times of declining membership. We certainly need to have user-friendly and appealing worship services, but we must not lose sight of our priorities. Worship is not a marketing strategy of the shopping mall called church. Worship is our recognition and celebration of the divine presence in our lives; it is an event of connecting ourselves to the divine and the rest of creation; it is an event that renews our lives for living and mission. This is the main goal, and whatever we do to make it user-friendly must be directed toward this purpose, not for the purpose of growth in church membership. C. Kirk Hadaway puts it in a proper perspective: "Enhancing worship is only relevant in terms of transformational effect it has on the people who attend."[46]

43. Hall, *Why Christian*, 135.

44. Messer, *A Conspiracy of Goodness*, 22.

45. Ibid., 17.

46. Hadaway, *Behold I Do a New Thing*, 34.

Getting our priorities right is crucial if we are not to fall into goal displacement. We need to deal with the issue of the church's reason for being. This is basically asking the question about mission. It is mission that gives us the right orientation in everything we care and do, from worship, to fellowship, education, and ministry. Even as we desire church growth, it is not the goal and mission of the church in general and of local congregations in particular. We must welcome growth, but "growth," contends Hadaway, "is a byproduct of institutional health and not our primary objective."[47] Shall we then expect growth as a natural consequence of vitality? Hadaway's response is more nuanced: "Vital churches that are clear about their reason for being tend to be growing churches, but growth doesn't lead to vitality. It's the other way around."[48] If our motivation for vitality is still growth, then I have to say that we still do not get it. Whether a congregation grows or not is not the heart of the matter. The heart of the matter is that it is alive in God's spirit and has embodied what it means to live out its calling in the world.

Various factors can be identified to take account of the present predicament of many churches, particularly the once mainline denominations. I am in agreement with Cobb that the issue at heart is deeply spiritual, though my account of our current spiritual malaise has taken on a different nuance, especially in accord with my critique of globalization.[49] The idols of market and misguided nationalism, particularly in the U.S., have claimed the primary allegiance of many church members, while the demand of the gospel and its call to carry out the *missio Dei* has been relegated to the lower rung in the list of priorities. Squeezed spiritually by the idols of the global market and narrow nationalism while being isolated from a caring and prophetic community, church members are left with no more spiritual juice for the life of the church. They go to the church for nourishment, but a church occupied with self-preservation and falsely oriented toward the idols of the market cannot provide the much-needed spiritual nourishment and an alternative moral imagination. No wonder church members have become spiritually dry or lukewarm as the whole church is suffering the same lacking.

47. Ibid., 27.
48. Ibid., x.
49. Cobb, *Reclaiming the Church*, 2.

RE-ORIENTING THE CHURCH:
TOWARD THE REIGN OF GOD

In the previous section, I explored the many dimensions in which the church has experienced dis-orientation and goal displacement and the need for re-orientation. The church needs re-orientation in the direction of its reason for being. This re-orientation is critical for the life and ministry of the church. It is critical as well for this project because I consider the re-orientation of the church as a requirement for re-imagining the church. I contend that the church can only experience re-orientation when it re-orients itself toward God's *basileia*. Without being oriented to God's *basileia*, the church remains without compass and becomes vulnerable to the sway of the various idols of death. God's *basileia* counters the sway of the god of mammon and provides the compass for the church to come to an understanding of what it is and what it is called to be about. It helps the church to stay focused and navigate carefully between the Scylla and Charybdis of life. In the midst of the world of mammon, Jesus is saying: "But strive first for the kingdom of God and his righteousness, and these things will be given to you as well"(Mt 6:33).

The phrase "kingdom of God" has been considered by many as problematic. It conveys a worldview that is kingly and hierarchical. Instead of "kingdom of God," some scholars prefer the phrase "reign of God." But an objection has been raised because it puts the emphasis on God's controlling power. Another possibility is to use the phrase "realm of God," but the term "realm of God," comments Cobb, "does not make clear that the reference is to this world as we hope it will be."[50] With these limitations, a growing number of theologians prefer to use the Greek term *basileia*. Regardless of one's preference (kingdom of God or reign of God or *basileia*), we need to see it critically so as not to reinforce imperial thinking and practices. We need to see this discourse not in the sense that the kingdom of God is higher than any earthly kingdom, which simply affirms the validity of the earthly kingdoms, but that the Kingdom of God that Jesus proclaimed was radically different from and in opposition to the kingdoms (empires) of this world. This interpretation recognizes that there is no space to theologize outside of the imperial sphere of influence, but even in the

50. Ibid., 69.

midst of empire it refuses to be swallowed and it continues to assert its subversive power.[51]

Central to the message of Jesus is the reign of God: he lived and died for the reign of God. "All else in his message and ministry," claims Norman Perrin, "serves a function in relation to that proclamation and derives meaning from it."[52] In like manner, Dermot Lane makes the point that "everything that Jesus says and does is inspired from beginning to end by his personal commitment to the coming Reign of God into the world. The controlling horizon of the mission and ministry of Jesus is the Kingdom of God."[53] Jesus did not preach or speak of God in a generic fashion, but God in God's activity of building the reign of God. To put it differently, he was not simply "theocentric" or God-centered, but "regnocentric" or reign-of-God-centered.

Jesus' central message of the reign of God also discloses to us the kind of God he proclaimed. For Jesus and for any authentic Jewish prophet, "God is a God-*of*, a God-*for*, a God-*in, never* a God-*in-himself.*"[54] This is the God that cannot be understood apart from the reign of God and cannot be divorced from the God whose activity is building the reign of God here on earth. "[T]he Abba whom Jesus proclaimed," argues Paul Knitter, "could not be known or worshipped apart from the *Basileia*—the Reign of God." Claiming to know God apart from this reign, he continues, "was to know a false God."[55]

C. S. Song also speaks of the centrality of the reign of God in his various works, especially in *Jesus and the Reign of God*. The vision of God's reign is, for Song, the all-encompassing principle, lens, or foundation from which we need to evaluate everything that Jesus did and said. The vision of God's reign, in Song's words, is

> the *hermeneutical* principle of the life and ministry of Jesus. It is the *ethical* standard of his lifeview and worldview. It is the *theological* foundation of his relation to God and to his fellow human beings. And it is the *eschatological* vantage-point from which he relates the present time and the end of time.[56]

51. See Rieger, *Christ and Empire*; also, Wiley, "Paul and Early Christianity," 49.

52. Perrin, cited in Song, *Jesus and the Reign of God*, 4.

53. Lane, cited in Knitter, *Jesus and the Other Names*, 89.

54. Sobrino, cited in Knitter, Ibid., 89.

55. Knitter, Ibid., 90.

56. Song, *Jesus and the Reign of God*, 2.

The temptation to preach Jesus without the reign of God has been common in the history of the church. While Jesus preached the reign of God, the church preached Jesus and often without his vision of the reign of God. We commit a serious mistake, says Song, if we remove the vision of the reign of God from the man Jesus of Nazareth, which is the case in many christologies or the doctrine of Christ. When Jesus is preached in isolation from his message of the reign of God, the result is a disastrous distortion: a cult of Jesus is developed. Jesus becomes a safe cultic object of worship, veneration, and speculation but dispossessed of the message that calls the world to repentance and to costly discipleship. As the cult of Jesus divinizes him, so he is also detached from the very people with whom he became one.[57]

If there is a danger in speaking of Jesus without the reign of God, Thomas Finger warns the opposite: a reign of God without Jesus could easily fall into equating one's historical project with the reign of God.[58] This was the case in the nineteenth century, notes Finger, when the reign of God was abstracted from Jesus and defined in Western cultural terms. In other words, the reign of God was swallowed by the imperialist impulse of the time, and certainly a possibility in our times when we separate the reign of God from the life and ministry of Jesus.

Finger's warning is critical: the notion of the reign of God is dangerous when abstracted from Jesus. It is of paramount importance that we not separate the reign of God and Jesus. We know what the reign of God is like in the life and ministry of Jesus. Conversely, we know who Jesus is only in relation to the reign of God. Jesus lived and died for the reign of God. The central focus of Jesus is the reign of God, not God as such, much less himself. In other words, the Jesus whom the church has called the Christ, is not himself christocentric.

Having the above point in mind, it has been argued that the corrective for ecclesiocentrism (church-centeredness) is not christocentrism but "regnocentrism" (reign-of-God-centered). This distinction is a critical one, contends Song, for christocentrism has led to Christ-centered exclusivism. However, because Song, like Finger, sees the inseparability of the reign of God from Jesus, he does not speak of "regnocentrism" without Jesus. In order to avoid christocentrism

57. Ibid., 16–19.

58. Finger, "A Mennonite Theology," 69-92; also, see Heim, "Elements of a Conversation," Ibid., 212.

and affirm the centrality of the reign of God that cannot be divorced from Jesus, he calls his theological stance "Jesus-oriented" christology. "Orientation," in Song's understanding, is open to relationship and is expansive instead of constrictive.[59] A Jesus-oriented christology calls us to focus on Jesus who in turn focused our attention on the reign of God. Thus, from Song's point of view, a Jesus-oriented-christology is reign-of-God-centered.

The Church Mission: Critique in Light of the Reign of God

Taking our clue from the life and ministry of Jesus, we can say that the church's reason for being can only be properly understood in relation to the reign of God. "Without the shining forth of the kingdom of God," says Dorothee Sölle, "the church is an association like any other, structured in hierarchy, imposed by blind pressures and misuse of office." "The criterion," she argues, "for what the church is remains the kingdom of God; the church arises out of its proclamation, and organizes itself in its direction."[60] The church is truly a church only when it serves the reign of God. The church's relationship to the reign of God is analogous to the relationship of John the Baptist to Jesus. In fact, it must always bear in mind its "provisional status" and its "advancing elimination" in relation to the coming reign of God. It has been said, Jesus proclaimed the reign of God, and the church proclaimed Jesus. It is true that the temptation of the church has been to proclaim the proclaimer, but this can be re-directed. The church must proclaim the proclaimer who proclaimed the reign of God. In other words, the church's knowledge of and commitment to the reign of God is through Jesus of Nazareth. As Jesus is oriented to the reign of God, so must the church be. The church must place itself at the service of the reign of God, not for its self-preservation and legitimation. It is called to manifest and foster the reign of God in its own life and ministry.

The history of the church shows that disastrous consequences arise when it becomes dis-oriented from its reason for being. When the church is not oriented toward the reign of God, self-preservation and legitimation become the focal concern. The self-centeredness of the church comes to its destructive height when it identifies itself with the reign of God or when it confines the reign of God within its walls.

59. See Phan, *Christianity with an Asian Face*, 157. Emphasis supplied.

60. Sölle, *Thinking About God*, 136–37.

Rather than saying "outside of the reign of God there is no salvation," it affirms the mantra "outside of the church there is no salvation." When the reign of God is equated with the church or swallowed by the church, it can only mean that the reign of God is present in the world only insofar as it is made present by the church. In this regard, the spirit of Christ or the Holy Spirit is denied any activity in the world apart from what the church is doing. Also, the church assumes itself to be the exclusive container of God's activity in the world.

This grave distortion has been challenged by both Roman Catholic and Reformed theologians. Leonardo Boff's work, *The Church: Charism and Power*, offers a powerful criticism of the Roman Catholic Church in light of the reign of God.[61] Boff calls the church to stand under the scrutiny of the reign of God, exposing its predilection to confuse the reign of God with the institutional church. On the Protestant side, Jay Rock reminds us that this confusion has been sharply challenged by Reformed theology.[62] Rock cites a statement by the Inter-Church Inter-Faith Committee of the United Church of Canada to advance his point: "All that God is doing in the world . . . is not accomplished only, or even primarily, through the Church . . . The mission of God is larger than the Church, but the Church has its part to play."[63]

It is not my intention to deny the presence of the reign of God in the church. I entertain the idea that the church can be interpreted as a sacrament of the reign of God in the world. I also look forward to the day when the church more truly embodies the reign of God. But the reign of God in which the church seeks to embody is not its possession; rather, the church has to be possessed by it. Rather than becoming arrogant, for the church to embody the reign of God is to stand in judgment of its norms and to be constantly open to its healing grace.

When the church finds its true orientation in the reign of God, things find their proper place. Its organizational structure, daily life, and operations are defined by this orientation. This is clearly visible in how it views mission and ministries. A church that has a distorted understanding of its reason for being, which is mission oriented to the reign of God, thinks of mission as primarily to plant churches. On the contrary, a church whose understanding of mission is *basileia-*

61. Boff, *Church: Charism and Power*.

62. Rock, "Resources in the Reformed Tradition," 46–68.

63. Ibid., 61.

centered, thinks of mission not primarily for the purpose of planting churches but planting the seeds of the reign of God. Planting churches occupies an important place, but planting churches is only important for the purposes of building the reign of God.[64] Howard Snyder articulates quite clearly the contrast between *basileia*-oriented church or the "regnocentric" church and a church-centered church:

> Kingdom people seek first the Kingdom of God and its justice; church people often put the church work above concerns of justice, mercy, and truth. Church people think about how to get people into the church; Kingdom people think about how to get the church into the world. Church people worry that the world might change the church; Kingdom people work to see the church change the world.[65]

A church revitalized and re-oriented toward the reign of God can both be a symbol of the reign of God and a center of activity striving for the reign of God. Being both, a symbol of hope and a center of activity for the reign of God are not separate. A church cannot be an effective symbol of the *basileia* it proclaims if it has not embodied what it hopes for. Vice versa, the church cannot be the center of activity for the reign of God if it has not been empowered by the Spirit of the reign of God. Cobb puts in a more tangible way how these two dimensions (symbol of the reign of God and center of activity of the reign of God) are present in the life of the church:

> When the church becomes less patriarchal, less hierarchical, more inclusive, and more energizing of its members, it is helping them to gain some of the qualities of life in the *Basileia* and, at the same time, it is functioning as a symbol of the *Basileia*. When preaching not only proclaims that *Basileia* but also helps the hearers to envision it and see how their lives can be ordered to it, the church is both symbol and active agent of transformation.[66]

64. Knitter, *Jesus and the Other Names*, 109.

65. Snyder cited in Knitter, Ibid, 110. Also in Bosch, *Transforming Mission*, 378.

66. Cobb, *Reclaiming the Church*, 72.

WHAT IS THE FUTURE OF THE CHURCH?

The magazine *Christian Century* was named to herald a Christian century. There were several reasons for this optimism. The church coffers were fat as investment returns soared and donations flowed; missionary societies bloomed and sent mission workers to far flung areas of the world; church denominational leaders imagined big things; national church organizations were full of personnel; and money for church programs abounded. We became accustomed to the notion of a Christian century or Christian era, and now we are shocked to know that the future we expected to happen is not what we are likely to get. The Christian century did not deliver what it had celebrated. As Arthur T. Clarke has said about postmodern society at large, we are surprised and shocked to realize that "[t]he future ain't what it used to be."[67]

There have been many ups and downs, much confusion, and distractions from its course as the church has journeyed or sailed through the years. An image that has remained vital for the church is that of a boat. This boat continues to sail, sometimes when the sea is calm and at other times in gusty winds and soaring seas. The church is no stranger to those times when it has been in the eye of a perfect storm. Those familiar with ship travel across the ocean, especially in stormy weather, will agree with Clark Williamson and Ronald Allen's advice: find a spot where you can see out, such as on a deck with a view or through a porthole. Extend your sight to the horizon to get a wider perspective and a sense of balance. Translating this to the life of the church, this is what Williamson and Allen have to say:

> We must keep our eyes not only on the immediate circumstances but also on the purposes of the church, the spreading in the world of the love of God and the love of the neighbor, the formation of a servant people, the needs of the vulnerable neighbor, and the loving grace of God that both empowers and commands us to attend to all things contained in the good news.[68]

The church needs liberation from being pre-occupied with its immediate circumstances, usually for purposes of self-preservation, in order that it may see the horizon as set by the reign of God. Programs of mission are not enough to correct its preoccupation with self-pres-

---

67. Clarke, cited in Hall, *The Future of the Church*, 1.
68. Williamson and Allen, *The Vital Church*, 20.

ervation, but the church, in the words of Gregory Leffel, must itself be "fundamentally reconceived as God's missionary movement into the world."[69] More particularly, it is a missionary movement toward the reign of God. The immediate circumstances are not completely ignored and immediate needs have to be addressed, but the critical point is to focus on the horizon—the reign of God. Staying focused on the reign of God is a constant struggle, for temptations along the way are plentiful. On sunny days and in the midst of plenty, we tend to be complacent; and in the midst of crisis we tend to panic and fall into duct-tape securities. I believe it is not enough to challenge the church to focus on the horizon. Our ability to focus on the horizon—the reign of God—is also a matter of faith and personal trust: it is trusting that the One who has called us to set our eyes on the reign of God has been with us along the way; that the One who has commanded us to "go" is already ahead of us; and that the One who has called us to invest our lives for the coming reign of God is the One who also said, "the kingdom of God has come to you." We cannot simply trust our own strength and expect to remain focused on the reign of God. We must put our trust in the One who said, "Follow me."

We can learn from the old navigators of Polynesia on the matter of focusing on the horizon and trusting. Kaleo Patterson, a Kanaka Maoli (indigenous Hawaiian) who gave me an experience of canoe surfing on the island of Oahu, shared this story of the old Polynesian navigators sailing in stormy seas. When winds are too strong and the waves are getting rough, the last thing you want to do is get *pu'iwa* (panic). Do not panic. If you get *pu'iwa* you will likely die. It is important that you focus your thoughts on that one star *Ka Haku* (God). First, you have to tie everything together. Next, you fill the canoe with water until it floats just below the surface of the water. That is right, sink your canoe. Those old canoes were designed to float no matter what. Even when you fill them with water they float just below the surface of the ocean. Then you have to tie yourself to the canoe as you emotionally and spiritually tie yourself to *Ka Haku*. In this way you become one with the ocean and one with *Ka Haku*. Of course you will be wet, but you will be safe with the canoe. So this means, says Patterson, you have to hang on and ride the storm out. And when the storm is *pau* (finished), you bail the water out of the canoe and

---

69. Leffel, "Churches in the Mode of Mission," 65.

continue your merry way. Remember, you have to focus on the same star.[70]

What is the future of the church? Whatever shape or form the church of the future may take, its future lies in finding its orientation or focus on the reign of God. Apart from this orienting horizon, it can only be gobbled by the forces of globalization and set adrift not knowing where to go, while obsessed with its own life. Thus, the church must have its sight focused on the reign of God. The church authenticates itself as the church of Jesus the Christ when it continually submits itself to the demands of the reign of God in its life, mission, structure, and resources. What better way to end this chapter than to quote Matthew 6:33 for the second time: "But strive first for the kingdom of God and his righteousness, and all these things will be given to you as well."

---

70. A story shared by Kaleo Patterson.

4

The Church as a Translocal (Glocal) Community

Catholicity and Mission in a Globalized World

WITH THE REIGN OF God providing the orienting horizon for the church's existence (chapter 3), the way is now prepared for reimagining the church in response to globalization. What I would like to reimagine first is the notion of the church as catholic (*kath'holon*) and its bearings on the life of local congregations. It took me a long time to reclaim the term "catholic." Even after learning that the term "catholic" has a broader meaning than its usual association, it was difficult for me to dissociate the word from the Roman Catholic Church. I grew up in a predominantly Roman Catholic country in which to be catholic means Roman Catholic; consequently, the person who is not a Catholic (RC) must be something else, such as a Protestant. On the other hand, the term "catholic" served as a handy word for Protestants to name the teeming majority who needed conversion. They were the objects of their evangelistic efforts. This chapter is my attempt to reclaim and articulate the term "catholic." In particular, I reclaim and articulate catholicity in response to the challenges of our globalized world.

The church is catholic. It is one of the classic marks of being a church that ecumenical Christianity has affirmed since its early beginnings (unity, holiness, and apostolicity being the others). Today, in the face of the intensifying pressure of globalization and the growing reality of world Christianity, the question of the church's catholicity or universality is again at the front and center of its concern. How shall we speak of the church's catholicity in light of globalization and

Christianity's demographic extension throughout the world? How shall we speak of catholicity in our highly interconnected world, with its shared vulnerabilities and hopes? How shall we speak of catholicity in a global village that is experiencing the pain of global pillage and global fragmentation? How shall we articulate the catholicity of the church in a world unified by a system that continues to promote social inequalities? How shall we articulate catholicity that takes into account our unity as well as honors and celebrates plurality? How shall we speak of catholicity without homogenization? Are there ways of speaking about catholicity that are non-dominative, that is, ways that promote mutual communication and exchange and do not choke the local? How shall we speak of catholicity that recognizes the interweaving of the global and the local in the life of every congregation and locality? What does it mean to be a church that embodies in its very identity the interweaving of the global and the local? What does this interweaving of the global and the local mean in terms of the relationship between international and national church bodies and local congregations? What does it mean for a local congregation to embody the interweaving of the local and the global in its own identity and presence in its specific community? What directions does globalization, the growth of world Christianity, and new ways of thinking about catholicity have to offer in relation to how we think and do mission and ministry?

CATHOLICITY IN THE CHRISTIAN TRADITION: FINDING ROOTS AND WINGS

The questions posed above will guide us as we explore what it means to be a church catholic in the face of the challenges and possibilities posed by globalization and the growth of world Christianity. I see rich and new possibilities for articulating ecclesiology, particularly the notion of catholicity. The wings for articulating these new possibilities, however, cannot fly high without deep roots; hence, the importance of tradition. It sounds contradictory, but it is not. Tradition gives us both roots and wings: roots that draw nourishment from the history of our community, and wings to soar and imagine new possibilities.[1] Without being deeply rooted in our tradition(s), our imagination cannot soar to new heights. For this reason, we need to find the roots of catholicity

1. See McDaniel, *With Roots and Wings*, 23.

in the tradition, even if we cannot be exhaustive about it here. Indeed, the term "catholicity" itself implies dealing with tradition, especially if we think of catholicity as that which "was believed" (starting with the past, as well as everywhere) and the fullness of faith.

Of course how we view tradition can either pull us down or give us wings. Scholars of the Christian tradition trace the beginnings of the term "catholic" in relation to the church with Ignatius of Antioch (around 110 CE) who said: "Wherever the bishop appears, there let the people be; as wherever Jesus Christ is, there is the catholic church"(*Smyr 8,2*).[2] There are two poles associated with the interpretation of catholicity, with one emphasizing the earthly and the other with the spiritual and eschatological dimension. Orthodoxy and the Reformation have continued to emphasize the spiritual and eschatological dimension. In spite of the many ways Ignatius has been interpreted, the meanings of catholicity would circulate around these two poles of universality and orthodoxy (orthodoxy in the sense of *pleroma* or fullness of faith).[3]

Following a broad sketch by Robert Schreiter, the term catholicity acquired new connotations in accord with its changing circumstances and fortunes.[4] When Christianity was formally recognized and declared the official religion of the Roman Empire (313 CE), catholicity took increasingly "geographic" connotations or overtones. (We should not overlook the fact that Christianity became an official religion of Ethiopia and Armenia in the fourth century. The earliest is Armenia, around 300 CE.)[5] The reach of the Roman Empire also became Christianity's reach; the limits of the Roman Empire became its limits; the entire inhabited world (*oikumene*) under the Roman Empire became its inhabited world. In other words, the catholicity (universality) of the church became identical with the Roman Empire. Of course, the world was much larger than the reach of the Roman Empire, but it was outside the *oikumene* of the Roman Empire or the *civitas romana*. The *oikumene* of Christianity shrank with the rise of Islam and the conquest of the Eastern centers of Christianity. Without

---

2. Schreiter, *The New Catholicity*, 121.

3. Ibid.

4. Ibid., 119–22.

5. See Jenkins, *The Next Christendom*, 18.

Constantinople, by the time of Charlemagne (800 CE), the Christian world was reduced and synonymous with Western Europe.[6]

When the Church of Rome gained more status over other centers of Christianity, particularly the churches of the East, catholicity experienced another metamorphosis: it grafted the "juridical" aspect to the notion of catholicity. This "juridical" aspect was nurtured throughout the Middle Ages and reached its peak at the time of the Reformation with, not surprisingly, the Church of Rome as the center and the bishop of Rome (the pope) at the top of the church hierarchy. Catholicity in this "juridical" sense means "uniformity" through communion with the Bishop of Rome. In other words, whoever is not in communion with the Bishop of Rome does not belong to the Catholic Church. Furthermore, Pope Pius IX (nineteenth century) added to the already juridically strangulated notion of catholicity the attribute of "immutability." In short, catholicity embraced into its original notion of catholicity such dimensions as geographical reach, juridical control, uniformity with the center, and immutability.

The mystical/eschatological dimension of catholicity was still present but remained sidelined in the Roman Catholic Church. Catholicity in the mystical/eschatological sense means that the church visible (earthly) is incomplete (not full) and broken (not whole), but it already participates in the Church invisible. In other words, its fullness and wholeness would be actualized in the fullness of time. While this dimension of catholicity was sidelined or eclipsed in the Roman Catholic Church (and has experienced revival), it continued to flourish in the Eastern Church and has been central to the churches of the Reformation.

CATHOLICITY AND MISSION UNDER THE COLONIAL-MODERNIST FRAME

With the medieval world fading, a new era emerged around the fifteenth century. It was an era of exploration, conquest, occupation, and colonization of new lands and people by European nations. Spain and Portugal were among the first explorers, conquerors, and colonizers. They were followed by the United Kingdom, France, Germany, and much later the United States. The reach of Portugal, Spain, and the United Kingdom extended to Africa, the Americas, and Asia, which

6. Ibid., 16–17.

was far greater than its Roman Empire predecessor whose dominion was more limited to the Mediterranean world. And, wherever the Western imperial powers went, they carried the Christian banner. In other words, wherever there was conquest and colonization there was Christian mission. Mission and colonization were intertwined: to colonize was to missionize and to missionize was to colonize.[7] This was the prevailing understanding.

As noted in the previous chapter, the advent of the Enlightenment brought some changes in the thinking and practice of mission. The theocratic ideal (marriage of church and king) was under assault and the burden of mission work shifted to the hands of mission societies. Nevertheless, even if mission was no longer under the direct patronage of the king or the state, colonialism and mission continued to be wedded. Decolonization (starting with Spanish colonies in the Americas) further withdrew the "protective umbrella" that the mission enterprise received from state patronage. Decolonization (national independence) did not, however, automatically lead to the autonomy of the then-missionized churches. Neocolonialism does not warrant that understanding, not to mention the long process of decolonization that must take place. Colonial administrative structures are easier to dismantle than are habits of thinking.

What this account of church mission and its direct or indirect alliance with Western powers before and after decolonization tells us is that catholicity, in Schreiter's way of framing the subject, is basically construed as "expansion," and that the main justification for the "expansion" is "civilization," while the form of church response is global mission. In essence, the well-known age of global mission is also the age of Western expansion. What the empires saw as an opportunity for expansion, the church saw as an opportunity for expansion by planting churches (*plantatio ecclesiae*). Just as imperial powers saw expansion as an opportunity to civilize, the church saw expansion as an opportunity to Christianize the pagans or to engage in *conversio animarum* (saving souls). *Plantatio ecclesiae* and *conversio animarum*, which circumscribed the church's sense of mission, became the means of the church's expansion (catholicity).

After the Second World War (1945), following Schreiter's periodization, mission and the notion of catholicity identified with it were

7. Bosch, *Transforming Mission*, 303.

severely criticized. Mainline Protestant churches called for a moratorium in global mission (1960–1970). New discourses on mission emerged, discourses that were informed by ideas about development and energized by the new-found optimism of the period. The new expression of the church's catholicity came under the name of "solidarity," and with it came new mission expressions, particularly in Latin America: *promoción* (advancement), *inserción* (commitment to enter the life of the poor), *acompañamiento* (walking with the people), and *liberación* (liberation).[8]

CATHOLICITY UNDER THE MCDONALD'S TWIN ARCHES

As the notion of catholicity acquired different nuances with changes in our world, a new era of globalization is again calling us to articulate catholicity in relevant and prophetic ways. As noted in chapter 1, the new era of globalization is loaded with irony: an intensification of connections along with intensification of fragmentation and violence, homogenization and the reassertion of difference, ecological connection and disasters, medical advancements and neglect of the health of the many, global village and massive diaspora, religious encounters and religiously motivated violence, and a predatory global economics in the form of a unified global economy, the dominance of transnational corporations, and footloose or homeless capital. This footloose capital is free to move around wherever it finds a "home" (favorable investment climate) but also free to depart and seek other "homes." A unified global economy is impossible without advancements in technology, transportation, and telecommunications. Through vast, fast, and efficient telecommunication networks, the universal reach of global capital is made real in every locality. It is for this reason that Schreiter names communication as the mode of universality, with global capital as the main carrier.[9] With communication as the new mode of universality, it is not surprising that access to technology and control of information and its dissemination are crucial.

How shall we think of catholicity in a world unified by the global market and dominated by global capital and whose mode of universality is communication? If the church follows the global market or allows the global market to define its catholicity, then we have a church

8. Schreiter, *The New Catholicity*, 126.
9. Ibid., 126–27.

that is like a transnational corporation (TNC) with international networks and centers at various locations. Using McDonald's as an image, catholicity would mean the reach and extension of the global church through its "franchises," the local congregations. Or, to use Microsoft as a model, autonomous or independent churches would be extensions of the global church because they would continue to be dependent on the hardware and software of the Microsoft church. The "operating system" and "programs" are designed and controlled by the central church of global North; local churches simply adapt them to their specific contexts. Even after buying the products, the Microsoft church continues to exercise control through upgrades; this includes a way of locking up or freezing the computers/churches if they fail to get the latest upgrade.

Catholicity through contextualization or inculturation also becomes distorted under the McDonald's church in its strategy of "glocalization." An example would be that of McDonald's serving rice with burgers in Manila, spam or *saimin* (noodle soup) in Hawaii, and McVeggie in India. Glocalization gives the appearance that the global has adapted to the local context, but the adaptation is primarily for the purpose of gobbling the local. The local does not find its fulfillment in the global but finds itself fulfilling the insatiable appetite of the global. Like a mouse in the claws of a hungry cat, it finally ends up in the mouth of the global. In other words, a catholicity that follows the model of predatory globalization and transnational corporation is deceptive and it violates the aspirations of the local. Thus, we need to explore new ways of thinking catholicity that counter deceptive glocalization or contextualization.

OPENINGS FOR THINKING OF CATHOLICITY IN NEW WAYS

How shall we think of catholicity that is not gobbled by globalization? How shall we think of catholicity that does not reinforce hegemony of the global market? How shall we think of catholicity that refuses to be outflanked by the ubiquitous and cunning postmodern Empire understood as "network power," which includes dominant nation-states and supranational institutions?[10] Put positively, how shall we think of catholicity that subverts universalistic claims of the market and profit?

10. Hardt and Negri, *Empire*. See also, Hardt and Negri, *Multitude: War and Democracy*.

Globalization certainly can or should inform how we think about catholicity in creative and responsible ways, but it must not dictate the theological and moral direction of catholicity. We need to study the ways of globalization not in order to fit catholicity into it, but for catholicity to deal creatively and responsibly in relation to the challenges of globalization.

Unified and Interconnected World: Shared Challenges and Hopes

In spite of the many positions and disagreements regarding what globalization is, there is one point of agreement among various interpreters: heightened connections and interweaving of our lives. John Tomlinson speaks of globalization as "complex connectivity" which he describes as "the rapidly developing and ever-densening network of interconnections and interdependencies that characterize modern social life."[11] Anthony Giddens speaks of a similar point by articulating globalization as "the intensification of worldwide social relations which link distant localities in such a way that local happenings are shaped by events occurring many miles away and vice versa."[12] In line with the heightening reality of our connectivity or interrelatedness is the heightening awareness of our interconnections or the increasing recognition that our lives are intertwined, and that we have shared vulnerabilities and hopes even if we have suffered unevenly.

With or without globalization we have, of course, always been connected. Globalization has only heightened these connections and made us more acutely aware of them. With connections heightened, so are the consequences of our actions on others, even to those who were once geographically far. With our abilities to reach and connect heightened, so are our abilities to affect the lives of others, for good or for ill. The easy mobility of people allows for the easy mobility of pathogens and the spread of diseases. With the fast and efficient delivery of goods, it is possible for those in temperate climates to enjoy tropical produce all year round. This also means, however, increasing dependency and vulnerability to what happens in other places. The highly toxic materials that the global North sends to the global South

11. Tomlinson, *Globalization and Culture*, 2.

12. Giddens, *The Consequences of Modernity*, 64. Also see Netland, "Globalization and Theology," particularly pages 18–23.

are coming back to the kitchens and dining tables of homes in the global North. Fast and efficient technology has made investing in the global market much easier, yet, there is also a downside. What happens in the global market affects all. The present economic recession in the United States is felt by other countries as well. Unrestrained access to the cheap labor of the global South has made it easier for people of the global North to satisfy their increasing appetite for the big and cheap, but not without adversely affecting them in return. Many victims of downsizing in the global North know painfully well the connection of downsizing, overseas outsourcing, and the poorly paid workers of the global South. Farmers have experienced in a painful way the interconnections of our world when cheaper imported goods undermine the price of their local produce. The question, "Who is my neighbor?" is becoming more complex and difficult to answer.

We may try to run away from our global interconnections, but such a strategy is limited and not completely possible. We are blessed as well as cursed by our interconnections. If this is our global reality, then the move is not toward disconnection, but creative and life-giving connections. If the forces of the global market are making us race to the bottom, then we must form creative interconnections that counter downward spiraling. We must be proactive in forging alternative forms of interconnections. My hope is that we will rise to the occasion and make the challenge of our shared vulnerabilities an opportunity to act for the common good. I will pursue this point in articulating a new understanding of catholicity. At the moment, however, I want to underscore that the interconnections and interdependencies of our lives provide a clue as to how we may think of catholicity.

The Resurgence and Growth of World Christianity

Another opening for thinking about catholicity in new and creative ways is the growth of world Christianity or the world church. Without discounting the growth of other religions, I focus here on the growth of Christianity. Claims that we are moving toward a post-Christian world seem to contradict global reality. It may be the case that we are moving toward a post-Christian world when we view it from Cambridge or Amsterdam, but the picture is different if we view it from Manila, Mexico City, Seoul or Nairobi. It would not be easy for us to convince Christians in these parts of the world that Christianity is dying when the main challenge is to have a building that can house 20,000 worshippers on a Sunday morning. At the same time, few Christians of the global North know of the flourishing of Christianity in the global South and, as one noted with ironic surprise, "Not even Anglicans and Episcopalians are looking South, although that is where virtually all the growth is occurring in their Communion."[13]

And so, in the next few pages we are "looking South," for this is where Christianity, in its diverse forms, is experiencing phenomenal growth. Let us begin with Africa as we attempt to imagine Christianity's resurgence and growth. By 1985, there were more than 16,500 conversions a day, or an annual rate of more than six million on this continent.[14] In a 2001 edition, *World Christian Encyclopedia* reported a net increase of 8.4 million Christians a year, or 23,000 a day, of which 1.5 million are net new converts. Some sources say that Christians already outnumber Muslims: Africa has become a Christian continent.[15]

Statistics also show a stunning growth of certain forms of Christianity in Asia, the Pacific islands, and South America. A congregation like The Full Gospel Church in Seoul claims to have half a million members. This is the world's largest single congregation. The Kwang Lim Methodist Church had 150 members in 1971, but at the end of the century, it had 85,000 members. A similar trend is found in Vietnam where there are around 80 million Christians, and the numbers are rising. If we shift our focus to South America, the church is also experiencing tremendous growth, especially among Pentecostals. Pentecostal churches are growing at the rate of 20 million new members a year.[16]

Viewing this numerical growth of world Christianity in a longer historical perspective, another trend becomes apparent. At the beginning of the twentieth century, 83 percent of Christians lived in the global North. Around 1970 a major change occurred: more of the world's Christians lived in the global South.[17] It is no longer the old European and North American precincts of Christendom but Asia, Africa, and South America. In the year 2000, 61 percent of the world's

13. Jenkins, *The Next Christendom*, 5.

14. Sanneh, *Whose Religion is Christianity?* 15.

15. Jenkins, *The Next Christendom*, 56.

16. Cox, *Fire from Heaven*, xv.

17. Cox, cited by Netland, "Globalization and Theology," 23.

Christians lived in the global South. The prediction is that by 2050, 70 percent of the world's Christians will be in the global South.

What does this account tell us? It tells us that Christianity is not waning; rather, it is experiencing tremendous growth, though unevenly. While churches of the global North are struggling to survive, churches of the global South are experiencing explosive growth. Moreover, it tells us that the center of Christianity's demographic growth and vitality already has shifted to the global South, even as power (narrowly understood) still remains in the global North. Put differently, if we read global statistics carefully, what we see is not the march toward a post-Christian world, if by world we mean the wider world. We may consider the post-Christian claim only if we mean the traditional Christian West, and only if by post-Christian we mean the demise of Christian hegemony in the West. From the perspective of the global South or the Two-Thirds World or the global South diaspora in our midst, what is happening is not so much the death of Christianity as much as it is the de-Europeanization or the de-Westernization of Christianity, even the de-Westernization of Christianity in the West. Or is it? After all, when did Christianity become Western?

The journey of Christianity is not over. The Christianity of the global South is coming to the global North through the diaspora communities, and they are re-Christianizing and redefining Christianity in the global North. Focusing our attention to our specific context, I say that they are re-Christianizing and redefining Christianity in the United States. Diana Eck's *A New Religious America* is often cited to support the idea that the United States is fast becoming "the world's most religiously diverse nation" because of the presence of the newcomers in our midst.[18] I agree that the U.S. is fast becoming a religiously diverse nation, but the countries of the historic Christendom, such as France, Germany, and United Kingdom, are proportionally more diverse than the United States.

I appreciate Eck's research on the growing religious diversity of our context, but her work does not address the reality that many of the newcomers to the United States are Christians. Stephen Warner takes account of this phenomenon. Mexico, the largest sending country, is an overwhelmingly Christian nation as are other countries of Latin America. Eastern Europe, the Philippines, Korea, Vietnam, India,

18. See Eck, *A New Religious America*.

and Lebanon also send a great percentage of immigrant Christians. Half of those who arrive from Korea are Christians, and another half of those who arrive from Korea with no religious identity become Christians. The end result is that 75 percent of Korean Americans are Christians. There is also a widespread conversion of Chinese. Warner notes that Chinese Christian converts predominate to the extent that an "estimated one third of Chinese Americans, across all generations, are now Christian."[19] Though recent statistics show a rising trend of immigrants from other religious traditions, Christians from other countries continue to reach our shores in great numbers as well.

So, what about this growth of world Christianity? I am not interested in simply providing information. We must challenge our ways of thinking, particularly about the church and its catholicity as well as mission and ministry. How shall we take account of the catholicity of the church that takes seriously the demographic shift of Christianity from the global North to the global South? And how shall we take account of the catholicity of the church when the diaspora Christians of the global South are already in the geographical heartland of the global North, even at the doorsteps of our churches? How shall we take account of the coming of the once missionized people, including the religious fundamentalism that the Western church exported, to the center of the global North? We explore these questions in the next sections.

ALTERNATIVE WAYS OF ARTICULATING THE CHURCH'S CATHOLICITY

I have found articulating the catholicity of the church in light of our new circumstances quite daunting. It is daunting because I would like my account of catholicity to be catholic too: encompassing in scope, yet profound in depth and fully cognizant of the plurality of voices. Perhaps, it is expecting too much of a single chapter. Perhaps I can include that as an aspiration. After all, eschatological aspiration is at the core of catholicity. Suffice it to say, I aspire that my account, following Avery Dulles, will be able to embrace the breadth, length, depth, and height of catholicity.[20] I aspire to take account of catholicity in a catholic way that includes reach/extension and the ability to draw together, celebration of difference while affirming unity, respect

19. Warner, "Coming to America," 21.
20. Dulles, cited in Groome, *What Makes Us Catholic?*, 247–48.

of the universal while respecting the integrity of the particular/local, proclamation of wholeness and healing of brokenness, celebration of openness while affirming deep convictions, and connection with the past while anticipating the unfolding of the new tomorrow.

Catholicity as Interdependence and Solidarity

We are living in an interrelated and interconnected world. That is the fact of our lives and always will be. Even our ability and the effectiveness of our acts to disconnect presuppose connection. We often use the ocean to speak of distance and separation, but the ocean is actually a great connector. The expressions of disconnection that we see daily only attest to the reality of interconnections and the interweaving of our lives. Globalization, as I said earlier, has made our connections more acute and has made us more aware. Though we have suffered unevenly, our interconnections mean shared vulnerabilities as well as hopes. Unfortunately, the discourse of shared vulnerabilities has elicited more fears to many, which has spiraled into more and sophisticated acts of disconnection. Our day-to-day realities and the news headlines point in this direction.

If interconnections and interweaving as well as shared vulnerabilities and hopes are our common lot, it is crucial and relevant that they inform or shape our understanding of the catholicity of the church. Significant in articulating a theology of the church and its catholicity is embraced by the notions of interconnections and solidarity. Interconnections and solidarity are catholic because they are our common lot. The church embodies this catholicity in sharing and connecting with the sufferings of all. It embodies catholicity when it reaches out and connects the pain of one with the pain of all; the dream of one with the dream of all. The church's catholicity reminds us that we cannot experience salvation outside the realm of our interconnections; that we cannot experience salvation apart from each other. Outside of our interconnections and interrelationship there is no salvation. Our well-being is intertwined with the well-being of our fellow humans and the rest of God's creation.

The particular shape of the church's catholicity is embodied in the life and ministry of Jesus and in the sacraments of the church, particularly the eucharist. In the act of incarnation, God's universal love became particular in Jesus, which is an affirmation that particularities are not beyond the reach of God's love. In fact, the only way to love universally is to love in the particularity. In the particularity of the life of Jesus, God's love is made real to all and in the various circumstances of their lives. If God, in the life of Jesus, shared and suffered our common lot, so God also shares our hopes. We have made this shared suffering and hope into a sacrament in the eucharist. In the eucharist we are one creation, one people, one community, and one bread that is broken for all. The eucharist is symbolic of our oneness with the earth, solidarity with one another, shared plight, and shared hopes.

Catholicity as Wholeness and Hospitality

Much as we celebrate our interconnections in the global village, our reality has also been that of global pillage, global fragmentation, global disconnection, global diaspora, global conflicts, and global walls rising. The global market that has unified us has also become an instrument for breaking the bond of our shared humanity, for lording over and denying others of the means to live life fully. It has become a means of breaking the backs of others and maintaining asymmetrical power relations. Predatory globalism has brought enormous wealth to some but poverty to most, and it has divided and uprooted communities. Displaced people, particularly from the impoverished global South, have come in hordes to the global North, and host communities have often reacted to the presence of the newcomers with alarm. Thus, instead of bridges of connections, hearts are constricting and walls of division and exclusion are rising. Violence is everywhere, which is a manifestation of a globally systemic violence.

In the context of global pillage, fragmentation, brokenness, and walls of inhospitality rising, it is not enough to affirm catholicity as the interconnecting and the interweaving of our lives. This is a foundational affirmation; however, it is not sufficient in itself. Yes, we are connected and we have shared vulnerabilities, but there are deeper questions: How just and life-giving are our connections? How open are our socio-economic and political systems to the participation of all? In other words, along with affirming our catholicity through interconnection and solidarity, we need to view catholicity as hospitality and just social relations. Catholicity is about our relationship with our neighbors. For Thomas Groome, catholicity is about "how open is our hearts, how wide our concern, whom will we welcome, and include?"[21] If I may use a different metaphor, catholicity is about the size of our hearts and who they include as neighbor. It is about the heart's capacity to embrace the other in the ministry of care and in the ministry of transforming and opening inhospitable social structures. Put differently, catholicity is about hospitality and the creation of hospitable communities and global society. It is about the removal of walls of division and systems of exclusion that marginalize and oppress others. Catholicity is about resisting unjust social structures and promoting just relations; it is about busting exclusionary laws and practices and welcoming all to the banquet table.

The church is called to embody wholeness and hospitality in the light of Jesus' life and ministry. In his life and ministry, Jesus showed the people what is at the center of God's heart: radical love and radical hospitality. In light of the coming reign of God, Jesus dared to take the risk, offended the gatekeepers, scandalized traditional piety, broke laws of exclusion, healed the sick and dying, proclaimed release to the captives, and welcomed the social outcasts. The egalitarian meals that Jesus performed symbolize not only the coming reign of God, but also what the church is called to be about. It is called to be egalitarian, hospitable, just in relationship, and caring for the broken and the marginalized. When the church embodies these values in its life, worship, organization, and ministries, it truly becomes a sacrament of the church's catholicity as wholeness and hospitality.

Catholicity as Creative Balance of Plurality and Unity

The issue of plurality and unity or of the one and the many is a perennial one but, like interconnections, has become more acute in the era of globalization. With globalization comes hegemony and homogenization. With it comes a unified global system that requires uniformity and conformity for efficient functioning. Globalization means the flattening of the world and the imposition of a monoculture and monolanguage, which are heavily influenced by the global market and the global North. In the history of the world it came under different labels: globabelization, globalatinization, anglobalization, global-americanization, and so on. For many, predatory globalization is another term for imperialism. But the predatory, hegemonic,

21. Groome, Ibid., 241.

and homogenizing globalization has also generated plurality, intense search for and articulation of identities, assertions of particularities, and defense of the local. As homogenization spreads, movements of various motivations countering homogenization are also rising.[22] Universalism, both secular and religious, has encountered the rise of a stubborn particularism in the guise of resurgent nationalism. Put differently, predatory globalization has generated antiglobalist reactions and resistance of various kinds such as ethnification, primitivism, and counterhegemonic movements, which I distinguish from "antiglobalism." Though it may seem paradoxical, even the antiglobal extremists or "guerilla antiglobalists," as Mark Juergensmeyer calls them, have global networks of antiglobalism.[23] Given these challenges, how then shall we speak of the one and the many and of the one world and the many worlds? More particularly, how does this inform the way we think of the church's catholicity?

I suggest, along with others, that we articulate the church's catholicity as that which upholds the delicate and creative balance between unity and plurality, between the many and the one. Catholicity, suggests Dulles, is present in the church's ability to hold things together in tension with one another.[24] Catholicity is not unity at the expense of diversity and vice versa. It is not colorless uniformity at the expense of variety and vice versa. Diversity is as central as unity. It is not a challenge to be overcome or a problem to be solved. There may be different emphasis in the spectrum of unity and diversity, but the framework should locate diversity and unity as inseparably intertwined. Though speaking in particular of the ecumenical movement, Michael Kinnamon's words offer help in articulating the balance of unity and diversity: "If monolithic unity is the Scylla of the ecumenical movement, 'autonomous diversity' is its Charybdis. By autonomous diversity, I mean an approach to community that loses sight of its given wholeness in favor of the particularity of its parts. Diversity, understood as constitutive of unity, is a blessing. Diversity, seen as an end in itself, is simply another expression of the sinful human tendency to organize reality into homogenous enclaves."[25]

22. Lochhead, *Shifting Realities*, 100.
23. Juergensmeyer, "Religious Antiglobalism," 135–48.
24. Dulles, *The Catholicity of the Church*.
25. Kinnamon, *The Vision of the Ecumenical Movement*, 59.

The harmonious balancing of unity and diversity should not be interpreted to mean smoothing out of crucial differences. Harmony cannot be achieved when unjust relationship exists. In a deeper sense, harmony presupposes a just social order or a just form of relationship. Harmonious balancing of unity and diversity does not mean spineless blending of differences, but demands taking a stand when greater well-being is at stake. Catholic ecumenism, in Dulles' interpretation, has taken this prophetic stance. While it is committed to the unity of incompatibilities, there is a point when it says no. It says no when life and truth are at stake, and it says no to "reductionist ecumenism, that is an ecumenism that would achieve unity by discarding what is distinctive of each tradition."[26]

The physical body is an image often used to articulate the inseparable connection of the one and the many. In fact, it has been used to speak of the church—the Body of Christ. In the Body of Christ metaphor we have a framework for understanding unity and diversity that is characterized by mutuality and common direction. The well-being of one member is the well-being of all; the full expression of one is the full expression of all; the unity of the whole is an expression and joy of all. Unity is not a threat to diversity but an expression of the health of every member acting as a whole. The gifts or charisms of various members are affirmed by the whole, and the whole unifies the various charisms for the benefit of the whole body.

This creative interweaving of unity and diversity in the life of the church is articulated in a larger setting through the image or vision of the Pentecost. Pentecost presents to us a vision of a church that embodies catholicity as creative unity and plurality and a society that is just, abundant, and colorful. The growth of world Christianity and the presence of diaspora communities are already providing the conditions for a world characterized by Pentecostal plurality. It is up to us to discern and follow the movement of the Spirit so that we become participants in the birthing of a Pentecostal tomorrow. The various tongues of the world are already in our localities, but a "miracle of the ear" must happen.[27] We may not be able to speak all the languages that are in our neighborhood, but if we have experienced the miracle of the

---

26. Dulles, *The Catholicity of the Church*, 78–79.

27. Wink and Keener-Wink, cited in Law, *The Wolf Shall Dwell with the Lamb*, 45–51.

ear, then we have acquired the ears for understanding, listening, and caring. When the spirit has given us these ears, we will have the mind of a heart that knows how to navigate and communicate in the one and many worlds in just and respectful ways.

Catholicity as Communication, Reception, Exchange, and Integration of the Gospel

If, as Schreiter suggests, the new mode of universality in our current phase of globalization is communication, it also provides a helpful clue in articulating the church's catholicity. Without communication we cannot speak of the catholicity of the Christian message and of the catholicity of the church. More fundamentally, the church would not even exist, for the church is born out of communication and is called to embody the life of communication. But there is something more: in the act of communication that which has been communicated must have been received and an exchange of communication ensued. If mutual exchange happened, then I assume that the integrity of each participant must have been honored. Otherwise, the response of the one who has been communicated to would not be genuinely true to one's self. When the integrity of each is honored, mutual communication becomes an expression of the length, depth, breadth, and height of one's being. This means the depth and texture of one's individuality and identity, the length of one's historical connections, the breadth of one's context and socio-cultural relations, and the height of one's faith and hope. When this form of communication, reception and exchange happens, then we can say that the integration of the gospel has become a reality, and that catholicity is shining forth brightly.

The matter of catholicity as communication, reception, exchange, and integration of the gospel or the Christian message has been normally dealt with under the topic of inculturation or contextualization. "Inculturation" has been the preferred term in the Roman Catholic circles, while the churches of the Reformation prefer the term "contextualization." While the term "inculturation," as it is interpreted by many Roman Catholic theologians, embraces culture and the issue of liberation, the term itself seems to focus on culture. On the other hand, the term "contextualization" carries better this double nuance of culture and an emphasis on liberation. Whenever I use inculturation, I mean it to convey this double nuance. It is with this understanding that I use contextualization or inculturation as a vehicle for expressing the catholicity of the church.

Pursuing our interpretation of catholicity in light of communication and exchange and through the process of inculturation or contextualization, my claims about catholicity in general apply to inculturation in particular. Inculturation is present when communication, mutual exchange, creative and faithful reappropriation and integration are present. Groome interprets the teachings of Vatican Council II on inculturation along this line. Inculturation happens in the context of "living exchange" between each native culture and the Christian faith and enriches both. It must be a two-way street (between faith and culture) for inculturation to occur. As he puts it, *"Today inculturation can be understood as an exchange of gifts whereby Christian faith, remaining true to its core, becomes native within each culture, thereby enhancing both the local culture and the mosaic of Christian faith with a unique expression."* What emerges, he continues, will be "a unique expression of the Christian faith, enhancing the church's catholicity."[28]

If I may pursue further Groome's interpretation, I say that the gospel is distinct from culture but not apart from culture. The gospel would not make sense apart from culture, so the gospel is only gospel in relation to culture. We understand the gospel in and through culture. This means that inculturation or contextualization is more than a way of finding cultural media for communication; likewise, it is a mode of apprehending the world. We apprehend the gospel in and through our context, and it is through our context that the gospel of salvation or liberation becomes saving and liberating to us. The emphasis on becoming native to a place is only one dimension of inculturation. Beyond it, inculturation is about the de-envelopment of communities from everything that envelops. Using a liberationist perspective in reading inculturation, I say that liberation comes through the medium of culture even as liberation itself is an expression of culture responding to the Divine in and through culture.

Although it is slow in coming, inculturation has been going on in many quarters of Christianity. I view popular religiosity as an expression of sophisticated inculturation at the popular level. The inseparability of culture and liberation or of the medium and the message is

---

28. Groome, *What Makes Us Catholic*, 258–59. Groome's emphasis.

important especially if we accept popular religiosity as an expression of inculturation. It is easy for a centralizing or Romanizing church to dismiss popular religiosity or to classify it as a second-class religiosity, because it does not often conform to the Western Enlightenment habits of thinking. It would be easy to suspect the religious expression, particularly of the people of the global South, as syncretistic. After all, the church has for many years labeled as syncretistic those religious expressions that are not native to the global North or West. While syncretism points to the unresolved tension-filled mixing of the Christian message with the local culture, I follow Sanneh's suggestion that, "unless we use it as a judgment against our own forms of religious practice . . . [we] drop it altogether."[29]

To encapsulate insights on communication in relation to inculturation or contextualization for understanding catholicity, I say that the church is catholic when inculturation is present in the various aspects of the church, such as liturgy, theology, morality, and institutional organization. Catholicity is present to the extent that a "living exchange" characterized by mutuality is happening between the Christian faith and each native culture that enriches both, and at the same time, transforms both. The church embodies catholicity to the extent that its ways of communication and exchange are able to speak universally in a manner that honors the particular stories, struggles, and aspirations of the local. Catholicity happens where the church has become native to each locality, while at the same time connected to the wider church and the wider world. In fact, becoming native to a locality does not mean localized isolation, for locality is wider than the immediate local. Locality is both immediate and beyond. More than that, locality is simultaneously local and global or an expression of the interweaving of the global and the local. I must now turn to this dimension of catholicity.

Catholicity in the Sense of Being Translocal or Glocal

As suggested in the previous section, locality embraces both the immediate and the wider context. The image here is the reach and coverage of one's locality. One is always a native of the immediate local as well as the wider local. To use a much wider imagery, we are all natives to the world and to the earth. But there is another way of viewing

29. Sanneh, *Whose Religion is Christianity?* 44.

the relationship between the immediate and wider context other than length or extension. Instead of the imagery of extended reach, as in immediate *and* beyond, it sees locality as *simultaneously* an expression of the interweaving of the local and the global.

The term "glocal," which integrates the local and the global, carries the understanding of a reality or a context experiencing the simultaneous interweaving of the local and the global. Simultaneous interweaving is my way of taking into account the multidirectional flow. The flow between the global and the local is not linear, and it is not one way. Many accounts of the relationship between the global and the local follow the linear, one-way traffic approach. It comes with this question: What are the impacts of globalization in the local neighborhood? This question needs to be asked, but this is a one-dimensional, one-directional approach. We must do more than reverse the question; we must ask the question that helps us see the multiple interactions. What glocalization does, says Charles Van Engen, is help us see the "interrelationship between the local and the global in their multifaceted, multidirectional, interactive dynamic influence one upon the other."[30]

As I have repeatedly stated, in a globalized world the global is lived locally and the local is lived globally. The global is not simply out there; it is also in here, wherever our location is. The global has no reality *apart from* the local, even as the reality of the global is more than the sum of the locals. The local constitutes the global even as the global is not equivalent to the sum of all the parts. The slogan "think globally and act locally" is not as simple as it sounds. Through the local we see the global, not outside the local. In fact, awareness that one is seeing through the local is constitutive of seeing the global. Global thinking is located thinking; it is not nowhere-thinking. After all, nowhere-thinking is somewhere-thinking that has forgotten it is thinking from, in, and through somewhere. To articulate the slogan differently, "thinking globally demands seeing locally." Nonetheless, we must underscore the converse as well. If we want to see the local, we have to see it globally even if only through locally. The reality of the local would only come to full light when seen globally. Only in seeing globally is the local taken seriously. Seeing globally is seeing through the local but using a wider frame that is able to analyze the

30. Van Engen, "The Glocal Church," 159.

various threads in their systemic interconnections. Apart from seeing the systemic or structural interconnections of the locals, we have not really taken the local seriously.

Glocalization offers a clue for a way of thinking about the church, particularly in relation to catholicity. The church is catholic not only because of its worldwide reach (extension), especially with the growth of world Christianity, but because every local church is a living embodiment of the universal church. We have no way of seeing the universal church apart from the local church. The universal church has no reality apart from the local congregations. The local churches constitute the universal church even as the universal church is more than the sum of all the parts. The bearer of the universal church is the local church. It is where the fullness of the church comes to expression. The local church is not *pars pro toto* (part for the whole), but it is whole and full, even if it is not the totality of the church.[31] The fullness of the church is found in the local church. Integrating the concept of interculturation, the universal church is a communion of inculturated churches and "each Christian community constitutes its own unique expression of Church, and the completeness of the local community is an instance of Christian *catholicity*."[32]

While I have underscored the idea that the universal church has no reality in itself apart from the local church, and that the primary bearer of the universal church is the local church, we should not lose sight of the fact the local church is truly local only because it is part of the universal church. David Bosch puts it this way: "It is true that the church exists primarily in *particular* churches, . . . but it is also true that it is *in virtue of the church's catholicity* . . .that the particular exists."[33] A particular church exists by virtue of the church's catholicity. The fullness of a particular congregation is negated when it is not connected to the universal. In other words, it ceases to be a local congregation of the church catholic when it is detached from its wider connection. Like a branch that is cut off from the tree, a local congregation ceases to be catholic.

31. Ibid., 163.
32. Groome, *What Makes Us Catholic*, 246. Emphasis in the original text.
33. Bosch, *Transforming Mission*, 457.

Catholicity in Vision and Hope: The Eschatological Dimension

In the previous sections we explored the church's catholicity in matters of reach (extension), connections, wholeness and hospitality, unity in plurality, communication and integration, and translocal or glocal identity. At this point, we continue the exploration of catholicity through the eschatological lens, which is one of the dimensions of the church's classical understanding of its catholicity. What do we mean by catholicity in the eschatological sense that takes into account the challenges of globalization? Or, how does globalization and eschatology inform the way we articulate the church's catholicity? To answer these questions, we begin with eschatology.

Eschatology is generally equated with that which is yet to come, the future. Although the future suggests something within the historical frame, the future that eschatology speaks about is also transhistorical. By embracing the historical and transhistorical, eschatology points to the fulfillment of the new tomorrow in the future in God's own time. But eschatology, while it is commonly understood as a discourse about the future (the not-yet), is also a discourse about the past and the present. Eschatological imagination is wingless when not rooted in the past and committed to the present. Even as eschatological expectation looks forward, it does not forget the past, especially the memories of those who died before their time. Eschatological imagination remembers. Consider the manner in which some South Pacific islanders gesture when they speak of the future: when speaking of the future, they gesture toward the past. This South Pacific gesture finds resonance among some Africans. An ethnic group in Kenya that speaks Kalinga expresses it this way: "The past lies before us and the future lies behind us." The future is unknown (behind us) and the past is what we know (before us).[34]

It is not my intention to polarize the past and future orientation. After all, the past is not always a sure guide to the future, although we can learn from it. Of significance is that the eschatological orientation embraces the past and the future through faithfulness in the present. The dismembered still have their future, and their future is tied to the present in our acts of *anamnestic* solidarity and creative action in the present. Likewise, eschatological orientation not only embraces the future of the past, but also the future of the not-yet—the future of

---

34. Cited in Lederach, "The Mystery of Transformative Times," 265.

those who are still to come or to be born. This is of crucial significance if we agree with the ecologists that we no longer inherit the earth from our parents, rather, we borrow it from our children.

What better way to speak of the catholicity of the church than to speak of its ability to carry the past into the future through creative and faithful actions in the present? What better way to speak of the catholicity of the church than to embrace the future of the past with the future of those who are still to come? As the church's catholicity is affirmed in the shared pain of the past and the present, so it is catholic in affirming our shared hope. As the church's catholicity is affirmed in its historical reach, so the church catholicity is affirmed in its transhistorical reach. In the church's catholicity, the communion of saints—living and dead—is affirmed.

Lastly, I cannot imagine a better way of talking about the church's catholicity without being aware of our failings and to speak of catholicity as an "aspiration of humanity at its best, calling us to oppose sectarianism and chauvinism of every kind and to practice solidarity and interdependence instead."[35] How uncatholic would it be to speak of the church as already fully catholic when historical reality continues to negate that claim? This would be the height of the church's arrogance and idolatry. "Catholic," contends Groome, "is not an accomplishment of any denomination but a vision for what Christians—Protestant and Catholic—should become together."[36] All the dimensions of catholicity that I have identified are, after all, eschatological aspirations that only God can finally fulfill.

WORLD CHRISTIANITY AND THE WORLD CHURCH: EMBODYING CATHOLICITY IN THE INSTITUTIONAL LIFE OF THE CHURCH

The growth of Christianity in the global South and its spread to the global North through diaspora communities is creating opportunities, following Sanneh's distinction, for the birthing of "world Christianity" in contrast to "global Christianity." Sanneh describes global Christianity as "the faithful replication of Christian forms and patterns developed in Europe," which echoes Hilaire Belloc's infamous

---

35. Groome, *What Makes Us Catholic*, 243.
36. Ibid., 247.

statement, "Europe is the faith."[37] Global Christianity carries vestiges of a Christendom church that reaches to the farthest corners of the world, with local churches as expressions of its socio-political and religious reach. Moreover, its connotations parallel with "economic globalization, with the same forces of global trade and the Internet revolution fueling the spread of a seamless environment of information and exchange without borders."[38]

On the other hand, "world Christianity," Sanneh contends, "is not one thing, but a variety of indigenous responses through more or less effective local idioms, but in any case without necessarily the European Enlightenment frame."[39] World Christianity is not a faithful replication of Western Christendom or a mere extension of Westernized Christianity. It is connected with the West, may even be related to a Western mission work and informed and nourished by that connection, but it is also the direct fruit of the work of the free Spirit, a Spirit that is present before the arrival of the missionaries and a Spirit that is beyond the control of the institutional church. World Christianity is native to its locality as it is native of the wider world through its connections. To use different imagery, it is not a "potted plant" from the West that has been transported and transplanted to the East. It is not even a "grafted plant" of a Western tree that has been transported and transplanted to the East. World Christianity is a native plant of its locality but connected to the same atmosphere and rain that nurtures every plant.

Enthusiastic as I am with Sanneh's distinction between global Christianity and world Christianity, I hesitate to claim that world Christianity, as he describes it, is already a reality. Yes there are manifestations of it, but has Christianity moved away from Western or global North hegemony? The expressions of world Christianity are present, but it appears to be more of an aspiration than a reality; more transformative work needs to be done. This is what many Christians are struggling to do: they struggle to articulate and give birth to a "world-church," an idea that has been articulated by some theologians.[40] World-church, in essence, is a communion of local, in-

---

37. Sanneh, *Whose Religion is Christianity?* 22.

38. Ibid., 23.

39. Ibid., 22.

40. See Bianchi and Ruether, *A Democratic Church*, 253–60. Also, see Hines,

digenous churches, each embodying the fullness of the church in their particular locality, and whose unity makes up the universal church.

Integrating insights from my account of the church as a translocal community and on inculturation, I say that the world-church is a communion of inculturated churches, each wholly church in their distinct particularities. In this account it follows that the world-church is in the first instance a local church; it is the diverse local churches that constitute the universal church. If we pursue this point, the church is constituted from the ground up, not from the top down. This should inform the way we think of the church's institutional structure and its power and authority. This should guide us in the direction of democratic restructuring of the church which, for Rosemary Radford Ruether and Eugene Bianchi, needs to be guided by these five principles: participation, conciliarity, pluralism, accountability, and dialogue.[41] The world-church cannot be governed by Roman centralism, but by a more democratic, participatory, and collegial form of governance.

The notion of world-church and the works of many to give birth to it as well as the growth of world Christianity are complementary and, it seems to me, are converging. The demographic growth of world Christianity is already challenging the church to free itself from its various forms of captivity: captivity to Western or global North hegemony, captivity to Western-modernist-secularist assumptions, captivity to wealth and control, and so forth. Meanwhile, advocates of the world-church, especially in the global North, have intensified their efforts in giving birth to a democratic church vis-à-vis the centralizing efforts of the church. We can only hope that these two converging energies will lead us closer to our aspirations of a church that is truly and fully catholic.

CATHOLICITY IN A GLOCALIZED WORLD: IMPLICATIONS FOR OUR COMMON MISSION AND MINISTRY

I have articulated the multiple dimensions of catholicity as well as its implications for how we may restructure the institutional life of the church. Now, we explore catholicity as it relates to the shared mission and ministry of churches. How shall a church understand its part in

"Community for Liberation."

41. Ibid., 176.

the shared mission and ministry? How shall a local church understand its place in relation to other churches and to the whole? What insights from the notion of catholicity and glocalization would inform the churches role in the shared ministry of the whole church? Finally, what is this shared ministry, or how would we characterize this shared ministry in our glocalized world?

Our account of the church—in the first instance a local church, that the universal or world-church is a communion of indigenous local churches, and that they are wholly church in their particularities—points not only to the direction in which we need to articulate the relationship between the local church and the larger/wider church in general, but also to their respective roles in the shared or common ministry in particular. I would like to appropriate this for the Protestant churches of the mainline denominations. If it is true that local churches constitute the church denomination and that the denomination is, in the first instance an expression of local congregations coming together, then there is no denomination apart from local congregations. The congregation is the primary bearer of the church's very being. In this regard, the denomination is an expression of local congregations communing together, and it exists to serve the congregations in their shared as well as distinctive life. If the church is, in the first instance, the local congregation, then it is also the primary bearer of the church's mission and ministry. The denomination exists to support the ministry of congregations at the local level, and the denomination supports the ministry of local congregations at the wider (shared, national and worldwide) level. The shared expression is crucial for local congregations: it is only through a widely/nationally/globally coordinated expression that the various local congregations can respond powerfully and effectively to nationalized and globalized concerns that are ubiquitously real locally. Empowering the ministry of local congregations (local, national, and worldwide) must be the concern of all members of the household of God. An empowered congregation cannot do otherwise than to support local, national, and global ministries because they are expressions of their very identity and calling as the primary bearer of mission and ministry. This also means that local congregations must have a greater say in the shared/wider/national/worldwide expressions of their ministry.

Having articulated the part of each in relation to the common ministry, let us explore the scope and thrust of ministry of the church catholic. Integrating the insights from my account of the church's catholicity, I say that the scope of the church ministry is worldwide; the depth is glocal; the mode of presence is interconnection and solidarity; the mode of relationship is mutual exchange and dialogue; the substance is radical hospitality that overcomes unjust relations; and the vision or *telos* is Pentecostal plurality and unity. Its main message (substance and thrust) is not that God has revealed Godself only in Jesus the Christ, but that God has revealed Godself in Jesus for the sake of the whole creation. This is the distinctiveness of the Christian experience and message—a message that must be proclaimed with passion and confidence without drowning other religious faiths.

With this overarching scope and thrust, let us consider ways of thinking and doing ministry with a church that is fully aware of its catholicity or is self-aware of its translocality in a glocalized world. Self-awareness of its own glocality is crucial for the church's understanding of its ministry and how it needs to proceed. Doing ministry must be in sync with a church's self-understanding if it is to have integrity, effectiveness, and sustainability. Congregations that have embraced a translocal identity are in a better position to carry out their mission and ministry in our globalized world given that their self-understanding matches with the character or dynamics of the wider reality. So, what is a church that is self-consciously translocal? A church that is self-consciously translocal adopts an understanding that its very being is an embodiment of the simultaneous interweaving of the local and the global; that what is happening in the world is happening to itself; and that whatever it does (or does not do) affects the larger whole. Likewise, a translocal church adopts an understanding that the local congregation is the primary bearer of the church and that every congregation embodies the fullness of the church in its locality.

Because a translocal church sees the presence of the world in its own local identity, it participates in God's mission to the world with the understanding that it is both a subject (although derived) and an object of mission in light of its being a part of the world. It thus considers openness to the Spirit's transforming work as a continuing posture even as it participates in the mission of the church for the world. With the understanding that its very own local identity mirrors the interweaving of the local and the global, a church with a translocal sensibility carries out its ministry in ways that seek to overcome a double split: a local-universal church split and local-global context split. In being a local church in a specific context, it is embodying the universal church; in doing ministry locally, it is doing ministry globally. Conversely, in relating to the universal church, it becomes truly a local church; in doing ministry globally (wider context and connections), it is doing ministry locally.

It is of course not easy to overcome the double split. Our habits of thinking that view the relationship of the local and the global context as well as the local and the global church in a linear fashion have made it difficult for us to overcome it. Even the notion of a two-way street that we have used to speak of communication and catholicity seems inadequate. A linearist way of thinking about global mission is still pervasive, such as the use of the term "outreach." Continuing this pattern of thinking, it feels natural to locate the starting point of mission and ministry from the local and then reaching out to the global or to the farthest corner of the world. What is also presupposed here is a center that sends or reaches out, even if this center may entertain the idea of receiving. If we follow a linearist way of thinking, we may end up not reaching out. If we do reach out, often times the manner of reaching out is dictated by the center. Also, if we do reach out, it is easy to feel being spread thin and, finally, to feel stressed out.

A translocal or glocal self-understanding is meant to overcome the linearist-centrist-unidimensional way of thinking and doing mission or ministry. Glocal mission or ministry is multidirectional and multidimensional in character. In this way of thinking, acting internationally is acting locally, and acting locally is acting internationally. Doing mission globally is doing mission locally; and doing mission locally is doing mission globally. This way of thinking and doing seeks to overcome the tendency to focus on one's domestic affairs, especially when funding is low, or when the church is experiencing a budget crunch. Many times we have to act internationally to care for the local; and there are times when we have to act locally to have an impact internationally, as in advocating policies that affect the wider world.

Pursuing further the implications of the translocal or glocal, if the church is glocal and the social reality is glocal, then there is a way of doing mission not only to "foreign lands" afar, though connected, but to structures that unite us all and that weigh us all down. The World Council of Churches in Canberra in 1991 puts it well: "There is an urgent need today for a new type of mission not into foreign lands, but into 'foreign' structures. By this we mean economic, social and political structures which do not at all conform to Christian moral standards."[42] Ministry with those who are geographically far from our location does not always mean crossing the seas but may take the form of seeking to transform predatory foreign structures or global systems that connect us all. In a world of glocalized space which is characterized by the "fading of the state" or the "fading" of nation-states vis-à-vis nationalist reassertions, the mission of the church may take the form of working with other stakeholders in the creation of what Susanne Hoeber Rudolph calls "transnational epistemic communities whose members share common worldviews, purposes, interests, and practices" to address transnational/transborder common interest.[43]

The journey of taking account of the catholicity of the church in response to the challenge of our globalized/glocalized world has been long, but it has yielded new and alternative ways of thinking about the church and mission and ministry. I hope we will pursue exploring the bearings of a translocal/glocal self-understanding of the church and a glocalized understanding of the world to help our church become more truly catholic in length, breadth, depth, and height.

42. Cited in Johannes Nissen, "Mission and Globalization," 38.
43. See Rudolph, "Religious Transnationalism," 189, 191.

5

The Church as Community
with a Burning Center and Porous Borders

Naming Our Globalized Spiritual Crisis

W E ARE IN THE midst of a deep crisis. When global wealth soars to an enormous height but leaves many in squalor and dying in abject poverty, something is terribly amiss. When technologies make it possible to produce more food, but the majority of the world's population still goes to bed hungry, something is woefully wrong. When communications technologies make it possible for people to communicate and dialogue but instead are used to disseminate false information and foment hatred, without a doubt we are in trouble. When the rhetoric, hoopla, and euphoria of the global village continue while walls of division and exclusion continue to rise, there is a deep crisis. Symptoms of our deep crisis are everywhere: they are present when people live under the sway of the religion and god of the global market; when the values of society and the identity of people are defined by possession and consumption; and when consumers are consumed by possession and consumption.

Our global society's deep crisis is manifest in its body politic. A sickly body politic is a manifestation of a deep crisis. When nation-states use more of their resources in policing dissent, the prison system, and in armaments over against education and health care, there is a deep crisis. When people know more about playing war than about playing peace, certainly a deep crisis is present. A deep crisis is present when migrants are met with xenophobia and hostilities; when religion becomes an ideology to support religious bigotry and militant fundamentalism. When the ecosystem is sacrificed in pursuit of short term economic benefits, usually for the few, a deep crisis is present, and it is a spiritual one.

Our crisis is a spiritual one: at the heart of the various manifestations of our current crisis is a denial and a violation of life. At the heart of our crisis is a distortion of our very being—of who we are, whose we are, what we are called to be and to do, and what we hope for. At the heart of our crisis is an egregious distortion of our core values, of what truly matters, and what affirms and nourishes life. At the heart of our crisis is the breaking of the web of life in which we all are woven. All these symptoms of our crisis point to the denial of the presence of the life-giving Spirit.

NAMING OUR DARKNESS—OUR DEEP CRISIS

> Once upon a time Abba Lot went to see Abba Joseph and said, "Abba, as much as I am able I practice a small rule, all the little fasts, some prayer and meditation, and remain quiet, and as much as possible I keep my thoughts clean. What else should I do?" Then the old monastic stood up and stretched out his hands toward heaven, and his fingers became like ten torches of flame. And he said, "Why not be completely turned into fire?"[1]

Yes, "why not be completely turned into fire?" But what shall we do to be on fire? We must learn the fundamentals of building a fire. To make fire we need materials, like firewood. We cannot make fire, however, unless we allow air to move in and out freely. Analogously, we cannot experience the fire of faith without the Spirit. Air, breath, and fire are a few of the symbols associated with the Holy Spirit. Without the Spirit (air) dwelling in us, we cannot experience being turned into fire; without fire we cannot emit light; without light we cannot shine. I speak not of a dim and flickering light, but of a light shining brightly, steadily, and boldly when something deep inside burns mightily. Apart from the Spirit that creates and sustains the blaze within us, we can only be swallowed by darkness, an ever deepening darkness.

There is deep darkness around us. Worse, the general public seems not to recognize it. William Stafford considers it "cruel, and maybe the root of all cruelty to know what occurs but not recognize

---

1. Cited in Chittister, *The Fire in These Ashes*, 32.

the fact." Therefore, insists Stafford, "It is important that awake people be awake . . . [T]he signals we give—yes or no, or maybe—should be clear." Even our naming of the "gray" areas should be clear. Our signals should be clear, lest the circus of our mutual parade might not find the park, much less follow the right God home, for "the darkness around us is deep."[2]

SPIRITUAL HUNGER OF OUR TIMES:
A MARKET OF SPIRITUALITIES

Our crisis may lead to new possibilities. Our spiritual crisis is creating an opening: it is creating a spiritual hunger. While this is an encouraging and hopeful sign, it is also fraught with dangers. Modernity, particularly secularism and positivistic science, kicked the spirit out, and now it is back in multiple ways. "Exile the human being's religious instinct to the sphere of the supernatural, the eternal, or to the private life of the individual," warns Raimon Panikkar, "and you force it to return, in a hundred different, not always wholesome, ways, to the agora of political and social life, not excluding the economic."[3] We are now experiencing and must deal squarely with the myriad deformities of spirituality.

The global market is always on the look-out for what it can sell, and spirituality is no exception. Spirituality is a growth industry. Spirituality is a hot commodity. What used to be non-marketable is now marketable: personal growth, serenity, and spirituality. Further, it appears that all the hype around spirituality is more likely to be found in the U.S. and Europe than in the global South. More specifically, there is more talk about spirituality among the middle and upper classes than among those who are barely surviving. Without a doubt, the market is more than happy to sell people of goodwill, big consumers of spirituality, the type of spirituality that suits their tastes.[4] And what are the requirements of cultivating such spirituality? One must be able to set aside a chunk of time at a quiet and comfortable environment, away from traffic noise and smelly dump sites or from anything that will break the spell of the pleasant. Those who have the financial means can travel to distant and famous monasteries for spiri-

2. Stafford, *Darkness around Us Is Deep*, 135–36.

3. Panikkar, *Cultural Disarmament*, 43.

4. See Gebara, "A Cry for Life," 115.

tual nourishment, places beyond the reach of the disinherited people of the land.

What kind of spirituality is it that the big consumers of supermarket spirituality receive for their money? This spirituality is narrowly associated with meditation techniques for relaxing the mind and body. In these meditation techniques we learn a mantra or focus on our breath; but rarely are we instructed to focus on an image of people scavenging for anything valuable on a mountain of trash. Roger Gottlieb names the consequence of this kind of spirituality: "it is not openness to life that we learn, but another version of the pursuit of pleasure. Meditation becomes a relaxation technique and not a source of spiritual development."[5]

We need to give direction to the spiritual hunger of our times. We need to guide it to a spirituality that takes seriously the earth and all its inhabitants; to a spirituality that is not a pursuit of pleasure but one that confronts the god and religion of the global market. We need to guide the spiritual hunger of our times to a spirituality that cares for the disenfranchised and the broken; to a spirituality that speaks truth to power; to a spirituality that embodies the dream of a just, abundant, colorful, and sustainable tomorrow; to a spirituality that plants and cultivates seeds of hope; and to a spirituality that empowers the church to live out its calling in the world. The church needs to be reawakened to this kind of spirituality if it is to be truly and vitally faithful as well as responsive to the monstrous threats we are facing today in the era of globalization. Reawakening is, of course, primarily the work of the Spirit. All the same, the church—composed of believers with endowed human agency—can help prepare the soil so that we can be receptive to the presence and work of the Spirit.

CRISIS IN THE CHURCH: RESPIRATORY FAILURE

Sadly, the church is not outside of the crisis: it is part of the crisis. Congregational studies are in concert in speaking of a crisis particularly at the heart of "mainline" Protestant churches. Some call it a sickness, and statistical projections indicate that it is a sickness unto death. Mainline Protestant churches are losing members. Sunday worship attendance is down. Financial giving in general is weak and the support

5. Gottlieb, *A Spirituality of Resistance*, 15.

for wider ministries in particular is on the wane.[6] Unless a major turn-around happens, it is argued, we will be seeing the gradual death of "mainline" Protestant denominations.[7] It may not be death in the literal physical sense of disappearance, for great institutions rarely disappear without a trace; rather, it may be "death" to these "mainline" churches as they once were, and becoming instead "oldline" churches. No doubt "oldline" churches continue to do great things and serve real needs. Even so, "as a group and on the whole," contends John Cobb Jr., they are "lukewarm" and "inspire no passion."[8]

Now that bites! A fire is raging in my heart. Part of me says no, it is not true. On the other hand, I feel it is right on target, and it needs to be expressed with passion. In the ups and downs of life, "oldline" Protestant churches have been present as vendors of services to both members and non-members alike, but on the whole we can say that they have not been very effective in producing passionate disciples who are committed to the mission of the church. If this is the case, what on earth is wrong? And, of course, the next question is: What are we going to do about it? Against the background of pervasive and contagious lukewarmness, how do we develop congregations with burning hearts and porous borders?

It is easy to fall into false panaceas in moments of profound cri-sis. Too eager for a quick turn-around, many declining or plateaued congregations are ready to grab for any silver bullet or "faithful fix" for our illness. As in most quick-fix solutions, the diagnoses are often in-adequate. The diagnoses lack comprehensiveness and depth. They fail to see the interrelationship of factors and the central challenge. What kind of solutions can we expect from inadequate diagnoses? They are solutions that do not address the root cause of the illness and simply treat the symptoms; thus, the illness remains or keeps coming back, and more complications happen in the long run.

It is my belief that mainline Protestant churches can live again if we are open to a major rethinking; if we are willing to let go of old hab-its of thinking; and if we are willing to take risks. A return to old-time religion will not suffice to form a burning center. As it is commonly understood, return to old-time religion, to use the words of James

---

6. Dick, *Revolutionizing Christian Stewardship*, 6.

7. See Schieler, *Revive Your Mainline Congregation*, 9.

8. Cobb, *Reclaiming the Church*, 4.

Luther Adams, "restores only the ashes and not the fires of faith."[9] A revitalized church is possible if we are willing to make a fundamental and paradigmatic change in our perceptions. The time has come to take a serious look not only at what and how we are doing, but why we are doing what we are doing. Asking why we are doing what we are doing may trigger a shift in perspective and help the church to move beyond maintenance.

As can be expected, a variety of reasons have been advanced as explanations for the decline of the church in the global North. Along with these reasons are prescriptions notably from an increasing number of congregational development and vitality gurus. Depending on one's field of expertise, various fixes are prescribed to an ailing or dying church. Since many of the gurus have been trained in the secularist-scientific-medical-corporate settings, not surprisingly, prescriptions reflect their background. Those shaped by the corporate-organization culture see the church as an institution to be governed and managed; those shaped by the therapeutic world see the church as a patient to be cured or healed; and those shaped by the care-giving world see the church as a hospice facility. This is not to discount completely the contributions of the corporate, therapeutic, social-scientific knowledge, but the irony is that the one crucial matter that would make the church into a living-breathing being has been sidelined, forgotten or neglected: the transforming experience of the life-giving Spirit. Without the transforming experience of the life-giving Spirit, what can we expect? We can only expect a respiratory failure and, without significant help, death. N. Graham Standish describes this death-journey trajectory: Because "we no longer breathe with the breath of the Holy Spirit, we neither *aspire* to become open to the Spirit nor allow ourselves to be *inspired* by the Holy Spirit. As a result, our churches eventually *expire*."[10] No amount of strategic planning, fund raising, leadership training, and various forms of ministry can restore life to a congregation unless the members experience the transforming presence of the Spirit. No amount of well-researched, well-crafted, and well-delivered sermons can bring vitality to an ailing congregation without the experience of the Spirit.

9. See Beach, *The Essential James Luther Adams*, 43–44.

10. Standish, *Becoming a Blessed Church*, 31. Emphasis his own.

Similar to Peter Ustinov's drama, *Beethoven's Tenth*, in which a resurrected Beethoven evaluates a young composer, Pascal Fauldgate, Beethoven tells the young composer that he is doing fine, and there is nothing wrong with his technique. The problem, he said, is that "you have nothing to say, and you say it quite well."[11] While we must be grateful that we can draw from the spiritual capital of those who have gone before us, we must have our own spiritual experience. We cannot continue to live on borrowed faith alone. We cannot hitchhike on others' spiritual journeys, much as we might like to do so. When church leaders lack spiritual oxygen, so it is with their congregations. We cannot give what we do not have. We can try to fake it, and it may work for a while, but it will not last. Bill Easum joins with others in naming this lack of spiritual oxygen as "the primary reason so many of our churches function more like hospices and funeral homes."[12] The church needs more than strategies and techniques if it is to be alive in Christ again: it needs a profound spiritual experience if it is to regain vitality.

A growing recognition of the crucial importance of spirituality in the life of our churches, on the whole, is a positive step. Spiritual practices and church vitality seminars are some of the expressions of this growing recognition. An abundance of materials have been written and published on the topic of how to become a vital congregation; indeed, several congregations have been identified as experiencing new vitality. Nonetheless, before we get too excited we must ask ourselves, on what basis are we classifying congregations as vital? Is it because a congregation is experiencing numerical and financial growth? Is it because a congregation has reached to the level of a mega-church? Is it because a congregation offers a variety of services and has plenty of paid staff? If so, is there not something spiritually amiss in talking about a spiritually alive church but still being driven by numbers and statistical figures? Is there not something spiritually awful about the comparisons pastors often make with one another, noting who has the biggest of the three B's (building, budget, and bodies or membership)? Is there not something spiritually stinky in talking about a spiritually vibrant church that is generally complacent and silent with regard to the destructive works of the predatory global market? Is there not something spiritually hollow when we speak of a spiritually vibrant

11. Cited in Messer, *Contemporary Images of Christian Ministry*, 127.

12. Easum, *Put On Your Own Oxygen Mask*, 28.

but segregated white congregation in a colorful neighborhood? Is there not something spiritually obnoxious when the health checklist for vital congregations does not include these concerns? What kind of Spirit and what kind of spirituality are we talking about?

Without negating other legitimate expressions of congregational vitality, we need to embrace a form of congregational vitality that makes our congregations measure their health in terms of their prophetic responsiveness to our hurting world. It is time that we sideline numbers, statistics, and marketing-driven-make-yourself-comfortable-worship and focus on what truly matters: how to be faithful and responsive to the challenges posed by our ailing world. To be sure, when this posture is integrated into a congregational health checklist, a congregation has taken the risk of offending members and the wider public. Yet, the risk must be taken. The choice is not between maintaining ourselves by avoiding serious questioning of our deeply-held practices and commitment on one hand and losing members by engaging in critical reflection and taking a stand on the other; rather, as Cobb puts it starkly, the choice is between having losses caused by decadence and having losses caused by faithfulness. If we continue to perform as we are now, the losses may be gradual, but there is no end in sight. On the other hand, while there is no guarantee of numerical growth if we follow Christ faithfully, there is a "chance that the renewed authenticity will attract new people and become the basis for a new beginning."[13] More than numbers, though, the crucial matter here is authenticity, faithfulness, and responsiveness. We will do our share, and let the Spirit do its part.

VENI CREATOR SPIRITUS: COME HOLY SPIRIT, RENEW YOUR CREATION, RENEW YOUR CHURCH

Veni Creator Spiritus is both a plea and a prayer. Of course, the Spirit is always present. From the human perspective, however, there are times when we feel the absence of the Spirit. It is in this sense that we pray for the Spirit's coming. As stated earlier, an expression of the hunger and presence of the Spirit is the growing search for spirituality. If this is so, how can we talk about spirituality without talking about the Spirit? Is not spirituality an expression of the Spirit's presence in our lives? Is it not that spirituality walks with and in the Spirit? Is it not

13. Cobb, *Reclaiming the Church*, 31.

that a spiritual life is a life empowered by the Spirit? If so, we cannot proceed to talk about the spiritual life without attempting to articulate what the Spirit is and its role in our lives and the world. The upsurge of literature on Spirit (pneumatology) is an indication of the widening recognition of this crucial point. This upsurge has been mostly associated with the feminist movement, the ecological movement, and the interfaith movement, and also in emerging articulations of ecclesiology or the doctrine of the church.

It is difficult, if not impossible, to take account fully of the nature and manifold expressions of the Spirit. The Spirit has been given various names, such as the creative energy, the breath of life, the mighty wind, the comforter, the healer, holy fire, and sanctifier as well as advocate.[14] That said, there are at least two major categories to map the theological discourse on the Spirit: the Spirit as the source of life and the Spirit as an agent of renewal or transformation. The four cardinal elements associated with the Spirit (earth, wind, water, and fire) illumine these two categories in varying ways.[15] With regard to the Spirit as a source of life, the four cardinal elements are key components or symbols of embodied life. Life would be impossible without these four cardinal elements. The earth is our home; wind (air) provides the oxygen that we breathe; water quenches our thirst and nourishes other creatures; and fire renews the earth. The pinecone, for example, may remain dormant for years until awakened by fire. Wind, water, and fire make up the earth that feeds and nourishes us all. Put differently, the Spirit symbolizes the source of life. It refers to the wellspring of life. When we speak of the Spirit we allude to the creative energy that brings forth creation. When we speak of the Spirit we refer to the power that nourishes every living creature. When we speak of the Spirit we speak of life and of that which brings forth and affirms life.

The same cardinal elements, however, viewed from another angle, also symbolize the Spirit of renewal. The earth is evolving and dynamic; the wind brings change and renewal; water not only quenches but also cleanses; and fire both purifies and transforms. The same Spirit that is symbolized as viridity (from the Latin *viriditas* or verdure—greenness of the earth) is symbolized, too, as the winnowing fire of renewal and burning commitment (red). In addition, the

14. See Prichard, *Sensing the Spirit*, 125.
15. Wallace, *Finding God in the Singing River*, 36–37.

life-giving and nourishing Spirit is the mighty purifying fire. The ebb and flow of the ocean, the changing seasons, the birth and migration of various flora and fauna, the laughter and cries of innocent children, and the struggles to change dehumanizing systems are all expressions of the same life-giving and renewing Spirit. Put differently, the Spirit who is the source of life is the same Spirit who is the power of renewal and transformation. The Spirit is the power that is continually at work in the renewal of creation and in the transformation of society. There is no space or event—not even hell—that is outside the reach and ubiquitous presence of the transforming Spirit. The destructive forces may, from our perspective, seem to be on the loose and unchecked, but the Spirit of renewal is alive and present. When people raise their laments in public, the Spirit of renewal is present. When people oppose destructive systems and their practices, the Spirit is at work. When people take courage in spite of the immense risk to their lives, no doubt the renewing Spirit is mightily at work. Waging hope in the face of the durability and pervasiveness of the forces of death is an expression of the power of the Spirit of renewal. Birthing, nurturing, and renewing the whole of creation and society are the works of the Spirit.

With the above account of the Spirit as both source of life and renewal, contrary to the common dualistic understanding, I say that the opposite of the Spirit is not matter but death. Matter cannot be the opposite of Spirit because matter is enfleshed or embodied Spirit; rather, the opposite of Spirit is death. By death I do not mean simply the cessation from our current physical existence, because dying is part of life. My understanding of death is anything that negates and violates life. Systems that deny the majority access to food, clothing, shelter, and medical health are expressions of death. Practices that perpetuate injustice are practices of death. These systems and practices work counter to the Spirit, the source of life and the power of renewal. The Spirit of life and renewal is at work against these forces of death, and it has chosen (not exclusively) to dwell in a fragile earthen vessel we call church. This utterly free Spirit who is not confined to the walls of the church has made its distinctive presence in the church. It is to this dimension that I now give focus.

THE CHURCH: A COMMUNITY BIRTHED BY THE SPIRIT

There is no doubt that the church, particularly in the day-to-day affairs of leading a congregation and maintaining its various forms of ministry, is a sociological entity with an organizational reality. It is composed of people from varied walks of life with common and conflicting interests. To carry out its avowed mission effectively it needs to have a sound organizational structure, able and skilled leadership, material resources, and other logistical support. Signs of trouble appear, however, when in the midst of being occupied with an important task of running an organization and doing the ministry, that which makes a church a distinct reality is glossed over. While the church is a communal-organizational reality birthed by the Spirit, it is the Spirit that is giving birth to the church, and it is the Spirit that is making us experience church. The life and ministry of Jesus of Nazareth would have come to naught without the Spirit, for it is through the agency of the Spirit that his life and ministry are made not only contemporaneous but also convicting and transforming. The Pentecost account is a testimony to the work of the Spirit in converting and empowering the once reluctant group into zealous followers: followers who committed themselves to living out the central message of God's radical love in Jesus in their day-to-day lives and in spreading the gospel wherever the diasporic wind brought them to various shores. Of course, the Spirit had been at work before the Pentecost event, but this event highlights in a dramatic way the role of the Spirit in birthing communities of faith.

The spiritual reawakening of the church can happen only when it realizes that it is first and foremost a community birthed by the Spirit; only when it realizes that it is first and foremost an event of the Spirit. When this spiritual foundation is simply assumed and, consequently, taken for granted, the church is terribly at risk. An institution called church may remain, but the organism is dead. Visible structures may exist, but life no longer permeates. An aggregate mass of people may exist, but the communal spirit is gone. To our surprise, the neglect of this spiritual foundation may be happening even when a church has received the accolades of success: a secure budget, highly trained clergies, management sophistication, and well-designed projects.

The transfiguration story is instructive here (Mk 9:2–9). After the ecstatic religious experience up on Mt. Tabor, the three disciples

(Peter, James, and John) did not know what to say. Nonetheless, typical of Peter, he spoke to Jesus, "Rabbi, it is good for us to be here; let us make three dwellings, one for you, one for Moses, and one for Elijah" (v.5). Peter's instantaneous response to the profound religious encounter was to dwell on it and put up a religious dwelling, a place of worship or a temple or a shrine.

While there is nothing inherently wrong in dwelling on mountain-top religious experiences, the common temptation is to capture, bottle, and institutionalize it. And it is not long until we fall into the temptation of substituting spiritual encounter with the institution we have created. This was the case with Peter as it is with the churches of our times. Peter, in Joan Chittister's powerful account, sought to express spirituality through "building temples and enlarging the office and saying proper prayers or praying properly and floating above the fray." Like Peter, the temptation in Christian ministry is to "play church, to dabble in religion, to recite the creed without feeling any moral compulsion whatsoever to render it in flesh and blood."[16] No sooner had Peter decided to be a church bureaucrat, strategic planner and fund-raiser, and organizational gate-keeper, than Jesus dashed his thoughts in midair. Instead of identifying with David the king and Aaron the priest, Jesus identified with Moses and Elijah.

Then, as the transfiguration story goes, Jesus began to lead Peter, James, and John to the edge of the cliffs and down into the plain where the crowd was waiting. Once there, the people raised their complaints to Jesus about his disciples' inability to expel demons, heal the sick and the dying. And Jesus, in Chittister's prophetic words, answered: "This kind can only be driven out by prayer . . . This kind can only be driven out by insight, by vision, by contemplation and the compassion that comes from it, not simply by technique, not by organization niceties and canon law and clericalism."[17] All the much vaunted academic degrees and religious titles have no power to drive out demons and heal, for they can only be done by putting on the mind or heart of Christ. The churches of our times may have "silver and gold," but they may have lost the power to make the lame and the sick "rise up and walk" (Acts 3:6).

16. Chittister, *In the Heart of the Temple*, 116.
17. Ibid., 121.

THE CHURCH AND COMMUNAL SPIRITUALITY

After taking account of the church as a community birthed by the Spirit, there is no need to belabor the point that spirituality must be understood communally. Nevertheless, I do not want to leave it to chance. Hopeful signs toward an ecclesial/communal understanding of spirituality are visible; even so, the journey remains an uphill climb. Elements that contribute to creating this uphill climb for congregationally-based spirituality is the unholy alliance of twin distortions: individualism and commodification. The two live in parasitic relationship to each other. By and large, the church has left individual members to scavenge for anything to nourish themselves spiritually and, not surprisingly, many have fallen prey to self-help spiritual junks that the market delights in selling to them. Michael Budde laments that Catholic and mainline Protestant churches have left their members to cobble together their own version of eclectic spiritualities embracing a whole shebang drawn from pieces of the Christian tradition, the world of the market, and nationalist-imperial ideologies.[18] What can we expect if not spiritualities oriented toward individual comfort and feeling-good?

The church shoulders the burden of responsibility of reorienting spirituality toward a communal/ecclesial experience. Christian spirituality needs to be rooted in the communal life of the church, stewardship, discipleship (formation), and the matter of salvation. Richard Crane is on target, and what he says of North Americans is true of others as well: although often the corporate Christian life is viewed as peripheral, if not antithetical, to spirituality and the struggle for justice, "connecting Christian spirituality and an authentically Christian social witness depends upon the recovery of the ecclesial character of both discipleship and salvation."[19] Given the distortion of spirituality to feed individualistic self-salvation, there is an urgent need to recover and advance, continues Crane, a "more comprehensive soteriological vision, one that insists the gift of salvation is joyous participation in a reality greater than one's own life. The gift of salvation is life together in community.[20]

18. Budde, *The (Magic)Kingdom*, 87.
19. Crane, "Ecclesial Discipleship," 60.
20. Ibid., 68.

The gift of salvation as life together in community is under assault. The prevailing notion of salvation that many Christian churches articulate is a version of rugged individualism projected onto the next life. Other religious traditions seem to fare better. In the Mahayana Buddhist tradition, the Boddhisatva cannot imagine going to nirvana alone. The Boddhisatva postpones going to nirvana for the sake of others. This is not the case for a Christian whose notion of salvation is an expression of individualism. Salvation is a reward that an individual gets, and it cannot be shared: it is his or hers alone. Speeding up to claim his or her prize, the Christian can only say, "Sorry, but I have to go. Good bye."

The following powerful story subverts the possessive-individualistic eternal reward motivation that is prevalent among Christians. The Talmud tells of a Rabbi who threw a great party in his house. A friend asked, "Why is there a celebration here? No one has been born or married. Why are you all singing and dancing?" The Rabbi responded,

> Yesterday, I was about my business with the elders of the village when a woman approached and asked me to come to her home because her daughter was ill. I could not interrupt my appointment with the village elders, so I told her to go home and wait. When I got to her home that evening, to my great dismay, the girl had died. I went home, and during the night I woke up and prayed. I said to God, 'Please let me resurrect the girl tomorrow! If she lives, may my name be taken out of the Book.' And God accepted my offer. This morning, I went to the girl's house and resurrected her. And now I am celebrating with all my students and all of my family and friends."
> "What are you celebrating?" his friend asked.
> His face beaming, the Rabbi answered, "*I am celebrating my freedom. For the first time in my life, I can serve God not for the sake of any rewards but for the sake of my love for God.*"[21]

When spirituality is liberated from consumeristic-individualism, the way toward an ecclesial spirituality is opened. When spirituality is liberated from individualism, the gift of salvation is understood as a life together in community. And when the gift of salvation is understood as life together in community, then we can say that the congregation as an ecclesial body has caught the fire of the Spirit, and we can say that

21. Cited in Selmanovic, *It's Really All About God*, 216–17. Emphasis supplied.

it has become a community with a burning center. It is this communal experience of a burning center that keeps everyone burning. Detached from this burning center, each one cannot continue burning. As an Oromo proverb of Ethiopia puts it, "One stick may smoke but it will not burn."[22] Conversely, the individual fire makes the ecclesial fire to burn mightily and to shine brightly.

THE CHURCH: A COMMUNITY OF BURNING CENTER WITH POROUS BORDERS

"Were not our hearts burning within us while he was talking to us on the road, while he was opening the scriptures to us?" (Lk 24: 32). These were the words of two of Jesus' followers after they recognized that they had encountered the risen Jesus on the famous road to Emmaus. An encounter with the Christ in Jesus creates a burning experience, both individually and communally. Let us listen to the words of The Gospel of Thomas: "Whoever is near me is near the fire, and whoever is far from me is far from the kingdom."[23] We have records from the New Testament of individuals turning into followers because they encountered the Christ in Jesus. These individuals were fired-up by the encounter, so they formed a movement around the life and witness of Jesus. Their stories of burning hearts are our heritage, but we must have our own burning heart experience if we are to revitalize the church and carry out its mission.

When a church as a body experiences the burning encounter, I say that the church has become a community with a burning center or a burning heart. Heart, both in Latin and French (*cor* and *coeur* respectively), means core or center.[24] The heart is the center or the innermost core of who and what we are. Rita Nakashima Brock identifies the heart as the "center of all vital functions" and "the seat of self, of energy, of loving, of compassion, of conscience, of tenderness, and of courage."[25] Heart, as a metaphor for center or core, unites body and spirit, reason and emotion, thinking and acting. Randi Jones Walker speaks of moving "our vision from our brain to our heart." By no means should this be interpreted, she argues, that we stop thinking

22. Healey and Sybertz, *Towards an African Narrative Theology*, 124.
23. Saying 82, cited in Fuellenbach, *Church: Community*, 203.
24. Brock, *Journeys By Heart*, xiv; Williamson, *Way of Blessing*, 253.
25. Brock, *Journeys By Heart*, xiv.

clearly, but that our thought "serves our heart."[26] This resonates with what the great spiritual leaders of the church advocated when they spoke of "keeping the mind in the heart."[27]

Is it not true that what we know best, we "know by heart"? Is it not true that when we truly remember something, we "remember it by heart"? Is it not true that when we take something seriously we "take it to heart"? Is it not true that when we speak with passion and honesty we speak "from the bottom of our hearts"? Heart-to-heart conversation means sincere and honest conversation. When one does something outrageously abhorrent, we say: "Where is your heart?" When we are discouraged, we "lose heart." Conversely, when we have gained courage we also have "found our hearts." When we are filled with joy, we "feel it in our hearts." And, when we have learned by heart, we act on what we know.

The church as a corporate expression of deep spiritual experience is a community with a burning heart or center. We know what the church is because it is a community whose center is burning with the spirit of Christ. Detached from this burning center, it is nothing but an organization with members who do some good things. Moreover, as John Fuellenbach puts it: "Without a burning center and a closeness to Christ and his vision of the kingdom such a community will be swallowed up by the values and standards of the society that surrounds it."[28] It is only in maintaining this burning center that the church can remain true to its being called *ekklesia*, that is, called out of the world or as a community set apart from the world. It is only in remaining connected to this burning center that the church as *ekklesia* remains a counter-cultural community.

Being a church with a burning center is always a challenge when the constant temptation is to accommodate to the world. Conformity is a temptation when the domination system exercises its coercive power with brazen brutality and calloused impunity, as in countries around the world that have become the top violators of human rights. But conformity to the domination system is no less a temptation when

26. Walker, "Lessons for a New America," 196.

27. Edwards, "Living the Day," 55.

28. Fuellenbach, *Church: Community*, 203. His image of the church as one with a burning center and open borders finds resonance in Martin Marty's image of the church as one with "magnetic center" and open edges. See *The Fire We Can Light*, 220.

the surrounding world appears more benign and, to some extent, when it presents itself as a patron of the values that Christian communities aspire to and emulate. This can be more dangerous to the health of the church than what we may recognize at first. Perhaps, this is the kind of social atmosphere that Christian communities in the global North have been breathing in and breathing out, and it has rendered their olfactory nerves less capable of smelling the highly toxic but heavily perfumed social atmosphere. It appears that many churches have become too comfortable with or so inured to their surrounding world that they have lost their identity as a distinct alternative community. Driven by the desire for relevance and seduced by the much-coveted three B's of success (building, budget, and bodies), churches have played footsies with the wider culture without realizing soon enough that they have ended up going to bed with the culture of domination, privilege, accumulation, and consumption.

When there is no difference between being a church member and not being one, then what is the point in remaining in the church? William McKinney and Wade Clark Roof suggest in their sociological study that people drop out of church life altogether because the mainline churches have become "something of a 'culture religion,' very much captive to middle class-values and somewhat lacking in their ability to sustain a strong transcendent vision."[29] Being closely identified with the mainstream culture means that church members can easily drift from institutional religion without the sense of having suffered any serious loss whatsoever.[30]

At this point we might ask, what is the purpose and direction of this burning center? Is it to maintain the community's purity unstained by the world? Is it to say we are saved by the cleansing fire of Christ? If the focus of a church with a burning center is inward, we are on dangerous ground, for this can lead to fundamentalism and fanaticism. The burning center needs to work in tandem with porous borders. An authentic burning spirituality is possible only when windows are open. A burning heart needs an open door; a burning heart is as large as the world. A burning heart needs another heart to engage in dialogue on a continual basis. A burning heart must be open in order not to burn others. When we live in constant threats and insecurities,

---

29. McKinney and Roof, *American Mainline Religion*, 22.
30. Williamson and Allen, *The Vital Church*, 21.

the temptation is to assert our certainties. Yet, when we assert our certainties, others may suffer. Our certainties can be lethal and can create troubles around the world. If we speak of certainty, it must be the
certainty of a leap of faith. We have experienced enough trouble when
two absolutely certain groups meet; they collide and clash. Extremely
religious people (e.g., burning for Christ and impassioned by Allah)
may be burning with hate against each other.

Putting in tension the notion of a burning center and open borders is important. It is a useful warning against a Christian community
that is bent on preserving its distinct identity but closes its doors to the
world. It is a warning against a church that focuses on preserving its
identity to the point of becoming a fortress community. On the other
hand, it is a warning against the liberal temptation to be relevant to
the current context and as a consequence ends up flattening its message and being swallowed up by the world. In a world globalized by
the forces of the market, there is no doubt that the church is called to
be a "contrast society" or an "alternative community."[31] The church,
however, can be a contrast without being a fortified colony of resident
aliens.[32] The image of the church as "burning center" with "porous
borders" conveys a posture or stance of faithfulness without being
closed off. It is also a stance that makes a witness to the world, and yet
refuses to be swallowed by the world. Churches need to learn how to
be open without loss of identity and how to be centered without being
closed off to the great issues and questions and human suffering of this
present death-dealing age.

THE CHURCH: A COMMUNITY
OF WORLDLY-HOLISTIC SPIRITUALITY

A community with a burning center and porous borders embodies
an integral or holistic understanding of spirituality. Contrary to the
understanding that to be spiritual is to be otherworldly, the new life
that the Spirit brings is not different from this life here; rather, it is
the power that makes our life here different. It is an earthly life lived
differently while we have life. Life in the spirit does not abolish bodili-
ness; it renews it for eternal livingness. When the Spirit dwells in us
we become truly earthly, and we acquire a new sense of earthiness and

31. See Borg, *Jesus, A New Vision*, 142.
32. See Hauerwas and Willimon, *Resident Aliens*.

sensuousness. When the Spirit dwells in us we are reminded that we are earthlings, citizens of this earth. The world around us is not an obstacle to a life in the Spirit. It is only because of the world and through it, not in spite of it, that life in the Spirit is realized. This Spirit keeps us in touch with our bodies and makes us experience the ground of the web of life through the sight, smell, and caress of other bodies, in both the human and the natural world.

The world around us and our social relations, though they do not always give us the kind of nourishment we are expecting, cannot be bypassed by those who seek to live a life in the Spirit. Sören Kierkegaard, a nineteenth century Danish philosopher, wooed Regina Olsen for several years before she finally said, yes. No sooner had she done so when Kierkegaard had second thoughts. He came to the conclusion that to marry Regina would distract him from loving God unreservedly. Out of loyalty to what Kierkegaard considered a "higher" love, he decided to relinquish the "lower" one. In order to love God truly, he wrote, "I had to remove the object [Regina]."

Martin Buber unravels in a marvelous way what it truly means to live in the Spirit in his comments about Kierkegaard's decision:

> That is sublimely to misunderstand God. Creation is not a hurdle on the road to God, it is the road itself. We are created along with one another and directed to a life with one another. Creatures are placed in my way so that I, their fellow-creature, by means of them and with them, find the way to God. A God reached by their exclusion would not be the God of all lives in whom all life is fulfilled . . . *God wants us to come to [God] by means of the Reginas[God] has created, and not by renunciation of them.*[33]

To live with the Spirit means becoming fully alive in our relating and in our acting. When the Spirit dwells, says Jürgen Moltmann, life "wakes up" and "becomes wholly and entirely living, and is endowed with the energies of life."[34] The Spirit of life breaks through the indifference of our hearts, our inner numbness, and our emotional frigidity. From calloused hearts of stone, we acquire the hearts of flesh, with undivided love for life and sharpened senses. With the Spirit rousing our vitality, we can cry out again, weep again, laugh, and dance again.

33. Cited in Brown, *Spirituality and Liberation*, 104–5. Original italicized.

34. Moltmann, *The Source of Life*, 11.

And we can be outraged again, outraged at the wrongs being done against the whole of creation, outraged because we care and because we hope. The Spirit of life transforms us into true ecological beings, consciously living interdependently with other beings, celebrating, and courageously defending the web of life.

Being alive in the Spirit does not pull us away from the social body, certainly not from our engagement in the body politic. Naming our pains, breaking our silence, articulating our soaring hopes, and giving wings to our moral imagination are integral to our religious life. For a truly religious person, there is no religion that is a purely private affair, as the more secular Western culture likes to believe. What Mohandas Gandhi said of Hinduism is equally true of Christianity: "The bearing of this religion on social life is, or has to be, seen in one's daily social contact. To be true to such religion one has to lose oneself in continuous and continuing service of all life."[35] Serving our communities is a spiritual act. Action for justice is a spiritual act. It is no less spiritual than practices commonly identified as spiritual, such as prayer, fasting, and retreat. Acts of mercy are spiritual acts. Howard Rice makes the point that "[w]hen we engage in such spiritual activities we open a window to the divine. We discover the reality of God in the person of those most in need."[36]

A COMMUNITY THAT CULTIVATES
AND PRACTICES SPIRITUALITY

Once a man was asked if he knew taekwondo, and his quick response was "Yes, I know taekwondo." Then, there was a follow-up question: "Do you practice taekwondo"? His answer: "No, I do not practice taekwondo." Without practice, we may have an idea of taekwondo, but we cannot perform it. To know taekwondo is to practice it. In like manner, communities of faith must be practitioners of holistic spirituality. "To say that spirituality is practiced," following Robert Wuthnow, "means that people engage intentionally in activities that deepen their relationship to the sacred . . . Broadly conceived, spiritual practice is a cluster of intentional activities concerned with relating to the sacred."[37]

35. Gandhi, "Selections from His Writings," 92.

36. Rice, *The Pastor*, 130.

37. Wuthnow, *After Heaven*, 169–70.

Diana Butler-Bass identifies three categories of this cluster of intentional spiritual practices.[38] I list them here in a slightly different order, namely: (1) anthropological, (2) moral, and (3) ascetical. Anthropological practices include practices that people do in their day-to-day lives, such as eating, meeting, greeting, and reflecting theologically. Moral practices include such activities as hospitality, caring, healing, doing justice, stewardship, and dying well. Ascetical practices include various forms to deepen the connection with the Divine, such as contemplation, silence, and so forth. I highlight the first two categories because they often fall under the radar screen of what are commonly considered spiritual practices. My study on Filipino popular religiosity/spirituality points to the crucial importance of the anthropological in people's survival and psychological health even in the face of wanton poverty, natural and not-so-natural calamities, and oppression.[39]

As well noted in various studies, congregations that do intentional spiritual practices are experiencing new vitality. In a fitting manner, these congregations have been called "intentional congregations" or "practicing congregations." These congregations are finding new expressions of vitality by being more intentional in their spiritual practices. Butler-Bass defines this intentionality as "marked by mobility, choice, risk, reflexivity, and reflection."[40] These congregations intentionally reflect about what they do and why they do the things they are doing in relation to the larger Christian story, the longer Christian tradition, their own congregation's story, and the context in which they are located. In addition to intentional reflection, they "reflexibly engage in practices" that best foster their understanding of their identity and mission as a congregation. These "intentional" practices, with their faith-as-pilgrimage orientation, stand in contrast to the "accidental" nature of spiritual practices in plateaued mainline congregations with their chapel-oriented-low-spiritual-demand kind of church going.[41]

---

38. Butler-Bass, *The Practicing Congregation*, 65–66.
39. Fernandez, "Filipino Popular Christianity," 37–60.
40. Butler-Bass, *The Practicing Congregation*, 80.
41. Ibid., 81.

SPIRITUALLY ENERGIZED AND LED MINISTRIES

Spiritual vitality does more than provide self-nourishment for the congregation. Spiritual vitality finds expressions in the ministry of the church. Ministries are expressions of the Spirit's guiding and empowering the Body of Christ to live out its calling in the world. It is inconceivable to have vital ministries without the vitality that comes from the Spirit. Conversely, vital ministries feed into the spiritual life of the congregation. Like a human body, if physical exercise nourishes the body, ministry nourishes the members of the Body of Christ. Carl Dudley names this reality: "The act of touching another person means being touched in return, and in that physical contact participants feel spiritually nurtured."[42] When the Spirit is experienced and the church follows its leading, the church is opened to doing ministry in new and radical ways. It becomes empowered to take risks—to move beyond the tried and the familiar. And when the Spirit is experienced, ministry flows in directions that respond to the deepest needs of the world. Creative responsiveness would mark the ministries of a Spirit inspired congregation.

Creative ministries would not, however, happen without specific spiritual practices. An important practice that is crucial for ministry creativity is the practice of discernment. In common parlance, discernment is often identified with the idea of finding "God's will." I am reluctant to use this term because of the many destructive practices that have been done under its name. It seems to suggest that "God's will is a fixed, immutable plan" in which we have to "crack the code" through the process of discernment.[43] Discernment has nothing to do with this. Instead, discernment is a way of opening and attuning ourselves to God so that God's longing may be realized in us and our longings match with God's. I concur with Ben and Andrew Dreitcer that "[i]n the process of discernment we seek to uncover our truest and most profound longings, which, we trust, touch God's longings for us."[44]

Ministries become effective ministries that address real needs only through the practice of discernment. Discernment is one of the practices of a church that seeks to be vital and responsive to the needs of members and the wider community. Discernment is crucial in identifying and lifting up the various charisms of the members of

42. Dudley, *Community Ministry*, 169.

43. Johnson and Dreitcer, *Beyond the Ordinary*, 100.

44. Ibid., 101.

the Body of Christ. The term "charism" is derived from the Greek term *charis* or *chairein* which means gratuity or God's gift to a person.[45] Each member has one or more charisms. No member of the community is without charism; there is no noncharismatic member. When the charisms of members are identified, used as an organizing principle, and directed toward mission, they lead to the edification of the church and to its ability to do effective ministry. When there is a match between gifts and callings, without a doubt a congregation is able to do great ministries and solid programs.

Again, we must remind ourselves of the constant temptation to confuse creative and spiritually nourishing ministries with having more programs, services, and activities. It is easy to confuse vital ministries with big budgets, a large staff, and a sophisticated organizational chart. Even ministries that serve real needs of members and the wider community are not free from becoming spiritually arid when they are detached from the deep spiritual wellspring. Standish has this reminder: "it is important to define our service to God first in spiritual, rather than purely functional, ways. The functional is an important component, but it must emerge from a spiritual yearning and aspiration to do God's will."[46] Everything that a church does, including meetings and planning sessions, needs to be seen in this light. Meetings must become spiritually nourishing rather than simply a way to plan and accomplish tasks. Environmental scanning, strategic planning, and asset mapping must be made into spiritually nourishing experiences. This must be true with the work of social analysis. Understanding the immediate and wider context of the church is not only a practical necessity but a theological/spiritual necessity. Doing social analysis is an expression of spirituality. It is our way of seeking to understand God through the mediation of the world, particularly through the cry and the needs of the people. When our sociological surveys and critique, asset-mapping, resource generation, and skills training flow from our individual and corporate spiritual depth, they become practices that are spiritually nourishing, rather than draining. When the church sees its organizational and administrative life as expressions of the Spirit, they become spiritually nourishing rather than mere instruments toward something else.

45. Boff, *Church, Charism and Power*, 156.
46. Standish, *Becoming a Blessed Church*, 91.

SPIRITUALITY FOR THE LONG HAUL:
KEEPING THE FIRE BURNING

Spirituality is not something one finally possesses or arrives at. It is a continuing journey and it needs cultivation; it needs rekindling or nurturing. The journey is long, the challenges immense, and the durability of the forces of death pervasive. We must be prepared for the long haul. The work of social transformation is not a few days' event, and not even in one's life time. The Christian tradition tells us of a conversation between Abba Anthony and an unnamed interlocutor: "What must I do to please God?" And the old man replied, "Pay attention to what I tell you. Whoever you may be, always have God before your eyes; whatever you do, do it according to the testimony of the Holy Scriptures; in whatever place you live, do not easily leave it. Keep these three precepts and you will be saved."[47] This conversation captures the dimensions of spiritual life that are too easily forgotten. Spiritual life is about seeking God, doing the Gospel, and persisting in pursuit of the two. Persistence is an expression of the spiritual life. Persistence needs persistent cultivation.

Joan Chittister tells us about what Gaelic speakers call *grieshog*, a process of burying warm coals in beds of ash at night so as to preserve the fire for the next day's cold morning. When this is done properly, a family would not need to start a whole new fire—a process that would take much of its precious time needed for other important works of the day. With *grieshog* the family will have a ready fast-starting fire the next morning. In short, the primary intention is not to let the fire of yesterday burn out completely at the end of the day but to carry it through the night for the next day.[48] It is likely that a similar kind of practice is present in other cultures. Translating it into our lives, Chittister has this to say: "it is not the cold that kills, it is the inability to rekindle the flame that once we held within the breast and now have left to smother that damps the heart and confuses the mind, wearies the body and slays the soul."[49]

We have heard or known many who are burning with passion for the ministry and the work of social transformation, but they have not been able to sustain this passion in the long run. They have suc-

47. Cited in Chittister, *The Fire in These Ashes*, 90.
48. Ibid., 37.
49. Ibid., 40.

cumbed to "compassion fatigue" and burnout. "People can exhaust themselves," warns Rice, "by ceaselessly doing good. Activity as an end in itself can drain us of our vitality. Some have found themselves depleted by work for social justice and have retreated into a highly privatized form of spirituality, reacting their way into a spirituality of retreat."[50] Burnout is more than being tired from being busy. Burnout is giving what we do not have; it is giving when our wellspring is dry. It is giving or doing when the act has not nourished us back.

Self-care is not selfishness; it is an essential practice for nourishing ourselves and the ministry to which we are committed. Self-care is a holy act; it is a spiritual act. Self-care has not been an easy practice in my life, and there are times when it is sidelined in the thick of doing something more. My team-teaching work in an integrative course with a colleague, Barbara Ann Keely, has been a blessing in making me more attentive to the importance of spiritual practices. Among other things, in that class she has reminded me that self-care is a form of spiritual practice. Her idea of incorporating it into the course requirement has challenged me to exercise responsibility for my own self-care, much more so if I wish to teach with authenticity. I relish the words of an Afro-American woman who, after participating in a Montgomery Bus Boycott, said: "My feets is tired, but my soul feels good."[51] Even then, I still wish that she had someone to massage her feet. Again, it is important to be reminded that self-care can become an act of privilege and open to abuse, especially in our therapeutic culture of self-care. James Gertmenian raised this caveat: "I am concerned about [those] whose view of self-care makes them so intent on avoiding burn out that they never experience the ravaging joy of being on fire with their calling."[52]

Hence, cultivating our spiritual life must be intentional. In addition to regular retreats and set aside practices, it is important that we see and experience spirituality in the mundane, the banal, and the ordinary, if we are to prevent burnout, numbing, and bitterness. It is in this sense that the notion of integral or holistic spirituality can offer a particular contribution. It not only integrates what has been dichotomized, an integrated spirituality is the only way to sustain ourselves in

50. Rice, *The Pastor as Spiritual Guide*, 131.

51. Cited in Baker-Fletcher and Baker-Fletcher, *My Sister, My Brother*, 147.

52. Gertmenian, *Convocation Address*.

the journey. The whole pastoral spiral or praxis (social insertion, social analysis, theological reflection, pastoral planning, and then back to insertion) is an expression of a spiritual life. Resource generation to support projects that we care about is an expression of spiritual life: it is stewardship. Stewardship is not primarily about our activity of fund-raising to support the programs of the church; it is about the care, nurture, and the cultivation of all that we have and all that we are so that we live lives of radical gratitude, extravagant hospitality, and overflowing generosity in the service of our participation in God's mission, which is also the mission of the church.

Caring or nourishing ourselves spiritually for the long-haul is no doubt both individual and communal. Again, Gaelic speakers have another custom associated with *grieshog*. Besides burying hot embers in a heap of ash to preserve the fire for the next day's peat fire, they share the fire from home to home as well. When a family moves or when a young person marries, he or she takes the fire from the first hearth to start the first fire in the new hearth. Irish know that no fire lasts forever, that new fire comes from somewhere, that fire energizes our homes, and that the fire that has served us in the past is worthy of serving us in the present and in the days to come.[53]

A similar practice can be found in Kenya with the Kikuyu tribe, which my Kikuyu student, Joseph Kimotho, shared with me in class discussions and personal conversations. The Kikuyu word for fire is *mwaki*.[54] A community was identified as *mwaki* from the way it made and shared the fire. When the fire had been lit in one home, all other homes in the community would take their fire from that one home. The sharing of this fire identified them as one community. In addition, *Mwaki* was symbolic of other forms of sharing and communing, such as family and community celebrations, local ceremonies, and in discussions of communal issues.

Community support is crucial if we are to continue burning and be a light to the world. Only "a good supply of wood keeps the fire burning through the night," according to a Sukuma proverb of Tanzania.[55] We must bring our individual sticks together to create a burning light so we can exorcise the deep darkness around us. The

---

53. Chittister, *The Fire in the Ashes*, 174.

54. Healey and Sybertz, *Towards an African Narrative Theology*, 124.

55. Ibid.

darkness is deep, the cold severe, and the tempest strong. We can survive and thrive only in the company of others. We must all be fire tenders; we must tender each other's fire. We must develop and nurture spiritual companions. Without the support of a spiritually nourishing community, our fire will not survive the dark and stormy nights or give warmth during the bleak mid-winter.

SIGNS OF THE SPIRIT, SIGNS OF HOPE

The spiritual crisis is real and pervasive. The forces of reaction are strong and pervasive. Ironically, however, when the forces of reaction grow stronger, they are themselves signs that the Spirit is working mightily. We only need a different lens, again a gift of the Spirit, to see what is hidden and revealed in the ordinary and in the outrageous. As the forces of reaction are globalized, so the life-giving, transforming, and subversive Spirit is globalized. New paradigm shifts are challenging highly entrenched and hierarchical ways of dwelling and acting. The shift toward holistic ways of thinking, particularly holistic spirituality, is a sign of the Spirit—a sign of hope. The trend toward pneumatological ecclesiology is a sign of hope for consumer-oriented-marketing-driven as well as hospice care churches. Congregations that have experienced new vitality are expressions of the Spirit. The rise of renewal movements and movements of transformation are signs of the Spirit at work in mysterious ways. Women's movements testify to the power and work of this Spirit, and in the ecological movement gaining momentum all over the world, the recovery of the role of the Spirit has been central. Likewise, this is true in movements committed to interfaith dialogue and movements helping to midwife a just and colorful society.

We cannot underestimate our deep crisis—our deep darkness. On the other hand, we must not underestimate the presence and power of the Spirit. The Spirit is at work in all places, and we had better attune ourselves to those places where we might least expect the Spirit to do its mysterious work. I can see this Spirit in the waves that keep rushing to the shore; in the crocus that comes out to greet the coming spring; and even in the dandelions that keep coming back in my yard no matter how hard I work to root them out. The Spirit is at work in the mundane and the odd, in the highways and the off-beaten paths, in the lofty and lowly. I have seen this Spirit in the religiosity of the common people. I recognize this Spirit among those who can still see the clouds even when their lives are at the moment gray. As long as the fire is aglow in our hearts and we still greet each day with verve and zest, the Spirit is present. The Spirit's hope is wedded to ours; it is invested in us. But we must come to recognize that there is hope not simply because of us, but because the Spirit is at work in us, through us, and beyond us. There is hope because the Spirit is sustaining us on the way. There is hope of an arrival at our "spiritual destinations" because we are being "led."[56] Because the Spirit leads, there is hope. Where the Spirit is, there is hope! Where we see signs of hope, the Spirit is present!

56. Holmes, "The Spirit Holy, Hip, and Free," 106.

6

The Church as a Household of Life Abundant

Another Economy Is Possible

ONE NIGHT A FRIEND and I were served a meal by a poor peasant-farmer family in the village of Buenavista on the island of Bohol in the Philippines. The meal included rice, *pancit* (rice noodle mixed with small slices of pork), *tinula* (boiled fish), and *linamaw nga butong* (young coconut sweetened with condensed milk) for dessert. In spite of our earnest request that we eat with our hosts, they insisted that my companion and I eat first. After a long travel and without snacks, I was ready for a hearty meal. Still wanting more after eating one side of the whole fish, I turned it over to start eating the other side. As I was doing so, I remembered a story about a little girl who, in a hushed and worried voice, said to her mom (Cebuano language), "*Nay, ingon ka dili balihon ang isda. Gibali na man lagi nay*" (Mom, you said that the man would not turn the fish over, but now he is doing it. Is he going to finish the whole fish?). I took a few more bites and finished my meal with enough food left on the table. I found out later that the family did not set aside extra food for themselves. That night, I went to bed thinking of table manners.

If ecology (also derived from *oikos*) is the structure of the household, and politics is the power dynamics of the household, economics is the table manners of the household. Given that the root of the term economics is *oikos* (household), the language of table manners is an apt and down-to-earth way to address issues of economics. Contrary to the superficial appearance that this down-to-earth-way is simplistic, it is actually profound in its simplicity. Economics is about table manners in the household, a household that is now acutely globalized.

147

We must ask ourselves, how are the table manners conceived in our various households and the global household? What is the overarching structure that frames how we formulate the table manners? What are the norms that guide the table manners of our household? Do our table manners promote the flourishing of all? Do all have equal access to the table? Are we creating impediments that prevent others from receiving their fair share? Are the table manners of our household causing others to die before their time? These are the questions we need to ask.

PREDATORY GLOBAL TABLE MANNERS: NEOLIBERAL ECONOMIC MODEL

Without a doubt, the global market has produced immense wealth. Global daily financial transactions total in the trillions. Technological advancements have led to increased production and distribution of goods and services. Even with the report of a declining harvest of crops and a shortfall in the catch of fish, enough goods exist to feed the people of the world. Notwithstanding all these achievements, why is it that many are without basic necessities and many are dying of hunger? Approximately 50,000 die of under-nutrition and poverty-related cases every day.[1] Five times as many children die in poorer countries of the global South before reaching age five (five per hundred) than in higher-income countries of the global North (less than one per hundred).[2] What is going on with our global household? What kind of table manners does neoliberal economics have?

Global hunger does not exist by itself. It is related to another global reality: massive global poverty. The issue is not a lack of food supply, as some would like us to believe, but massive poverty. People are too poor to purchase the available food in the market. Almost half of the world's people live on less than $2 per day, and conservative estimates say that approximately 1.3 billion people live on less than $1.00 a day.[3] Contrary to the image being projected that poor people are lazy, many of the people who are living in poverty are hardworking. They work in a fast-paced job and a highly-monitored working envi-

1. Held, "Becoming Cosmopolitan," 11.

2. Brubaker, *Globalization at What Price?* 45.

3. Mather, "Combining Principle with Profit," 31. Cf. Held, "Becoming Cosmopolitan," 11; Wallis, "Changing the Wind," 117.

ronment.[4] And how much are they paid? A garment factory worker in the Las Mercedes Free Trade Zone in Managua, Nicaragua, earns 31 cents an hour, a total of $14.88 a week. Yet his or her weekly total expenses, which include round trip bus fare, breakfast, lunch, rent for sharing a room, and water, is $15,04. If we add electricity, wood (for cooking on an outdoor stove), powdered milk (for infants), childcare, and school (text book and supplies), the total is $29.34.[5] This does not include food for dinner, clothing, and medical care. What this worker is receiving is not a living wage; rather, it is a death wage. Meanwhile, the big capitalists are reaping enormous profits.

Death has been the plight of many amidst the rhetoric that economic globalization provides salvation. Many are dying slowly due to sickness and starvation, while others are left with no other options but to die quickly. This is the fate of some farmers in the Indian village of Bhimnagar Tanda. The farmers of this village borrowed money to buy pesticides to eliminate the caterpillars that infested their cotton crop. Even after several applications of the pesticide, the caterpillars did not die. There was a bad harvest that year, and the farmers were not able to pay back their debts. As the story goes, the moneylenders pressured the indebted farmers to commit suicide so that they could pay their debts out of their liquidated assets. More than 150 farmers killed themselves by swallowing the pesticide.[6]

The poverty and the death of the many only prove the sinister side of the much trumpeted rising tide of economic globalization. It is not a rising tide that is going to lift all boats on an ocean of poverty. No less than the Central Intelligence Agency's (CIA) 2000 report made the projection that the "rising tide of the global economy will create many economic winners, but it will not lift all boats."[7] As I noted earlier, contrary to the belief that "a rising tide raises all boats," the reality has been that "a rising tide raises all yachts."[8] While the poor fisherfolks of my hometown have experienced being caught in a perfect storm, death caused by storms is infrequent among fisherfolks, nor are shark attacks a frequent cause of death. The sharks that are killing

4. Bacon, "Maquiladora Workers," 147.

5. Bonilla, "A Trade Unionist," 145.

6. Shiva, "Stealing," 226.

7. Cited in Delgado, *Shaking the Gates of Hell*, 77.

8. Borg, *The Heart of Christianity*, 141.

fisherfolks do not live in the deep blue sea but on land—the "loan sharks," whether big or small. Likewise, in the day-to-day Filipino discourse the killer crocodiles or alligators (*buayas*) do not live in the rivers but in high public places. They devour the government coffers and people's money.

Delivering the massive poverty and the death of the many is a system of organized greed and a system of organized inequality. "The earth provides enough for everyone's need," says Mohandas Gandhi, "but not for everyone's greed."[9] We are not speaking of a simple personal greed but organized corporate greed in alliance with governmental institutions. Behind the massive poverty and death of the many is a system of onerous capital-labor relations and various forms of exploitative practices. Behind the labels and brand names of famous clothing and footwear are the overworked and poorly paid workers, sometimes including child laborers. Such was the case of the three hundred Vietnamese who were brought to American Samoa to work in sweatshops that produce clothing for J.C. Penny and other retailers. Their daily meal typically consisted of a watery broth of rice and cabbage. They were kept thirty-six to a room, with two workers sharing a thirty-six-inch-wide bed. Workers were sometimes beaten with pipes. When they were discovered, the workers were like "walking skeletons."[10] We need not go outside of the U.S. mainland to encounter a similar phenomenon. On August 2, 1995, seventy-two female Thai nationals were discovered in virtual slavery in El Monte, California (Los Angeles County). They worked seventeen hours a day for about sixty-nine cents per hour. The clothes they made were sold in famous department stores—Target, Mervyn's, Sears, and even up-scale Nordstrom's.[11]

We may think that these are isolated instances, but my argument is that these oppressive practices are manifestations of a system of organized greed. The neoliberal market has created a system that favors the capitalist and transnational companies and continually dis-empowers the laborers. With footloose capital's ability to move wherever favorable investment climate is, what we can expect is the race to the bottom of the majority. With the system of organized greed

9. Gandhi, cited in *Treasury*, 39. Modified.

10. Peterson, "Sweatshop Fact Sheet," 159.

11. Cited in Brubaker, *Globalization at What Price?* 60.

and inequality deeply entrenched, we can expect that the economic disparity between individuals and between nations will continue to widen. In the United States, the poorest 20 percent own no wealth, while the top 20 percent own over 80 percent. The top five percent own more than half of all the wealth. The poverty rate in the United States has continued to rise. It went up from 7.6 million families (10 percent) in 2003 to 7.9 million families (10.2 percent) in 2004.[12] Even worse, some nations have experienced a drop in human development index according to the United Nations (Human Development Index 2003).

When economic disparity and massive poverty become the order of the global household, we can expect negative consequences: poor health, short life span and high mortality rate, high illiteracy rate, stagnant communities, increased criminality, and rampant depression. Poverty begets disease and disease begets poverty. Those who cannot afford to buy nutritious food and have no access to safe drinking water, sanitary living conditions, basic health care, and good education are more likely to get sick. When they are sick, they cannot support their families; thus, the cycle of poverty and disease continues. In considering a society as a whole, we find that the greater the economic disparity among its people, the worse the overall health of the people in that society. Poor communities lack good educational opportunities for advancement; hence, the likelihood of being buried in their miserable situation is high. Furthermore, social inequity, economic disparity, and massive poverty lead to socio-political instability and a host of social maladies. Socio-political instability leads to extremism of various sorts and to violence. In short, the overall quality of life of the people suffers.

Let us not forget that it is not only the marginalized of society who suffer, but also the earth itself. Along with the impoverishment and death of human communities is predatory globalization's assault on the ecosystem. The global system of organized greed and inequality has raped and violated the earth. A Philippine government ad in *Fortune Magazine*, for the purpose of luring investors, shows the destructive character of economic progress: "To attract companies like yours, we have felled the mountains, razed jungles, filled swamps, moved rivers, relocated towns, and in their place built power plants,

12. Delgado, *Shaking the Gates of Hell*, 62–63.

dams, roads . . . all to make it easier for you to do business here."[13] In pursuit of business and profits, we are losing a billion tons of top soil every year due to erosion because of deforestation, overgrazing, electrification, mining, and corporate agriculture. In pursuit of progress that does not benefit the overwhelming majority, we have accelerated toxic pollution and global warming. The whole inhabited earth—our household—is railing from our household management and table manners. Our table manners have not served the community well and have been destructive to the earth.

CHANGING THE WIND: MOVING BEYOND NEOLIBERAL ECONOMICS

"The direction of the wind has changed," my late father said as we observed the typhoon. My father's observation meant that the *timog* (south wind) had arrived, and it was a sign that the typhoon was on its way out. The arrival of *timog* was for him a sign of promise that new and better days were going to replace the stormy ones. He could hardly wait for the *timog* to finish its course before getting his fishing gear ready, especially given that the few days immediately after a typhoon usually promised a better catch. The majority of the world's people and the earth have been waiting for the *timog* or the wind of change to come and blow in the right direction. They are waiting for the fresh wind of change to blow away the toxic air of predatory globalization. Unlike the natural *timog* which is beyond our control, however, the wind of societal change lies to a greater extent in us. We must help change the direction of the wind and unfurl our sails to catch its spirit.

Jim Wallis asks: How do you distinguish a Senator or a Congressperson when they are in a crowd? He says they are the ones "who are always licking their fingers and putting them in the air to see which way the wind is blowing."[14] We often make the mistake of thinking that we can replace one wet-fingered politician with another wet-fingered politician and everything will be all right. Then, when no significant change happens, we are disappointed. Wallis insists, however, that if we really desire significant change, "we must change the wind" because the wind has been blowing in the wrong direction. Changing guard-

13. Bula-at, "Kalinga Women," 91.
14. Wallis, "Changing the Wind," 117.

ians while leaving our political-economic system intact is not enough. We must strive "to change our whole perception of things."[15] We must change our fundamental understanding of the world, particularly of the political-economy.

Yes, we must change the direction of the wind: a wind that will blow away the toxic air of neoliberal table manners that have produced socio-economic inequality and tremendous suffering. Changing the direction of the neoliberal economic wind requires more than changing the guards; we must change the economic model—a change in the overarching framework or, to use a different metaphor, a change in the undergirding structure of our understanding of how we dwell together in the household. Let us stop deceiving ourselves that economics is only about Gross Domestic Product (GDP), and that when the GDP is up we should all be dancing and feasting. We have watched nation upon nation post high GDPs while the living conditions of the general populace worsened. Let us not be deceived when Dow Jones and NASDAQ reach new heights for they are not the true indicators of socio-economic well-being. GDP does not tell us who is receiving the largest share of the household pie and who is starving to death while scavenging for crumbs. GDP does not make a distinction between what is harmful and what is not. A harmful event may even have a higher economic value because of the volume of financial exchange involved. An increase in robbery, assault, and murder may cause the GDP to rise because of the cost of litigation, hospitalization, policing, and maintenance of the prison system. Finally, GDP does not take into account the depletion of natural resources or the deterioration of air, water, and soil at the front end, that is, as an intrinsic part of an economy.[16] We must move past GDP as the dominant or the only way to measure economic progress and articulate an alternative way of thinking about economics.

ARTICULATING AN ALTERNATIVE ECONOMIC MODEL: THE ECONOMY OF CARE

We need an alternative economic model to the current neoliberal economic model. In contrast to the chrematistics economics of the neoliberal model which deals with the manipulation of property and

15. Ibid.

16. McFague, *Life Abundant*, 80.

wealth in order to maximize short-term monetary gains for the owners, economist Herman Daly and theologian John Cobb Jr. articulate a
model of economics understood in the sense of *oikonomia* (economics for community). This understanding of economics affirms three
important guidelines: (1) It takes seriously the long-term interest
rather than the short-term gains; (2) business transactions take into
consideration the costs and benefits to the whole community, not
only the benefits of the transacting parties; (3) instead of prioritizing
abstract value and its stimulus for unlimited accumulation, *oikonomia*
focuses on concrete use value in relation to specific needs that can find
objective satisfaction.[17]

I would like to add a fourth criterion to Cobb and Daly's three
criteria of economic well-being: ecological sustainability. Adopting
this fourth criterion makes it possible for us to speak of *oikonomia*
economics as, following Sallie McFague, "ecological economic."[18] We
cannot talk about a real alternative to neoliberal economics without
putting ecology and justice (right relation) at the heart of it. From the
ecological economics' point of view, nature is not simply a resource but
has its own integrity. Furthermore, we need to interpret justice within
the wider purview of ecology. Not only must the two precede any talk
about allocation of resources, even justice must be understood in the
context of right relation among creatures. In other words, any discus-
sion of just allocation of resources must take into account the matter
of ecological well-being. When we have embraced this fundamental
starting point at its depth, it will come to light that ecological well-
being does not stand counter to just allocation of resources. On the
contrary, just allocation is best served when ecological sustainability
is assured.

What Cobb and Daly refer to as economics for community
(*oikonomia*) and McFague calls ecological economic resonate with
Bod Goudzwaard and Harry de Lange's "economy of care."[19] To speak
of an economy of care is to speak of a community of care or of a
caring community. An economy of care happens only when we see
human beings as persons-in-community. Economy is geared toward
the care of the community, both human and other beings. Success,

17. Cobb and Daly, *Common Good*, 139.

18. McFague, *Life Abundant*, 99–123.

19. Goudzwaard and de Lange, *Beyond Poverty*.

as an economic criterion, is based on what builds and supports the community as a whole. If well-being is the defining norm for both production and consumption, then care is a fundamental economic category. Economics is not simply a matter of production, but primarily of care: care for the overall well-being of human beings and the rest of creation. Care is a basic element in the oldest definition of the Greek word *oikonomia* or economy. Our conception of economics must recover this dimension.

What is this economy of care and how does it view human beings in relation to economic forces? In a "postcare" economy, such as our present dominant economy, "we engage," according to Goudzwaard and de Lange, "in the highest possible consumption and production and only afterwards attempt to mitigate the mounting care needs, often with extremely expensive forms of compensation."[20] This economic model subordinates human and ecological well-being to production and consumption. An alternative to "postcare" economy is "precare" economy. Goudzwaard and de Lange describe "precare" as an economy that places income and consumption in service to care needs. It does not consider the care needs of the people only after production, income, and profits have been secured; rather, it puts care at the forefront of economic decision-making.[21]

When care is at the core of how we think of economics, other aspects find their rightful place, such as our understanding of work/ labor, our relationship to time, and our relationship to commodities. Let us begin with labor. If care is at the heart of economic activity, we will view labor differently. Labor in the dominant model has been reduced to a commodity and given value according to the criteria set by chrematistics economics. The economy of care offers an alternative perspective. While the value of labor in chrematistic economics is a function of accumulation and to perpetuate class stratification, the value of labor in the economy of care is what contributes to greater well-being. The value of labor is seen in relation to its contribution to the building of the community and not simply in terms of monetary transaction. With this as a guide, we will arrive at a different norm of evaluating labor.

20. Ibid., 63.
21. Ibid.

Neoliberal economics has skewed the conception of labor by devaluing those forms of labor that cannot be easily transacted in the market and assigned a monetary equivalent. Goudzwaard and de Lange call these devalued forms of work "transductive labor."[22] Works that are classified under transductive labor are not geared toward the production of goods for the market; rather, they are oriented toward care of the community, social relations, and the ecosystem. Such forms of work may include housekeeping, taking care of children, volunteering in civic organizations, providing food and care for the hungry and the needy, community organizing, and caring for the ecosystem. As these forms of work are not easily quantifiable, they are not considered in factoring economic gains. Perhaps the fact that some things are beyond being easily quantifiable explains the failure of dominant chrematistic economics from taking account of transductive labor. At this juncture, I would like us to open ourselves to a feminist critique.

Hiding beneath the cloak of normalcy is the gender bias of neoliberal economics' account of labor: it is an account of labor that operates on a patriarchal worldview and male bias. If we analyze it carefully, the types of work that are normally classified under transductive labor are predominantly the types of work that women perform. These are in the informal sector of the economy and reproduction. A way to bring to the surface the gender bias is to adopt the term "reproductive labor."[23] Reproductive labor—taking care of the children, cooking, cleaning, shopping, and so on—is crucial for the survival and quality of life of the human species, yet it does not normally fall under wageable labor or, if wage is involved, it is poorly paid. As crucial as it is, reproductive labor is an area that patriarchal economics is reluctant to consider seriously.

Transductive/reproductive labor is essential to any society. Without it chrematistics economics would collapse and society would fall into chaos. The forms of work or services classified as transductive/reproductive labor have, in many ways, provided the much needed "safety nets" for the victims of corporate greed. And while the poorly paid workers of the world have in many ways benefited from the "safety nets" that various individuals and organizations provide, they are not the only users of the "safety nets." When we look at it at a

22. Ibid., 57.
23. Jarl, *In Justice*, 16.

systemic level, big corporations have been living on these "safety nets." Business corporations have continued their greedy pursuit of profits at the expense of the poorly paid workers because of the transductive labor of non-governmental organizations (NGOs) and faith-based organizations (FBOs). Who says there is no free lunch in America? What of the corporate welfare fathers who receive government subsidies, bailouts, and transductive safety nets provided by civic and religious organizations?[24] Without discounting the significance of the services that churches provide to the wider society, they need to be aware how their best ministries can function to prop up the dominant economic system by providing cushion (safety nets) to the devastating impact of the predatory market.

Whether we call it *oikonomia* economics (Cobb and Daly) or ecological economics (McFague) or economy of care (de Lange and Goudzwaard), we are talking about an economy of life. The economy of life calls us to use a different way of measurement than what GDP can provide. A better alternative that has been used by the United Nations Development Program (UNDP) is the Human Development Index (HDI). The HDI measures three combined dimensions embracing life expectancy (population health and longevity), literacy (educational attainment), and standard of living (measured by the natural logarithm of gross domestic product per capita at purchasing power parity). The position of the United States in the HDI profile makes it clear that a high GDP does not necessarily lead to a high HDI rating. It is appalling that a country like the United States which has a high GDP actually occupies a place at the lower tier in HDI among countries of the global North. Canada has been ranked the highest eight times, Norway six times, and Japan three times. Undoubtedly, the HDI is an improvement from GDP. Nevertheless, HDI has its shortcomings: it does not take into account ecological health; it presupposes that material amenities would suffice as the criterion for human development; and it does not take into account spiritual and moral development.

It is into this neglected dimension that a theological account offers something beyond what socio-economic and political analysis can provide. The issue of economics is not simply about production and allocation of goods and services; it is about a way of being in the world. It is about what we care about or what truly matters to

24. See Moore, *Downsize This!*.

us, about faith and what we confer ultimacy, about moral values and about care, and about the good and the beautiful. In other words, the matter of economics is a theological issue because theology deals with economics, and Christian theology, in particular, talks about God the economist.

DIVINE ECONOMY: CREATION, NURTURE, AND LIBERATION

God the economist does not have the common ring as God the king, sovereign lord, ruler, governor, law-giver, and judge. Political metaphors for God have dominated traditional Christian theology. This may be due to the higher status that the ancients accorded to *homo politicus* in contrast to the economist (*homo economicus*), which was associated with steward (Middle English: *stigweard* or *styward*) or the one who kept the pig.[25] Given this background, it would be difficult for believers to imagine speaking of God as an economist. Yet being an economist is an apt metaphor for speaking about God, for it is central to what God is and what God does, particularly the God we know in and through Jesus. God's relationship and dealings with creation is an expression of divine economic activity.

The God we know in Jesus is an economist in the most profound sense of the term *oikonomia*, the whole inhabited household of God. In this household God is the householder/economist who brings forth the whole household into being, sustains and liberates it, and brings it to its fulfillment. The classical trinitarian formula can be seen through the lens of divine economic activity of creation, sustenance, and liberation. God's trinitarian embodiment is an expression of God's economic acts in the form of creator-life giver, sustainer, and savior. God the economist is a creator-life giver whose economic acts promote life. God the economist in the mode of the Spirit sustains and nourishes life. God the economist in the mode of Christ acts in order to save or liberate creation. God the economist saves. The overall economic activity of the triune God aims to bring the whole household to its fulfillment.

It is within this larger divine economy that we must see God's economic activity of building the whole *oikoumene* (household). God the economist builds the household on the foundation of right rela-

25. Meeks, *God the Economist*, 76.

tion or justice, and God manages the household in ways that are just. As Meeks puts it, "Within the all-encompassing horizon of creation as household, the economy of God, most briefly put, is the distribution of God's righteousness."[26] The just economist makes sure that everyone has access to the goods that support life. The just economist manages the household in such a way that every creature lives in harmony. God the just economist secures the earth as a home for all by establishing justice and peace among all inhabitants.

The narrative of our faith points to a God whose activity is one of establishing justice in God's household, an activity that often takes place through human participation. When the oppressed Israelites raised their anguished cry to the heavens, God raised prophets in their midst to proclaim God's justice and to lead God's people out of oppression. Faced with the idols of the imperial Rome, God raised apostles and martyrs of the faith to speak of God's new economy in opposition to the economy of Caesar. In other words, God's economic activity does not annul active participation from members of the household; rather, they are called to participate with God the economist. To be created in the image of God is to be an economist as God is. God's economic acts call forth economic acts on the part of human beings. Meeks rightly states that "being human is an economic commission to join God the Economist in distributing righteousness so that the world may live."[27]

JESUS: GOD'S CHOSEN ECONOMIST

If we want to get a clearer view of God's economy, we need to see the economic activities of Jesus. Jesus' economic activities must be understood in light of his commitment to the coming God's economy vis-à-vis the economy of imperial Rome. While the economy of imperial Rome was founded on the resources of colonized nations and the labor of the slaves, the economy of the *basileia* that Jesus gave witness to is founded on right relation. While the economy of imperial Rome triumphed on the back and marginalization of the many, Jesus bore witness to an economy of radical hospitality. The new economy that Jesus proclaimed welcomed the outcasts to the banquet table, such as the destitute poor, the hungry, the homeless, the sick and crippled,

26. Ibid., 77.
27. Ibid., 90.

and prostitutes. Jesus' feeding and healing acts point to the kind of economy he was commissioned by God the economist to help give birth to: the economy of care.

Committed to the birthing of the economy of care, Jesus had to embody in his very own life the manner in which the new economy is to come: it comes not by power and might but by way of servant-hood. Jesus the economist "did not count equality with God a thing to be grasped, but emptied himself, taking the form of a servant" (Phil 2:6–7). Unlike those who became rich and powerful working for the poor and the downtrodden, Jesus became a servant. He became a servant of the *basileia* economy—the economy of care—so people would no longer be servants to the imperial economy. He took the lowest and the dirtiest job: cleaning God's household of sinful structures and practices. That is not an easy job. It is a 3D job: demanding, dirty, and, above all, dangerous. Moreover, we can say that his job belonged to the category of transductive labor, that is, it was not given monetary worth because it did not contribute to the GDP of imperial Rome.

The clash between Jesus' commitment to alternative economics and imperial economics led to his death, to his crucifixion. It is a reality that is repeated every time the reigning economic system is challenged to its core. Those who labor to clean up the reigning economic arrangement often times end up crucified. Examples abound. Imperial economics kills by the thousands in its day-to-day functioning. Furthermore, it kills brazenly when anyone attempts to undermine it. What happened to Jesus is a reminder of what the dominant economic system is capable of doing: crucifixion. But the crucifixion need not only be seen as an outcome; it is also the way of God's economics. Crucifixion means that *basileia* economy, the economy of care, is an economy of solidarity: it is self-giving at its core.

THE CHURCH AS A HOUSEHOLD (OIKOS) OF GOD

If God the economist commissioned Jesus as an economist of the *basileia*, what can we say about the church? If the church is to be true to the God it has known through the economic activities of Jesus, then we can and must speak of the church as a community of Christ's economists. To appropriate the root of the term economics (*oikos*), we must speak of the church as the household of God (*oikos tou theou*) or, more specifically, the household of Christ. In fact, this is what the early Christians did: they spoke of the church as household of God (Eph 2:19). It is not, of course, a surprise that the early Christian communities (particularly those initiated by the Apostle Paul) would use the household metaphor to speak of the church, after all, they gathered in the homes of members and named their groups in relation to these households: "the church in the house of" (Prisca and Aquila—Rom 16:3–5; Chloe—1 Cor 1:11; Nympha—Col 4:15; Philemon, Apphia, Archippus—Phlm 1:1–2). But there is more to it: the early Christians and the Apostle Paul used the metaphor of household for the church to speak of a new reality. They wanted to convey the profound meaning of the term *oikos* (household) as well as the character and practices of the new community whose main identity is an *oikos* of God.

Like Jesus who embodied *basileia* economics vis-à-vis imperial economics of his time, the early households of God were self-consciously aware that they were to embody a new economy vis-à-vis the imperial economy of its time. But, beyond saying what it is against, what shall we say it is about? What is the nature, shape, and character of the *oikos* of God when viewed through the lens of God's *basileia* economics? Following the Apostle Paul, I say that the "cornerstone" (Eph 2:20–21) or the foundation stone of the household is the crucified Jesus. In Jesus the crucified One, the "dividing wall of hostility" (2:14) has been broken down and a new household has been formed whose foundation is radical self-giving love. This is a love that is oriented toward the well-being of the other (Phil 2:4). This is the love that defines relations among members of the household. To be sure, there are conflicts and contradictions in the household, but it remains that the well-being of all is everyone's concern because all are one in Christ the crucified One. As one in Christ, the pain of one member is the pain of all, and the joy of one is the joy of all (1 Cor 12:26). Bearing one another's burden is a mark of God's household (Gal 6:2). With the crucified and risen Christ as the cornerstone of the household, actions to support the well-being of all members must assume the posture of humility (Eph 4:2). All members of the household are expected to care for one another in humble service. This service does not put down the recipient; instead, it is characterized by magnanimous concern to help the other increase in stature.

If the foundation of the household of God is Jesus the crucified One, then the organizational structure of the household of God is built on justice or right relation. Right relation is the basis of order in the household; it is not the other way around. Order in the household must be predicated on just or right relation. An order without right relation is an order of *disorder*. We can extend this point to the concepts of harmony and mutuality. Harmony in the household of God must be based on right relation. The native Hawaiian word *pono* conveys in a profound way the meaning of harmony: justice, righteousness, balance, and right relation.[28] Harmony among members of the household exists when there is justice. Authentic harmony and order are possible only in the context of just (right) relation among members. Similarly, true mutuality can only exist under a just relation. Without it, mutuality is farcical. Mutuality also presupposes a relationship among equals. By equal I do not mean exercising the same function in the household but having equal status as members of the household.

Oikos is an ecclesiological key for speaking of the church as a household of God in the most profound sense of the term household. In using the term *oikos*, we view the church as an embodiment and sign of God's economy. The church, Christ's household, is a new household whose story is the narrative of God's economic activity; whose foundation is the crucified Christ—a buster of the dividing walls of inequality; whose organizing principle and power dynamics is right relation; whose table manners reflect distribution of righteousness and respect of ecological integrity; and whose mission is to live out God's economy within and outside its space vis-à-vis the stultifying complacency and submission of the stupefied many to the global market religion. The church, whose existence is for the new economy, can only be effective in its mission when it is faithful to Christ the economist in its very own life. It must then become, following Meeks, "a peculiar sphere of distribution because it has a special meaning of social goods derived from the life, death, and resurrection of Jesus Christ. Its household rules of distribution are meant to conform to God's own distribution of righteousness."[29] In the words of William Cavanaugh, Christians must help "create concrete alternative practices that open up a different kind of economic space—the space marked by the body of Christ." The whole body of Christ, he continues, must embody in its own life a "different kind of space and to foster such spaces in the world."[30]

28. See my *Reimagining the Human*, 188.
29. Meeks, *God the Economist*, 180.
30. Cavanaugh, *Being Consumed*, viii, ix.

SACRAMENTS OF THE ECONOMY OF CARE

The sacraments of the church point to a new economy. Baptism liturgically and formally symbolizes the acceptance of the baptized into the household of God. In the act of baptism, the church members welcome the new member to a new life in Christ and into a new household characterized by love, care, support, respect, and right relation. The sacrament of baptism symbolizes the members' commitment to covenant with one another to make sure that everyone would be cared for, and that no one in the household would lack the basic necessities of life while other members wallow in opulence. As a member of the household, the baptized is offered access or place at the table. The support that members express in the act of baptism points to their commitment to exercise power in a manner that uplifts rather than puts down the new member. Moreover, baptism means participation in the mission of the household. As a member of the household, the baptized undergoes the process of discipleship for the mission of making God's economy a reality in our world and, more particularly, of distributing righteousness.

Along with the sacrament of baptism, the sacrament of the eucharist is helpful in understanding God's new economy. There is no doubt that the eucharist points to the ugly reality of our world. The broken bread and the cup of wine symbolize what the forces of death can do. Bread broken and cup poured point to the reality of the breaking of the web of life; they point to the broken relations brought about by interlocking forms of oppression. Nevertheless, while pointing to the world in need of healing, it also offers a vision of a healed world. Out of a broken body has emerged a vision of a mended body. The broken body of Jesus, symbolized in the broken bread of the eucharistic celebration, is broken open for the many that all may experience healing and liberation. The body is broken open as a symbol of openness, service, and hospitality. Out of the broken body, ritualized in the eucharistic celebration, comes the invitation to dine at a common table.

The common table, particularly the meal table, is an important direction. As a symbol, the eucharistic table points to the common meal table of the household. "Like all households," as Meeks accurately puts it, "God's household is structured around a table."[31] The meal table is central to the household: it is here that the members of the household

31. Meeks, *God the Economist*, 45.

are served, fed, and nourished. Important household conversations occur around the meal table. Instead of limiting our image to one of a single family sharing, serving and feeding each other, we imagine a meal in which all are invited. C.S. Song renames the Last Supper as the "people supper." It is a people supper prepared by the community for the whole community.[32] The community prepares and shares the meal. The people supper is a communal event. Imagine the difference if we chose to interpret the eucharistic celebration in this way.

In light of the New Testament background, I suggest that we view the eucharist through the lens of the egalitarian meals Jesus offered to all those around him throughout his ministry (Mt 14:13–21; Lk 9:10–17; Jn 6:1–14).[33] It was through one of these egalitarian meals that the people recognized the resurrected Jesus, as in the Emmaus story (Lk 24:13–35). It was in the breaking of bread that he was recognized by his sorrowful followers. Likewise, we recognize Jesus and recognize God wherever egalitarian meals take place. In egalitarian meals the crucified Jesus is resurrected, and in shared meals God's power is alive. As Jesus' presence is known in the breaking and sharing of bread, so we are known as disciples of Jesus and children of God whenever and wherever we celebrate egalitarian meals. McFague thinks that "[w]ere such an understanding of the eucharist to infiltrate Christian churches today, it could be mind changing—in fact, perhaps world changing."[34]

Inasmuch as God's household is beyond individual human households, it is fitting to speak of a meal table for the whole world (cosmic table). The egalitarian meals, in McFague's words, point to the "prospective" phase of Jesus' life and ministry. This prospective phase cannot be divorced from the "deconstructive" (parables) and "reconstructive" (healing) phase of Jesus' ministry. The egalitarian meals point to the radical vision of Jesus in which all are welcome at the banquet table. They offer both what she calls minimal and maximal vision: the exhortation that even when there is little food at the table, everyone must get their proper share, and they point to the hope of abundance—a feast that satisfies the needs of all.[35]

32. Song, *Jesus, The Crucified People*, 200–8.

33. Crossan, *Jesus: A Revolutionary Biography*, 179–81.

34. McFague, *Life Abundant*, 174–75.

35. McFague, *The Body of God*, 168–69; also, see her work *Models of God*, 45–57.

Fiesta is an image that is familiar to me when I think of the maximal vision. For the poor Filipinos who have barely enough to survive, like those who depend on *daing* (dried fish) and *bagoong* (salted fish) for food, what could be the best expression of the maximal vision if not a banquet—a fiesta? The fiesta is not only characterized by an abundance of food—*lechon* (roasted pig), *embotido, hamonado, relyenong bangus, pancit, calderita*, and various kinds of desserts—but joy, friendship, and sharing. In God's eschatological fiesta everyone has access to that which sustains life; it is an egalitarian meal.

On the other hand, when there is little food on the table, family members make sure that each one has their rightful share. In a Filipino idiom (Tagalog): "*Kung maiksi ang kumot, matutong mamaluktot*" (literal translation: If the blanket is short, one must know how to curl up). Poor families make sure that every member is present during meal time. Eating is an occasion for sharing not only food but life. Eating is a mark of relationship, of connection. In fact, deep connections among Filipinos are expressed through the language of food and internal organs. The word *kapatid* (brother or sister), suggests Melanio Aoanan, is a contraction of "*patid ng bituka*" (connected by a single intestine). Other Filipino languages, such as Cebuano (*sumpay sa tinai*) and Ilocano (*kapugsat iti bagis*), speak of this intestinal connection. Filipino theology, continues Aoanan, is truly an incarnational and, more specifically, an intestinal theology—a *bituka* (intestine) and *pagkain* (food) theology.[36]

Deepening the symbol of the eucharistic meal (people supper), Song suggests that the egalitarian people supper took place at a "round table."[37] The round table shows the egalitarian power dynamics, the positioning of all in relation to the food, the sharing of the meal, the communication that transpires among those around the meal table, and other related "table manners." In relation to ministry, Chuck Latrop has this to say: "Concerning the why and how and what and who of ministry, one image keeps surfacing: A table that is round."[38]

The people supper at a round table manifests not just the presence of food, but the miracle of sharing. The food is located at the center of the table, within reach of each member. The round table

---

36. Aoanan, "Teolohiya ng Bituka at Pagkain," 23–44.

37. Song, *Jesus, The Crucified People*, 204.

38. Latrop, "In Search of a Roundtable," cited in Russell, *Church in the Round*, 17.

shows us the positioning of persons in relation to the food: everyone is located at a spot that has direct access to the food. With each having direct access to the meal, the structure or system is already organized in such a way that sharing becomes possible. The giving and receiving of food circulates around the table. In the round table people supper, communion becomes a reality.

The people supper at a round table also points in the direction of hospitality. The round table is a "welcome table" to which those who have long been unwelcome are welcome. At the welcome table we can discern the longing that those who have long been excluded will someday sit at the round table. At the round table those once excluded can dine, enjoy the banquet, and participate in the table talk. The African-American church tradition gives us a glimpse of this passionate longing for the welcoming round table: "We're gonna sit at the welcome table! We're gonna sit at the welcome table one of these days! Alleluia!"[39]

People supper at a round table needs to be extended into a cosmic round table in which hospitality is understood in the context of the interdependent web of life. Hospitality within the framework of ecological sensibility means allowing others to have a space where they can live with integrity in relation to the overall harmony. Hospitality involves creating a home for each one to feel at home in the cosmos. This is in consonance with God's economy—in which God intends to make this world into a home for all.

People supper at a round table is a proleptic celebration of the promised future. It is a rich and deep symbol of who we are and what we are called to be. The bread and wine, produce of God's earth and products of human labor, come together in an act of communal liturgical celebration to reveal the interdependence and communion of God, humanity, and nature. The elements of bread and wine truly re-present the broken body of Jesus, because Jesus' broken body is one with the produce of the earth. In partaking of the elements, we truly re-member the broken bodies throughout the ages because they live in us—the living—and are one with us in our experience of re-memberment (being made whole). Through the eucharistic/egalitarian meals we experience a glimpse and a foretaste of the richness of a liberated and healed community of interdependent beings in a cosmic

39. Cited in *An Advent Sourcebook*, O'Gorman, 50.

body. The whole sacred celebration points to God's incarnation in the fullness of history and nature in which "God will be all in all" (1 Cor 15:28) and human beings will truly embody the image of God.

MINISTRY OF THE HOUSEHOLD

The vision of an alternative economics must find embodiment in the life of the congregations, informing how they do Christian formation (discipleship) and various forms of ministries. There must be congruence between vision and discipleship training that church members receive from their respective congregations. If money, property, and various forms of commodities exercise a powerful influence on a person's life, then there should be an economic component in every discipleship training and practice. Members must learn the right relationship between stewardship and the meaning of wealth. In a world tyrannized by the god of the global market, Christian formation (discipleship) must prepare members for an evangelism that confronts the idols of the market and help people in society develop a liberating understanding of wealth. Since these are issues at the heart of Christian identity, they cannot be left alone to the individual to sort out. Church members need communal help to sort out priorities, establish a table of values, and make decisions with regard to these crucial matters.

Learning and Practicing Household Stewardship

Christian formation on stewardship must be in accord with God's economics. Strangely, churches often talk about stewardship and stewardship campaign and education but usually do not connect them to God's economics—the *basileia* economics, as if we can be faithful Christian stewards within the confines of neoliberal economics. There is a prevailing socio-political naiveté that stewardship can be exercised in a vacuum and that stewardship does not involve critique of the dominant socio-economic arrangement. This is partly due to a narrow understanding of stewardship that is prevalent in many churches, which simply equates it with fund raising.

In contrast to the prevailing understanding of stewardship, the church needs to articulate a notion of stewardship in accord with the spirit of God's economy as care, distribution of righteousness, and ecological sustainability. In the context of God's economy, stewardship is not primarily about our activity of fund-raising to support the programs of the church as about our participation in the care, nurture, and cultivation of the whole web of life, and orienting our whole being so that we live lives of radical gratitude, extravagant hospitality, and overflowing generosity in the service of God's mission—that of making a just, hospitable, and sustainable household—which the church has been called to take part. Having the church's mission understood in relation to this grand notion of stewardship, I say that we are Christian stewards when we are faithful to the mission of the church.

With stewardship attached to the very purpose or reason for being of the church, we have put it at the center of the church's identity. If mission is not so much about what we do (though expressed in what we do) as about who we are, likewise stewardship is about who we are. It is an expression of our very center—of our very identity. Our gifts to and through the church emerge from who we are. This is not an inversion of the scholastic adage: *Agere sequitor esse*, "action follows being." Instead, it is the identification of action with being: *Esse est agere*, "to be is to act."[40] Or, we act because we are.

Educating the Household on Proper Relation to Material Goods

Money is a taboo topic of conversation in contemporary life. "Does your mom or dad make a lot of money?" is a much more awkward question to ask at a Thanksgiving dinner conversation than the innocent question of a young child: "Where do babies come from?" It does not mean, however, that simply because we are silent about it that it has ceased to play a powerful and pervasive influence in our lives. In fact, our silence suggests the opposite: it is central to our very identity that we do not want others to know about it. We want to claim it as our sole domain. James Hudnut-Beumler's words are on target: "When people have but one central operative value, they guard it carefully and surround it with mystery and taboo, lest that one value be taken away."[41] The money taboo "stems from money's central role as an expression and index of worth."[42] My encounter with this ugly truth came as a shock when I was asked: "What is your net worth?" Our value as an individual in a consumer-and-market-oriented society is measured in terms of our net worth. Since in a market-consumer society we are

40. See Knitter, *Jesus and the Other Names*, 169.

41. Hudnut-Beumler, *Generous Saints*, 2.

42. Ibid., 1.

what we do and what we consume (possess), we are loath to have our worth compared with others lest we fall short of other's expectations, much less our measurement of success.

There are, of course, a few places when we disclose our finances, but we do so only because there is no choice. The church is certainly not one of those places where people share their money matters. The car dealer may get financial information from a church member in 15 minutes, but not the beloved pastor—not even after several years as a pastor of a congregation. But, why do we not talk about money and its place in our lives in our churches? Why should we leave the money matter outside the church? Are we not in the business of dealing with the whole person—head, heart, and checkbook?

It is difficult to talk about money in churches, but it should be a topic of study because it has direct bearing on our ultimate commitments and Christian discipleship. Our relationship to money is an expression of our inner self. How we make our money and what we spend it on is a witness to others about who we are as persons. The choices we make on how we use our money reveals much about ourselves and what we value. These are matters that are properly theological and moral; hence, they are at the heart of the church's concern. If the church does not talk about money and its place in our lives, we are likely to make a verbal confession that we are following God's way, while in practice we leave money in a protected private space. Ironically, this protected private space is wide open to the god of the market and to Visa and Master Card as well.

The Christian tradition offers insights about our proper relationship to material goods in general and money in particular. It is important that churches study their tradition, for it offers guidance on proper attitude and relationship toward money and other forms of possessions. There are writings from the early church communities to the founders of contemporary denominations that provide a compass for members to examine themselves in relation to the issue of possession and consumption. They need to be exhumed and appropriated in a market-driven culture that has lost its proper orientation with regard to material possessions.

There is no need to belabor the point that material goods are not only a requirement for our existence: it makes us who we are. Wealth and property are not evil in themselves. Money, a form of easily exchangeable wealth, is not evil in itself either. In the words of

Chrysostom, "money is called *chremata* [from *chraomai*, "I use"] so that we may use it, and not that it may use us. Therefore possessions are so called that we may possess them, and not they possess us. Why do you invert the order?" [43] The problem, however, is that we invert the order. Instead of using money, money uses us. Instead of possessing it, we are possessed by it. Possessions possess us by defining us and making us into their own image. Money and other material goods exist for our use, and we must constantly be on guard lest we invert the order. *Chremata* (use), however, is not an adequate norm when it stands by itself. More than seeing one's relation to material goods in terms of *chremata*, the early Christian theologians also employed the twin concepts of *autarkeia* (self-sufficiency) and *koinōnia* (community). Clement says that properties are for our use and for the sake of *autarkeia* (self-sufficiency).[44] Self-sufficiency and self-reliance not only free us from being a perpetual burden to others, they are also marks of human dignity.

The quest for self-sufficiency, however, may run amok if left by itself. Self-sufficiency must be balanced by the quest for *koinōnia*. As Charles Avila puts it: "[T]he purpose of property, and of wealth, is not only to achieve individual *autarkeia*, but also to attain *koinōnia*," a fellowship that dismantles the death-laden differentiation between those who have more and those who have very little for survival.[45] If we are who we are because of our relationships, we cannot be who we are as truly human when in our affluence others are deprived of their most basic needs. In a covenanted community in which the journey toward an authentic humanity is a companionship, we can only find our humanity as real companions (*cumpanis=cum* [share with] + *panis* [bread]) who share bread as we journey together.[46]

The three categories—*chremata*, *autarkeia*, and *koinōnia*—are, however, not comprehensive enough in revaluing our relation to the world around us, especially with regard to the ecosystem. Ecological insights demand that we move beyond relating to the world of nature in terms of use, self-sufficiency, and communal human well-being. We must place *chremata*, *autarkeia*, and *koinōnia* within the larger

43. Chrysostom, *Inscriptionem Altaris et in Principium Actorum*, 69, cited in Avila, *Ownership*, 144.

44. Clement, "The Educator," 436, cited in Avila, *Ownership*, 145.

45. Avila, Ibid., 145.

46. Brown, *Persuade Us to Rejoice*, 67.

context of ecological right relation. The purpose of wealth and human knowledge is to promote just harmony and intrinsic interdependence. Wealth, which is derived from nature and human labor, must be used to promote the healing of the ecosystem.

Spiritual Formation and Consumer Education

There is no doubt that the global market is a powerful shaper of self-identity—an identity defined by possession and consumption. Possession and consumption can define who we are and how we are perceived and given value by others. We consume, therefore we are. Not only does possession and consumption define who we are, we are also considered spiritually alive when we consume more. At the heart of consumerism is a distorted spirituality. If consumerism is a distorted spirituality, then it must be addressed spiritually. Addressing consumerism spiritually requires not only that the spirituality of consumerism be exposed and opposed, it also requires that we expose and oppose the consumerising of spirituality. Beyond exposing and opposing distorted spiritualities, the church must articulate what spirituality means in response to commoditization and consumerism.

Spirituality is not simply the acquisition of relaxation techniques to ward off unpleasant thoughts, but liberation from commodity addiction for the sake of life abundant.[47] Spiritual direction must lead household members to see their self-worth beyond the worth given by the market. The church must provide opportunities and support for members who are struggling to develop a lifestyle not defined by consumerism. When members find life's meaning not in what they possess and consume, they become more open to the various gifts of the spirit. Instead of loading themselves with things, which only "thingify" people, they seek to be filled with the spirit. And when they are filled with the spirit, they bear "fruits of the spirit," such as "love, joy, peace, patience, kindness, generosity, faithfulness, gentleness and self-control" (Gal 5:22–23).

Spiritual formation to counter consumerist identity would not, however, be successful unless there are opportunities for people to make informed choices and programs that enable them to practice healthy lifestyle changes. Consumer education must be an important component in the ministry of the church. The church must design

47. Gottlieb, *A Spirituality of Resistance*, 15.

educational opportunities for people to become more self-aware of their lifestyle and its impact, such as taking stock of their consumer habits, which is a beginning step in changing behavior. This may be done by focusing on one area of life and then expanding gradually to other areas as well. Some of the guide questions are: Where do our consumer goods come from? How are they produced? What is the working condition of the workers? What are the alternative products that we can buy, or even better, what can we do with less? It is difficult to be a responsible consumer when we do not have the information and we do not know where to go. Churches can be "clearinghouses" of good, quality, ecologically-friendly, and fair trade products.[48] Moreover, churches can offer ways on how to dispose our consumer items.[49]

Ministry through Service, Socio-Economic Programs, and Advocacy

There are various services that the church can do in response to economic issues not only to the church members but also to the wider society. There certainly are many victims of the economic system that call for various forms of churches' services. The church and other faith-based organizations have been doing effective work in providing services, such as feeding the hungry and providing housing for the homeless. Beyond providing assistance to the immediate needs of the disenfranchised and victims of calamities, churches have launched various socio-economic initiatives. Churches have been at the forefront in helping communities start socio-economic projects to respond to the needs of the people.

There is, however, another form of ministry that churches must take if they are to address economic policies and structures that produce inequality, poverty, and suffering. Churches need to join with others in economic policy advocacy work and organizing communities to effect change. Beyond advocating for the implementation of the first-generation of human rights (political and civil rights), churches must work with civil society and other sectors in the implementation of the second-generation of human rights, which include economic, social, and cultural rights. Based on the second-generation of human

48. Example, Community Resources for Responsible Living, created by the First Unitarian Church of San Jose for their church members to share information on no-sweat clothes or shoes.

49. Owens, "Consuming Responsibly," 40–49.

rights (Article 25 of the 1948 UN Declaration), every person has the right to adequate food, clothing, housing, medical care, and other necessary social services. The second-generation of human rights are positive rights. This means that a society has the responsibility to insure that everyone's basic needs are met.

A NEW HOUSEHOLD IS POSSIBLE! SIGNS OF HOPE

There is no doubt that the mission of making the world reflect God's economy is a gargantuan challenge. The forces of domination and reaction are always present to stop any attempt to move our economy toward the economy of care. Nonetheless, there are signs of hope. In various places around the world, concerned individuals are forming what David Korten calls "communities of congruence" to address specific issues.[50] These "communities of congruence" are joining forces to form networks or coalitions of support to address common concerns across regional and national boundaries. Many of these networks have become global, which have become more promising in countering the move of predatory globalization.

The opposition against WTO in Seattle (known as Battle in Seattle) offers hope of what people can do against predatory corporate globalization. The synergy, massive street protest, and the rebellion of nations of the global South led to the spectacular collapse of the Third Ministerial Meeting in Seattle in 1999. Stuart Townsend, writer and director of the Battle in Seattle, said that he wanted to tell the story of what happened in Seattle because it was "a victory and there are so few victories . . . Seattle has become that feared reference point . . . But there will be another Seattle and it will be worse. It's inevitable as long as the system only favors a few. There will be more and more push-back eventually."[51] Bioethicist Michael W. Fox expressed his feelings of the WTO demonstration in Seattle: "I felt the dawning of a global ethical society. Arising from the ashes of corporate hegemony and government complicity and corruption, it links the rights and interests of all beings, human and nonhuman, with a healthy environment, a healthy economy, and healthy communities."[52] Yes, Seattle has become a reference point and

50. Korten, *The Great Turning*, 317. Also cited in Delgado, *Shaking the Gates of Hell*, 226.

51. Townsend cited in Postman, "'Battle in Seattle' brings back memories."

52. Endorsement of Janet Thomas's, "The Battle in Seattle."

an inspiration. On September 30, 2003, WTO negotiations in Cancun collapsed when delegates from the global South staged a walk out, which stalled the efforts of wealthy nations to extend free-trade on a global scale.[53]

Another seed of hope is associated with the name Cochabamba, a city in Bolivia. When the city's water supply was sold to Aguas del Tunari (a subsidiary of Bechtel), the already poverty-strapped Bolivians had to deal with another challenge: the astronomical rise in the price of water. But this was not the end of the story. The people of Cochabamba organized themselves and aired their protest. What happened in Bolivia became an opening salvo of the water wars and a symbol of a people's defiance to privatizing water for corporate greed. As a result Bechtel was forced to withdraw. The name Cochabamba has become a story of people's organized resistance against corporate privatization of a common trust, the people's hard-won victory, and the defeat of the privatizers. Cochabamba is a story of the first great victory against corporate globalization in Latin America. This story needs to be told, especially given that more water wars are on the horizon.

Motivated by their religious faith, many churches around the world have staked their share in planting seeds of hope through active involvement in caring for the victims of predatory globalization and in ministries of social transformation. Two stories, one from the Philippines and the other from the United States, have, in some ways, converged because they both involved churches taking a stand against the same multinational corporation—Nestlé. The United Church of Christ in the Philippines in Calamba, Laguna, has launched a community outreach ministry that defies the prevailing understanding and practice of community outreach. Its outreach ministry is a response to the effects of globalization, particularly in relation to the plight of workers in the nearby factories. An example was its ministry to Nestlé workers who went on strike.

Meanwhile, in Michigan, Nestlé Corporation became the target of protests, with the United Methodist Church and its members playing an active role. Several United Methodists spearheaded the suit against Nestlé Waters charging that its over-pumping of spring water had serious environmental cost. In November 2003, Judge Lawrence Rood ordered Nestlé to stop the water pumping. It was a victory. The

---

53. Delgado, *Shaking the Gates of Hell*, 225.

state, however, allowed Nestlé Waters to continue pumping in order to "save jobs." Short-lived as it was, the taste of victory became an inspiration to continue the struggle. In 2004, the West Michigan Conference of the United Methodist Church passed a resolution continuing to support a citizen boycott of fourteen brands of bottled waters sold by Nestlé.[54]

Another seed of hope that I have witnessed first-hand is the work of RELUFA (REseau de LUtte contre la FAim). RELUFA is a national network of ecumenical and secular non-profit organizations and mainstream churches in Cameroon. The member organizations come from all regions in Cameroon and have joined forces to develop common strategies against systemic problems of hunger, poverty, and socio-economic, gender, and ecological injustice. Though small scale, its comprehensive response to the challenges is inspiring. Its programs include food sovereignty, self-development (involving micro-financing), equity and transparency in the extractive industries (such as oil, mining, and logging), trade justice, gender justice, sharing of experiences through exchange visits between members, and publication of materials that promote values of solidarity. When I look at the work of RELUFA and the commitment of its workers, such as Valéry Nodem, who is working hard in demanding that extractive industries be more transparent and accountable to the people, I am graced to see signs of hope.

Seeds of hope are sprouting everywhere. We can see these seeds of hope among individuals, communities, and churches that have continued to believe that an alternative economic system is possible. We can see these seeds of hope among those who continue to believe that another world is possible and are conspiring to make it a reality. Yes, *otro mundo es possible!* "Another world is not only possible, she is on her way. On a quiet day, I can hear her breathing," says writer-activist Arundhati Roy, in Porto Alegre, Brazil.[55] There are signs of this new world around us: she is visible and audible for those who have the eyes to see and ears to hear. And this new world is not outside of us; we carry her in our hearts. She is growing this minute. She is emerging out of the old. She will not come, however, by herself, but only through our concerted efforts. Let our politically engaged spirituality usher her coming! Let our conspiracy of social transformation midwife her birthing!

54. Ibid., 238–39.
55. Roy, cited in *Yes*.

7

The Church as a Community of Peacebuilders

Exorcising Globalized Violence and Terror

A N ELDERLY MAN SAW some six and seven-year-old children at play, and asked, "What are you playing?" "War," responded the kids. "Why don't you play peace instead?" said the elderly man. The children stopped, huddled together and discussed something among themselves. Then they looked puzzled and finally ran out of words. One of them asked, "Grandpa, how do we play peace? We don't know the game." "How can we be so stupid as to play war when we know how horrible war is," the elderly man said to himself.[1]

Sad, so very sad, that our society teaches us more about playing war than about playing peace. Early in life we are exposed to a culture of violence. The general public enjoys watching war and violent movies, even if in reality it knows how destructive war is. Or, does it really? Does it really know the ravages of war, ravages that are not limited to the immediate physical destruction but include those that stay even after the formal ending of hostilities? Perhaps this is what Slavenka Drakulić refers to in speaking of the "other side of war" that her beloved homeland (Croatia) was not spared. Drakulić likens war to "a monster, a mythical creature coming from somewhere far away . . . Somehow you refuse to believe that the creature has anything to do with your life . . . Finally the monster grabs you by the throat. You breathe in death, it impregnates your sleep with nightmare visions of dismembered bodies, you begin to picture your own end."[2]

1. Mihalic, *1000 Stories*, 58.
2. Drakulić, *The Balkan Express*, 1–2.

I am blessed that I have not experienced the extreme ravages of war that others have suffered. It is difficult for me to imagine what it is really like to be in the thick of war, but my world of experience has not been sanitized from the world of violence either. Even from my limited experience, I know that war and other forms of violence come with a high cost, and I know that violence brings terror to a population. I still remember one early evening when several pirates terrorized our barrio. I did not know how it happened; out of fear I ended up crawling in the mud with the pigs. The pirates took the mayor of the town as hostage. He was paraded around our barrio and was forced to tell the inhabitants not to do anything that would force them to kill him. In 1972 Ferdinand Marcos declared Martial Law and draconian measures and terror were unleashed. From the early 1970s to the mid-1980s, my hometown became one of the areas of the armed confrontations between the New People's Army (NPA) and the government forces. The town hall was attacked twice by the NPAs, and, in one incident, several soldiers were ambushed and killed. The war between the New People's Army and the government has continued to this day.

Certainly wars or armed conflicts are not new in human history, and they occur for various reasons. But, at a time when our rhetoric about "global village" has intensified, so has violence escalated and intensified around the world at a horrifying level. In its 2000 report, Project Ploughshares documented that by the end of 1999 there were 40 armed conflicts in 36 countries. This record is higher than the immediate past two years, with 36 armed conflicts in 31 countries in 1998 and 37 in 32 countries in 1997.[3] By the end of 2007, Project Ploughshares reported a total of 30 armed conflicts. The regions of Africa and Asia continue to be the most ravaged by war, both hosting 12 and 11 armed conflicts respectively. This is followed by the Middle East.[4]

Most people in the global North are familiar with major armed conflicts that have become news headlines, such as the war of aggression by the United States against Iraq and its war against the Taliban in Afghanistan, the Palestinian-Israeli conflict, the war in the Balkan region, the bloody conflict in Rwanda and East Timor, and most re-

3. Project Ploughshares, Institute of Peace and Conflict Studies in *Echoes,* 14.
4. Project Ploughshares, Press Release.

cently in Sudan. Yet, these are only a few of the wars fought in recent years within and across national borders.

The continent of Africa has surpassed many parts of the world in the number of armed conflicts, to name a few: Congo, Nigeria, Liberia, Senegal, Sudan, Mozambique, Chad, Sierra Leone, Rwanda, Burundi, Kenya, Algeria, Somalia, Angola, and Ivory Coast. The civil war in Congo has been referred to as Africa's first world war.[5] Somewhere in what is known as the Horn of Africa, the Eritrea-Ethiopia war erupted in February 1998 and intensified in 1999, with deaths estimated in the tens of thousands. In Asia, to mention a few, Indonesia has experienced major armed conflicts between Christian and Muslim groups in the Molucca Islands, adding to its three other conflicts in West Papua, East Timor, and Aceh. India continues to be the location to three separate conflicts (Andhra Pradesh, Kashmir, and the Northeast region), and other Asian countries in similar situations are Myanmar (Burma), Philippines, Bangladesh, and Pakistan. Elsewhere, major armed conflicts have been experienced in the Middle East, Europe, and the Americas. In addition to the Israeli-Palestinian conflict that has continued to intensify, Iraq, Lebanon, Turkey, and Egypt have known violent conflicts. The Americas have, likewise, not been spared, with conflicts in Peru, Colombia, Panama, El Salvador, Guatemala, Nicaragua, Mexico, and Haiti. In Europe, the countries of Bosnia-Herzegovina, Croatia, Yugoslavia, Georgia, Azerbaijan, and the United Kingdom have all experienced armed conflicts. Finally, following a period of relative stability initiated by the 1996 truce, Russia renewed its war against Chechnya in 1999.

While reliable estimates are difficult to gather, most of the victims in current global conflicts are not combatants but civilians. This is worth noting especially when we compare the war-related casualties among civilians in major wars of this century. Civilian losses accounted for half of the war-related deaths in the 1950s, but it went up to three-quarters in the 1980s and then to 90 percent in the wars of the 1990s.[6] In spite of the use of "smart" and "precision-guided" bombs by the United States in its war against Iraq, for example, most of the casualties have been civilians. Many of the civilian casualties in recent wars and conflicts are not simply the result of accidental shooting or bomb-

5. Kobia, "Violence in Africa," 11.
6. World Council of Churches, *A Moment to Choose*, 23.

ing, but have become targets themselves. Men and women civilians are tortured, sexually violated, and killed to demoralize the enemy. A testimony from a Tutsi woman (Rwanda) who narrowly escaped a gang-rape shows the ugly and abhorrent character of this war:

> I was caught by a group of Interahamwe on 1 April 1994, along with about twenty other women, and we were held by them in Gatare sector. Some of them decided to rape us before killing us. Others of them refused to rape us. The ones that wanted to rape us began to rape the women one by one. About ten of them would gang-rape a woman, and when they had finished, they would kill her by pushing a sharpened stick the size of a broomstick into her vagina until she was bleeding and almost dead.[7]

Systematic or strategic rape has become an instrument of war for the purpose of making the soldiers fight better and as a way of humiliating the enemy and destroying community life. Gaining control over enemy women's reproductive ability is a major goal, and rape provides that opportunity. Sexual violence and rape for the purpose of humiliating the enemy are not, however, limited to women. The Abu Ghraib prison scandal provides a well known example of sexual violence against male prisoners of war.

GLOBALIZATION AND GLOBAL CONFLICTS

The escalation of armed conflicts around the world is not surprising in the context of predatory corporate globalization. I say not surprising because predatory corporate globalization can only thrive in violence, either through direct military action or in sowing seeds of violence and terrorism. The invisible hands of the global market need the fist of military might to suppress any opposition. Armed confrontations and violent conflicts, however, are not simply instruments of predatory corporate globalization; they are outcomes of predatory corporate globalization. Predatory corporate globalization breeds armed conflicts and terrorism because it creates and promotes social inequities, fatalism, and despair among its victims, undermines sovereign states, fragments communities and families, pollutes and destroys the ecosystem, desecrates sacred places for profit, and disperses population as migrants and refugees. The homogenizing work of predatory

7. Barstow, *War's Dirty Secret*, 93.

corporate globalization triggers antiglobalist sentiments among those who believe that the worldview and values it is propagating are morally outrageous. Predatory corporate globalization continues to breed violent confrontation by undermining global harmony and stability.

What may at the surface appear as purely ethnic conflict is related to predatory globalization. Civil or ethnic conflicts in Africa and the Balkans have their deep roots in artificial territorial divisions carved by the colonial powers. The tension in Fiji between the Indo-Fijians and the native Fijians has deep roots in its colonial history. This is also the case in the conflict between the Hutus and Tutsis (Rwanda) and among various clans in Somalia. The Hutus and the Tutsis had complex institutional structures during the pre-colonial times that not only allowed social mobility across class/caste lines but also across ethnic lines. Likewise, Somalia had a complex clan system that balanced the rights of grazing and water of different clans and a system of dispute resolution. These structures were destroyed during the colonial period and nothing viable took their place. Thus, when the colonial authority was gone, there was nothing to fall back on by way of institutional checks and balances.[8] So, while many armed conflicts are defined as conflicts of ethnicity, they should not be confused with identifying the causes of these conflicts. Woven into ethnic and national identity struggles are basic economic and social grievances that need to be addressed adequately.[9]

Moreover, armed conflicts are not simply instruments or outcomes of capitalist globalization: they are an inevitable expression of the economization of war. In other words, predatory globalization rests on the foundation of a war economy. From the point of view of a war economy, armed conflicts are in themselves profitable. Proliferation of armaments is an expression of globalization. In August of 2001 a report from the United States Congress stated that international arms sales grew 8 percent in the previous year to nearly $36.9 billion. U.S. arms manufacturers accounted for $18.6 billion or roughly half. Of those arms sales, 68 percent were sold to countries of the global South.[10] In 2008, U.S. arms sales reached a new record of $36.4 billion.[11]

8. Tandon, "The Violence of Globalization," 26.

9. World Council of Churches, *A Moment to Choose*, 36.

10. Brooks-Thistlethwaite, "New Wars, Old Wineskin" 276.

11. Reuters, "U.S. Heads for Record Overseas Arms Sales."

PREDATORY CORPORATE GLOBALIZATION
AND THE CULTURE OF VIOLENCE

The escalation of violent conflicts around the world is an expression of the pervasiveness of the culture of violence. The militarization of economies continues to fuel a culture of violence in a more direct way, but the proclivity of our society toward violence has deeper roots in a culture that breeds and nourishes violence. At home, in our local neighborhoods, schools, and the wider public, we are relentlessly exposed to a culture that nourishes and perpetuates violence. For many individuals, the home is the first locus of encounter with violence, which then expands to the local neighborhood, school, and the wider society.

Overtly or subliminally, our society promotes violence through various media: in song lyrics that encourage hatred against others and oneself, in films and visual arts that encourage violence as a way of solving conflicts, in many competitive sports, comic books and toys, and even in children's television cartoon series.[12] Parents are more likely to forbid their children from watching actual war footage. Studies show, however, that fictionalized television violence may have more influence on children's attitudes toward war and other forms of violence than news showing actual footage of bloody combat encounters.[13] Children's comic books may also play a similar insidious function. The heroes or the "good guys" of comic books seldom use nonviolent ways to resolve conflicts. Walter Wink describes the psychodynamics with this trajectory: the children identify with the "good guys" so they can think of themselves as good and then project onto the "bad guys" their repressed anger and rebelliousness. While they continue to identify with the "good guys," they also receive the privilege of vicariously enjoying their rebellious selves when the bad guys initially prevail. As expected, the "good guys" emerge victorious. The final death-blow is dealt to the "bad guys" who end up decimated. Salvation is achieved and the children have found salvation by identifying with the heroes or the "good guys." Furthermore, the satisfaction they feel in that salvation is intensified when the "good guys" use all

12. World Council of Churches, *A Moment to Choose*, 25.

13. McGinnis and McGinnis, *Parenting*, 47.

their might to shred the "bad guys" to pieces. This is the trajectory of the myth of redemptive violence.[14]

The children of the global South are not immune from the insidious influence of the media. In spite of pervasive poverty, television is widely used among the urban poor. In places where war and violent conflicts have continued to ravage the land, the encounter with violence is more direct. The sight of daily violence may have become normal for many kids. Others continue to live with the physical and psychological pain of the violence. In some areas children have been trained to use high-powered weapons and engage in wars. In the inner cities children are acculturated to violence through encounters with raw violence, usually between rival gangs. As a form of protection they join gangs.

The cultivation of a culture of violence through the media is gradual and steady. At first we are repelled by the violent act. Then, as we continue to watch more and more, we become numb to violence or become addicted to it. "The worst thing apathy to violence in the media does," contends Usha Jesudasan, "is that it stunts our conscience. When we no longer see it as something hateful and destructive, when we start making excuses for it, when we accept it as inevitable, then something terrible has happened to us."[15] In many ways, our world has been addicted to violence and we do not know other ways of settling conflicts except through violence. This is an addiction of individuals and communities, of small and large nations, and of terrorists and counterterrorists. The addiction to violence has done damage to our moral imagination in the direction of exploring ways of peace. Powerful nations, relying more on their military power than moral imagination, take even a further step in their violence through preemptive strikes. Indeed, the culture of violence has engulfed the land.

THE CHURCH IN THE MIDST OF VIOLENT CONFLICTS

The church is in the midst of violent conflicts, especially in the global South. Some churches have been abandoned or moved to new locations because of violent confrontations, or moved following the groundswell of refugees. The armed conflicts in the Philippines between the New People's Army (the military arm of the Communist Party of the

14. Wink, *The Powers that Be*, 49.
15. Jesudasan, "Entertaining Violence," 29.

Philippines) and the Philippine government as well as between the Moro Islamic Liberation Front and the Philippine government forces have placed churches in the midst of violence. In some instances, congregations have been caught in the crossfire. This was the terrible fate of the members of a United Church of Christ in the Philippines (UCCP) congregation in Rano, Sta. Cruz, Davao del Sur. On a fateful Sunday in 1987, church members (mostly of the indigenous Bagobo tribe) gathered in the parsonage after they heard gunshots. A paramilitary group took cover near the parsonage from the approaching group of New People's Army. After the exchange of gunshots, around 50 UCCP members had died, including women and children.

Many churches have been torn apart or divided because of violent conflicts. This is not because churches have become more courageous in their commitment to justice and peace—though some are—but because their identities have been tied to certain ethnic groups. With church members identified among opposing groups, whether along ideological or ethnic lines, the unity of the church has been seriously threatened. The unity of churches in Fiji, for example, has been seriously threatened by the relationship between native Fijians and Indo-Fijians, especially in the aftermath of the 1987 military *coup d'etat.* The United Methodist Church, which accounted for 90 percent of all Christians in Fiji and whose membership are mostly indigenous Fijians, was deeply divided, with most Methodists supporting the military coup.[16]

The involvement of the church in the Rwandan tragedy, whether by commission or omission, has not been widely circulated. Investigations by African Rights in London give evidence that some local Catholic, Anglican, and Baptist church leaders were implicated in the killings. One of the most egregious examples of church complicity is that of the Roman Catholic Archbishop of Kigali, Vincent Nsengiyumva, who was part of the circle of the hard-line fanatical anti-Tutsi clique around Habyarimana. His death, along with two other bishops and the vicar-general of Kabgayi diocese, at the hands of RPF soldiers, brought his role into sharp focus. A fair assessment of the complicity of the church, however, must be done within the context of a deeply divided church, "split by different views of the demands of simple justice *and* by ethnicity and regionalism. Put simply, the

16. See Premdas, "The Church and Reconciliation," 79–95.

church and its clergy, both missionary and indigenous, were far from neutral in their sympathies."[17] There were those who remained silent, but it was nevertheless complicity; for it was silence masquerading as prudence.

Another case of the church's complicity in ethnic strife is the war in the Balkan region. The Croatian Catholic Church and Serbian Orthodox Church were both complicit in the ethnic killings. Both remained silent, neither acknowledging the genocide nor seeking forgiveness. Obsessed with racial purity, during the last world war the Croatian fascist state murdered 600,000, mostly Serbs, but also Jews, gypsies, and others who were classified as racial inferiors or as political criminals. The name Jasenovac, the largest Croatian concentration camp, is as infamous for the Serbs as is Auschwitz for the Jews.[18] Serbs remember this genocide in deeply held memories. When the tide later turned in their favor, Serbians launched a campaign of genocide to avenge their ancestors killed in Jasenovac. Living with the wound that the passage of time never healed, they became ruthless butchers of their perceived enemies in a heinous crime popularly called "ethnic cleansing."

In the U.S., the pre-emptive war against Iraq has been contentious and divisive. While it is not a surprise that most conservative churches readily supported the war, many mainline churches easily found justification for supporting it. This support seems to be based on the unquestioned assumption of the compatibility between God and country (a clear symbol is the tradition of having the U.S. flag stand next to the cross in the sanctuary). Some churches even wanted to put up a flagpole as a sign of patriotism, which other members vehemently opposed. As one person at a church meeting in Ohio put it, "You've got to remember: we are Christians, but we're Americans first." Let us put it to the test, challenges Wink, "which would cause the greater outcry, removing the American flag from your church sanctuary or removing the cross?"[19] In addition, "God bless America" bumper stickers proliferated everywhere along with "Support Our Troops." Meanwhile, other important issues have taken a backseat as

---

17. Linden, "The Church and Genocide," 51.

18. Forrest, "A Dialogue on Reconciliation in Belgrade," 113.

19. Wink, *The Powers that Be*, 59.

debates regarding the war and homeland security have moved front and center.

WHEN WILL WE LEARN THE WAYS OF PEACE? JESUS AND THE COMING REIGN OF PEACE

We have progressed in technological sophistication and economic wealth (though with widening disparity), but we are lagging behind in learning the ways of peace. In fact, we have advanced our sophistication in justifying various forms of violence, for war is now waged in the name of peace. It may be possible through sophisticated technology and military power to track down international terrorists, but they are not going to be totally deterred. The social elites may create "fortress communities" to insulate themselves from the outside world, but they will soon realize (if they have not already done so) that they are not completely invulnerable. They may be wired to the global market through the cyberspace, but they do not know their local neighbors. Terrorists are aware of this vulnerability. A peace that has walls in our highly globalized world is no peace at all. We seem not to understand, or we refuse to understand, that lasting security can only be secured through just peace and not by war—even "just war." Why do we not get it? The philosopher Friedrich Nietzsche got it right: "The quest of power makes [one] cunning, the possession of power makes [one] stupid."[20] Power intoxicates, finally possessing its possessor. When power possesses, those possessed lose sight of what promotes life, which finally ends in self-destruction.

Jesus wept over Jerusalem, saying: "If you only knew today what is needed for peace!" (Lk19:42). When will we learn the ways of peace and true security? When will we know by heart the things that make for peace? When will we understand and gain the courage to address the roots of terrorism and counterterrorism?

Central to Jesus' life and ministry is his proclamation of the coming reign of God, which is the reign of peace, the reign of shalom (Rom 14:17). Jesus embodied in his life and ministry the vision of the peaceable kingdom. What is the foundation of the reign of peace that Jesus embodied in his life and ministry? I say that the foundation of this shalom is right relation: right relation with God, neighbors, and the whole created world. When right relation exists, shalom reigns and peace prevails

20. Nietzsche, cited in Smith and Watson, *De/Colonizing*, 210.

in the land (Is 32:17; Jas 3:18). The Decalogue, which Jesus summed up in two (loving God and loving the neighbor), crystallizes the message of right relation: right relation with God and right relation with neighbors, both near and far. Just relation is the foundation for peace and security. Justice or righteousness is the foundation of cosmic harmony and order. YHWH (God) created the world according to *sedaqâ* (righteousness). Douglas Knight makes the point: "When *sedaqâ* prevails the world is at harmony, in a state of well-being, in *šālôm*. An act of sin in the religious sphere or injustice in the social sphere can inject discord and shatter *šālôm*. It then takes a decisive act of *mispat*, 'justice' to restore the *šālôm* and reestablish the *sĕdāqâ*."[21]

"*Ua mau ke ea o ka aina i ka pono*" (The life of the land is perpetuated in righteousness) is the state motto of Hawai'i. Without *pono* (justice or righteousness, balance, right relation), there is no peace and harmony in the land *(aina)*. Only the practice of just relations and the righting of wrongs can restore harmony and bring security. Harmony exists when there is justice or righteousness and mutuality (balanced relation) among created beings. Only just or right relation can stop the curse of the vicious cycle of violence and disharmony.

THE CHURCH: FOLLOWERS OF THE WAY OF PEACE

The angels announced Jesus' birth as the reign of peace on earth (Lk 2: 14). This reign of peace, not the *Pax Romana*, is the peace of the reign of God that is seeking to actualize itself in history. The peace that Jesus proclaimed and witnessed (*Pax Christi*) is much more than the absence of war or a space marked out within the Roman peace; it is of a different origin altogether: It did not come from the world of domination and subjection. The gospel of John says: "Peace I leave with you; my peace I give to you" (Jn 14:27). Jesus, the "Lord of peace" (Eph 2:14–17), is the giver of peace. His Spirit is a Spirit of peace and his gospel is the good news of peace (Eph 6:15). Jesus, the Lord of peace, has broken down the dividing wall of hostilities (Eph 2:14).

Not surprisingly, the followers of Jesus (the Jesus movement) identified themselves as the followers of the way of peace. They were called peacemakers (Mt 5:9) or sons and daughters of peace. Peacemakers became a mark of their new self-identity. "Peace be to this house" was a common greeting practiced by the followers of the way of peace. In ac-

21. Knight, "Cosmogony," 149.

cord with their new identity, the followers of Jesus were "mandated" to be peacemakers. Jesus' gift of peace is not something to be received and appreciated; it is a new mandate (*novum mandatum*) to work for peace.

Walter Brueggemann underscores this mandate for the contemporary church: It "is mandated not just to do kind things, but to perceive the world differently, to know that the wave of the future is not in putting people down, but in *raising them up*."[22] The word mandate is not very appealing to many. Yet, Jesus' gift of peace is a new mandate (*novum mandatum*) to work for peace. This mandate or imperative is more than an external command; it is a mandate arising out of who we are or out of our very identity. We are capable of carrying out this mandate because we have experienced transformation in our lives. In other words, this mandate is a call to manifest what is deeply true to ourselves as followers of Jesus, the Lord of peace. Following Jesus is not simply following a commandment but becoming like him—becoming Christlike. Accepting the new mandate is bearing the message of peace and becoming Christlike: It is, as Sallie McFague reminds us, christomorphic.[23]

Following the way of peace cost the followers of Jesus much. They suffered marginalization and persecution under the peace and order imposed by the Roman Empire. They refused to be silent under the imposed peace of the empire; hence, they were considered enemies. In its long history and with changing fortunes, the church has not always been faithful to its identity and mandate. Colonized by the surrounding culture, many of its brightest theologians have concentrated their energies justifying war rather than working for peace. Yet, with the empowering work of the spirit, the church has not been left without faithful followers of the Lord of peace in all times and places.

CHURCH: EXORCIST OF THE IDOLS OF FALSE SECURITY

"If the fear of God is the beginning of wisdom," the fear for our security is the beginning of idolatry. Idolatry strikes so deep because it addresses our need for security. Fearful for our security, we cling to mundane goods, such as wealth and military force, to secure ourselves, and we give them the status of eternal securers—idols. But they are measures that do not lead to security and, in fact, continue to undermine security.

22. Brueggemann, *Peace*, 147.

23. McFague, *Life Abundant*, 184–85.

False security is what idols provide. Idols offer not lasting security but only duct-tape securities. Yet, when individuals and communities are controlled by idols, they fail to discern false securities. The idols' control may reach a point when people "live a lie."[24] The lying may become so deep that an individual or a community believes its own lie.

Idolatry operates on deception, and as a consequence, it is very much invested on the discourse of "truth." In the Central Intelligence Agency's (CIA) old headquarters building a New Testament passage is prominently displayed: "You shall know the truth and the truth will set you free" (Jn 8:32). I do not know what kind of "truth" the CIA is talking about. What I do know about the CIA, though, is that it is more invested in "concealing truth" and "manufacturing truth" than in knowing and revealing truth.[25] If, in the words of Thomas Friedman, "the market will never work without a hidden fist," it is equally true that the hidden fist will not work effectively without the cunning of "truth manufacturers."[26]

In all major wars, the first casualty is "truth." "Experts" are called upon to "create" (manufacture) truth to support war, and people are asked to trust in the power of armaments to restore peace and security. Before the guns are fired, the first battle is the battle for "truth." The first confrontation does not happen in the battlefield, but in the media: television, newspapers, radio, and so on. The citizens must be convinced that war must be waged at all cost for the security of their lives, resources, and way of life.

The God discourse is not exempt from becoming an instrument of idolatrous powers. In fact, God has become a convenient tool. Many wars have been waged in the name of God. If "truth" is the first casualty in war, the first to be enlisted is not Private Ryan (protagonist of Hollywood's movie "Saving Private Ryan") but God. God the almighty must be enlisted to crush the enemy and secure victory. God the truth must also be enlisted to expose the falsehood of the other. And this God must be on our side, not on that of the enemy. In this way, the universal God is transformed into a tribal God, a God identified with a nation and a protector of its interest. In times of war, nations do not have qualms identifying and enlisting God on their side.

24. McFague, *The Body of God*, 110.
25. See Griffith, *The War on Terrorism*, 239.
26. Ali, *The Clash of Fundamentalisms*, 260–61.

When nations enlist God on their side, this means that the God of one is the devil of the other. Then a hopeless battle for life and death ensues and the authentic coordinates of good and evil disappear. Everything becomes possible. In this regard, whoever said that when there is no God everything is permitted or possible is wrong (or, just partly right). On the contrary, everything is possible because of God. War, genocide, terrorism, and suicide bombings are possible in the name of God. Indeed, everything is possible because of God. The song "nothing is impossible when you trust in God" takes on a negative twist: to support heinous acts in God's name.[27]

Likewise, peace has not escaped from being used as an instrument of idolatry. Peace, like God, has become a unifying myth of our time. If wars are waged in the name of God, wars are also waged in the name of peace. Waging wars in the name of peace has become a convenient justification for wars. In our time invasions are identified as missions to establish global peace, justice, and security. Invasions are now called "Operation Just Cause" or carried out for the purpose of liberating a country ("Liberate Iraq"). The response of the citizens of the "land of the free and home of the brave" following the September 11, 2001 terrorist attack is an example of idolatrous nationalism. Terrified, the citizens of the "home of the brave" grasped anything that could restore their threatened security. The event of September 11 left the church in the U.S. shocked and disoriented, and its capacity to transcend the messy situation was compromised. Lacking both in substantive liturgical habits and theological grounding, many congregations easily caved in to the pressures of the moment. Experiencing a terrible pain, they reached for a reassuring symbol, the American flag, instead of a chalice or a Bible.[28]

We must exorcise the idolatrous nationalism that has engulfed the land. Let us exorcise this idolatrous nationalism by exposing its claim to the blistering critique of light. We must let our lights shine brightly in the midst of darkness. Muhammad Iqbal's lines are for us to ponder: "Thou didst create the night, but I made the lamp. Thou didst create clay, but I made the cup. Thou didst create the deserts, mountains and forests, I produced the orchards, gardens and groves. It

27. Duchrow and Hinkelammert, *Property*, 138.

28. Willimon, "What September 11 taught me," 106. Also, see Marshall, "When Listening," 170.

is I who made the glass out of stone, and it is I who turn a poison into an antidote."[29] The point is clear: God gave us the ability to turn the dark spots in our lives and society into light. So we must let our lights shine wherever we are.

THE CHURCH: A COMMUNITY OF WALL-BUSTERS AND BRIDGE-BUILDERS

The evangelists of globalization proclaim in tantalizing ways the message of global village. While they like to speak of capital without borders, they do not speak about hearts without borders. On the contrary their hearts are walling up, and this inside walling is finding expression in the building of physical walls separating the winners and the losers. The winners have constructed "fortress communities" to insulate themselves from the losers. The fortress, however, is not going to give them complete peace and security.

When people become imperialistic their hearts actually shrink. Wanting to have more and fearing for their security, their hearts constrict and construct walls of fear, walls of division, and walls of exclusion. They fail to realize that as they wall others out, they are also walling themselves in. They are imprisoned by narrow and self-serving nationalism. Some time in 1816, Stephen Decatur proposed the ultimate toast to narrow nationalism: "Our country right or wrong!"[30] The new global person with a heart as large as the world and with an alternative understanding of patriotism refutes Decatur's sentiment by emending it. Speaking against the extension of "Manifest Destiny" into the Philippines in 1899, Senator Carl Schurz of Missouri said, "Our country, right or wrong. When right, to be kept right; when wrong, to be put right."[31] The new global persons with hearts as large as the world are not imprisoned by narrow nationalism. They know, to paraphrase Albert Camus, that it is not a contradiction to love one's country and still love global justice.[32] In fact, I say that the only way to love one's country is to love global justice.

An embodiment of a global heart seeking to overcome narrow self-interest is found in the story of Mazen Julani and his wife and

29. Cited in Chittister, *Listen with the Heart*, 16.

30. Cited from Church, "We Need More Patriots," 12.

31. Ibid.

32. Camus, cited in Brown, *Saying Yes*, 8.

their three children. Mazen Julani (a 32-year-old Palestinian pharmacist) and his family lived in the Arab part of Jerusalem. One day, when he was with his friends, he was fatally shot by a Jewish colonist—an expression of revenge by an Israeli for an attack that day by a group of Palestinians. He was immediately taken to an Israeli hospital but did not survive. The Julani clan decided on the spot to donate his organs as transplants to those who needed them. This is how it came to be that in the breast of Ygal Cohen now beats a Palestinian heart.

Mazen's wife, whose name was not mentioned in the story, did not know how to explain to her 4-year-old daughter that her father had died. So she told her that her Daddy had gone on a trip and that on his way back, he was going to bring her a beautiful gift. To those around her, she whispered in tears: "In a little while now my children and I will visit Ygal Cohen in the Israeli section of Jerusalem because there lives the heart of my husband, the father of my children. And we will listen to the palpitations of his heart. And that will be for us a great consolation."[33]

Another story of hospitable hearts and wall-busting took place during the First World War. Soon after the devastation of the First World War, Quakers responded to the need of the impoverished people of Poland by distributing food and clothing. As the story goes, one relief worker contacted typhus and died within twenty-four hours. There were no other cemeteries except that of Roman Catholics, and canonical law forbade burying anyone not of that religious confession in consecrated ground. So the deceased worker was buried in a grave just outside the wall of the cemetery. But during the night the villagers took action: they moved the fence of the cemetery to include the grave.[34] This was a serious transgression of canonical law; nevertheless, the villagers decided to betray the law of exclusion even if it meant going to hell.

Being willing to go to hell for the sake of busting walls of division and creating hospitable communities was what Huck Finn did with his friend Jim, a runaway black slave. Raised in a culture that preached that helping a runaway slave was equivalent to spitting in the eye of God, Huck was faced with a difficult choice: betraying his friend Jim or suffering eternal damnation in hell. In what is arguably one of the

---

33. Cited in Boff, "It is Dark."
34. Steere, *Mutual Irradiation*, 7, cited in Messer, *A Conspiracy of Goodness*, 127.

greatest lines in Western literature, Huck decided: "All right, then, I'll go to hell."[35]

What do fence-movers and wall-busters do? They are willing to go to hell for the sake of busting the walls of societal division and the predatory laws of the global capitalist market. Fence-movers and wall-busters dare to dream, dare to hope, dare to struggle to break idolatrous fences of divisions and dare to forge more just, inclusive, and sustainable communities, both locally and globally. They are boundary crossers in the good sense, overcoming fences of various kinds. Fence-movers and wall-busters are the new human communities whose hearts are as wide and as large as the world. The church, a community of followers of the Lord of peace, is called to the task of breaking down walls of fear, division, and hostilities.

CHURCH: A COMMUNITY THAT PRACTICES FORGIVENESS

How can we break the cycle of violence whose roots are deep? Is it really possible to circumvent the vicious history of violence? How can we circumvent history?

Deep within the Christian tradition—though not its monopoly—is the notion of forgiveness and related notions of repentance and reconciliation. But, is forgiveness really powerful enough to circumvent deeply rooted animosities, more particularly between social groups and nations? Reinhold Niebuhr, a theologian who is known for his engagement in politics, answers this question with a big "No." For Niebuhr, when Christians talk about love and forgiveness in a political setting "they are likely to become sentimentalists, expecting too much of ordinary self-interested human beings."[36]

My engagement in the topic of forgiveness has not been long, as it has not been my favorite topic. My interest has been in social justice and, as one who sees our societal predicament at the systemic level, in social transformation. As I have continued to explore the relationship between forgiveness and social transformation, however, I have realized that my dream of a new tomorrow is not possible apart from forgiveness. In fact, it is a contradiction to speak of a new tomorrow—a tomorrow that seeks the well-being of all—without forgiveness. In other words, there is no new tomorrow without forgiveness; for

35. Twain, *The Adventures of Huckleberry Finn*, 273.

36. Shriver, *An Ethic for Enemies*, 7.

without forgiveness, no space has been created for commencing the journey toward a new and better tomorrow. Without forgiveness, the dreamed-for tomorrow is likely to devour its own children.

It is not only that forgiveness is tied to the notion of a new and better tomorrow: forgiveness is critical to the life of movements for transformation. Movements for social transformation, historical instruments for the eradication of the social expressions of sin, are necessary and good, but they are still the works of human beings; thus they are liable to human sinfulness. Forgiveness, as "gratuitous love," says Jon Sobrino, "is an important way of remaining true to what is at the origin of liberation movements: love, not vengeance or mere retaliation; keeping true to the purpose of liberation, which is a just and loving society for all."[37] As J. I. Gonzales Faus puts it, we must "make revolution as people who have been forgiven" and, with Sobrino's reminder, "that we carry liberating love in vessels of clay." This view can help heal "any tendency to authoritarianism, dogmatism, or power mania" that may be present in liberation movements.[38]

Forgiveness is not a one-time event but a process. It does not neglect justice but embraces it by taking seriously both the violation and the prospect of healing. It is a multidimensional process. Shriver compares it to "a twisted four-strand cable, which over time intertwines with the enemy's responses to form the double bond of new politics. No one element in this cable carries the weight of the action; each assumes and depends upon the others."[39] As a multidimensional human action, it can start at various locations. Moreover, any process to forgiveness must take seriously the context. Approaches vary in response to the context.

The growing literature on forgiveness presents complex and various approaches in relation to individual and societal forgiveness. While individual and social forgiveness are related, they are distinct and their relationship is asymmetrical, for the reason that society is not merely the sum of all individuals. It is possible to achieve individual forgiveness when social forgiveness is not yet present. However, although it is impossible to imagine social forgiveness without a good amount of individual forgiveness, social forgiveness is not simply the sum of individual forgiveness.

37. Sobrino, *The Principle of Mercy*, 66.
38. Ibid.
39. Shriver, *An Ethic for Enemies*, 9.

These four elements are normally present in the literature on forgiveness: (1) open naming of the wrong, (2) forbearance or drawing back from revenge-in-kind, (3) empathy, and (4) extending a tentative hand toward renewed community still in the future.[40] I consolidate these elements around three concepts: (1) prophetic memory, (2) intersubjective empathy, and (3) creative imagination.[41] These three concepts suggest temporality or modality of time: past, present, and future, respectively. While they are presented in this sequence, the interaction of memory, empathy, and imagination is not linear. This way of framing captures the complexity of the matter and the direction in which it needs to move. Open naming of wrong or truth-telling falls under the category of prophetic memory, the notion of forbearance under the category of empathy, and the new future under the category of creative social imagination.

These three must be woven together for the process of forgiveness to be complete. The absence of one leads to a distorted understanding of forgiveness. Forgiveness without memory is hollow; memory without empathy is cruel; empathy without imagination can lead to the imprisoning of a relationship within its past or present manifestation; and imagination without empathy can lead to failure to take account of one's social relatedness.[42] Empathy and imagination both lead to a different and liberating retrieval of memory. Forgiveness is our way to move forward. Forgiveness prevents us from becoming what we hate (the paradox of opposites). In other words, it offers hope for the birthing of a peaceful world.

A story from Sarajevo, in Eastern Europe, gives us a courageous account of forgiveness and, consequently, of hope. Zlatko Dizdarevic's *Sarajevo: A War Journal* tells a story of a three-year-old girl who was hit by a sniper's bullet while playing outside her home. Without delay, her horrified father brought her, bleeding and hovering between life and death, to the hospital. It was only after her father, "a big hulk of a man," as Dizdarevic described him, found a doctor to care for her did he allow himself to burst into tears and give words to his wounded heart. Two of his sentences, says Dizdarevic, will linger long past after the event: "The first comes when the stricken father invites the

40. Shriver, "Is There Forgiveness in Politics?" 131–49.
41. See Suchocki, *The Fall to Violence*, 144–60.
42. Ibid., 41.

unknown assassin to have a cup of coffee with him so that he [the assassin] can tell him, like a human being, what has brought him to do such a thing. Then he says, aware that this question may not elicit any human response: 'One day her tears will catch up with him.'" After sharing this painful story, the outraged Dizdarevic makes a commentary: "If the most barbaric act imaginable in this war, a sniper shooting at a three-year-old girl playing in front of her own home, elicits only an invitation to a cup of coffee and hope for forgiveness, then Bosnia-Herzegovina doesn't stand much chance to survive."[43]

Miroslav Volf offers a different reading of the tragic event. While Dizdarevic sees the man's invitation to the assassin to have a cup of coffee as the act of a sentimental fool, Volf sees a ray of hope. He is not about to suggest that we blur the line between the executed and the executioner, or to let the executioner continue the dastardly act. But he wants to suggest that the hope for Bosnia and, certainly, for the whole world tyrannized by the evil of exclusion, lies in men and women who, though they have suffered so much and have not forgotten their suffering, still gather enough courage to invite the perpetrator to a cup of coffee and inquire of him what has "brought him to do such a thing." While it is true that the "rifle butt in the back . . . shatters civilization" (Dizdarevic's words) and creates inhumanity, the "rifle butt in the back" of the avenger does not restore civilization and humanity either. For Volf, the hope for Bosnia and the hope for the world lie with men and women who have not allowed the "rifle butt" to colonize their souls and their social imagination. They are the men and women "who, despite enduring humiliation and suffering, have not given up on the will to embrace the enemy."[44]

CHURCH: COMMUNITY OF MEDIATORS AND RECONCILERS

I gave a distinct space for forgiveness because it is a central Christian concept, but it should not be confused with reconciliation. Reconciliation, in a much broader sense, includes the element of forgiveness and also of repentance.[45] John Paul Lederach narrates a conversation his colleague at Eastern Mennonite University had in one of their constituent congregations. The congregation asked:

43. Volf, "A Theology of Embrace," 30.

44. Ibid., 31.

45. Liechty, "Putting Forgiveness in its Place," 59–68.

"When will the Mennonite Church and its academic centers stop fussing so much about peace and justice issues and get on with the gospel?" Right on target, Lederach's answer was, "reconciliation *is* the gospel."[46] The gospel is that God was in Christ reconciling the world. As God was in Christ reconciling the world, likewise, the followers of Christ are entrusted with the ministry of reconciliation. The church is an "ambassador for Christ" entrusted with the mission of witnessing and spreading the message of reconciliation to all people around the world (2 Cor 5: 17–20). Not only is reconciliation at the heart of the Christian gospel, it is also crucial and urgent for our current context.

While many are calling for reconciliation, they may not be in agreement on what it means. Many dictators around the world have made appeals for reconciliation. The leadership of apartheid South Africa often made appeals for reconciliation, calling for black South Africans to live peacefully together. Black South Africans greeted the exhortation with a mixture of anger and hilarity, for they know that reconciliation among people is only possible when certain fundamental conditions are met.[47] Fundamental to reconciliation is the recognition of the harm done, and it must satisfy the demands of justice or right relation. Reconciliation does not replace justice; rather, reconciliation is predicated on justice. Without justice, there is no reconciliation of peoples; without reconciliation, there is no peace and harmony.

While it is true that reconciliation is predicated on justice, we need to act beyond justice (narrowly understood as retribution) for the process of reconciliation to take place in history. When the violation is deep, no call for the implementation of retributive justice can totally restore what has been destroyed or violated. Raimon Panikkar is sharp on this: "To believe that a simple reestablishment of the order that has been violated will right the situation is a crudely mechanistic, immature way of thinking. Lost innocence," he continues, "calls for a new innocence, and not a retreat to a paradise of dreams. No manner of compensation can undo what is already done. Peace is not restoration . . . The very cosmos, while it moves rhythmically, does so without repeating itself. The *status ante* is an impossibility."[48] The only way to move in the direction of peace is to move forward. Peace is not

46. Lederach, *The Journey Toward Reconciliation*, 159.
47. Wells, "Theology for Reconciliation," 4.
48. Panikkar, *Cultural Disarmament*, 23.

restoration or maintenance of the status quo but "our emancipation from this status quo and its transformation into a *fluxus quo*, toward an ever-new cosmic harmony."[49]

The only hopeful move is to move forward, but the actual journey toward reconciliation and peace is a difficult one, sometimes involving more backward than forward steps. Nonetheless, steps must be taken, and we can learn from those who have taken the journey. Lederach is one who has taken that journey. I cannot give justice to his thoughts in the space available here, but I will share his framework as it is useful in understanding the broad and complex dynamics of the reconciliation process.

Lederach's account is deeply theological and very practical. His theological rendering makes practical sense, and his practical account makes theological sense. He uses familial images to talk about the foundational theological and moral concepts of truth, mercy, justice, and peace and relates them to a historical timeframe: truth=past, justice=present, and mercy=future. Peace is both the mother and the child. Peace is the mother because it requires peace (negotiated peace) for the reconciliation process to start, but peace is also the fruit (child). There is, however, no peace without mercy, truth, and justice. Each of these concepts must have integrity in the process of reconciliation for peace to emerge. One cannot be sacrificed for the sake of another. Since this process does not happen in a vacuum, but in a particular space and time, attentiveness to the context and timing are crucial. Simply following a linear sequencing (past=truth, present=justice, future=mercy and, in addition, hope) is not possible when the people clamor for a different starting point. Thus, instead of a linear and monochronic approach to time, Lederach suggests that we adopt a polychronic approach. This polychronic approach involves two essential elements: "*multiplicity* of activities and *simultaneity* of actions, doing several things at the same time." This needs, Lederach notes, "a *systemic* rather than a *linear* perspective on people, relationships, activities, and context."[50]

49. Ibid., 16.
50. Lederach, *The Journey Toward Reconciliation*, 78.

THE CHURCH AS A PARTICIPANT IN CREATING
A CULTURE OF PEACE

It is easy to spend all our resources and energies merely putting out the fires of violent conflicts around the globe. Violent conflicts have deeper causes, however, that need to be addressed. We need to be more proactive in creating cultures of peace. The notion of "conflict transformation" offers a more comprehensive way of understanding and dealing with conflicts. It includes conflict management, conflict resolution, and structural reform.[51] The purpose of conflict management is to find ways of preventing the conflict from becoming more violent or from expanding into other areas, while conflict resolution means the removal, to the extent possible, of the inequalities between the disputants through mediation, negotiation, or some other means. Structural reform, on the other hand, seeks to address the roots of the conflict and to create an atmosphere and institutions conducive to peaceful relations.

The church has been and must be involved in the various dimensions of peacemaking. The church's impact in conflict management and conflict resolution has been significant, but it is short term. It is at the level of structural reform that the church can play a very significant role and with long-term impact. This is a dimension where the church can contribute much, especially with its rich theological resources and intentional communities. Creating a "culture of peace" belongs to this dimension. Such a culture creates and nurtures worldviews, values, and behavior that promote peaceable diversity of all living beings and mutual caring and equitable sharing of resources that sustain life.

The creation of a culture of peace requires intentional effort, especially now that the culture of war and violence has become pervasive. It requires what Panikkar calls "cultural disarmament." By cultural disarmament, he means the abandonment of the trenches in which modern culture has dug in, such as its vested and nonnegotiable notion and value of progress, techno-science, democracy, and the world market. Moreover, it means a change in the predominant myth of modern humanity—of that part of humanity that he names as the "most vociferous, influential, and wealthy, and is in control of the destinies of politics."[52]

---

51. Appleby, "Religion and Conflict Transformation," 439.
52. Panikkar, *Cultural Disarmament*, 34.

The work of cultural disarmament in order to create a culture of peace requires the building of a counter-mentality, which operates at the level of mythos. This counter-mentality, as James and Kathleen McGinnis advocate in *Parenting for Peace and Justice*, is an interdependent mentality that must begin at an early stage of a person's life. The McGinnises list some of the themes that are part of interdependence that must be introduced to children of all ages: "becoming comfortable with differences; developing a sense of oneness; understanding the systems or structures that influence people; and developing a sense of responsibility for strengthening ties among people."[53] Instead of the usual narrow nationalist pledge that children learn at school, the McGinnises endorse the World Pledge:

> I pledge allegiance to the World
> To cherish every living thing,
> To care for earth and sea and air,
> With peace and freedom everywhere![54]

In addition, a part of the continuing work of cultural disarmament is rereading and rewriting history through the hermeneutic lens of peace.[55] The culture of everyday life is largely peaceful, but the culture of historical record is overwhelmingly about warrior societies. Historical record revolves around stories of battles won and lost, of nations and states conquered or engaged in conquest. Violence, destruction, and sexual misconduct of top officials easily become news headlines, and they sell. On the other hand, wholesome community events and creative efforts for peace, unless done by top officials for political purposes, do not garner as much media coverage.

The church must play an active role in rereading and rewriting history to highlight peacemaking activities. This includes chronicling the lives of peace heroes, a practice that helps subvert the dominant notion that heroes are only those who have fought and died in wars to protect one's country. Since many peacemaking activities have come through the creative intervention of the church, synagogue, and mosque, it is essential that religious institutions consider it as part of their mission to write a history of various acts of peacemaking. This

---

53. McGinnis, *Parenting for Peace and Justice*, 50.

54. Ibid., 52.

55. Boulding, "Cultures of Peace and Communities of Faith," 96–97.

provides an occasion to counterbalance the historical emphasis on holy wars, such as the Crusades of the Middle Ages.[56]

The task of cultural disarmament cannot be done mono-cultur-ally. It must be done in companionship with others; it must be from the very beginning an ecumenical enterprise. We must do this on both epistemological and political grounds. On epistemological ground, we always view social reality from a certain location; thus, our under-standing of ourselves and our world is limited. We are not fully aware of our own myths. It is only through the help of other people and cultures that we can begin to recognize our own myths. For this to happen, we must "see our neighbor not only as some*thing* else, but as *alius/alia,* some*one* else—not only as an object of observation or cognition, but as another source of intelligibility, and an independent subject of our categories."[57] Beyond the epistemological benefit, we need the companionship of others so that we can unify our strength to address the complex and enormous challenge before us. Through ecumenical cooperation in services, advocacy, educational programs, organization and mobilization, and building alternative communi-ties, the church can contribute to the creation of a culture of peace. Through many of its intentional communities, the church can present models that give people a foretaste of what it means to live in a peace-ful community.

CHURCH: AN EMPOWERED COMMUNITY OF PEACEBUILDERS

While it is true, as an old saying goes, that "absolute power corrupts absolutely," it is also true that powerlessness corrupts and can be cor-rupted absolutely. When people feel powerless, they can submit easily to cynicism and to any corrupt power. Michael Lerner even makes the point that the problem is not so much the absence of power, but what he calls "surplus powerlessness."[58] When people feel that they are powerless, they become even more powerless than they actually are. The members of the Body of Christ are not an exception. In many peace advocacy works, such as writing letters to the U.S. Congress, it is not uncommon to hear church members say, "It is not going to make

56. Ibid., 97.

57. Panikkar, *Cultural Disarmament,* 36.

58. Lerner cited in Stockwell, "Cathedrals of Power," 85.

any difference." A critical way to counter cynicism, powerlessness, and hopelessness is in people's empowerment. When people realize that they are not powerless and that they have a different form of power (not military arsenals and huge budgets), they are empowered to act on their deepest convictions and hope. The church can perform its mission of peacebuilding only when it is empowered to do so.

Empowering the peacebuilding mission of a congregation through education is an obvious place to begin. Education is surely an endless task, and it requires more than what people normally receive from Sunday School. In addition to providing theological grounding for peace, a congregation's peacebuilding education program needs to include the learning of social analytical tools. These are critical tools for understanding a conflictive situation beyond its symptoms. These tools are helpful in understanding the context as a whole as well as in understanding the particular factors and players, power dynamics, what connects and divides, and the local capacity. They also help people see the connections of the many expressions of violence, such as structural violence and secondary form of violence. In addition to social analytical tools, the members of the congregation (though at different levels) need to have a basic knowledge of the many approaches or the nexus of peacebuilding approaches. This includes, according to Lisa Schirch, (1) waging conflict non-violently: monitoring and advocacy, direct action, and civilian-based defense; (2) reducing direct violence: legal and justice systems, humanitarian assistance, peacekeeping, military intervention, cease-fire agreements, peace zones, and early warning programs; (3) transforming relationships: trauma healing, conflict transformation, restorative justice, transitional justice, governance, and policymaking; and (4) building capacity: training and education, development, military conversion, research, and evaluation. Furthermore, members of a peace-church need to develop skills in dealing with conflicts in non-violent ways, skills in reducing direct violence, skills in transforming relationships (e.g., conflict transformation, trauma healing, principled negotiation, mediation, and restorative justice, etc.), skills in capacity building and relational skills (self-reflection, active listening, diplomatic and assertive speaking, appreciative inquiry, creative-problem solving, dialogue, negotiation, and mediation).[59]

59. Schirch, *Strategic Peacebuilding*.

Knowledge and skills become knowledge and skills only when they are integrated into the whole life of the congregation and only in the wakefulness of daily living and organized action.[60] The whole ethos of church life must cultivate a peace identity, a peaceful life, and peacebuilding skills. Peace must be incorporated into the worship life of the church and all liturgical celebrations. Major holidays, such as Memorial Day, 4th of July, Veterans Day, Thanksgiving Day, and the Christmas season need to be transformed from occasions for narrow nationalism, destructive militarism, and devouring consumerism into occasions for the building of a peaceful and sustainable world. Sermons, prayer, confessions, and the choice of hymns must be critiqued in light of their contribution to a peaceful life. What happens in the worship life must find support and reinforcement in other church activities, such as network building and advocacy. Moreover, the church must be a resource and a support for members and the wider community in living out the gospel of peace.

CHURCH: NURTURER OF A PEACEFUL HEART

Thich Nhat Hanh narrates a story about a walk for peace that he participated in New York. Because his group was slow in walking, the groups behind started to walk past them with impatience. "Many people like to participate in walks for peace," says Thich Nhat Hanh, but "there is no walk for peace; peace must be the walk . . . The practice is simply to embody peace during the walk. The means are the ends."[61] In our hurry to arrive at something better—peace, we do violence to that which we aspire toward, and we do violence to ourselves and to all those whom we encounter in our journey. We become ungrateful to those who have graced our lives, and we become unsatisfied with small accomplishments. In our hurry to something better, everything we desire falls from our hands and, ultimately, we fail to notice God.

If we are concerned about peace, we must embody peace in our lives; we must nurture as individuals and as communities a peaceful heart; we must cultivate a spirituality of peace. A peaceful heart is simple (not simplistic) in the sense of being undivided. It is not carried away by a multitude of conflicting concerns. The frenzy of activism, as

60. For strategies for building identity as a peacemaking church, see Lintner, "Building a Peacemaking Church," 165–78.

61. Hanh, *Creating True Peace*, 64–65. Slightly modified.

Thomas Merton reminds us, "neutralizes [our] work for peace. It destroys [our] own inner capacity for peace. It destroys the fruitfulness of [our] own work, because it kills the root of inner wisdom which makes work fruitful."[62] Cultivating our own spirituality of peace is crucial for the peace of the wider society; it is not only for the self. A peaceful heart will always have bearings on the outside world. If most people first learn the culture of violence at home, then there is enough reason why we should start learning peace at home and in our own selves. There is violence around us and we do not have full control of our surroundings, but we can choose how to respond. We can choose peace only as we practice the spirituality of peace. In choosing peace in the midst of violence we are creating that space that will become our entry point in breaking the cycle of violence.

SEEDS OF PEACE, SEEDS OF HOPE

I started this chapter with a story about our society's failure to nurture us in peaceful ways and the escalation of violence in our globalized world, but that is not the end of the narrative. While it is true that training in peaceful ways is lacking, it is not totally absent. Although the environment that I grew up with was and still is mired by violence, my parents and the church did not fail completely to impart the ways of peace, particularly in standing for justice and human dignity. As a child, I learned to stand up against the big elementary school bully, and I also learned to forgive. Individuals and communities have risen from the ashes of violence embodying and planting seeds of peace—seeds of hope.

A couple of images come to mind as I think about seeds of hope, seeds of peace. One image is that of a body of a downed World War II fighter plane that sat at the back of my uncle's house. My uncle cut portions of its body and made them into woks or frying pans. For several years we had a wok that came from the body of a fighter plane. By the gift of hindsight, I now realize that he made an instrument of war into an instrument for cooking—an instrument of peace. In a similar spirit, I remember that our barrio *kapelya* (chapel) converted the empty shell of a huge World War II bomb into a bell to gather people for church events. Again, an instrument of war was converted into an instrument of worship, into an instrument of peace. These images

62. Merton, *Conjectures of a Guilty Bystander*, 73.

reconnect me to the prophecies of the Old Testament prophets when they spoke of the coming of shalom when instruments of war will be converted into instruments of peace (Is 2:4; Mi 4:3). These images of peace have found embodiments in individuals and communities around the world. Their stories of embodying peace need to be told if we are to nurture cultures of peace.

Earlier in this chapter I noted the complicity of the church in the killings of Tutsis in Rwanda, a complicity that involved the top hierarchy of the church. That is only one side of the story. There is another side: it is a story of individuals and parishes who took the risk and some paid dearly for their commitment to the Christ of peace. The Episcopal parish of Gahini, consistent with its tradition of offering sanctuary for all those in danger, provided sanctuary for Tutsis running for their lives. Rev. Simon Banyanga, a Hutu, encouraged his parishioners to hide Tutsi refugees in the church. A similar story happened in the parish of Kaduha, Gikongoro province. Survivors are grateful for the work of a German nun, Sr. Milgitha Kosser, who fed, hid, and helped refugees to escape for safety. Not all survived to tell the tragic story. After the genocide, Sr. Milgitha and other survivors worked to put up a memorial for the twenty-thousand Tutsis who lost their lives at Kaduha church.[63]

There were those, however, who paid dearly for their commitment to the gospel of peace. Among the most celebrated martyrs of the Rwandan genocide are Felicité Niyitegeka, a Roman Catholic lay worker, and Fr. Jean Bosco Munyaneza, both Hutus. Both died under similar circumstances. When the genocide began, Felicité worked to provide Tutsi refugees with their basic needs, and she helped some to escape for safety. She refused to leave the Tutsi refugees at St. Pierre Center and so died with them when the Hutus attacked. Fr. Munyaneza suffered a similar fate. He was told by the advancing Hutus to abandon the Tutsis, but he refused and stayed with them as a good shepherd to his flock. Fr. Munyaneza and Felicité died as martyrs. In 2001 Felicité was recognized as a national hero.[64]

Another story of hope occurred in the Middle East. The life of Isaac Saada, a teacher who was involved in peace education in Israel and Palestine, exemplifies what it means to embody peace. His own

---

63. Cejka and Bamat, *Artisans of Peace*, 150–51.
64. Ibid.

children asked him how he could possibly work with the Israelis after all that the Palestinians have been through for years. He responded: "We have had to believe in peace and that peace would eventually come." Pursuing this point further, he said: "The worst thing that could happen to them and to the Palestinian people would be if they filled their hearts with hatred." Not long after saying these words, Isaac Saada died in a shelling that was meant for the so-called terrorist.[65]

In that same war-torn region of the world another seed of hope is the work of Rapprochement Center at Beit Sahour in Palestine. This Rapprochement Center was organized in 1990 under the auspices of the Mennonite Central Committee. The work actually began two years earlier when the community of Beit Sahour began inviting groups of Israelis to their town for discussions, worship, and meal-sharing for the purpose of breaking down the stereotypes between the two peoples. To make sure that the experience was positive, the community of Beit Sahour was organized to prevent violence when the visitors were present. There have been threats to the existence of the Rapprochement Center, such as harassment and killings by Israeli soldiers of Palestinians and suicide bombings by Palestinians, but the Rapprochement Center has continued as a testimony that there is another way besides violence.[66]

These are only a few of the many stories of hope around the world. There is no easy promise of success, but seeds of peace and seeds of hope are sprouting everywhere. The seeds sprout in the hearts of those who have not accepted the culture of violence as normal and inevitable; they sprout in the hearts of those who have mustered the courage to walk the peace in a world tyrannized by violence; they sprout in the hearts of those who have dared to live the hope of peace in the present in acts of empathy and forgiveness; and they sprout in the lives of those who have dared to tear down walls of fear and division. We can see the seeds and signs of hope in the hearts of those who have continued to believe and hope that peace is our future.

65. Moore, "Wounds of Hurt," 324.
66. Peck, "The Palestinian Center for Rapproachment," 96–109.

8

The Church as a Community of Radical Hospitality

Diaspora and the Strangers in Our Midst

I BEGIN THIS CHAPTER with a few vignettes or brief stories of real diaspora experiences in order to put a face on what appears as cold and, perhaps, numbing statistics. Behind the statistics are the lives of real persons who are participants in the massive phenomenon of global migration of peoples. Their stories need to be told so we can understand what we have become as a global society, and so we can explore ways to reclaim our social agency in the complex web of global socio-political and economic interactions in which we live our lives. Let us listen to the words of a diaspora:

> I never dreamed I would end up a domestic helper in Hong Kong. I had to leave my family because the salary I earned back home would not allow me and my family to live decently. I've been here for more than six years now. I want to return home but I cannot. No job awaits me there . . . each time I try to start saving (part of my salary), the price of oil at home rises. I am stuck.[1]

Turning to a migrant advocate, she said, "*Di ba, Ate? Para akong* toilet paper *sa tindahan? Kung mabili ka, okay. Kung hindi, diyan ka lang. At pag nabili ka naman, pagkagamit sa iyo, tapon ka na lang. Hindi ka naman kinukupkop.*" [Is it not true, Big sister, that I am like a roll of toilet paper in a store? If I am not sold, I remain on the shelf; if

---

1. Cited in Ruiz, "Diaspora," 39–59.

someone buys me, I get used up and thrown away afterwards. I am not cared for . . .].[2]

The plight and dream of this nameless Filipina domestic is shared by many diaspora people around the world. It is shared by Andrea, a sex worker from Sosúa, Dominican Republic. Though her immediate circumstances, opportunities, and values may be different from the nameless Filipina domestic helper, they both participate in the larger narrative of global diaspora, and they both share a common dream of moving out of a miserable situation toward a better life. Denise Brennan describes Andrea's life story of migration in this way.

> On the eve of her departure for Germany to marry her German client-turned-boyfriend, Andrea, a Dominican sex worker, spent the night with her Dominican boyfriend. When I dropped by the next morning to wish her well, her Dominican boyfriend was still asleep. She stepped outside, onto her porch. She could not lie about her feelings for her soon-to-be husband. "No," she said, "it's not love." . . . Andrea, like many Dominican sex workers in Sosúa, a small town on the north coast of the Dominican Republic, makes a distinction between marriage *por amor* (for love) and marriage *por residencia* (for visas). After all, why waste a marriage Certificate on romantic love when it can be translated into a visa to a new land and economic security?[3]

Likewise, the plight and dreams of the nameless Filipina domestic helper in Hong Kong and Andrea (sex worker from Dominican Republic) are shared by Veronica, a single mother of a 14-year-old boy. She lives with her sister and brother-in-law in Mexico City. Like many Mexicans, she dreams of leaving poor Mexico and crossing the northern border into the U.S. "*Pobre Mexico. Tan lejos de Dios y tan cerca de los Estados Unidos*" (Poor Mexico. So far from God and so near to the United States) is a common expression heard on the Mexico-U.S. border.[4]

In July of 2002, she made a decision to cross the border to "El Norte" (U.S.) with her nephew. Taking a bus to Northern Sonora, just south of the Arizona border, they and others, with the help of a "coyote" (a paid smuggler), attempted to cross the Sonoran desert. They began

2. Ibid.

3. Brennan, "Selling Sex," 154.

4. See Gill, *Borderlinks*, vi.

hiking late in the afternoon, although the temperature was still above 100 degrees Fahrenheit. They faced numerous potential dangers: untrustworthy coyote, dehydration or heat stroke, poisonous snakes, and "la migra" (the U.S. Border Patrol), as well as losing both their elusive hopes and all of the money they had invested in their journey.

After hiking all night and much of the day, Veronica began to feel weak and nauseous. Fighting a pounding headache, she could no longer keep up with the group. She had the classic signs of heatstroke. Her nephew stayed with her, while the rest of the group went ahead. Eventually, Veronica collapsed. Her nephew waited until dusk when the desert was a little cooler, and then began to carry his aunt vaguely in the direction he believed would take him to the nearest highway. Someone must have found them, for eventually they ended up in the emergency room of a Tucson Hospital. Finally, more than two weeks after her attempt to cross the border, the Mexican consulate helped to purchase a plane ticket for her to return to Mexico.

While waiting for her flight back to Mexico, Rick Ufford-Chase of BorderLinks, a program that educates people on Mexico-U.S. border issues, interviewed her. "Knowing what you now know," he asked her, "would you recommend others try and cross the border without documents?" Veronica was thoughtful about her answer. "In the end," she whispered, "I don't really feel like I have any other way to provide my son with the future he deserves. There is no work that will pay me enough to keep him in school, and there is little chance that his life will be any better than my own."[5]

These three stories are distinct, but they share several elements in common. While the specific contexts and circumstances of each person differ, they all are undergirded by the same global socio-economic and political dynamics of interaction. All three stories are woven by a shared overarching narrative and their themes resonate with each other. They all identify situations or circumstances that make them "stuck" (Filipina domestic helper) and from which they are struggling to be freed. An element of personal "choice" is present, but it is a "choice" the circumstances have forced on them. By no means is it a decision or "choice" that issues from the barrel of a gun; nonetheless, it is a forced one given that there are no promising options available closer to home. Andrea's "choice" may be seen in this light when she

---

5. Story narrated by Rick Ufford-Chase in Gill, *Borderland Theology*, vii–viii.

made the decision in favor of marriage for a visa (*por residencia*) and economic security instead of marriage for love (*por amor*), which she also cares about but is fully aware that such a marriage would make her a prisoner of her current circumstances. Compounding the "forced" choice, especially in the case of Veronica, is the pain of making a "choice" between two equally cherished values: to be with one's children to care and guide them, or to leave them for the sake of earning money for their education so they might have a better future.

I have heard of similar circumstances and encountered people with similar stories in my travels in Hong Kong, Tokyo, Seoul, Milan, Rome, Amsterdam, Utrecht, and in the place where I currently reside, Minnesota. Further, I have had the fascination of crossing national borders. While in Honduras, upon knowing that the Guatemalan border was only a few miles from the place we were visiting (Cópan Ruinas), I asked my host, Linda Hanson, that we cross to the Guatemalan side. I also had the opportunity to cross the border from Tucson, Arizona to the Mexico side of the Sonoran desert with the help of BorderLinks. Unlike Veronica, however, I took this trip as a privileged academician wanting to see what is on the other side. Even if I could say that my crossing was motivated by the noble idea of seeking to understand life on the other side in order that I could write and educate my mostly Caucasian students in Minnesota about it, still my crossing of the Sonoran desert came out of my privileged location. As much as I try to, I cannot fully understand what it is like to cross the border like Veronica.

Yet, even if my context and social location are different from Veronica, Andrea, and the nameless Filipina, writing about diaspora is not foreign to my own life and that of my siblings at some points in their lives. Out of eight brothers and sisters, only three have not experienced either being a migrant worker or an immigrant. This includes my older sister, who has never been a migrant worker herself, but was, for many years, supported by a migrant worker husband (sailor). Additionally, while writing this chapter in early 2008, I received a "text message" on my cellular phone from my brother informing me that he was working in Dubai, United Arab Emirates. Writing about diaspora, then, is much more than an academic or intellectual exercise; as I write about Veronica, Andrea, the nameless Filipina domestic worker, and others, I speak out of my own experience, my very own diaspora life, as one who is momentarily located in the U.S.

DIASPORA: A CONDITION AND DISCOURSE

The stories of Veronica, Andrea, and the Filipina domestic helper are just a few of the many true tales of diaspora. Diaspora (*diaspeiro*— scattering of seeds), in its common and loose usage, is the scattering of people from one place to another. It is often equated with the term migration. I embrace this common usage (migration) as part of the notion of diaspora, but diaspora is broader than this while specific enough to name a distinctive reality. Diaspora is a condition of people as well as a discourse. My discourse on diaspora embraces this common notion of migration (regardless of conditions, reasons, and intentions of "going home" literally or mythically). The general notion of migration includes various categories or types, such as migrants, immigrants, refugees, *au pairs*, students, tourists, and global investors. This chapter does not deal with the experience of the last two groups (tourists and global investors). Although they are expressions of globalization, I have excluded them, not for the sake of limiting my focus, but because they do not fit into my specific notion of diaspora.

Beyond this general notion, diaspora is about the experience of uprootedness, dispersion, displacement, and dislocation as well as the search for roots and connections. In addition, diaspora includes transnational relations or linkages (either to the original homeland or, laterally, with its counterpart overseas communities across the world) involving people, money, goods, services, information, and, in particular, religious practices. It includes as well (im)migrants' constructions of identity, belonging, home, and what it means to live together in the world that has become, for the diaspora people, not simply limited or bounded by the territory of one's country of origin. This diasporic construction of identity, belonging, and what it means to dwell together is perceived more acutely as a matter of human (social/ political) agency, especially when the host country challenges one's way of being and dwelling.[6] In this sense, diaspora not only signifies uprootedness, dispersal, displacement, and dislocation; it is a political discourse or, more particularly, a resistance discourse. The location of this resistance discourse has "now shifted," in Edward Said's words, "from the settled, established, and domesticated dynamics of culture to its unhoused, decentered, and exilic energies whose incarnation today is the migrant, and whose consciousness is that of the intellec-

6. Okamura, *Imagining the Filipino*, 13–29.

tual and artist in exile, the political figure between domains, between forms, between homes, and between languages."[7]

DIASPORA: A PERVASIVE PHENOMENON IN OUR GLOBALIZED WORLD

The diaspora of people all over the world has intensified at an alarming rate in recent years. While not a new phenomenon, the massive diaspora of people that we have witnessed in our times is more than a simple continuation of the migration patterns from the ancient past. It is a creature of modernity, colonialism, and postmodernity, particularly through the predatory global market. Modernity, the much-celebrated age of progress and reason, not only conquered, butchered, and colonized, but also uprooted and dispersed large segments of the native population. Many of those who survived the swords and guns of the conquerors were not fortunate enough to survive from the diseases brought by the conquerors, such as the case of the indigenous people of America and the Pacific islands.[8] In addition, many of those who did survive the sword and diseases did so only to suffer dislocation and displacement. A critical reading of the history of the encounter (*encuentro*) or, more appropriately, clash (*encontronazo*), between the forces of the imperializing West (global North) and people of the global South reveals that after discovery, conquest, colonization, and exploitation comes diaspora.[9]

I hasten to add that the dislocation and displacement that conquest and colonization bring do not always mean physical diaspora. In some instances, it is the nation-state borders that move. As in the case of the early Mexicans in California and Texas, it was not them who came to the U.S.; rather, it was the U.S. that came to them. Similarly, on a recent trip to Wroclaw, Poland (over the years Wroclaw was once part of Austria, Bohemia, Prussia or Germany) our host, Probst Andrzej Fober, spoke of how his ancestors had acquired multiple na-

---

7. Said, *Culture and Imperialism*, 403.

8. A well-documented case is the plight of the Kanaka Maoli (indigenous Hawaiians). With the introduction of whooping cough, influenza (1824–1826), mumps (1839), leprosy (1840), measles (1845–1849), smallpox (1853), and scarlet fever (1870), the Kanaka Maoli population of 135,000 (1824) was reduced to 43,000 (1893).

9. See Segovia, "Aliens in the Promised Land," 16.

tional identities even while staying in the same place. At one point, he said, they were Austrians, then Polish, then Germans, and then Polish. Clearly, national and ethnic identities are political constructs and can be fluid.

Except for certain places in the Pacific and the Caribbean, the era of direct colonization is over. Decolonization started with colonized countries in Latin America gaining independence from Spain, even while countries in Africa were being occupied and partitioned by colonial powers during the period that has been called the Scramble for Africa (1880–1914). In light of this context, it is no longer adequate to see diaspora as a direct result of conquest and colonization. With nation-states gaining independence and acting as the main players in international relations, nation-states also became the major players in facilitating the flow of people.

Today, however, again, we are undergoing a major change in which not only is the notion of nation-state under assault but also, as Stephen Castles suggests, the notion of citizenship and rights based on nation-states is being challenged.[10] We are now in the era of a unified global market and transnational global capitalism. So even where continuity in patterns of migration exists and the reasons for migration have not changed, the era of transnational global capitalism calls us to interpret diaspora in significantly new ways. Nation-states still play a crucial role, but it is the global market—through transnational corporations and transnational institutions (e.g., the World Trade Organization)—that has become the major player in the movement of capital, goods, services, and people. The global market is now the prime mover: it facilitates the exchange of commodities (e.g., goods, services, and people) and accords them their exchange value. With market exchange as the prime mover of people and the arbiter of value, it is but consistent, for example, that even what is commonly called prostitution is now seen in the context of sex trade and prostitutes as sex workers (laborers).

Intertwined with the predatory global market, various forms of political instability, such as human rights violation, persecution, and particularly war have triggered massive migration. In addition, wedded with socio-economic and political factors, environmental disasters have triggered massive migration. Environmental disasters have

10. See Castles, *Ethnicity and Globalization.*

displaced communities and forced them to migrate to other places both within and outside their country. The existence of island nations such as Maldives and Tuvalu are at stake due to the rising sea level as a result of global warming. The "environmental refugee" now joins the classic "political refugee."[11]

TENSIONS FROM MULTIPLE FRONTS: "BACK HOME," "NEW HOME," AND "ON THE ROAD"

When millions of people migrate from one country to another to resettle, these hordes of newcomers threaten the inhabitants of the receiving countries and intensify anti-immigrant sentiments. In various parts of the world, we have witnessed the rise of racist and xenophobic hostilities directed against newcomers. We have witnessed the rise of racism not only in rhetoric but also in legislation and the rise of hate crimes and police brutalities against newcomers and racial-ethnic minorities. The influx of diaspora people has threatened not only the dominant groups but also the already marginalized indigenous people. The interests of diaspora and indigenous people—uprooted, dislocated, dispersed, and marginalized by the same predatory global market and imperial projects—seem to be on a collision course. We can take the case of diaspora Filipinos in Guam and the *I Man Chamoru*, the Indo-Fijians and the native Fijians, and the Vietnamese in relation to the Kanaks of New Caledonia. The Kanaks (natives) perceive the influx of Vietnamese refugees as part of France's strategy to suppress their struggle for independence and, even worse, as a form of "genocide by substitution."[12] Compounding the xenophobia and racism of the dominant group and the tension between diaspora and the marginalized indigenous people is the tension between diaspora/ethnic communities. A painful example took place in South Central Los Angeles when Korean Americans saw the fruits of their years of labor turned into ashes by African Americans.

The experience and stories of diaspora people are mixed. Many are barely surviving, and others have acquired fortunes. Some immigrants have broken the glass ceiling in their adopted homelands. Yet, even after years have passed the sense of homelessness and the desire to go "back home" seems, for many diaspora people, not to fade away

11. Ibid., 129.
12. Uregei, "The Kanak Struggle," 66–69.

totally; it continues to shape their lives. The accomplished Filipina novelist Jessica Hagedorn writes: "I will probably write about the culture of exile and homesickness in one form or another until the day I die; it is my personal obsession, and it fuels my work."[13]

Meanwhile, "back home" (in migrants' country of origin), family life faces several challenges even as money flows to support the family. Though many diasporia families may adjust, the absence of a husband or a wife causes strain in the marriage. Weak relationships are all the more susceptible to stresses. One example is the story of Romeo (not his real name) and his wife. I had the opportunity to interview Romeo, an undocumented migrant, at a birthday party in Amsterdam in the Netherlands. He came to the Netherlands through the help of a wealthy relative who is operating a few "windows" (prostitution windows) in the Red Light District of Amsterdam. Before his move to the Netherlands, Romeo worked in Saudi Arabia for a construction company. He left his wife and son in Manila. While working in Saudi Arabia, his wife traveled to the U.S. on a tourist visa. Before her U.S. visa expired, she married a U.S. citizen in order that she could stay permanently in the U.S. Romeo heard all this unpleasant news while in Saudi Arabia. Compounding the pain of Romeo is that his former wife was able to bring their son to the United States. With sadness, Romeo shared that he had not seen his son for several years.

Also, what about the children? Even if many studies have shown that children of diaspora parents, in general, are adjusting well, we cannot discount the effects of the absence of one (especially, in most cases, the "transnational mother") or both parents on the children's development. The ability of each family to adjust depends on many factors, but most, to the presence of a strong family support network, such as surrogate parenting.[14]

The cost of diaspora on marital relation and the rearing of children is only one of the many aspects that need to be addressed. The social consequences of diaspora for the context back home are numerous, and beyond what I can attend to in this chapter. One case is the relationship of diaspora and the spread of HIV/AIDS. By no means am I claiming that this relationship is a relationship of cause and effect, but that diaspora contributes to the pandemic. Charles

13. Hagedorn, "The Exile Within," 178.
14. See Parreñas, "The Care Crisis in the Philippines," 39–54.

Hunt has noted that the terrible economic condition in Central and Southern Africa and the heavy reliance on migrant labor triggered the breakdown of family and sexual patterns, leading to the explosion of both prostitution and sexually transmitted diseases, a situation only worsened by the appearance of the HIV/AIDS virus. As Hunt puts it, "AIDS had, as a consequence of the migrant labor pattern of labor organization and the capitalist takeover of rural African agriculture, a ready population which suffered from an unusually high level of sexually transmitted diseases."[15]

FROM DIASPORA VIA BABEL TO PENTECOST: JOURNEY, PASSAGE, AND VISION

What is diaspora's challenge to our globalized world? Where is it leading us? What is it suggesting about who we are and what we are called to be about? Toward what possibilities and openings is it luring us? Where do we see these possibilities and openings? What are the signs of the times? How do we prepare ourselves so that we can be more receptive and pro-active in helping to midwife the new world? What imaginative frameworks do we need so we can transform the challenges into opportunities?

Diaspora, Babel, and Pentecost are three powerful biblical metaphors that capture the pain, struggle, and hope of diasporized people. To be sure, diaspora involves dislocation, disruption, displacement, homelessness, and marginalization, but that which is a cause of pain can also be a gift to the world. Before it can be a gift, though, the pain of diaspora must undergo the process of transformation and healing. When diaspora pain is reclaimed and transformed, it provides the condition and the possibility for birthing a new tomorrow as envisioned in the Pentecost. However, before this birthing can occur, there is a painful passage that we cannot evade—the deconstruction of Babel.

A familiar image, Babel is a symbol of imperial praxis, centralized, and cultural homogenization, particularly through mono-language. It is a symbol of "settled life" guaranteed by imperial power. What we must keep in mind is that the "myth" itself of the Tower of Babel is a creation of the diasporized Israelites vis-à-vis the Babylonian imperial myth—the Mesopotamian myth Enuma Elish. It was deployed by the diasporized people not to extol the Babylonian lords and their

15. Hunt, "Africa and AIDS," 3.

epic achievements but, ironically, to subvert the mono-language (discourse) or "univocal linguistic code" of the Babylonian empire.[16] If imperial control can thrive only through maintenance of a univocal linguistic code, then subversion's way must take the form of confusing and disrupting—through various linguistic codes—the empire's communication network. Lest we ourselves get confused, we can be effective in our subversive acts of confusing and disrupting imperial univocal discourse only when we do them with utter clarity, not by adopting a vague and confusing, to paraphrase Mark Lewis Taylor, "obscurantist poco/pomo-speak" regarding "alterity" and "difference" that dulls the liberationist edge of postcolonial-diasporic discourse.[17]

Diaspora—through the deconstruction of babylonian univocal linguistic codes and transgression of imperial hierarchical-binary categories—has now created an opening for the realization of the "originative" polyglossia of the Pentecost which has been aborted throughout history by imperializing projects under various brand names: babelization, hellenization, globalatinization, anglobalization, and McDonaldization. Pentecost confronts us with a choice: Which moral vision will be normative for us? Imperializing Babel or Pentecost? "[W]hat the new diaspora does," in R. S. Sugirthajah's words, "is challenge the old Kiplingesque paradigm of East is East and West is West, with no possibility of the two meeting, no possibility of weaving the religious and cultural traditions from home into the complex and varied cultures of the host country."[18]

What usually comes to mind when people hear or read about the Pentecost story is the "miracle of the tongue": the speaking of many languages. Wherever diaspora people are, so are many languages present. In this regard, diaspora has been an agent of the Pentecostal "miracle of the tongue." The Pentecost, however, is not primarily a "miracle of the tongue." More than that, it is a "miracle of the ear."[19] If we read the account with care (Acts 2: 6–12), we find that it is about a miracle of hearing, of understanding and, therefore, of caring and building a just, abundant, colorful, and sustainable tomorrow.

16. Croatto, "A Reading of the Story of the Tower of Babel," 203–23. Also, see Fernandez, "From Babel to Pentecost."

17. Taylor, "Spirit and Liberation," 46.

18. Sugirtharajah, *Postcolonial Criticism*, 185.

19. Wink and Keener-Wink, cited in Law, *The Wolf Shall Dwell with the Lamb*, 45–51.

We need to let the opening occasioned by diaspora lead us to the vision of the Pentecost by following the clue of the Pentecostal spirit—a spirit that blows and flows wherever it wills, jarring as well as transgressing our fixed, stable, pure, and ordered categories. Perhaps, it is here that hybridity complements diaspora in opening the creative "Third Space of enunciation" that Homi Bhabha speaks of in order that the vision of the Pentecost can be given birth.[20] What I see as the greatest threat, if not already wreaking havoc in our personal lives, *res publica*, and the global commons, is not so much "social contamination" as the defense of hierarchical, exclusionary, and binary categories of the pure against the impure, the stable against the transient, the solid against the fluid as well as the native against the alien/strange. The "clash of fundamentalisms" that finds its translation in terrorism and counter-terrorism is but one notorious example.[21] What diaspora-hybridity does is to subvert the purist/essentialist/binary/exclusionary foundation of sinister and violent fundamentalism, both religious and secular.

Diaspora-hybridity offers a way of articulating our longing for and vision of a just, colorful, abundant, and sustainable society.[22] Multiculturalism, a model that has gained wider acceptance vis-à-vis the melting-pot or assimilation, continues to operate on the assumption of a pure and fixed culture juxtaposed with others and, as is often the case, leaves the socio-economic inequality untouched. Diapora-hybridity helps us move beyond assimilation, multicultural-ism, "nativism," and postmodernistic celebration of difference which is oblivious of power relations. It is an antidote to nativism that "seeks to eradicate any form of impurity in the indigenous culture" and to the "postmodernist notions of hybridity" that "tend to sweep under the carpet the cultural and political impact of colonialism."[23] In this regard, diaspora-hybridity pursues the aspirations and struggles of the colonized and those who are marginalized by other forms of oppressive practices. It also stands in continuity with liberation movements in their insistence that no amount of postmodernist discursive suturing is enough unless we alter the reigning social relations of

---

20. Bhabha, *The Location of Culture*, 37.

21. Ali, *The Clash of Fundamentalisms*.

22. See Segovia, "Aliens in the Promised Land," 16.

23. Sugirtharajah, *Postcolonial Criticism*, 194.

production or, in the version of E. San Juan Jr., unless we "historicize power relations in concrete material conditions of production and reproduction."[24] Though diaspora-hybridity stands in continuity with liberation movements, it is not timid in exposing some of the shortcomings of liberation hermeneutics.

THE CHURCH AND THE CHALLENGE OF THE DIASPORA

How shall the church respond to the diaspora in our midst? How shall we respond to the cries of sojourners and exiles? What projects shall we embark on that are more effective in addressing the underlying reasons of people's migration? These are important questions. Nevertheless, we need to ask deeper and more pointed questions. The diaspora-stranger directs us, as Lester Edwin Ruiz puts it, not only to the question, "What is to be done?" but also to the questions: "Who are we, what [do] we hope for, and where [do] we go?" or "What does it mean to be a people under the conditions of Diaspora?"[25]

These are central questions that we must address if we are to take the diaspora challenge seriously. I direct the above questions to the church: "What does it mean to be a church under the conditions of diaspora?" Or, put differently, how shall we reimagine ecclesiology (doctrine of the church) under the conditions of diaspora? Diaspora poses a challenge to how the church must think of itself and how it must respond ethically to its current context, particularly to the presence of the Divine in the form of a stranger. Here, I present the diaspora not simply as someone whom we must see as a stranger who needs our kindness and help, but as someone who calls us to take account of who we are as a church.

RECLAIMING THE CHURCH'S DIASPORA-EKKLĒSIA IDENTITY

If the current diaspora phenomenon cannot be understood apart from hegemonic, imperializing, and globalizing power, neither can the church. The existence of the early Christian communities cannot be understood apart from their relation to the imperializing and globalatinizing power of its time—the Roman Empire. If the current

24. San Juan, "Postcolonial Dialogics," 70; also see McLaren, *Revolutionary Multiculturalism*.

25. Ruiz, "Diaspora," 50.

massive diaspora is a product of modern imperializing powers and of postmodern emergent Empire (in capital letters—Hardt and Negri) the church shares a similar plight.[26] The early Christian communities were communities diasporized by the Roman Empire, and the contemporary church continues to be shaped by imperializing powers (e.g., U.S.) and the global predatory market Empire. Diaspora and the church share common roots as the creation, product, and refuse of imperializing powers. When Christianity opened its young mouth, its language was shaped and informed by empire. If Christian diaspora communities were born in the crucible of empire, then there is no church's beginning outside of imperial condition, no pre-imperial Christianity.

Even as the early Christian diaspora communities were a product of Roman imperial order, they also stood in opposition to the empire of their time—many times using and mimicking imperial logic while at the same time subverting it. The early Christian diaspora communities were "alternative communities" (*ekklēsiai*) vis-à-vis the Roman imperial order, with roots in Israel's opposition to the *pax Romana*. "Ironic as it may seem," Richard Horsley pointed out regarding the *ekklēsiai* established by the Apostle Paul, "precisely where he is borrowing from or alluding to 'imperial' language, we can discern that Paul's gospel stands counter primarily to the Roman imperial order."[27]

Of course, as institutions and social movements respond to their environment, self-understanding undergoes change, and the early Christian communities were no exception. When the Christian diaspora communities earned the blessings of a "settled" life under the auspices of the Roman Empire, they slowly began to lose their diaspora-*ekklēsiai* identity. This "settled" mentality was reinforced under the auspices of modern Western colonial powers. In the colonization process the church's diasporic identity was overcome by the "settled," and its "originative" polyglossia was overcome, says Catherine Keller, by imperial theo-logos: "a metaphysical Babel of unity, an identity that homogenizes the multiplicities it absorbs, that either excludes or subordinates every creaturely other, *alter*, subaltern."[28] This colonized and colonializing church accompanied imperial conquests and diasporiz-

---

26. Hardt and Negri, *Empire*.

27. Horsley, *Paul and Empire*, 7.

28. Keller, "The Love of Postcolonialism," 223.

ing projects, and its local converts acted as "native informants" for the empire. By no means is the colonized and colonializing church over, for it has mutated into new globalizing forms with churches around the world acting as local "franchises" of global Christianity.[29]

We need to exhume and resurrect the diaspora-*ekklēsia* identity of the church, if the church is to be true to itself and if it is to have a future. When I say exhume and resurrect, I mean making diaspora a permanent posture or marker of the church's identity, not a temporary condition that we hope to overcome someday. This is different from Miroslav Volf's view that departure is a "temporary state" and that "departures without some sense of an origin and a goal are not departures" but "incessant roaming, just as streams that flow in all directions at one and the same time are not streams but, in the end, a swamp in which all movement has come to a steady rest."[30] To assume a diaspora identity (not a temporary condition) does not mean that one has no sense of "departure" or "beginning" and no sense of "arrival" or "ending"; rather, it underscores the point that there is no absolute or stable departure and arrival. In other words, there is no "un-originated origin" from which we can start life; we are born in the middle of things. When we search deeper, we find that beginnings are not absolute, pure or stable; neither are endings. For, beginnings are always beginnings from somewhere before me—before my own time, and endings are constantly new beginnings. The moment we think about endings, we are commencing already. It is in this context of the ever-flowing stream (not Volf's swamp) that human beings discover and exercise their subjectivity and agency, not outside of it. Subjectivity and agency are present when human beings construct their sense of "departures" and "arrivals" amidst the flow, not outside in some imagined stable and stagnant world.

Volf seems to think that the only way to talk about subjectivity and agency is to step outside of the continuing flow of history, which is not only not necessary but impossible as well. This is what he did in an effort to underscore Abraham's agency in response to the Divine call to go forth. But in doing so, he not only removes Abraham from the ever-flowing movement of history (like a fish out of the water), he reads the story as if Abraham had figured out in advance the religious

29. See Bellagamba, *Mission and Ministry*, 33.
30. Volf, *Exclusion and Embrace*, 41.

significance of his diaspora. He fails to understand that this is a story born out of discernment, and that his reading is a reading from hindsight. For the common flesh and blood migrants, recognizing their plight as a point of Divine call is most often the product of reflection in the midst of being thrown into and tossed about by the waves of the diasporic sea.

I presented this point in length because it is critical for the church to see diaspora as a permanent posture (like the stranger which I will present later). This is critical for the healing of the church and for reclaiming the experience of diaspora. When it is perceived as a temporary condition in which the final aim is to "settle," it is not a surprise that it is a dreaded condition, with hurtful consequences in the church's attitude and practices toward the new diasporas.

DIASPORA, HYBRIDITY, AND CHURCH IDENTITY

If diaspora-hybridity points in the direction of global Pentecost, it also points in the direction of how the church must constitute itself. Sadly, it is true that the day Christians go to worship the one God is still the most segregated day of the week. Though many have joined established congregations, diaspora people continue to form "ethnic churches" or "ethnic parishes" or "multinational congregations" (e.g., Spanish-speakers from different countries of origin), not multicultural-multi-ethnic congregations.[31] Yet, to limit the notion of "ethnic congregations" to diaspora congregations is to think white (in the U.S. setting), which is to remain oblivious to the fact that white congregations *are* themselves ethnic congregations and that, for many years now, we have been worshipping in "ethnic enclave congregations." Many diaspora people have joined predominantly white ethnic churches, only to experience being melted or assimilated into "white ethnic enclave congregations." Of course, there is a difference between diasporia ethnic churches and dominant white ethnic churches in the way they have functioned in the lives of members. For diaspora ethnic communities, their churches have functioned as a "safe space" that affirms who they are and nourishes them as they face the challenges of a different and, sometimes, not always hospitable world. In this sense, diaspora ethnic congregations may always have its place in society.

---

31. Stepick, "God is Apparently Not Dead," 20.

Whether diaspora ethnic churches continue to remain or more multi-ethnic or pan-ethnic congregations will be the trend, diaspora-hybridity is creating an opening for the churches to become truly the church of all nations, celebrating difference and taking account of social inequalities seriously. Diaspora-hybridity opens this possibility as it transgresses and subverts "nativism" that is so beholden to the racial-ethnic purity that has made our churches racially segregated. As noted earlier, when our reality is characterized already by plurality, "nativism" stands in the way of preserving the pure over the threat of the impure, which the diaspora communities are often identified with. Diaspora-hybridity does not call for the erasure of our distinctive differences. Instead, it opens new possibilities of relationship and partnership in the Body of Christ by transgressing binary-hierarchical categories and by allowing freedom and fluidity. Diaspora-hybridity is open to mixtures and fusions and new configurations and the emergent, which is quite threatening to our well-guarded, following Michel Foucault, "order of things."[32] Of course, as Volf reminds us in his critique of Said's contrapuntal reading method, this is not sufficient by itself. "Concurrence of theologically and culturally closed views," he argues, "often reinforces the mutual exclusion of conflicting views, rather than enriching them."[33] Diaspora-hybridity maybe perceived as a threat, in which case, the common response is wall-building (e.g., nativism) or, in the worse scenario, the annihilation of the diaspora-hybrid—the other (e.g., ethnic cleansing). Yet diaspora-hybridity has prepared the soil: it has created the conditions for and has offered some clues of what it is like to be a church that embodies our plural reality, and what it is like to be a church that embodies the vision of the Pentecost. Diaspora-hybridity offers a starting point and a way toward the development of what Hannah Arendt calls an "enlarged way of thinking."[34]

DIASPORA CHURCH, CATHOLICITY, AND TRANSGLOCAL CONNECTIONS

Diaspora has now diasporized the Christian faith. The once mission-ized Christians of the global South are already in the heartland of the

32. Foucault, *The Order of Things.*

33. Volf, *Exclusion and Embrace*, 211.

34. Arendt, *Between Past and Future*, 221. See Volf, Ibid., 212.

global North either joining established congregations or organizing their own. Diaspora churches are challenging the church to new ways of understanding itself and its calling in the world. They are posing an opportunity for the church to reimagine what it means to be truly worldwide and truly catholic.

Diaspora churches are sprouting everywhere. A diaspora church is emerging and growing in a place like rural southwestern Minnesota, which suffered abrupt farm population decline (mostly White settlers) because of the family farm crisis in the 1980s. In the rural area of Bigelow, Minnesota, a new and vibrant congregation has emerged out of the death of a congregation (Christian Reformed Church, founded in 1915) once comprised of refugees from the Netherlands. With "newer" Laotian and Vietnamese refugees settling in the area, especially due to agribusiness work opportunities, a new congregation (Asian-American Reformed Church) has been formed through the dedicated ministry of Pastor Ron Lammers who, after painstaking study, is now fluent in Lao. It has become a home church for Laotians and Vietnamese (and a few Caucasians). Immediately after Sunday worship the congregation gathers for potluck with their delicious and colorful variety of Vietnamese and Laotian food. While they are having potluck lunch in the church basement, another congregation (composed mostly of Guatemalans) shares use of the facility for worship.

What is happening in a congregation in the remote rural area of southwestern Minnesota is only one case of diaspora faith communities rising in our midst and transforming the religious landscape. They are making an impact not only on the demographics of Christian congregations but also the religious practices. At the same time, diaspora faith communities are leading the church to new forms of transglocal (transnational or transcontinental) exchanges, encounters, linkages, and partnerships. It is not only money, goods, and services that are crossing borders, but also religious practices and prayers. Along with the money that a migrant worker sends to his or her country of origin, she or he also sends her best wishes and prayers. Religious practices from the country of origin also find their way into the new location and, not surprisingly, undergo the process of appropriation. Beyond the transglocal flows of religious practices and prayers are various forms of social projects and social activism.

Diaspora—the stranger in our midst—is challenging the churches of the global North/West to free themselves from their Western (including secular humanism) captivity. The diaspora Christians—the neglected and marginalized—are already at the doorstep of the Western church challenging it to reclaim its diaspora-*ekklēsia* identity in order that it may truly be what it professes to be, following Lamin Sanneh's distinction, a catholic or "worldwide" church in contrast to a "global" church (read: globalizing and homogenizing).[35]

THE CHALLENGE OF THE STRANGER: THE DIASPORA CHURCH AS A STRANGER

Earlier I engaged in a constructive retrieval of the church as diaspora-*ekklēsia*. I argued that the retrieval of diaspora-*ekklēsia* identity is crucial for understanding the identity of the church (ecclesiology) which, in turn, is crucial for understanding what it is called to do (ministry). At this point, I advance the point that being a "stranger" is intertwined with diaspora identity. The diaspora is also a stranger or alien/foreigner; the displaced is also a stranger; hence, the coupling: diaspora-stranger. I claim that being a stranger is constitutive of the church; it is central to its identity. If the church fails to embrace this identity, surely it will fail in its mission and ministry.

The suggestion that the church identify itself as the stranger should come as no surprise, for Jesus was a diaspora-stranger, a displaced-stranger, a dislocated-stranger. He was the stranger that the Gospel of Matthew (25:35–36) speaks of: "[F]or I was hungry and you gave me food, I was thirsty and you gave me something to drink, I was a stranger and you welcomed me, I was naked and you gave me clothing, I was sick and you took care of me, I was in prison and you visited me." Likewise, he was the stranger in Luke's account in which even "[f]oxes have holes, and birds of the air have nests; but the Son of Man has nowhere to lay his head" (9:58).

The concept of stranger is so central in monotheistic religions (particularly Hebraic and Christian traditions) that the stranger is a classic Other, which is also a classic metaphor for the presence of the Divine. That is to say, the Divine has chosen the encounter with the Other or the real flesh and blood stranger as a condition for the Divine-human encounter. Put differently, how we see and relate to

---

35. Sanneh, *Whose Religion is Christianity?* 22–23.

the stranger is the litmus test of our faith or to any claim of having encountered the Divine. Marc Gopin puts it clearly and powerfully: "[T]here is no person of greater concern in the Bible than the stranger who is with us but not with us, whom we know but do not know, who is a source of great mystery and yet ancestral familiarity, whose treatment by us is ultimately a litmus test of whether we and our culture have succeeded or not in the eyes of God, and whose experience is essentially a yardstick of our moral stature."[36]

We need to recover and embrace the identity of the stranger for the church not as a temporary condition (something we can get over someday), but as a permanent posture. It is essential that we do this constructive retrieval with care, however, in order that we not diminish the seriousness, the pain, and the life and death risk that many diaspora people have suffered when they have been perceived as strangers/aliens. Diaspora communities have known by heart what it is like to be treated and to think of themselves as an alien/stranger. Diaspora communities in Australia, for example, have known the pain of being treated as Austr*aliens*. We are also aware of how the powerful missionary churches of the global North have introduced an alien and alienating Christianity in the global South.

With the above caveat, we must pursue the project of reclaiming the positive importance of the category of stranger. We need to recover the stranger as an important metaphor to speak of the church because it is central to the church's very identity and its narrative, and it has serious consequences for its ministry. Only through the stranger, not outside of it, can we experience salvation. Outside of the stranger there is no salvation. This is not to say that the stranger is a means for our salvation; rather, it is to say that our very own salvation is bound with the stranger. The stranger/alien is crucial for our liberation from our narrow worldviews, stereotypes and prejudices; we need more doses of the unfamiliar, the strange, and the discomforting to help us move into different ways of thinking, dwelling, and acting. I am in agreement with Volf that the main issue for the church is not about being a stranger/alien or foreign, as about "being a stranger [alien] in the *right* way."[37] We need a church that maintains its strangeness in relation to the culture of its time. Our biggest challenge in the era of global market is that we have a church that has become so much

36. Gopin, "The Heart of the Stranger," 6.
37. Volf, *Exclusion and Embrace*, 39–40.

at home (naturalized) with the dominant culture that it has lost its prophetic edge. We have a church that has lost its identity as a stranger and has become a "friend" to the reigning social arrangement.

As a culture, we have not been well-trained in how to deal with the stranger or the strange (also true of difference) in the right way. We either eliminate it or absorb it into our narrow world. I have been inclined to think that it would be easy for those who have experienced what it is like to be a stranger to be more open to strangers, but perhaps it is not natural. We know this from the manner in which diaspora communities have treated newcomers or new diasporas.

As noted earlier, a pain that is not healed is transferred. The pained or wounded may develop what Gopin describes as "negative identity," or an identity that has emerged out of one's own experience of being a stranger, particularly when the experience is negative. As he puts it, "If the rule of deep identity of the stranger is 'love your neighbor as you love yourself' (Lv 19:18), then the rule of superficial identity or negative identity is 'do unto others what they have done unto you, or before they do it unto you again.'"[38] It is, indeed, a difficult challenge to convert the stranger to something positive and liberating; nonetheless, it is a challenge that we must take, for the church's integrity is judged in relation to how it deals with the strangers in our midst.

THE CHALLENGE OF THE STRANGER IN OUR MIDST: ON HOSPITALITY

If "who the stranger is" is the "socio-analytical question," contends Ruiz, "how" we relate to the stranger is the "ethical" question.[39] The Christian answer to this question is hospitality, which is at the heart (*cor* and *coeur* in Latin and French, respectively) of the Crucifixion story—the expression of hospitality par excellence. If how we respond to the stranger is a "litmus test of whether we and our culture have succeeded or not in the eyes of God," the practice of hospitality is the plumb line by which we have to judge ourselves and our society; it is the yardstick, the litmus test by which our moral stature is judged. If, in the spirit of the Reformation, justification by faith is the article by which the church stands or falls (*articulus stantis et cadentis ecclesiae*),

38. Gopin, "The Heart of the Stranger," 17.
39. Ruiz, "Diaspora, Empire, Solidarity," 51.

Arthur Sutherland puts hospitality in a similar spirit: "Hospitality is the practice by which the church stands or falls."[40]

Hospitality in common parlance is basically about warm welcome and good reception. In the world of business, particularly tourism industry, hospitality is about fine dining, accommodation, and professionalized service and, of course for those who can afford it. The signature song, "Be Our Guest," of Walt Disney's animated film *Beauty and Beast* (based on a classic tale to overcome natural fear of strangers among children) has been co-opted, says Sutherland, to mean simply "having a good time." "The singing plates and dancing forks," he continues, merely want to give the impression or appearance that "hospitality toward guests means chasing away frowns, chirping about sunshine, and churning out glee by the gallon."[41]

We know, of course, that the market will use everything to make profits; that there is nothing outside of its corrupting and trivializing reach, including spirituality and, in particular, hospitality. It is for this reason that we must reclaim hospitality and rearticulate its profound and radical meaning. Here I found Henri Nouwen's distinction of the German and Dutch word for hospitality insightful: the German *Gastfreundschaft* emphasizes "friendship" with the guest, whereas the Dutch *gastvrijheid* emphasizes "freedom" of the guest. Integrating and re-appropriating these two distinct emphasis, Nouwen speaks of hospitality as "offering a friendship without binding [freedom] the guest and freedom without leaving him alone [friendship]." In this notion, hospitality is primarily a "creation of a free space" where the stranger can be at home and be a friend instead of a threat or an enemy.[42] I had an opportunity to confirm Nouwen's point in a recent trip to Germany when Andreas Fünfstück, a pastor in Vierkirchen (a municipality in the district of Görlitz), demonstrated to the group through cut-out letters how the stranger can be converted into a friend. He cut the letter "m" of "fremd" (German word for stranger) to produce two "n"s and then inverted the first letter "n." The result is the transformation of the stranger into "freund" (friend).[43]

40. Sutherland, *I was a Stranger*, 83.

41. Ibid., xiii–xiv.

42. Nouwen, *Reaching Out*, 71.

43. This visit happened on the occasion of Edward Ludwig Nollau's celebration in Reichenbach, Germany, July 1–4, 2010.

Hospitality transforms strangers into friends, but the stranger embraced as a friend is allowed free space. Hospitality is about creating a space for others to breathe, find their own voice, sing their own songs, and dance their own dances. It is about creating a space where strangers can be who they are in their strangeness. Conformity to our views, expectations, and practices should not be the basis of our hospitality. "*Freedom*," for Marjorie Thompson, "is the medium of human exchange in true hospitality."[44] Along with the creation of free space for the guest or stranger, hospitality is also about our openness and humility: it is about receiving the gifts of the strangers, and about opening ourselves so we can truly listen and learn from strangers.

Still we need to expand as well as go deeper with our notion of hospitality. Hospitality is about the creation of welcoming communities and resistance to practices that are inhospitable, such as zoning that favors those who have the economic means. Hospitality is about housing and having access to health care. In the context of the predatory global market and imperializing projects that are inhospitable to the needs of the many, hospitality involves critique and subversion of power differentials. Otherwise, acts of hospitality only reinforce the unjust system and the privilege of those doing the hospitable acts. Often drowned in our enthusiasm for doing something "good" for the diaspora stranger, we focus on the comfortable question "What can we do?" while failing to raise the more difficult and necessary question, "How might *we* be part of the problem?"[45] Even as hospitable acts of charity are commendable, we must move beyond charity toward acts of social justice; the unjust "table manners" of the global market demand it. While "faith-based charity provides crumbs from the table, faith-based justice offers a place at the table."[46]

Moreover, efficacious hospitality in the context of the predatory global market demands that it be linked to solidarity and resistance or struggle for social transformation, both locally and globally. To be hospitable is to be in solidarity with the strangers and the historically marginalized groups in our midst and to engage in transformative acts that would make it possible for all to have access to the table. Hospitality means subversion and resistance to imperial projects

44. Thompson, *Soul Feast*, 134.

45. See Rieger, "Theology and Mission," 214.

46. Moyers, cited by Messer, "More than Random Acts of Kindness," 88–89.

and transformation of the predatory and inhospitable global market. Pursuing this further, hospitality and solidarity, particularly through the notion of difference, should lead us to the understanding that solidarity and struggle cannot be reduced to sameness or to a single umbrella of struggle. Solidarity in the struggle must take various forms and address multiple fronts.[47]

THE CHURCH AS A COMMUNITY OF HOSPITALITY

If I, as I did earlier, argue for the coupling of diaspora and hybridity (diaspora-hybridity) and diaspora and stranger (diaspora-stranger), I contend that we do the same for diaspora and hospitality (diaspora/stranger-hospitality). If the church needs to reclaim the identity of a diaspora-stranger to be true to itself as a church and be responsive to the needs to our times, I say the same for hospitality. If the church is a creature of diaspora and was born a stranger, so is the church a creature of hospitality, born out of hospitality. Without hospitality there would have been no church. The diaspora/stranger faith communities of the early church were at the mercy of hospitable individuals and communities.

The Roman Empire (after years of persecuting the early Christians) presented its version of hospitality to the early Christian communities. It presented itself as a host, if not, as a patron and protector of Christianity. We know the rest of the story. The host (imperial Rome) made the guest (Christianity) hostage. Its version of hospitality to Christianity was enslaving and suffocating. In other words, imperial Rome did not "create a free space" for Christianity to be true to itself—to be a stranger. Imperial Rome "befriended" Christianity and sought to make it into its image.

Of course, the history of imperial powers and dominant cultures shaping Christianity to conform to their image and likeness has continued in our present times. But, as I articulated earlier, even as the *ekklēsia* has been subjected to incessant assault by the powers that be, it has not been completely domesticated, and its notion of radical hospitality is alive still. We must retrieve and nourish this generous and radical hospitality, for it is central and formative of the church's identity. When the church opened its young mouth, it cried hospitality, was nourished by hospitality, and practiced hospitality. It was well

47. See Fernandez, *Reimagining the Human*, 31–52.

known for its hospitality. In addition to the preaching of the Word and the breaking of the bread, the early Christian communities had a remarkable growth, as Mortimer Arias noted, because of the extraordinary quality of their hospitality. Arias calls this inviting character and practice of the early Christian communities "centripetal mission" or "evangelization by hospitality."[48] I assume that the early Christian communities practiced hospitality not as bait and switch or a tactic to increase membership, but because it was truly at the heart of their identity, and it was an act of faithfulness to the gospel of Christ. It was in their acts of hospitality that the gospel shone brightly, and the people saw them; hence, these acts of hospitality paved the way for their membership in the Christian communities of their time.

THE CHURCH AS A HOME AWAY FROM HOME:
A COMMUNITY OF BELONGING

Hospitality is as inviting and relevant today for the viability and vitality of the church as it was in the early years of Christianity. Discerning congregations of today have reframed their evangelism thrust basically along the category of community and belonging. As one puts it, "Evangelism is about helping people belong so that they can believe. Most people do not 'decide' to believe. In community they 'discover' that they believe."[49] This is not to discount the importance of communicating the gospel in ways that are coherent and convincing, but it is generally the case that people join a community not simply because of a convincing argument but because of a profound hospitality they have received. People join a group or community because they believe that the group or community cares, which for them has more veracity and validity than the force of words. In the end, we are again led to hospitality: hospitality is about "showing how much [we] care for another person [or community] before expounding on how much [we] know."[50]

The sense of belonging is a basic human need, but this is rendered more acute in the context of a diaspora life. Living as a diaspora and seeking to both survive and to thrive in the context of a relatively white Minnesota (at least in the immediate area where I live), I have learned to find a home among people not limited to my Filipino eth-

---

48. Arias, cited in Thompson, *Soul Feast*, 127.

49. Cited in Lee, "Hospitable Household," 136.

50. Halverson, *The Gift of Hospitality*, 28.

nicity, particularly among people who know what it means to love their country and still love global justice. It is among these people that I have found a home and have received hospitality. Even so, there continue to be times when I long for a larger home, and so I seek connections with the wider world, even volunteering to teach during my precious sabbatical time in countries of the global South. And, as a Filipino diaspora, there are times when I long to hear the familiar sounds, smell the familiar aromas, and taste the familiar foods of my country of origin. How sweet it is to hear the sound of one's native language and the jokes (that often loss their power in translation) that make one belly laugh.

So I imagine a church—a hospitable church—as a space, place, community, and an event where one finds a home, where one's memories, stories, struggles, and hope find expression and are connected with others—not melted. Diaspora "ethnic churches" provide this sense of home away from home, a sense of community of belonging. It may be for this reason that we will always have diaspora "ethnic churches." But there is also that broader community (church) in which we desire to belong, more diverse and hospitable to difference. We may in our present times call this church (community) multicultural or pan-ethnic or the emergent Pentecost church of tomorrow: the crucial point is that we need a hospitable church where we can be truly at home. Being at home in a hospitable church does not mean absence of struggle and contradictions; it means finding a home in the struggle within a church that provides a home for struggle.

DIASPORA MINISTRY OF SERVICE, ADVOCACY, AND ORGANIZING

Diaspora people, especially the newcomers, are in a precarious situation that needs support and services. They need basic support so they can adjust quickly to the challenges of the diaspora life, which includes transportation, housing, schools (if they have children), finding the nearest grocery and medical clinic, processing travel and working documents, finding work, and so forth. The church often becomes the first place where diaspora communities seek support. This was true in the past, and it is true now among new waves of diaspora. It is a joy to see the increasing number of churches responding to the needs of migrants.

Migrant ministry takes many forms or expressions. It includes services that help newcomers to adjust quickly as well as addressing migrants' religious needs and offering pastoral care and counseling. It includes sponsoring refugees and providing host families for them. Beyond services, churches with diasporic commitments need to be involved in community organizing; they need to join with faith-based organization (FBOs), nongovernmental organizations (NGOs) and other concerned citizens in advocating for migrant and immigrant rights, affordable housing, and even transnational issues that involve human rights and peace. The venue of this advocacy may be local (such as advocating for health care benefits for migrants) or global (such as against a WTO ruling, trade agreement or testifying at a global summit), but the two are intertwined. It is not enough to offer services when we know that the issues are systemic and global. Services must become a springboard for advocacy, organizing and mobilization, both local and global.

MINISTRY BACK HOME: MINISTRY TO THE LEFT BEHIND

When we think of diaspora church and ministry, what we often overlook is the community and the church back in the home country. Diaspora, as I noted earlier, has an impact not only in the place of destination but also on the place of origin. The diaspora, even for those who have decided to immigrate, has left a family, a barrio, a hometown, and a country, and whose departure has psychological, socio-political and economic impact back in their homeland. It is for this reason that when we think about what it means to be a church and what it is like to do ministry in light of the challenges of diaspora, we also must consider the place of origin.

When I was working as a pastor on the island of Leyte, in the Philippines, I had church members who had children in diaspora, such as the U.S., Canada, and Hong Kong. Some members had children living in other areas in the Philippines, such as Cebu City and Manila. While the congregation could survive with our local resources, a large amount of the church financial support came from the diasporized children of church members. The dependence of the church on foreign support became more obvious when it had infrastructure projects (for the church building and parsonage) or during special occasions, like the church's anniversary.

While our local congregation was thankful to our diaspora supporters, we did not know in a deeper sense the life of a diaspora. Diaspora Filipinos tend not to share their not-always-rosy life with nosy Filipinos. I simply assumed that they had a good life in diaspora and that they were making lots of money. Perhaps this was the case with our diaspora supporters from the U.S. and Canada (nurses, business folks, and highly paid employees in private companies), but it was not likely the case with the domestic worker in Hong Kong. At that point in time, I knew little about diaspora, except that they sent money to our church. Since that time I have come to realize that churches back home need to know the issues related to diaspora and the lives of diaspora people in general and of diaspora members and supporters in particular. The plight and stories of diaspora people must be incorporated into the life and worship of the church. A Diaspora Sunday must be incorporated in the church calendar. Churches need to develop ministries of service to members of diaspora families and advocate on issues that deal with the plight of diaspora people. Furthermore, churches need to network with NGOs, FBOs, and government instrumentalities in some forms of "re-integration" projects for migrants into their communities. There are too many cases in which migrants, after working for many years abroad, have not saved enough for their eventual return. In many cases, the remittance money has been spent on consumer goods, the construction of a house, and education of children, but not invested in income generating projects.

DEVELOPING AND CULTIVATING DIASPORIC SPIRITUALITY

The church needs to reclaim and develop not only its diaspora identity; it must also reclaim and develop a diasporic spirituality. As I said earlier, when the church sees diaspora as a permanent condition, diaspora is converted from being a dreaded condition that must be overcome to a posture of life understood as a journey and characterized by the willingness to take risks and be open to new possibilities. When the church embraces this journey spirituality, it is more able to be what it is: free to respond to God's call wherever it is sent because it has not been "settled" by possessions, wealth, and power. It is free to go, venture, and speak its mind without the burden of wealth and possessions because it knows how to live with the generous hospitality of others. Of course, the diaspora church needs material blessings to carry out its ministry, but material blessings are its feet and wings, not a load to carry.

A metaphor of journey is central to diaspora experience and, therefore, to diasporic spirituality. To think of life as a continuing journey is not something given; it is learned and cultivated. It is easy to succumb to a "settled life" and to become at home in it. The sense of security that a "settled life" offers is very appealing. On the other hand, a life of spiritual growth is a life that involves movement, the pain of departure and arrival and departure and arrival again, and again, and so on. In the journey we encounter more risks, we are more vulnerable, we are more at the mercy of others, we are surrounded by unfamiliar people, and we face many uncertainties. This is the context in which diasporic spirituality is born: it is a spirituality that has found a home in the journey; a spirituality that has found a home wherever we are. And if God is everywhere and God is in the journey, then to find a home in the journey is to find a home in God, and God has found a home in us.

Being at home wherever we are, or making every place our home is a crucially much-needed posture for our world today. As a person in diaspora, I will forever cherish my home "out there" (Philippines), but I also have found a home in the journey, and I have found a home in other lands. Places that I have had the opportunity to work as a teacher (such as Myanmar, Honduras, and Cameroon) have a special place in my heart. I still continue to affirm that my mother is the best cook (of course in certain dishes, like the mongo bean soup with *malunggay* [*Moringa oleifera*] and *par-ok*—taro leaf with coconut milk and seasoned with shrimp paste). Yet, I also have learned that other mothers are good cooks too, and I have learned to like other foods such as *pho* (Vietnamese), *shushi* (Japanese), *champong* (Korean), taco and seafood enchilada (Mexican), mutton *dum biryani* (Indian), minestrone soup and prosciutto (Italian). I still love to sing the *Bayan Ko* (my native land) and my heart leaps with gladness when I listen to Michael Dadap's solo guitar or Yoyoy Villame's songs, but my diaspora life has been equally nourished by a new song/hymn: *This Is My Song* (tune: *Finlandia*). My heart beats with hopes and dreams for my adopted land; nonetheless, it is also true that "other hearts in other lands are beating with hopes and dreams as true and high as mine." The skies of my diaspora location are "bluer than the ocean," but "skies are everywhere as blue as mine."[51] Diaspora has taught me how to care deeply for my new home here (U.S.) even as I continue to care deeply

51. "This Is My Song," *The New Century Hymnal*, 591.

for my home "out there" (Philippines), and other places in the world. This is an expression of a diaspora heart, a heart that has grown in size: it is a heart whose size is as large as the world. In making the U.S. my home, I see not only its imperialistic foreign policy but also the real flesh and blood people who are starving, bleeding, crying, and laughing. I oppose the war in Iraq and Afghanistan, but I also cry when a U.S. soldier is killed, and I am outraged at a government that sends soldiers to war but does not take care of them when they return home maimed and/or psychologically devastated as veterans. To my mind, this is what it means to have a diaspora heart that has made every place a home.

Would it not be critical for a church to have this diaspora heart, this diasporic spirituality? Certainly! We need churches whose hearts are as large as the world. We need churches that care deeply for its place but also care deeply for other places. We need churches whose loyalty is not to a nation-state but to the God in Christ who cares for the whole world, especially those who are dying before their time.

SEEDS OF DIASPORA, SEEDS OF HOSPITALITY: SEEDS OF HOPE

It seems apropos to end this chapter with seeds of hope, after all, diaspora is about seeds, and more specifically, seeds scattered. The scattering of seeds happens in various ways, some blown by the wind, carried by animals, and others by human hands. For those whose lives are deeply "rooted" to the ocean, like people of the South Pacific, "drifting seed" (Tahitian: *hoto painu*) has become a natural metaphor for diaspora.[52] Seeds are tossed by waves and scattered wherever ocean currents take them to various shores, some fertile and receptive, while others are not. Many seeds die in transit while others "take root," survive, and even thrive in new locations. It is certainly a delight to see these seeds thrive, but whether they die or thrive, they are our seeds of hope.

There is no doubt that it is difficult to see seeds of hope. Yet even in the mist of stormy seas and deep darkness, our ability to see the darkness is already an affirmation of the presence of hope. Yes, drifting seeds of hope are diasporized everywhere. They are in our churches and among Christians who have reclaimed the *ekklēsia*-diaspora spirit. I have seen these seeds of hope among individuals, social move-

52. Hoiore cited in Pearson, "Criss-Crossing Cultures," 5.

ments and faith-based projects through their services, advocacies, and organizing works. We can see these seeds of hope in the programs that our churches are involved in and have supported, of which I can only mention a few.

One such program is the Samaritan border patrol in Arizona. In July of 2002, The Reverend John Fife (also known for his involvement in the Sanctuary Movement), pastor of Southside Presbyterian Church in Tucson, Arizona, along with nine representatives from faith-based communities founded a program—Samaritan patrol—began to respond to the needs of border-crossers in the Mexico-US border. The mission of the program is to render humanitarian assistance to those who are trying to cross the Sonoran desert to the U.S. border, such as giving food, water, and medical assistance. During the summer months, also known as "season of death," Samaritan volunteers patrol the desert border seven days a week. Fife is clear on the "bottom line": "save as many lives as possible." Helping migrants, however, is only one aspect of the mission. In addition, it encourages Arizona residents to practice hospitality and oppose the U.S. government's "beef-up-the border" policy. The hundreds of deaths and millions of captures of undocumented border-crossers only demonstrate a failed policy. It is evident that no walls (whether physical walls or border patrols) can deter desperate migrants from crossing the border.[53]

Seeds of diaspora and seeds of hope are sprouting and growing everywhere. I have seen these seeds of hope in the Filipino migrant ministries in Hong Kong, Seoul, Milan, Rome, and the Netherlands. I have seen these seeds of hope in the joint ministry of the United Church of Christ in the Philippines (UCCP) and the Presbyterian Church in the Republic of Korea (PROK) that addresses the needs and issues of the Filipino migrant communities in Seoul. The Redemptorist missionary society's ministry with migrant Filipinos in Rome is a seed of hope. Another seed of hope is embodied in the ministry of La Puerta Abierta, a United Methodist congregation in St. Paul, Minnesota, which offers various forms of services to Hispanic migrants. We must nurture these seeds so they may blossom and bear fruits—bearing fruits in our postcolonial practices that are organically related to our faith communities and people's movements wherever we are finding "home" and "taking root" in our current journey.

53. Presbyterian News Service.

9

The Church as Community of the Earth (Green) Spirit

The Challenge of the Ecological Crisis

WALT WHITMAN'S POEM, "THERE Was a Child Went Forth," speaks to me and my relationship to my hometown.[1] I am that child who "went forth every day" and the place "became part" of me. My current geographical distance only makes me realize more than ever that I belong to my hometown as the hometown is in me. I live daily with the nostalgia of a childhood home in Canipaan, Hinunangan, Southern Leyte, Philippines—a place where the ocean and the river kiss and embrace. I recall that in the month of June, especially around St. John the Baptist Day (June 24), the high ocean tide would cause the river to flood our yard. Our house had a bamboo floor high enough that the water did not reach it. As a child, fishing was an integral part of my life. I recall the times when I fished from our back porch and caught a few big ones—usually mudfish. I also learned how to watch for signs of freshwater clams by observing the water ripples that their breathing made, especially with the first rush of the rising tide.

With the ocean only fifty meters or so away, it was easy to switch from the river to the ocean. The ocean, of course, had much to offer— fish, shrimps and prawns, crabs, squid, and octopus. I did not have to go deep to catch fish and crabs. There were times when a fish would accidentally land on the shore while trying to elude a larger fish. At times schools of small fish, most often *bulinaw or dilis* (anchovies),

---

1. Whitman, "There Was a Child Went Forth," 234–36.

would visit the ocean of my childhood in such miraculously great numbers that even non-regular fisherfolks would join fishing. Since they were without fishing equipment, they used their mosquito nets to catch fish while standing waist-deep. During those times, the ocean was like a fiesta.

My hometown was also rich in flora and fauna. Our swampy backyard had what we called *milyapi* trees and vines that connected one tree to another and on which I used to play Tarzan. Early in the morning I often watched the *uwak* (crows) making their daily journey from their resting place (among the trees near the town cemetery) toward the northern mountains and back at dusk. Hawk (*banog*) soared freely. I had to watch out for the hawk and *bayawak* (monitor lizard)—predators of our hens and chicks. There was also the *tikling* (*Gallirallus philippensis*) and the little *tamsi* (*Arachnothera longirostra*), which I hunted with my slingshot. With such abundant flora and fauna it was not a surprise that there were times when we had unexpected guests such as snakes and centipedes. One of our favorite pastimes was removing the *tungaw* (tiny reddish ticks) from their favorite parts of our bodies.

Such was the idyllic place of my childhood. The rivers and ocean sustained us with the food we needed. We fished for food and for livelihood, not for sport. Some days my companion and I had to awaken at 2 o'clock in the morning and paddle our canoes to reach the fisherfolks in the ocean to buy their catch for the market. It was not the kind of sporty-fun canoeing that my seminary colleagues imagined during our sailing experience at Bar Harbor, Maine. Our lives had a different rhythm, though it was not a lackadaisical life. To be sure, even as marine life was abundant, there were seasons when we had little catch. Moonlit nights (especially those around the full moon) may be good for lovers, but not for fisherfolks. And the times when *amihan* (northeasterly wind) and *dumagsa* (eastern wind) would strike also led to lean seasons. Consistent strong winds and waves could last for several days before a respite, enabling the people from the islands of San Pablo and San Pedro to come to the mainland of Leyte for provision. Typhoons were also frequent visitors.

I carry this once-upon-a-time place deep within, even more so now that I live in a place in the middle of a large continent. From my office window in New Brighton, Minnesota, I sometimes imagine the white snow as the white caps of the ocean. Wanting to share my childhood home with my children, I took them for a visit. Maybe, I thought to myself, they could experience what I experienced as a boy. As it turned out, the visit was not enjoyable, as it was full of family tension. My hometown had, of course, changed, and I had as well. Some changes were welcome, but others were alarming. There were few fish in the nearby ocean. Fisherfolks had to sail far away into the open Pacific for their catch. And sadly, the ocean of light coming from the kerosene lamps of the fisherfolks is no longer visible from the shore of Canipaan. In addition, the ocean had claimed several meters of shoreline; even the seawall that my late father helped build as a construction foreman could not protect it. The rising ocean had claimed the huge tree that the barrio inhabitants called *hambabago* as it advanced closer to the houses.

The ocean and marine life were not the only ones that had suffered ecological destruction. Two landslides in my home province (Southern Leyte) had claimed the lives of people. A couple of weeks of continuous heavy rain would be more than enough to soften the bald mountaintop that was once a tropical forest. In recent years the island of Leyte has suffered serious ecological disasters: a flashflood in Ormoc City (1991), a landslide in Punta, San Francisco (2003), and a landslide in Ginsaugun, St. Bernard (2006). The latter wiped out the whole village and buried its children at a nearby elementary school. I visited the place a few months after the disaster with a medical mission group that my wife and I had helped to organize. I returned in July 2009 to visit the people in the relocation site and could not help but ponder the ecological tragedy. I thought to myself: Is there something good that can come out of this tragedy?

PREDATORY GLOBAL MARKET AND ECOLOGICAL DESTRUCTION

I assume there are others like myself who are nostalgic about their once upon a time ecologically idyllic, diverse, and abundant hometown. For years I thought that one day I would be able to return home to an ecologically healthy place. I was wrong. My hometown has suffered ecological disasters: the ones that hit the headlines were the landslides. The common default explanation for such disasters, by insurance companies and others, is to call them "acts of God." But are they?

It took me years to understand that what seemed like purely "natural" catastrophic events that my hometown had suffered were not purely natural, that the natural was intertwined with the socio-economic and political, and that they were not isolated cases. The rising tide that claimed our beautiful shores and the stronger typhoons that lashed our neighborhood are some of the "fingerprints" and "harbingers" of a major ecological tragedy for which human beings are greatly responsible—global warming. Global warming's fingerprints include record-breaking warm weather, severe heat waves, ocean warming, rising sea levels, melting glaciers, and the warming of the Arctic and Antarctic. With these fingerprints come the harbingers: the spread of diseases through animals, coral reef bleaching, movement and death of animal populations, heavy rain and stronger storms, drought, and wildfires.[2]

It is against this wider backdrop of ecological and socio-political connections that I now view the catastrophic events of my hometown and the inhabitants' contribution in the unfolding of these events. Certainly, the population growth in my hometown has led to over-fishing to keep up with the increasing demand for food. But there are other causes, including destructive fishing practices of various sorts—dynamite, *sahid* (nets with small holes drawn by people from the shore), poison, and big fish trawlers. The death of the mangrove plants has destroyed the breeding place of various forms of marine life, and agricultural chemicals that flow from the ricefields to the rivers and finally to the ocean have killed various forms of marine life. Additionally, years of *kaingin* (slash and burn) and logging have denuded the forest of Leyte, leaving the ground more vulnerable to landslides, especially during the rainy season.

We cannot continue blaming our ecologically destructive practices on God. We all have participated in varying ways in the ecological destruction. As a young farmer, I contributed to the creation of this ecological imbalance through use of agricultural chemicals in our ricefield, and particularly with the introduction of new breeds of rice. I was captivated by the magical power of chemical fertilizer. In a couple of weeks the fertilizer could turn the brown field green. I contributed to the ecological disaster further with our use of *lagtang* seed and *tubli* root that poisoned the fish. And there were times we

2. Watt-Cloutier, "Climate Change," 97–99.

used the ocean as our toilet, which delighted the hungry fish because we had given them something to feast on.

Without doubt the common people of my hometown have contributed to the ecological destruction by the way they live, but what is their share compared to the global imperial market's mess. This ecologically destructive imperial market mess has reached to the bottom of the Philippine Deep. Below the ocean surface is a mountain of global market trash—the market mess. Liberalized trade conditions have increased the volume of trade, thus accelerating the depletion of natural resources and the destruction of the natural environment. Around the world, forests are being cleared for timber, agriculture, and grazing. They are also flooded for dams and hydroelectric power. Rivers, lakes, and oceans have become dumpsites for booming industries. And the ocean has been overfished to support ever-increasing demands both domestic and international.

An encounter with fisherfolks in Laguna de Bay in the Philippines underscores the ecological challenge we are facing. After a modest meal of rice and fish one evening, in the fisherfolks' hut in the middle of the lake where my immersion group rested for the night, one of the fisherfolks shared his fears tearfully as he thought about the death of the lake due to pollution coming from the nearby factories. The lake is a source of livelihood and the future of his children. With a deep sigh, he asked: "How will I support my children and what will happen to them?" Of course, the question was a rhetorical one. He was not asking for a quick answer from my group. His question was his way of sharing with us his precarious future.

The plight of the fisherfolks in Laguna de Bay is shared by fisherfolks in the Visayas and Mindanao. The destruction of coral reefs by illegal fishing and the death of mangroves have adversely affected the ocean's ability to support the lives of the fisherfolks and their families. One must sail far to the open sea for a catch that will support them. As fisherfolks in the Visayas and Mindanao put it: "*Daghan pa ang mangingisda kay sa isda*" (There are more fisherfolks than fish). In Pasil (Cebu City), for example, a different form of *mananagat* (literally, one whose livelihood is associated with the ocean) has evolved. When I heard the word *mananagat*, I immediately associated it with fishing, as people commonly do. So, my question to the wife of a *mananagat* was, "What kind of fish does your husband usually get?" Her answer surprised me: "My husband 'fishes' or dives for scraps of iron or steel that fall into the ocean floor somewhere near the pier. Whatever 'catch' he gets, he sells them by the kilo to the buyers." What a frightening image of the future: the ocean, from this story, is not breeding fish but iron junk as a result of the market's relentless pursuit of profits.

Further devastation of the earth has occurred with logging for export; it has been a major culprit in the destruction of forests around the world. Forests have also been destroyed for grazing, mining, and the construction of hydroelectric dams. They have been cleared to give way to pasture lands. Strip mining has destroyed several thousand hectares of forest. Chemicals used to process the minerals flow to rivers and streams and kill plants and animals. The ecological assault continues as the global market pushes for more areas to mine. The Asian Development Bank, for example, pressured the Philippine government to adopt the Philippine Mining Act of 1995, leading to the massive influx of foreign mining corporations. This Mining Act allows the companies to lease lands for seventy-five years with the freedom to repatriate 100 percent of their profits.[3] The construction of hydroelectric dams and thermal plants has been destructive to world's forests as well.

With the destruction of the forests comes the destruction of various species of plants and animals. One expression of destruction is the displacement of the indigenous people in the areas affected. The much-touted development and jobs for the poor have not translated into positive change for the lives of the poor who are affected by the big projects. Such was the promise of the Chad-Cameroon Oil and Pipeline project, which I was privileged to visit in 2007. This pipeline (1,070 kilometers in length) cuts through Chad's most fertile agricultural region and Cameroon's Atlantic littoral forest to an offshore loading facility in the Atlantic. This area is rich in biodiversity and home to the Bantou and the more vulnerable tribe *Bakola/Bagyéli* (pygmy).[4] The construction of the pipeline forced them to leave their traditional homelands, which radically altered their way of life. Uprooted from their source of livelihood, the *Bakola/Bagyéli* people must push deeper into the forest to hunt for game while waiting for the promised compensation. I recall one afternoon when, through the

3. Tebtebba Foundation, Ibid., 159.
4. Ibid., 165–66.

work of RELUFA (a network of people's organizations in Cameroon), I met some of them and learned more about their miserable plight.[5] Will the promised compensation of the oil and pipeline project remain a pipedream?

Industrial growth in general has contributed to the overall pollution of the ecosystem through discharge of toxic effluent, poisonous fumes, dusts, and particles. Many of these are now part of the earth's global circulation and many resist breakdown.[6] They also interact with one another, thus multiplying their power and effects. In due time these chemicals accumulate in our food, water, and bodies. A study conducted by scientists in the mid-1980s with samples of breast milk from Inuit women in the Canadian Arctic had an alarming result. Expecting to find the milk relatively free from toxic chemicals, they were surprised to find that milk from Inuit women was not pure enough to be used in controlled studies. This result helps explain what scientists call hydrologic cycles. As polluted water evaporates, water vapor forms into clouds and is carried by winds around the globe. In the Arctic it is deposited as toxic rain or snow. The Arctic has become a resting place for volatile chemicals. Additional studies reveal that these persistent chemicals can reach a high level of concentration and can be magnified a million times as they circulate around the globe and up the food chain. With seals, polar bears, and humans up the food chain, it is no surprise that a high concentration of these persistent toxic chemicals have been found in them.[7]

The agriculture and food industry is an area where we can see further ecological destruction and its consequences. Mono-cropping and heavy use of synthetic fertilizers and pesticides are trademarks of the unified global market. Mono-cropping is the global market's way of producing in massive volume. Huge tracts of lands are planted with crops primarily for export, but what is often overlooked is the high cost involved. Mono-cropping's heavy dependency on chemicals carries serious risk: these chemicals seep through the soil and may reach the water table, eventually ending up in our kitchens through agricultural produce and drinking water. Mono-cropping is a culprit against diversity—a principle of life that is a crucial defense against

---

5. www.relufa.org.

6. Rayan, "Theological Perspectives," 223. See Delgado, *Shaking the Gates of Hell*, 38.

7. Delgado, *Shaking the Gates of Hell*, 38.

pests and failed harvests. It is harmful not only to ecological health, but also increases the people's vulnerability to market forces. Focused on producing export-oriented crops for cash, they often neglect the cultivation of plants for domestic consumption, which is a cushion for failed harvests. And, even when the harvest is a success, the people are still vulnerable to the whims of the market.

Tampering with the ecological balance for the sake of greater harvest and profit compounds the issue. An example is the introduction of blue tilapia (*Oreochromis aurea*) into Lake Effie in Florida. When blue tilapia was introduced in 1970, it consisted of less than 1 percent of the total biomass of Lake Effie, but by 1974, the blue tilapia accounted for more than 90 percent of the biomass. This is a sudden change in the ecosystem of Lake Effie. A similar case took place with the introduction of opossum shrimp in Flathead Lake, Montana. With an eye for a great harvest of Kakonee salmon, opossum shrimps were introduced into several lakes upstream of Flathead Lake between 1968 and 1975 to improve food sources for the Kakonee salmon. Unbeknownst to those who sought to improve the situation, the opossum shrimps were voracious predators of zooplankton (an important source of food for the salmon). When zooplankton declined, the salmon population declined and, consequently, the salmon catch plummeted. The introduction of opossum shrimps into Flathead Lake had a Frankenstein Effect.[8]

The much-sought progress of produce and profit could become a nightmare. For many, it already is. We are putting the whole ecosystem at risk and, with it, the whole of humanity. While the risk belongs to the whole ecosystem, ecological destruction is more acutely felt in poor neighborhoods and developing nations. Oddly, the ones with light ecological footprints suffer disproportionately. General statements about shared suffering and general responsibility only add insult to the injury of the most vulnerable. It is indeed true, as Thomas Berry puts it, that "when nature goes into deficit, then we go into deficit . . . Neither economic viability nor improvement in the life conditions of the poor can be realized in such circumstances." But what appears unequivocally clean at an abstracted and generalized level has flaws when analyzed closely through the lens of the interlocking forms of oppression. We must not forget that the poor have been living in

8. Shiva, *Stolen Harvest*, 52.

deficit long before the elites have realized that when nature goes into deficit a worse catastrophe is going to happen and affect all.[9]

Powerful nations have dumped hazardous and toxic wastes on the poor. Nations of the global South, indigenous people around the world, and poor communities have been the target of "environmental terrorism" by powerful nations. Arguments have been made that many poor and racial minorities actually choose to settle in dump site areas. Well, what is the choice: to die slowly of toxic contamination or to die quickly of hunger? Besides, dump sites, like the Smokey Mountain in Manila (mountain of trash), have become a source of livelihood for many of the world's urban poor. Yet, with the help of Mark Molina of the Visayas Primary Health Care, I have come to realize that the much-despised scavengers have done something for the common good: in their scavenging work they have become the segregators and recyclers of the public waste—our mess.

THE CHURCH AND THE ECOLOGICAL CRISIS

The ecological crisis poses a challenge to the church. It is a challenge not only because its members are a part of a world facing ecological crisis, but also because the ecological issue is at heart a matter of faith. It is theological because ecology is about our understanding of who we are in the whole of creation: it is about knowing who we are and our role in the whole; it is about finding and practicing our rightful place in the overall scheme of things; and it is about how we dwell and treat others. The ecological crisis is at heart a matter of faith because it is about our covenant with the rest of creation; it is about common dwelling and common flourishing. The ecological crisis is one of living in right relation.

Our failure to live in right relation with each other and with the whole of creation is what we call "sin." The ecological crisis is an expression of sin. It is a form of "living a lie": it is living a lie in relation to other human beings (us versus us), living a lie in relation to other animals (us versus them), and living a lie in relation to nature (us versus it).[10] All three dimensions of sin point to the interconnection of life. The life and well-being of human beings, animals, and nature depend

9. Fernandez, *Reimagining the Human*, 161.
10. McFague, *The Body of God*, 112–29.

on this interconnection. We may call this interconnection the web of life. Sin is an act of breaking the web of life.

Naming our ecological crisis as sin may not be popular among many Christians, but calling it as such names the depth and gravity of this crisis, and hence, the possible responses. What is involved in the crisis is not simply a lack of understanding or a matter of the intellect but, as Mark Wallace argues, a matter of the heart. By this he means that "[t]he problem is not that we do not know how to avoid our current plight, but rather we no longer experience our co-belonging with nature in such a way that we are willing to alter our lifestyles in order to build a more sustainable future."[11] We certainly are not lacking in theological materials articulating our interdependency, shared vulnerabilities, and hopes. Nonetheless, as James Cone reminds us about the relationship between racism and ecology, "if white ecologists really believe [in co-beloging and altering our lifestyle], why do most still live in segregated communities?"[12] Of course this indictment applies not only to white ecologists.

If the ecological crisis is comprehensive and radical, then our response must be comprehensive and radical as well. We must be speaking of a *metanoia,* that is, a radical conversion of our ways of thinking, dwelling, and acting. In relation to the immediate task of this book, it means a turn-around in our theological habits of thinking. A necessary step in this direction involves detoxifying or decontaminating ourselves and our churches of habits of thinking that are manifest in our doctrines, liturgies, worship, ministries, and various practices.

THE CHURCH:
DETOXIFYING TOXIC THEOLOGICAL HABITS

While I cannot be exhaustive at present, nevertheless, I will identify certain major theological toxins that we must confess in order to detoxify ourselves. Ian Barbour identifies four dysfunctional theological habits from which to start. First is the separation of God from nature. God is a being outside of nature even as God acts in nature. Acting from the outside, God relates to the world primarily in terms of saving acts in history. Second is the separation of humanity from nature, which is modernity's primary mindset. Human beings stand apart from

11. Wallace, *Finding God,* 27.
12. Cone, "Whose Earth Is It," 31.

and above other beings. All other living creatures have instrumental value in relation to humanity. Third is the separation of the doctrine of redemption from the doctrine of creation. Salvation history is primarily about the one God who acts in history to redeem humanity, with creation as a backdrop or a stage in the drama of salvation. Salvation is primarily one of personal fulfillment rather than the fulfillment of the whole of creation. The fourth is hierarchical dualism: human beings and nature, men and women, mind and spirit, and so on.[13]

These four theological habits have a common point: the separation of God, humanity, nature, creation, and redemption and the corresponding move of hierarchization. Separation goes along with hierarchization. Dualistic and binaristic thinking is hierarchical thinking. As in other forms of dualism, the dualized categories are also hierarchized. Karen Warren noted this point: "Oftentimes . . . hierarchial thinking has been applied to conceptual dualisms, so that one side of the dualism is valued 'up' and the other 'down.'"[14] And that which is valued up, or that which is at the higher scale of the hierarchy, establishes itself as the norm in relation to that which is at the bottom of the hierarchy. This norm has the "power to oppress," Elizabeth Dodson Gray rightly points out, "because it is an expression of a social hierarchy or pyramid of status or power."[15] The norm is a creation of power; power produces norm; it is a creation of the power-knowledge nexus. The "valuing up" and "valuing down" also acquires the status of the sacred because it is seen as part of the natural order created by God; thus it becomes more difficult to change. Anyone who attempts to change this hierarchical dualism or holy order is going against the natural order and is, therefore, an enemy of the Creator.[16]

This dualistic hierarchical thinking is the overarching worldview that undergirds various expressions of ecologically toxic theological thinking. It finds expression in anthropocentrism, which elevates human beings above other beings and instrumentalizes other creatures; in patriarchalism, which puts the male specie over female who are more closely identified with nature; and in the assault against the

13. Barbour cited in Hessel, "The Church Ecologically Reformed," 187–88.

14. Warren, "Feminism and Ecology," 3–20, cited in McDaniel's *Of God and Pelicans*, 116.

15. Gray, *Green Paradise Lost*, 131.

16. Ibid., 7.

poor and indigenous people, who are considered earthier. Dualistic hierarchical thinking finds expression in an understanding of God as an interventionist who comes to act only in historical events. It leads to a failure to recognize God in creation. It finds expression in the elevation of the spirit over the material, which neglects the material condition and leaves it to the control of the powerful; in the focus on redemption in another life beyond at the expense of creation; and in the treating of the earth as a hotel that will be abandoned for another true home. Dualistic hierarchical thinking finds expression in the separation or breaking of interconnections. It comes to expression in what I articulated earlier about our view of sin and, therefore, of forgiveness. Moreover, it fails to understand that sin is a sin against God, because it is a sin against God's earth and God's people.

The challenge now is to articulate alternative ways of thinking, dwelling, and acting vis-à-vis destructive theologies. Non-theologizing will not drive away deeply imbedded toxic theologies. If Christian theology is an expression of the church, then the whole congregation must be actively involved in theologizing. Theology is too important to be left to professionals. Sadly, even many pastors have been led to believe that theologizing is the job of professional theologians. Many have failed to understand or have failed to carry out the vocation that pastors are the resident theologians in their congregations.

THE CHURCH: COMMUNITY BIRTHED
BY THE GREEN SPIRIT/SOPHIA

When we think of the birth of the church, we think of the Spirit and, in particular, of the Pentecost. Typically, when we think of the Pentecost what comes to mind is the Spirit appearing in tongues of fire. Not surprisingly, the liturgical color of the season is red. Indeed, it has become automatic to associate the Pentecostal Spirit with red, but what if we also think of the Pentecostal Spirit as green? It may at first appear jarring, but red (fire) and green (plants) complement each other perfectly well, for they both are symbolic of the life-giving, nourishing, empowering, and transforming Spirit. Red and green are among the colors that can represent the four primal elements associated with the earthy Spirit—earth, wind, water, and fire.[17] Certainly fire kills, but fire also cooks, warms, and actually makes some plants grow, as a student

17. Wallace, *Finding God*, 9.

reminded me with the example of the jack pine pinecone seed.[18] After a forest fire, the pinecone that has been dormant for years responds to the enormous heat and opens its hard cone. The dreaded fire that destroys gives way to green vegetation.

The Christian tradition is rich with images of the green Spirit. Rebecca Button Prichard's work makes this point: "If we dig more deeply into the ground of scripture, we will see that the Spirit's creative presence is portrayed . . . in vivid visual imagery, the imagery of greenness, of verdure, of viridity."[19] Her study reveals a cluster of words that support our claim: greenness and growth (*'arek/'orek*), verdure (*chatzir*), green growth (*desheh*), luxuriant growth (*ra'an/ra'anan*), herbage (*'esev*), and sprout (*tsmach/tsemech*).[20] Greenness is a symbol of God's creative and sustaining presence, of God's continuing care and blessings, and of God's renewing power. It is a symbol of God the Spirit nourishing the weary, refreshing the thirsty, and feeding the hungry through the green meadows, still waters, and luxuriant harvest. Greenness is a symbol of the Spirit that restores our souls—a symbol of our coming back to health and right relation. The green Spirit that brooded over the waters in the creation account is the same Spirit who is actively present in the renewing of creation—making streams flow and sending rain to water dry and parched lands, letting flowers bloom and trees to bear fruits as well as providing food for the animals.

The green pneumatology (doctrine of the Spirit) is found in early articulations in the work of Hildegard of Bingen. Hildegard offered a nature-based model of the Spirit in contrast to the prevailing cultural metaphors, particularly linking the Spirit with *viriditas* (greening). In relation to the other two members of the Godhead, she spoke of the Spirit as "eager freshness" proceeding from both and sanctifying the "waters by moving over their face in the likeness of an innocent bird, and streamed with ardent heat over the apostles."[21] Hildegard linked, according to Elizabeth Dryer, the Spirit to the "flow of water on the

---

18. Lyn Pagliarini, a student in my class at United Theological Seminary of the Twin Cities, New Brighton, Minnesota.

19. Prichard, *Sensing the Spirit*, 33.

20. Ibid., 33.

21. Hildegard of Bingen, *Scivias*, 418.

crops with the love of God that renews the face of the earth, and by extension the souls of believers."[22]

This green Spirit of creation is the red Spirit of the Pentecost, the event commonly associated with the birth of the church. The red fire of the Pentecostal Spirit is an activity of the green Spirit renewing life and communities. If the Pentecostal event is the work of the green Spirit in the form of renewing and empowering fire (red), then the church is an event of the green Spirit. If the green Spirit has given birth to the church, then it thoroughly makes sense to imagine its offspring (the church) as having a green DNA. We can say then that the church is a community of the green Spirit or the church is a community of the Earth-Spirit.

THE CHURCH: THE BODY OF THE GREEN SPIRIT, FOLLOWER OF JESUS

If the Spirit is green and the church to which it has given birth is a community of the green Spirit, how shall we articulate a christology that moves along with green pneumatology? For years I had difficulty imagining a link between ecology and christology, particularly in relation to the person of Jesus of Nazareth. I easily connected Jesus' option for the poor and radical message of the reign of God but had difficulty relating it to ecology. Part of my difficulty was my predisposition to look for specific narratives in the life of Jesus that dealt directly with ecological matters. I am grateful for the works of scholars who have helped me acquire a theological lens for reading christology ecologically. There are two theological moves involved in this christological reading.

The first move constitutes a pneumatological reading of christology. Christology is the shape of the Spirit in Christ. The presence of Christ is the presence of the Spirit. The Christ in Jesus is the Spirit embodied in a specific gestalt. The New Testament portrays Jesus as one not only anointed by the Spirit but also porous and obedient to the leading of the Spirit. He became an embodiment of the Spirit. If the Spirit as we know it—the green Spirit present in creation and in the Pentecost—is the same Spirit that found embodiment in Jesus, then what we have is a Jesus who embodied the green Spirit—the green Christ. The Christic gestalt that Jesus embodied is the green sensibility. Jesus is the green Spirit enfleshed, bearing the consciousness of

22. Dryer, "An Advent of the Spirit," 134. Also, see Wallace, "Crum Creek," 127.

ecological sensibility and committed to the mission of restoring viridity to the earth.

The second move demands that we enlarge the coverage of the green Spirit's incarnation. The cosmos and the whole inhabited earth is the green Spirit's incarnation; it is Christ's incarnation. God the green Spirit is incarnate in the web of life. Incarnation (becoming flesh), argues Dennis Edwards, is not "restricted to humanity. The flesh that is embraced by God is not limited to the human. It includes the whole interconnected world of fleshly life and, in some way, includes the whole universe to which flesh is related and on which it depends."[23] So, if incarnation is not restricted to humanity, it cannot be restricted to one expression of humanity—Jesus of Nazareth. This is the christological point here: Jesus is significant not because he is the sole incarnation but because as Christians we see in him a God who "becomes a vital part of an ecosystem and a part of the interconnected systems that support life on Earth."[24]

When we see incarnation and, in particular, Jesus of Nazareth in this way, our apertures are prepared for a more radical and extensive way of reading christology ecologically. The struggle and suffering of Jesus mirror the struggle and suffering of the green Spirit—the Spirit intrinsically connected to the earth. The Jesus who bore the mark of human sin mirrors the estrangement of humanity and the rest of creation. As Jesus bore the cross, so now the green Spirit bears the cross of our ecological sin. "[T]he lash marks of human sin cut into the body of the crucified Son of God," Wallace contends, "are now even more graphically displayed across the expanse of the whole planet as the body of the wounded Spirit bears the incisions of further abuse. The Spirit in the earth, the body of God for us today, is being crucified afresh."[25]

If the whole inhabited earth is the context of our interpretation of the crucifixion, it is also the case with our interpretation of the resurrection. Resurrection symbolizes the resurrection of all flesh—the whole of creation, not only human flesh. If in the crucifixion of Jesus the whole earth is crucified, so Jesus' resurrection mirrors the resurrection of the whole earth—the whole web of life. The resurrection of Jesus, the new Adam or the firstborn of creation in the likeness of

23. Edwards, *Ecology at the Heart of Faith*, 58.

24. Ibid., 59.

25. Wallace, *Finding God*, 24.

human being (Phil 2:7), points to the deep longings of all earthlings (including humans) and the assurance that creation will experience redemption. Redemption is the resurrection promise for the whole of creation, not just for humanity. Though distinct, Sallie McFague views creation and salvation as one: "creation is not one thing and salvation something else; rather, they are revealed as scope and shape, as space and form, as place and pattern. Salvation is for all creation."[26] Creation is the scope of salvation and the direction of salvation.

If the green Spirit is incarnate in creation in general and in Jesus of Nazareth in particular, what does this mean for the church, a follower of Jesus? As Jesus was fully porous and obedient to the green or earth Spirit, so must the church be a community birthed by the green Spirit and follower of the Spirit-led Jesus. If Jesus embodied green sensibility, so must the church. The church as the Body of Christ assumes an embodiment that reflects that of Jesus—an embodiment of the green Christ. Christian discipleship must then be evaluated in light of how we live out the green Christic-gestalt.

THE CHURCH AS AN OIKOS (HOUSEHOLD) IN AN OIKODOME

After taking account of the green Spirit (pneumatology) incarnate in creation in general and in Jesus in particular (christology) and giving birth to the church (ecclesiology), I now focus on articulating the gestalt or shape of the green church. Following Geiko Müller-Fahrenholz's suggestion, seeing the church from an "ecodomical" perspective or in the context of an *oikodome* may help us understand better this alternative ecclesiology. An ecodomical perspective sees the church as an *oikos* (household) or a community within the whole inhabited earth (*oikoumene*). The ideas that I have pointed out about the Spirit enfleshed in the whole of creation in general and in Jesus in particular and the church embodying the same, warrant that we see the church as intrinsically part of the *oikoumene*—the whole inhabited earth. The *oikoumene* is not simply the context in which the church is located; rather, the church belongs to the *oikoumene*. It is an expression of the *oikounome*, and only through the *oikoumene* can it be properly understood. The *oikoumene* is its home. Members of the body of Christ have no other home but the earth: they are earthling

26. McFague, *The Body of God*, 182.

Christians. This means that the plight and destiny of the church is bound with the earth. Since, as I articulated earlier, the scope, direction, and location of salvation is the earth, this must be the witness of the church. The church must witness to the good news of salvation that in Christ we are at home again—reconciled with the earth.

Unfortunately, we have been taught in Sunday school and catechism classes that we are citizens of another world and that this world is simply a backdrop to God's mighty action in history, which will involve snatching us away to the world up yonder. Müller-Fahrenholz notes a historical shift from an "ecodomical" interpretation (the world understood as home) of the term *oikos* (household) by the early Christian communities, toward a construal of the term *oikos* as *paroikia*, which means "living away from home."[27] In the context of the persecution of the early Christian communities, the idea that Christians are aliens and exiles or "resident aliens" (*paroikoi*) in a hostile world and that their true home is in heaven was crucial (compare 1 Pt 2:11). It helped them hold onto their faith in the face of persecution. We need, however, to recover the ecodomical perspective, without abandoning the *parokia* perspective.[28]

THE CHURCH AS A COMMUNITY OF THE WEB OF LIFE: THE INSIGHTS OF HOLON

A concept that might help us better understand the church as an intrinsic and vital part of the *oikoumene* as well as the relationship between communities is offered by the theory of holons. A holon cannot be pinned into one expression: it is not a kind of matter or a wave; it is neither a particle nor a process. As integrated and presented by Ken Wilber, a holon is whole and part simultaneously. Whatever exists is always whole/part. Every whole is a part and every part is a whole simultaneously and indefinitely.[29] It does not matter if a holon is a single cell or an organism: it is always part/whole. As more fundamental holons (whole/part) embrace other holons (whole/part), holons of greater depth emerge. A living human body, for example, contains not only atoms but also molecules, cells, and organs. But a human being

---

27. Fahrenholz, *God's Spirit*, 109.

28. Fernandez, *Reimagining the Human*, 190–91.

29. Cited in Wessels, *The Holy Web*, 57.

is a human being only in relation to the larger holon, which we can imagine only as something complex and infinite.

The theory of holons discloses to us how crucial and central relationship is—a relationship that is intrinsic and indefinite—even as we recognize individuality and self-agency. Every creature is a creature only in the context of being part of the whole or in relationship with others. Every creature has its beginning and life only in the web of relationship. There is no life outside of relationship even if it is true that many forms of relationship are destructive. If this is the case, right relationship must characterize the web of relation; otherwise the web of life becomes the web of death. We can learn from the plight of *Brighamia insignis*, a plant that grows on the cliffs of Hawaii. When the plant started to disappear, the people wanted to know what was behind this loss. Studies were conducted to discover the factors that led to this phenomenon. Scientists found that the birds responsible for pollinating the plant had become extinct. Without the birds, the *Brighamia* was left without a means of reproduction. Thus, it was slowly becoming extinct as well.[30]

It is in the context of the web of life—the web of right relation—that we can see properly the issue of intrinsic worth. The idea of intrinsic worth has been used to argue against instrumentalist thinking. While this approach is understandable, I have concerns. Given the individualistic predilection of the West, I am concerned that the notion of "intrinsic worth" remains captive to individualism. It remains vulnerable to the "absolutization" of an individual entity by virtue of the claim to intrinsic worth. Without throwing out intrinsic worth completely, we can prevent individualist thinking from co-opting it if we see intrinsic worth along the holon line. Individual mountains, animals, plants, and human beings have intrinsic value, but this value is inseparable from their being part of the whole web of life.

With insights drawn from the theory of holons, we have acquired a new set of eyes to see the church in a new light: the church is a holon within the larger holon. The church's being or identity can be understood only properly as whole/part. It exists in relationship and can thrive only in mutual relation. It possesses, according to Cletus Wessels, the characteristics of holons: capacity for self-preservation,

---

30. Moore, *Ministering with the Earth*, 51.

self-adaptation, self-transcendence, and self-dissolution.[31] As having
the capacity for self-preservation, a holon preserves its own wholeness. Each holon exercises its autonomy and agency. But as part of
the whole simultaneously, it also has the capacity for adaptation. For
example, hydrogen is whole, but in right relationship with oxygen it
turns into another holon: water. When holons of greater depth merge
with holons of greater depth, a new being emerges. Furthermore, even
as holons have the capacity of building up, they also have the capacity
to break down. These characteristics of holons mirror the characteristics of a church in a world understood as holoverse.

These insights from our account of the identity and characteristics of holons shed light on many aspects of what it means to be
a church. While I cannot be exhaustive, I will identify a few central
points that reveal in a profound way the kind of organizational structure and dynamics of power relation that must guide the church of
Christ. As an alternative to the more prevalent pathological hierar-
chies, we can follow Wilber's word, "holarchy."[32] The power dynamics
in the church of the green Spirit is characterized by holarchical mode
of relationship. There are beings with basic holons and beings of more
complex formation of holons, but the relationship is not that one is
of greater value than the other. The more complex holons are, in fact,
more dependent than the less complex, but the less complex also find
their actualization in the more complex ones.

Furthermore, insights from the theory of holons shed light on
the organizational relationship of various church bodies (local congregations, and regional and central religious bodies), the catholicity
of the church, and the matter of inculturation. The local congregation
may be construed as a more basic holon, but it is not simply a part: it is
whole/part. The local church embodies the fullness of the church even
as the totality of the church is more than the sum of local churches.
Holon also sheds light on the issue of the catholicity of the church.
The church is catholic by virtue of its being whole/part. It is catholic
in the sense of translocal/glocal because it is simultaneously whole
and part, local and global. We cannot speak of holon informing the
notion of catholicity without at the same time informing inculturation. In the complex and highly differentiated and varied bioregions

31. Wessels, *The Holy Web*, 57–61.
32. Cited in Wessels, Ibid., 60.

of the earth, each is coherent within itself and yet intrinsically and intimately related to and in concord with the whole, providing a lens through which to understand a church that is rooted in its locality and yet connected to the wider church. This account, contends Wessels, provides a "useful analogy that points out the great variety of local and regional Christian churches, differing in culture, language, ritual, and theological expressions. Each church is coherent within itself and yet intimately related to the others."[33]

THE CHURCH: LITURGIST/WORSHIP CELEBRANT OF THE EARTH

Who can relate to nature and marvel at its complexity, diversity, unity, beauty, and mystery without experiencing enchantment? This is not a simple romantic enchantment; it is an enchantment that leads to worship, thanksgiving, and celebration. "Enchantment with nature," writes Leonardo Boff, "opens us to our specific mission in the universe, that of being priests celebrating and giving thanks for the grandeur, majesty, rationality, and beauty of the cosmos and everything in it."[34] Sean McDonagh, one of the prophets of ecological praxis, says something similar: "Our unique human vocation is to celebrate the beauty and fruitfulness of all life on Earth."[35] The church is a community that celebrates and gives thanks for the beauty and majesty of God's creation. It is a community that leads the whole inhabited earth in praise and adoration for the web of life in which we all belong and derive our being. Unfortunately, many congregations still prepare liturgy and do worship without much intentional incorporation of the elements of nature. At best, nature is incorporated as a backdrop, not an active participant in the liturgy and worship.

A transformation in the way we prepare liturgy and do worship needs to happen along with our theologies. Troy Messenger puts it strongly and well: Our "[e]arth theologies cannot be effective without transformed worship. Worship is an essential companion to environmental justice because theology happens first and foremost in worship. Worship is primary theology."[36] If theology happens first and

33. Ibid., 144.

34. Boff, *Cry of the Earth*, 200.

35. Cited in Edwards, *Ecology at the Heart of Faith*, 113.

36. Messenger, "These Stones," 174.

foremost in worship, then we better make sure that our liturgies and worship embody the green theology we are attempting to articulate. If the green Spirit is truly enfleshed in the various forms of life on earth, then we must invite the earth as our partner in worship. When we do this, the Spirit is fully in us and among us. Only churches that take seriously the earth as their partner will develop truly earth-centered liturgies and worship.

THE CHURCH: CELEBRANT
OF THE CHURCH'S EARTHY SACRAMENTS

Along with liturgy and worship, we need to articulate an ecological vision of the sacraments. The eucharist and baptism point to the ecological identity and mission of the church. Analogous to the Trinity, the bread and wine of the eucharist symbolize the perichoretic relationship of the earth, humankind, and God. In the bread and wine of the eucharist we have the fruits of the earth, products of human labor, and God's life-giving and sustaining power coming together. In a symbolic-liturgical way, the eucharist gathers the earth and its fruits, human activity, and God's creative and sustaining power. Every time we celebrate the eucharist in remembrance (*anamnesis*) of Jesus, we are reminded of the One who reconnected us to God, to one another, and to the earth; we are reminded that we are a part of the 4.7-billion-year history of the earth. At the same time we are reminded of the daily crucifixion of the earth through our ecocidal acts. Every time we celebrate the eucharist in remembrance of Jesus, we are reminded of the One who embodied the hope of a new creation. In short, the eucharist plays out an ecological vision in a ritualized form.

The sacrament of baptism also plays out an ecological vision, though this has been eclipsed by narrow understandings of baptism. Most common is the understanding of baptism as something like inoculation. Parents want their children baptized to protect them against evil diseases. Baptism is also narrowly understood as a way of "welcoming into the club." Against these narrow understandings we need to retrieve and articulate a notion of baptism that affirms our intrinsic connection with nature, with each other, and with the Divine. Baptism is a symbol of our immersion into the body of God. It is a symbol of our connection to the earth, a symbol of our belonging to a community, a symbol of our deep connection to the wellspring of life. Baptism affirms that we are individuals only in community. Through the baptismal water we are reminded of our need for the living water that quenches all thirst, and we are reminded of our need for cleansing. The baptismal water reminds us that we are constituted by water and what happens to water happens to us. Water is a testament of our oneness with the earth. For Paul King and David Woodyard "[t]he water in baptism is a statement of solidarity and mutuality with all creation: it is essential for earth-healing and producing, and a bearer of sacred spirits."[37]

THE CHURCH CALLED TO MISSION AND MINISTRY OF ECOLOGICAL CARETAKERS

All of my ecological interpretations of the church, its theology, liturgy, worship, and sacraments must come to expression in mission and ministry. It is exciting that missiologists have now included ecological concern as one of the five marks of global mission, namely, (1) to proclaim the Good News of the Kingdom of God; (2) to teach, baptize, and nurture new believers; (3) to respond to human need by loving service; (4) to seek to transform unjust structures of society; and (5) to strive to safeguard the integrity of creation and sustain and renew the life of the earth.[38] A summary report from the World Evangelical Forum and *Au Sable* Institute Forum speaks strongly of this ecological mission: "the church needs to do what it can do best: 'to proclaim the full truth about the environmental crisis in the face of powerful persons, pressures and institutions which profit from concealing the truth'; and to strive for reform and replacement of practices and institutions that degrade God's creation."[39] This is a powerful statement that underscores our responsibility as stewards of the ecosystem, although it may not be satisfactory for those who are not comfortable with the language of stewardship given that it runs the risk of an inflated view of humankind. While our primary stance should be one of harmony with creation, the use of stewardship or caretaker underscores agency, especially that we are the creatures who have the ability to destroy— and to destroy with wanton intentionality.

---

37. King and Woodyard, *Liberating Nature*, 124.

38. Walls and Ross, *Mission in the 21st Century*, xiv.

39. Cited in DeWitt, "To Strive to Safeguard," 93.

With mission informed by ecological sensibility, the church must proceed to articulate the ministry directions and expressions congruent with it. Our ministry response must be comprehensive and must include service, education, advocacy, organization, mobilization, building sustainable communities, adoption of appropriate technologies, and lifestyle change. There is a saying, "If you give a person fish it will feed him or her for a few days. But if you teach a person how to fish, it will feed him or her for the rest of his life." In light of the ecological challenge, however, when there are no more fish, it is not enough to teach the person how to fish. We must teach the person how to take care of the lake, river, and ocean. We must teach the person how to care for the ecosystem. This means educating and acquiring skills and organizing people for specific programs or activities. Moreover, caring for the earth may lead to advocacy and mobilization when deeply entrenched powerful interest groups resist change.

THE CHURCH: A COMMUNITY THAT PRACTICES ECOLOGICAL SPIRITUALITY

I opened this chapter by sharing my childhood memories of living near the river and ocean. The ocean, in particular, has been formative to my identity. Now I understand why in my travels to coastal towns and cities of the world that I like, whenever possible, to see the ocean, if not swim. I cannot, however, enjoy my life in diaspora with the continuing nostalgia of the ocean of my childhood. Diaspora life has taught me to find new geographies to nourish my soul. The wide expanse of Lake Superior (U.S. and Canada) has helped nourish my oceanic sensibility—my connection to the vast expanse of water. Also, I cannot continue to live with the nostalgia of a once-upon-a time rural place with abundant flora and fauna. It took me more than a decade to understand that diaspora—though an experience of uprooting—is not simply about being rootless; it is also about becoming "rooted" to the place where our journeys take us. With this realization, I began to connect to the world in my new neighborhood in Fridley, Minnesota. I started to recognize and learn the names of some flowers, distinguishing the annuals from the perennials. What a delight. They lift up my spirit when I am down. What a glorious morning it becomes when I am greeted by the morning glory. And let me not forget the crocus that restores my focus while the ranunculus lures

me away from the frenetic pursuit of the ridiculous. With this new attentiveness I learned to distinguish not only a peony from a daisy but
also a coreopsis from a heliopsis. To my astonishment, I have become
an amateur (French for "one who loves" or "for the love of") gardener.
A diaspora like myself has become connected to the place.

Yes, I have become native because I am acknowledging my root-
edness and connection to my new place. This is possible because I have
learned to be porous; I have learned to listen deeply. Initially I dreaded
it, so I tried to avoid deep listening by immersing myself in my work.
Sensing what is present, feeling what is inside and around us, seeing
what is unfolding before our eyes, smelling the aroma of the changing
season, savoring the fruits of the earth, and listening to the manifold
sounds of the universe all require that we open ourselves to the world
around us and in us. They require opening our hearts—our center—so
we can hear, smell, feel, taste, and see the enfleshed Spirit. Opening
our hearts is at the core of cultivating spirituality in general and an
ecologically attuned spirituality in particular. It is about our willingness to be touched, to be vulnerable, to learn, and to be changed. In
this spirituality of opening our hearts, says Joan Chittister, "all of life
becomes a teacher and we its students. The listener can always learn
and turn and begin again. The open can always be filled."[40] And we can
be changed and transformed.

Deep listening is transforming. It has transformed my life and
it has nourished my day-to-day life. In deep listening we are changed
ontologically—we realize our ontological identity. Jay McDaniel articulates this ontological change: "In moments when we truly listen
to others, the sharp dichotomy between subject and object falls away,
and we realize that we are more connected to others than we might
otherwise have imagined."[41] This is true of my new understanding of
the ocean. Beyond conventional interpretation, ocean does not separate us but connects us. The ocean is a great connector. I am connected
to the Pacific Ocean of my childhood even as I take a dip or fish in the
Atlantic. We may not see easily this connection, but I am connected
to the Pacific Ocean as I wade in the Mississippi River in Minnesota
because its water flows to the Gulf of Mexico and joins with other

40. Chittister, cited in McDaniel, "In the Beginning," 26.
41. McDaniel, "In the Beginning," 30.

oceans, including the Pacific. The ocean of my childhood is our ocean; it belongs to the world.

Historical geographer Epeli Hau'ofa puts it well: "The ocean unites us, and is our common heritage . . . The sea is constantly flowing. No boundary can contain it, or stop its movement within a confine. The same body of water washes all shores . . . The ocean is our supreme metaphor."[42] Indeed, the ocean is our supreme metaphor, a metaphor for connection and interdependence. It circulates the Spirit-enfleshed body—the earth; it circulates in our bodies and in our cells. It is a metaphor for life, a metaphor for God. The strong waves of the ocean can be unforgiving, especially for the sailors caught in the eye of a perfect storm. But, like the fisherfolks of my hometown, I continue to affirm with them, saying, *"Ang kalooy sa Dyos sama ka lapad sa dagat"* (God's mercy is as wide as the ocean). Even if God's mercy does not always bring us to safety, we know that in death or in life, we belong to God—the ocean. And, as the saying goes, "If God were an ocean, what is a shipwreck?"

Moreover, listening—deep listening—does not only lead us to the realization of our deep connections, but also to the task of transformation. Knowing our deep connections, we can embrace the pain of the earth and engage in transformative acts. Listening is not simply wishing that something terrible would go away. McDaniel sees two aspects that a life of listening includes: "attunement to actuality and possibility: *to the way things are* and to *the way things can be in the future,* given the way things are."[43] Ecocide is the prevalent way things are, but it is not the way of the future, and it should not be. We must muster courage to prevent our march toward ecological destruction.

SEEDS OF GREEN, SEEDS OF HOPE

Ecocide is everywhere. The green Spirit's enfleshed earthly presence is undergoing crucifixion; it is flowing with the blood of ecological violence. The green ecology is red in the blood of destruction; it is also red in the blood of those killed because of their commitment to a green future. The destructive power of predatory globalization has crushed those who have opposed its ecologically destructive projects.

42. Hau'ofa, "A Beginning," 131, cited in Victorin-Vangerud, "From Metaphors and Models," 82.

43. McDaniel, "In the Beginning," 31.

But out of the red blood of destruction a green seed of hope is rising. Out of the bloody cross has evolved a green cross. Like the blood of the early martyrs, the blood of the ecological martyrs of our times is like a seed—seed of a green tomorrow. Seeds of green tomorrow are sprouting and growing everywhere.

Somewhere in the obscure river town of Zapuri in Acre, Brazil, lived Francisco "Chico" Mendes Filho.[44] Mendes, a rubber tapper by trade, organized and mobilized three hundred thousand rubber tappers and one million farmers and hunters, all victims of World Bank and Brazilian government-supported cattle ranching and hydroelectric projects that had stolen and destroyed their lands. He also forged an alliance with Brazilian NGOs and First World allies. Mendes and representatives of indigenous, environmental, and human rights organizations traveled to the United States in 1987 and did advocacy work at the U.S. Congress and the World Bank. They demanded the creation of "extractive reserves" under the management of local rubber tapper communities. On December 22, 1988, Mendes was murdered in his hometown Zapuri (Brazil). Nevertheless, the struggle for extractive reserves went forward and the Brazilian government finally created nineteen extractive reserves covering nearly three million hectares of rainforest.

Another powerful story and seed of hope is the work of The College of Maasin—Community and Extension Development Program (CM-CEDP), a college of the United Church of Christ in the Philippines, and the Asuncion Fisherfolks Organization in Maasin, Southern Leyte. The Asuncion Fisherfolks Organization started as a small group of fisherfolks seeking to help each other, especially those lost or capsized by strong storms in the open seas of Leyte, Bohol, Camiguin, and Surigao. With educational, material, and financial support from CM-CEDP, the group evolved into a strong organization that responded to the wider needs of the members, needs such as food, boats, gasoline, and other fishing supplies. It further developed programs such as the fish-aggregating device (FAD), which is used to provide shelter for pelagic fish. In addition, it facilitated the creation of a fish sanctuary. Furthermore, as an organized group, it helped deter big fishing boats with huge and deep fishing nets. What the fisherfolks

44. See Brecher and Costello, *Global Village*, 92. Also, see Messer, *A Conspiracy of Goodness*, 79–80.

have accomplished may not be grand in scale but, as Zuriel Tiempo, director of CM-CEDP, modestly expressed it: "it has made the lives of the fisherfolks better."

The greening of consciousness is growing in our churches, including the evangelicals and the Pentecostals. Many evangelicals have joined the ecological movement and embraced ecological concern as an important ministry. For David Gushee, a robust orthodoxy includes a "robust and contextually sensitive theology of creation that actually plays a working role in our daily practical theology."[45] He argues further that a robust orthodoxy cannot speak of a "pro-life ethic" without being pro-creation. Care for creation is consistent with a pro-life ethic.

An encouraging example of this evangelical ecological commitment coming to life is with the Full Gospel Churches of India, particularly in their ministry in the Krishna river delta of Andhra Pradesh. Following the Pentecostal heritage, they started their ministry in the area focusing exclusively on evangelism (read: "saving souls") and church planting. As they learned more about the area and its people, the evangelists were shocked by what they found: poor and disease-ridden people eking out a living and destroying the coastal mangrove swamps. This led the evangelists to redefine their mission. The Full Gospel Churches of India launched a ministry under the name Christian Coastal Development Project. Starting with church planting, the ministry of the church now includes education, medical services, rural development, and ecology rehabilitation.[46]

The ministries of various Christian communities on ecological care are seeds of the green Spirit, and they are seeds of hope. The green Spirit is at work. Only the green Spirit can make the plants grow and bear fruits, but we have a role to play. We are to align ourselves with the work of the green Spirit in planting and nurturing the seeds of green or earthwise churches. Let us do our part and trust that the Earth Spirit will bless our efforts.

45. Gushee, "New Frontiers," 46. Also Gushee, "Opinion: Our Theology of Ecology."
46. Bookless, "To Strive to Safeguard," 94–95.

10

The Church as a Community
of Mending Healers

Mending the Sickly State of Global Health

O UR HEALTH FACES SERIOUS threats in the era of globalization, particularly by the predatory global market and global hegemonic
forces. Many speak out strongly of a global health crisis. How does
globalization affect people's health and health care around the world?
What are the signs of globalization's impact on health and health
care? What happens to health when predatory globalization promotes
policies and practices that heighten the economic disparity of nations
and people? What happens to health when private corporations rule
the world, including the delivery of health care? What happens to
health when profit takes precedence over the right of each person to
adequate health care? What happens to health when the production
of medicine is controlled by corporate interest? What happens to the
health of the poor and the vulnerable? Where do they go for health
care? What happens to health when ecology is destroyed in pursuit of
greater profit? What happens to health when genetically modified organisms (GMOs) are introduced into farming practices and the food
market? What happens to health when the much-needed resources
are spent for the production of armaments of war? What happens to
health when borders become more porous and people and viruses become more mobile? These questions demand a serious response. Most
certainly they demand a serious response from the church. How does
the challenge of globalization to health inform the way we think about

the church and of its mission and ministry? What are the resources in our Christian tradition that may help us imagine how to be a church in light of the challenges of globalization to health? This chapter seeks to articulate a view of the church (ecclesiology) that takes seriously the challenges that globalization poses in relation to health.

PATHOLOGICAL BODY POLITIC, SOCIAL INEQUITY, AND HEALTH

In the Philippines, I used the following humorous yet serious story of a person who consults a medical doctor to underscore the crucial importance of reading context before giving any treatment. *Mang* Juan complains to the doctor that he has not been to the toilet for three days. After a quick examination, the doctor prescribes a medicine to loosen his bowel. *Mang* Juan laments that he does not have the money to buy the medicine. The kind and generous doctor gives him money to buy medicine. After a couple of days, the doctor sees *Mang* Juan at the *mercado* (town market) with his friends drinking *tuba* (coconut wine). The doctor asks *Mang* Juan, "How are you? Did the medicine work? Have you been to the toilet after taking the medicine?" "Yes, I finally went to the toilet." "Good," said the doctor. But *Mang* Juan continues, "I hope you will not get upset. I did not use the money to buy your prescription. Instead, I used it to buy rice to fill my empty stomach. Finally, I had something for the toilet."

A sound treatment of a disease is impossible without an adequate medical diagnosis. An accurate diagnosis is crucial for treating the disease, not just the symptom. Yet, even a good diagnosis of a specific form of illness may be limited in scope. It may address a specific disease but not the circumstances that contributed to the formation of the disease. While diagnostic focus is crucial for effective medical intervention, it may not address the larger pathological basis of the disease that a person or community is suffering. I recognize the limits of what a medical doctor can do in specific cases and circumstances, but we need to see disease and healing in relation to the larger context if we are to address the larger pathology that is undermining health. The larger pathology that I refer to is our body politic. Our body politic is sick—terribly sick! It is sick at the very core. A sick body politic makes the people sick. People die before their time. The facts pointing in this direction are indubitably irrefragable.

Jean-Bertrand Aristide has a story of this sick global body politic that is making people die globally and in his home place—Haiti. He tells of a morgue worker who was preparing to dispose of a dozen corpses. To the morgue worker's surprise, one soul lifted himself off the table, shook his head and declared, "I am not dead!" The morgue worker responded, "Yes you are. The doctors say that you are dead, so lie down."[1]

The physicians of the global market have already declared millions of people around the world dead. Thousands are dying day after day of preventable diseases. Thousands are dying every day because they do not have access to medical services; thousands are dying every day because they have no financial resources to buy food and other basic necessities. What is heart-rending and appalling is that this is happening when our medical and technological capabilities have reached a level of sophistication that is more than adequate to respond to the need. What is heart-rending and appalling is that these deaths are happening when huge pharmaceutical corporations, health insurance companies, and health maintenance organizations (HMOs) are reaping humongous profits. What is heart-rending and appalling is that we have let the genocide (particularly HIV/AIDS) continue by our silence and indifference. Moreover, what is heart-rending and appalling is that so many are not yet appalled, certainly not the churches. What on earth is going on?

I say that what is going on is a sickness of our society's soul. What is going on is a sickness of the heart. What is going on is that we have created a market society that values profit over the health and well-being of all. What is going on is that we have created a market society that negates health care as a basic human right and transforms it into a commodity. Moreover, what is going on is that we have created a market society that institutionalizes individual and corporate greed. Still further, what is going on is that we have created a global market society that promotes and perpetuates social inequity.

This social inequity is lethal. It is a lethal divide: it destroys health, particularly of the most vulnerable. If the fundamental prerequisites of a healthy society include access to the basic necessities of life, such as adequate and nutritious food, clothing, housing, education, sanitation, and health care, then there is a correlation between economic status and health. Even if we take into consideration other factors beyond socio-economic resources (psycho-social interpretations),

1. Aristide, "Globalization: A View from Below," 10.

studies have shown that there is a "strong and consistent relationship between income distribution and health: A greater difference between the incomes of the rich and the poor within a country meant worse overall health."[2] This has led Stephen Bezruchka and Mary Anne Mercer to conclude that "inequality is the fundamental cause of poor health and premature death. Global inequality has produced a world where millions die of preventable causes every year."[3]

With the economic situation of many countries, especially of the global South, worsening under the era of corporate-led globalization, what can we expect? With income disparity among individuals within a nation and between nations widening, what can we expect? Expect bad news: a worsening health situation. Evidence of the correlation between corporate-led globalization and declining health can be found in many countries, especially if we compare health statistics between the 1980s and the 1990s (when corporate globalization became more entrenched) from the 1960s and the 1970s. Statistics from nations of the sub-Saharan Africa from 1970 to 1997 offer a stark and grim example. Hardly surprising, "By 1997, countries with proportionately greater debt had significantly higher infant mortality than countries with lower debt."[4] This is the result when debt servicing takes priority over the health care needs of the people.

THE GLOBAL MARKET AND CORPORATE ASSAULT ON HEALTH AND HEALTH CARE

The corporate assault on health, particularly its goal of privatization, further compromises the health effects of social inequity. Transnational corporations, in cooperation with the World Bank, are aggressively pursuing the goal of privatizing health care by undermining public health care, including primary health care. The World Bank, for example, has used its economic and political muscle to pressure governments around the world to play limited roles in financing and providing public health care and allows for the broader role of the private sector. Through a carrot and stick approach, those who are willing to cooperate get loans and aid while those who are not receive various forms of threats and punishments. Of course, the World Bank

2. Bezruchka and Mercer, "The Lethal Divide," 13.

3. Ibid., 11.

4. Ibid., 16.

and transnational corporations attempt to portray the situation as one in which national governments are in control. In the words of a senior African ministry health official, "They say they want to put us in the driver's seat. But sometimes I feel that I am sitting in the front seat driving a taxi, and they are still telling us where to go."[5]

Numerous cases of the World Bank and transnational corporations' assault on global health exist; I cite here a few. The United Nations' World Health Organization (WHO) was under severe corporate threat when it introduced an Action Program on Essential Drugs (1978) and the International Code on Breastmilk (1981). Guatemala adopted the WHO-UNICEF Infant Formula Marketing Code into laws which prohibit companies that sell infant formulas from using advertising labels that make their products appear to be healthier than breast milk; they were forced to back down when Gerber gained U.S. support to challenge Guatemala at the World Trade Organization (WTO) tribunal.[6] Again, in 2003, the U.S. sugar industry tried to undermine the WHO's recommended health guideline for sugar intake by co-authoring a report with the Food and Agriculture Organization named "The Expert Consultation on Diet, Nutrition and the Prevention of Chronic Diseases." A trade group (the Sugar Association) went so far as to lobby members of the U.S. Congress to challenge the US$406 million contribution to the WHO as well as demand that the international health organization remove an early draft of its report from its Website.[7]

If countries and United Nations bodies are not free from corporate assault, then ever more vulnerable are the community-based health initiatives that address the root causes of the health crisis and support the struggle of the marginalized for holistic health. In fact, corporate interest works in tandem with other groups, such as medical and nursing establishments that have entrenched interest in the control of knowledge related to healing. Many primary health care workers have been harassed and arrested. In some countries people merely found in possession of David Werner's trailblazing book, *Where There Is No Doctor*, suffered arrest and brutal treatment.[8]

---

5. Cited in Hong, "The Primary Health Care Movement," 35.
6. Shaffer and Brenner, "Trade and Health Care," 82.
7. Hong, in *Sickness and Wealth*, 33.
8. Ibid., 28–29.

GLOBAL MARKET AND HUMAN ORGAN TRAFFICKING

If the global market can commodify sex and health care, what would prevent it from commodifying human organs? With a desperate population ready to sell whatever it can, the buying and selling of human organs has become a profitable industry. India and the Philippines, for example, are among the hotspot countries in kidney trafficking. A recent document reports that poor Filipinos who sell their kidney to Arab or Western buyers receive about US$3,000.[9] This amount sounds much higher than what many of the poverty-stricken organ donors actually receive. If so, brokers must be making a killing off the transaction.

While others survive after the nephrectomy to taste the money they have received from selling their kidneys, some do not live to tell the story. In some cases the poor are lured for a job placement abroad and are told to submit themselves to a medical check-up. They are "usually held for a few days in a flat. Then they [are] told to pass medical tests and receive jabs." Unaware of the evil plot, they are killed and their body organs taken for sale to those who can afford them. This gruesome story happened to Makhbuba Aripova's husband, Farkhood, and his relatives from the central Asian republic of Uzbekistan. Makhbuba saw her husband for the last time when he prepared the necessary documents for his departure to Canada, with the intention that she and her child would join him later. His body and those of his relatives were found in plastic bags in their hometown of Bukhara.[10]

MILITARIZATION, WAR, AND HEALTH

Militarization worsens the health consequences of economic inequality and the privatization as well as the commodification of health care. The most obvious link between militarization and health is that of war. If we are unable to respond effectively to the health-care needs of the people in peaceful times, war compromises their needs all the more. With more destructive technologies of war, we can also expect more casualties, and continuing war means more and more casualties. The use of pathogen or biological products (biological war or bioterrorism) not only raises the number of casualties but also heightens the

---

9. Carney, "Why a Kidney," 1.
10. Franchetti, "Dozens Killed for Body Parts."

link between war and health. However, the destruction of war extends far beyond the immediate victims (both combatants and civilians), and the number of postwar casualties is often much higher than during the war itself. War causes collateral damage that takes a wider cast and extends for a longer period of time.

War destroys the community's economic and socio-political infrastructure. If we consider economic sanctions as an instrument of war, which we must, then the collateral damage spreads even more. The loss of economic infrastructure leads to unemployment, poverty, and lack of means to buy the basic needs for sustenance. The destruction of the socio-political infrastructure means chaos and, therefore, more violence and death. War leads to the destruction of health infrastructure, disease-control programs, and sanitation systems. When these are destroyed, it means more death in the affected population.

Post-traumatic and related illnesses and deaths are also post-war casualties. Victims of war, terrorism, and torture suffer post-traumatic illnesses long after the actual event. The horrible events remain deep in the psyche of the person, and no one can simply forget and drive the ghost of these past experiences away. Adults and children alike are not immune from post-traumatic illness. Children who have grown up in villages that had been destroyed by war and whose parents were killed in their presence have developed serious post-traumatic illnesses. These illnesses manifest in many ways. John Paul Lederach tells of a case of a woman in Latin America who manifests deep post-traumatic illness. Unable to sleep at night, she wanders around and screams. She complains of a monkey inside her stomach that she is trying to force out. She and her family are looking for a *brujo* (witch doctor) who can get the monkey out.[11] And as we now know, post-traumatic illnesses are not limited to civilian victims: Soldiers suffer them as well.

The collateral damage of war extends far beyond what we often recognize because war is more than an instrument of predatory globalization. War is destructive to life and particularly to health at the most fundamental level because it is an expression of the militarization of the economy. The militarization of the economy continues to destroy health and kill not only in times of actual war but also in "normal" times because it supports the social and political infrastructure that promotes inequity, and it prioritizes the production of the

11. Lederach, *The Journey*, 74.

armaments of death over the instruments of health. Furthermore, the collateral damage of war and militarization extends to the ecosystem. Militarization and war have left toxic legacies, thus affecting the health of people. The nuclear fallout in the Marshall Islands and unexploded landmines that remain buried in a country like Cambodia are only two notorious examples.

GLOBALIZATION, MOBILITY, DIASPORA, AND HEALTH

Global mobility and diaspora compound and aggravate the health crisis. Easy mobility means easy movement of various pathogens from one geobiological region to another. Further, the diaspora of people poses new challenges to health and health care as well. This is more obvious in the case of refugees and migrants. War, civil strife, and environmental destruction create a groundswell of refugees within and across borders that worsens the already compromised and volatile health condition of the refugees as well as that of many of the receiving communities. Many communities are not prepared to respond to the health-care needs of the sudden influx of refugees and migrants. Without support from international governments and nongovernmental bodies, the outbreak of an epidemic could easily occur in the place of departure as well as the place of destination.

Though less dramatic than the sudden flow of refugees, the regular diaspora of people presents a serious challenge to health. The movement from one place to another itself has significant consequences to the health of the traveler or the settler. Adaptation into the host country means new health challenges. It means increasing exposure to new health stresses. Moving or resettling implies changes in one's lifestyle, food habits, daily routine, relationships, and physical exercise; it imposes psychological and other forms of emotional stress and a certain degree of isolation. The stress of the individual migrant or permanent settler is compounded with the stress that other members of the family are experiencing. Each of these factors can affect the health and well-being of the traveler or settler and can have potential physical and mental health consequences.[12]

Among (im)migrants are medical doctors, nurses, and other health professionals. Many of them have left the global South for the global North in search of a better life, leading to the shortage of medi-

12. See *Unnatural Causes*.

cal practitioners in their countries of origin. The Philippines offers a good example. Because nursing is the best route to finding work abroad, many medical doctors have abandoned their profession to pursue nursing. With the Filipino propensity to create jokes out of a serious situation, I heard someone say that "one of the requirements for the nursing degree these days is the M.D. degree."

GLOBALIZATION, ECOLOGY, BIOTECHNOLOGY, AND HEALTH

When the predatory global market's pursuit of profit leads to ecological destruction, the health of all living creatures is at risk. As we witness the destruction of the forest through logging and hydroelectric dams to support the electricity needs of the industries, we are confronted with industrial wastes and other consequences. Dams, large-scale irrigation projects, and industrial wastes provide breeding places for disease-carrying insects, such as Anopheles mosquitoes, which carry the malaria germ. Compounding the situation, there is a body of research showing that agricultural pesticides have not controlled the mosquito population. On the contrary, Anopheles mosquitoes have developed resistance to some of the pesticides, including DDT. Thus, malaria is on the rise again in many countries.[13] Malaria was a disease I knew only through statistics until I found out that it was one of the main reasons some of my students, who came from various places in Africa (Nigeria, Ivory Coast, Benin, Togo, Democratic Republic of Congo, Republic of Congo, and Rwanda), were absent from my class in Yaoundé. More lethal than malaria is dengue, which is another disease borne by mosquitoes (*Aedes aegypti*)—a type of mosquito that thrives in areas without good sanitation.

Pollution from toxic chemicals circulating in the environment poses another health challenge. As noted earlier, studies show that more than 73,000 synthetic chemicals are circulating in the environment, and many of them resist breakdown.[14] Furthermore, they interact with one another, thus multiplying their power and effects. These chemicals accumulate in our food, water, and bodies, making us vulnerable to diseases. Air pollution has also contributed much to the rise of respiratory-related illnesses such as asthma, allergies, and lung

13. Holtz and Kachur, "The Reglobalization of Malaria," 138–39.

14. Delgado, *Shaking the Gates of Hell*, 38.

diseases. More affluent regions of the world have not been spared.[15] Studies have reported a forty percent increase in asthma deaths among people between the ages of five and 34 between the mid-1970s and the mid-1980s in many affluent regions, including Europe and the United States.[16]

The food supply is another area in which corporate globalization, ecology, biotechnology, and health intersect. The United States banned DBCP (1979), an extremely toxic pesticide that is known to cause sterility among farm workers, yet it exported the pesticide to countries that grow bananas for U.S. owned or operated corporations.[17] Aggravating the health risk is the introduction of genetically modified organisms (GMO) to the food supply. GMOs may enhance food production—and the profits of the few—but they raise the possibility of genetic pollution, which can have lasting and destructive consequences beyond the immediate gains. When released into the environment, the genetically modified plant or animal may breed new plants and animals that cause new diseases to emerge among the people in the area, diseases that are highly resistant to antibiotics.[18]

GLOBAL MARKET, DISTORTED DIET, AND HEALTH

When food supply and food consumption are dictated by the goal of what makes profit, the health of the people will be at risk. When the majority of the world's poor do not have even enough food to eat, corporate interest compounds the already worsening situation by creating a culture of food consumption that is counter to proper nutrition. By spending millions on food advertising, corporations lead consumers to believe that they are buying food items that are needed for their physical nourishment. Food conglomerates are successful as well in shaping the minds of consumers to take advantage of convenience foods (fast foods), bulk purchases, and super-sized portions. Making it all the more ridiculous, government resources (e.g., the United States) are used even by corporate welfare fathers to subsidize corporate advertising for nutritionally empty and harmful food products.

15. Brennan, *Globalization and its Terrors*, 35.

16. Ibid.

17. Delgado, *Shaking the Gates of Hell*, 41.

18. Brennan, *Globalization and its Terrors*, 61.

The poor of the global South have not been spared from the reach of multinational food conglomerates. In fact, the poor have bought into the idea of buying highly processed food items because of their association with affluence and of their association with the global North/West. It is a dream come true to have food products of the affluent and westernized world, products such as cola drinks, highly processed but poor-quality meat products like Spam and hot dogs, and bread made of highly refined flour. It is no surprise that when I visit a family in the Philippines whose home is surrounded by a pineapple plantation, I am served canned and syrupy Dole pine-apple instead of fresh-sliced fruit. When, after a year's absence in the Philippines, my heart longs for the *gabi* (*taro*) and *palawan* (a kind of root crop) and the *ginataang pako* (fern cooked in coconut milk), it is no surprise when I am served angel food cake, deviled eggs, food for the gods cake, and spaghetti (the Filipino way—sweeter, mixed with hot dogs, and with banana ketchup as sauce).

The consequences of unhealthy food and diet are enormous. The poor suffer not only from double but a triple or fourfold wham-my. Not only do they not have enough income to buy an adequate amount of food, but the pittance of their hard-earned income is used often to buy products with empty and destructive calories. This may be truer among the poor of the global North: "the poor people are malnourished because they do not have enough to feed themselves, and they are obese because they eat poorly, with an important energy imbalance . . . The food they can afford is often cheap, industrial-ized, mass produced, and inexpensive."[19] Meanwhile the rich, while not completely spared from corporate advertising, are spending their money on diet and exercise programs, more expensive organic foods, guided meditation and relaxation techniques, medical tour-ism to other parts of the world, and various forms of makeover, such as liposuction, eye-lid lift, and so forth.

SICKNESS OF THE SOUL: IMPERIAL BLOWBACK, IMPERIAL SICKNESS

The health crisis that predatory globalization brings, especially that brought about by war, is more than physical, and it hurts not only the victims but also the perpetrators. One obvious example of imperial

19. Golson, *America's Eating Disorder.*

blowback that strikes at the soul of the citizens of imperializing nations is post-traumatic stress syndrome and the high rate of suicide among war veterans. A study by the Centers for Disease Control in Atlanta reports a high rate of violent deaths of Vietnam veterans, including cases of suicide, medicine overdose, car accidents, and homicide.[20] The rate of suicide among veterans of the Gulf War is rising also. In addition, around 300,000 U.S. soldiers suffer from depression and post-traumatic stress after their tour of duty in Iraq and Afghanistan.[21]

An account by George Orwell may partly explain the veteran's turmoil. Orwell recalls how his feeling of repugnance of the imperial abuses of British rule was compromised by his own role in perpetuating it, when a part of him felt that "the greatest joy in the world would be to drive a bayonet through a Buddhist priest's guts." [22] This kind of feeling may be considered a "normal byproduct[s] of imperialism" because, as David Spurr interprets it, "the maintenance of authority depends on an inherent enmity, a constant vigilance for signs of resistance among the colonized. The signs of resistance in *oneself* are alternately repressed and expressed in irrational ways."[23] Imperial blowback, however, moves beyond what happens to military veterans of imperialistic wars. It also takes a toll on the larger population and manifests itself in complex sicknesses of the soul. Again, interpreters of Orwell say that he brings to the surface the symptoms of the deep religio-cultural crisis that the West is suffering: an instrumentalist view of nature, the reification and "thingification" of social relations, "created loneliness," the constant need to show masculine posture over a colonized population who are perceived as children, and the suppression of one's self for the sake of maintaining imperial identity.[24]

Overall, the market society is manufacturing deep psychosomatic sickness of various sorts. Writing of the ravages that her beloved homeland suffered, Slavenka Drakulić speaks of "the other side of war" that is often forgotten in taking account of the cost of war. "War," writes Drakulić, "devours us from the inside, eating away like acid, how it wrecks our lives, how it spawns evil within us, and how we tear the liv-

20. Bower, "Deadly aftermath for Vietnam."
21. *Stepping Up*, 8.
22. Cited in Spurr, *The Rhetoric of Empire*, 191.
23. Ibid.
24. Ibid. Spurr citing Nandy, *The Intimate Enemy*, 40.

ing flesh of those friends who do not feel the same way as we do . . . In the war death becomes a simple, acceptable fact. But life turns to hell."[25] It is the side that cannot be measured simply by weapons of mass destruction and direct casualties of war but instead by the destruction of the human spirit. Human history is deeply scarred not only by direct violence, but also by meaninglessness, ennui, and boredom.[26] Perhaps the growing number of certain types of depression, high rate of suicide, drug and alcohol addiction, and violence, particularly school shootings (e.g., Columbine High School and Virginia Tech), are symptoms of the devastation and annihilation of the human spirit.

THE HEALTH CRISIS: A CHALLENGE TO THE CHURCH

Our short account of the current health situation shows that we are facing a crisis of epic proportion. It is a crisis that strikes at the heart of how we think about ourselves in relation to the world. It is a crisis that is an expression of a fundamental distortion in our understanding of the world, life, and relationship, and of what we truly value. In the traditional Christian term, we call this fundamental distortion "sin." If this is indeed a sin, then the health crisis is, at its heart, a theological issue. It is at heart a matter of faith or unfaith, of the God of life and the idols of death. It is about our view of God and creation, alienation, brokenness, salvation or liberation, and our dream for a new tomorrow.

The health crisis is a church crisis. The health crisis poses a challenge to the church's understanding of its identity and its theologies. It poses a challenge to its theologies, particularly those that have contributed to the health crisis—theologies that are toxic and hazardous. It poses a challenge to how the church might reimagine itself so that it can be part of the solution, which is healing. It poses a challenge to the church's understanding of mission and ministry.

THE HERMENEUTICAL TASK: HERMENEUTICS, MEDICINE, AND HEALING

Interpretations are not simply interpretations. We live by our interpretations and according to our constructed world. Interpretations matter. If they do not promote life, then they must promote the opposite.

25. Drakulić, *The Balkan Express*, 84.
26. Ruiz, "Cultures of Peace," 4.

Interpretations contribute to the making of the sickness; they add pain to the injury. Interpretations hurt; interpretations kill. Church leaders at the World Council of Churches consultation in Nairobi, Kenya, in 2001, made an emphatic statement that underscores this point in relation to HIV/AIDs: "our interpretation of the scriptures and our theology of sin have all combined to promote stigmatization, exclusion, and suffering of people with HIV or AIDS."[27] It is for this reason that hermeneutics or interpretation must be viewed as constitutive of the healing ministry. Hermeneutics is not a prelude to healing but constitutive of the healing process.

Healing is an ancient and noble calling of hermeneutics. Based on Greek mythology, hermeneutics is the science of Hermes, the god whose task was to transmit clearly to human beings the results of the stormy deliberations on Mount Olympus. Hermes also had other roles. As the patron of merchants and thieves, Hermes was responsible for commodity exchange and was influential in effecting currency exchange. Hermes was also the protector of physicians or those who work to restore the fullness of life to those who are sick and threatened by death. Georges Casalis notes four dimensions of hermeneutics: (1) it translates a divine message into human words, (2) it transposes what was said "at that time" into contemporary categories, (3) it reclaims possession of the text and its meanings from those who have locked them away, and, finally, a medicinal one: (4) it revives or resurrects texts that are about to die in order that people who are suffering and struggling experience healing and liberation.[28] These four dimensions intertwine. While one dimension receives the medicinal designation, all four dimensions comprise the medicinal function of hermeneutics.

Of course, we know that not all interpretations promote healing, just as not all medicine necessarily cures or heals when it is used. The term *pharmakon* suggests both a cure and a poison. Hence, part of the hermeneutical project that is committed toward healing is to expose interpretations that are hurtful or death-giving. Part of the hermeneutical project is to name and expose interpretations that create and exacerbate the disease as well as condemn and isolate the patient. Put positively, the hermeneutical project is about articulating and promoting interpretations that contribute to greater well-being and health.

27. Cited in Messer, *Breaking the Conspiracy of Silence*, 24.
28. Casalis, *Correct Ideas*, 61–66.

Before we go too far and, perhaps, do more harm than heal, we need to examine seriously our perspectives, analytical tools, skills, and resources. We are familiar with many stories of good intentions that produce bad effects. Initially, I considered Henri Nouwen's *The Wounded Healer* as a title for this chapter; I chose to modify it when a colleague from United Theological Seminary of the Twin Cities said, "Eleazar, it better be on the mending side."[29] Yes, it had better be on the mending side, otherwise the wounded will continue to wound others even as he or she aspires to be a healer. We better take to heart Richard Rohr's reminder: "Pain that is not transformed is transferred."[30] On the other hand, we cannot wait until complete healing has occurred before we act. To wait for such a time is to wait forever and not lift a finger. After all, health may be more a matter of degree in a continuum rather than simply an either-or, that is, either sick or healthy.

We must view the health situation from different angles to get a wider perspective, but there is one crucial perspective that offers a serious alternative to our current health malady. Sadly, this is also the perspective that is oftentimes overlooked. It is easy in our excitement to assume the perspective of the healer. No one wants to be ill or sick. Whether or not we actually lift a finger to do something, it feels better to be on the giving-doing side than on the receiving side. This is the perspective from which the classic story of the Good Samaritan has been commonly interpreted. While it is true that reading the story from the point of view of the Samaritan healer (marginalized and outcast) is already radical and subversive in itself, its subversiveness is co-opted quickly given that it feeds into the desire and imagination of virtue, control, and privileged agency. It feeds into our ideal of a modern self-assertive person, a heroic helper who is autonomous and in control of his or her destiny.

Robert Wuthnow offers an incisive critique on this point in his work, *Acts of Compassion*.[31] The Good Samaritan story draws us in with special magnetism because, in Wuthnow's words, "it is essentially, in our modern view, about individual virtue . . . For most of us the story remains an illustration of individual compassion. We let it reinforce our individualism because we neglect even the institutional

29. Nouwen, *The Wounded Healer*.
30. Rohr, cited in Yoder, *The Little Book of Trauma Healing*, 30.
31. Wuthnow, *Acts of Compassion*, particularly pages 157–87.

focus it once had historically."[32] Drawn into the virtue aspect, the general public fails miserably in taking account of deeper issues, such as the societal and systemic dimension. For example, most do not ask the listener to identify with the injured or the marginalized person; most do not ask the listener to imagine being a part of a community that collectively encourages and supports charitable behavior; and most fail to ask what social upbringing, social support, and resources that a person may need to perform compassionate acts. Moreover, the overwhelming majority fails to see the institutional connections that made this kind of care possible in this particular context.

Taking seriously both the institutional critique and the point of view of the sick, Patricia Benner is on target in saying that the vantage point of the healthy helper is a "poor starting point" in dealing with health and health care. It is a "poor starting point" on various grounds: It creates a false sense of immunity; it creates a false separation between the sick and the healthy; and it creates an adversarial relationship between the two groups. As an alternative, Benner contends that the starting point in health care "should be the universal human reality of vulnerability and suffering . . . Suffering and vulnerability are the common fates of finite human beings. We each might need a fellow human being to respond with compassion to our needs for protection and comfort."[33]

JESUS THE RADICAL HEALER

The temptation to read from the point of view of the privileged healer is present in many of our interpretations of Jesus. I, myself, am tempted to jump quickly to point out the healing acts of Jesus while forgetting that this healer was also wounded. It is easy to assume that Jesus did not suffer illness; after all, there is no record of him becoming ill. He was killed at the prime of his life, but common interpretation does not see that as sickness. He did speak of himself, however, as someone who was ill and in need of healing (Mt 25:31–46). In other words, he took the perspective of the vulnerable, and he suffered as a vulnerable person against the mighty power of the Roman Empire. With this perspective in mind, let us now take account of Jesus' acts of healing and exorcism.

32. Ibid., 176–77. Also, see Benner, "When Health Care Becomes a Commodity, 127.

33. Ibid., 126.

Without recounting the details of Jesus' acts of healing, it is important to point out that the New Testament is replete with such stories. What I want to emphasize is that the acts of healing and exorcisms—like Jesus' teaching and preaching—are not simply sporadic acts; rather, they are acts performed by Jesus in light of the coming reign of God. Healing and exorcism are at the heart of the Good News of the reign of God (Mt 4:23). This is the context and horizon in which we must read Jesus' acts. His ministry of healing and exorcism was in obedience to the vision of the reign of God. In other words, Jesus' acts of healing and exorcism are part of the larger project of radical transformation guided by the vision and values of the reign of God.

If the acts of healing and exorcisms of Jesus were done in light of the Good News of the coming reign of God, then they were as much political as physical. In fact, we can say that the larger target of Jesus' acts of healing and exorcising was the sick body politic of his time. The miracle stories, for Rita Nakashima Brock, "point to the political implications of disease and to the social-psychic nature of much sickness. They present inclusive and sophisticated metaphors for understanding the relational nature of sickness and suffering." Brock uses the term "brokenheartedness" as a metaphor to capture in a comprehensive way the interweaving of sickness, political oppression, and the damage to the self due to various and "complex forms of destruction in our culture."[34]

A body politic critique of disease has led biblical scholars to study closely some of the healing and exorcism accounts, such as the story of the Gerasene demoniac in the Markan account (Mk 5:1–20). Scholars, particularly those using postcolonial discourse, have interpreted the demoniac's words ("My name is Legion; for we are many") to refer to the Roman legions. If the legion refers to the Roman army of occupation, Stephen Moore's interpretation makes sense that the demoniac may be identified "as the land and people under occupation." This may explain why the demons earnestly entreat the exorcist "not to send them out of the country [exô tês chôras]." Being sent out of the country to fight for the imperial wars of their colonial masters had been the plight of the colonized and imperialized. This is the likely scenario that the Gerasene demoniac dreaded.[35]

34. Brock, Journeys by Heart, 76.
35. Moore, "Mark and Empire, 135–36.

Sharon Betcher's work, *The Spirit and Politics of Disablement*, offers another meticulous account of the connection between sickness, healing, and body politic. Taking seriously scholarly accounts of the preponderance of the imperial powers' ancient practice of large-scale enslavement, mutilation of male prisoners, and rape of women prisoners, Betcher calls us to interpret the healing accounts in light of this historical background. With this background in mind, the biblical accounts of the lame walking, the blind seeing, and the deaf hearing (Is 35:5–6, Lk 7:22, Mt 11:4–5) will likely have had the ancient imperial practice in mind. If this is the case, then it must change our reading of the healing miracle texts "from an issue of perfect health and wholesomeness to an issue of socio-political critique-of the colonizing nation, its colonizing of bodies, of persons living under empire."[36]

THE CHURCH: FOLLOWER OF THE RADICAL HEALER

The church cannot speak truly of itself as a healer without being a follower of Jesus the radical healer. The church can only claim to be a follower of Jesus if it also assumes the identity of the healer. Indeed, the church as a healer has been a mark of its identity. The disciples of Jesus and the early Christian communities were identified and known as healers—radical healers. When the people heard that disciples of Jesus were present, they asked to be healed. An account in Acts describes how people brought out the sick into the streets and placed them on mats and cots in order that "Peter's shadow might fall on some of them as he came by" (5:15). The crowd also gathered around Jerusalem with their sick and those possessed by evil spirits for exorcism and healing (5:12–16).

As the early Christian communities grew and spread, their health ministry evolved and acquired distinctive shapes. The leaders appointed deacons to care for the needy and the sick. The writings of Paul (Rom 16:1–2) claim Phoebe to be the first visiting nurse. By the third century, organized groups of deacons were caring for the sick. Around the fourth century, we can observe the early beginnings of hospitals staffed by nurses. The private homes of deacons became the settings of these hospitals.[37] An account by the historian Eusebius of a devastating plague reveals how concern for health and well-being is

36. Betcher, *Spirit and the Politics of Disablement*, x.
37. Shelly, "Nursing," 46.

central to the early Christian communities: "The Christians were the only people who amid such terrible ills, showed their fellow-feelings and humanity by their actions. Day by day some would busy themselves attending to the dead and burying them; others gathered in one spot all who were afflicted by hunger throughout the whole city and gave them bread."[38]

Care of the sick continued to be a ministry of the church. The early monasteries became places for caring for the sick. A large number of hospitals in medieval Europe were directly affiliated with monasteries, priories, and other religious institutions. This concern for healing continued in the mission age when churches sent not only missionaries but also missionary-doctors: they established schools and hospitals. Thus, to speak of the church as a covenanted community of healers is simply to retrieve its tradition and identity. It is to claim that which is at the heart of its identity: a follower of Jesus, the radical healer.

THE CHURCH: DIAGNOSTICIAN AND EXORCIST OF CONTEMPORARY MADNESS AND IDOLATRY

A Hasidic story speaks of an isolated kingdom where the grain harvest one year turns poisonous. Everyone who eats it will become mad. Yet there is no other food available. Finally, the king turns to a trusted counsellor. "We must all eat, or we will die," he said. "But you, try to eat less. Preserve enough sanity to enable you to remind us, through the long dark period ahead, that we are mad. Tell us. Again and again. The time will come when we are sane again."[39]

The king in this story appears wise, but he may have underestimated the grip of madness once it has become pervasive. He could have learned from one of the desert fathers, Abba Anthony, who said: "The time is coming when people will be insane, and when they see someone who is not insane, they will attack that person saying: You are insane because you are not like us."[40]

Our society is under the grip of a certain kind of madness that often escapes our scrutiny. Even those who have recognized this madness are reluctant to name it for fear that they may be labeled insane and

38. Ibid., 47.
39. Cited in Shriver, *An Ethic for Enemies*, 63.
40. Nomora, *The Desert Wisdom*, 15.

would face the threat of being sent to a mental asylum. But this madness must be named and exorcised in order to pave the way for healing and greater well-being. This madness will be difficult to dislodge for it has clothed itself with the dominant rationality of our times. We often think of madness as lacking reason. Quite the contrary, as G. K. Chesterton argues, "The madman is not the man who has lost his reason. The madman is the man who has lost everything except his reason."[41] Yes! What breeds this madness or insanity is reason, and more specifically a particular kind of reason: linear, instrumental, and calculative rationality. It is no wonder that logicians become insane. Chesterton got it right: "The poet only asks to get his head into the heavens. It is the logician who seeks to get the heavens into his head. And it is his head that splits."[42]

Madness is intellectual tunnel vision and submission to *idée fixe*. Madness is a disease of modern rationality and of those who are imprisoned by lunatic straitjacket logic, which may be compelling but constricting. Rationalistic and constricting madness has killed or imprisoned imagination. It has imprisoned health to cure and skewed health to physicalism. It has limited medicine to that which can be quantified. It has controlled the regime of truth in medicine and sidelined or muted other healing traditions. It has relegated others to quackery. In other words, while successful in curing many diseases, this rationalistic madness of modernity does not take the health of the whole person in relation to the larger society.

This reductionistic-physicalistic way of thinking is in unholy alliance with the religion of the global market and its god (profit). They work in tandem perfectly well. A reductionist notion of health fits perfectly with the main drive to increase profit at the expense of the whole person. A reductionist notion of health eliminates or disqualifies the so-called "extra" expenses that are associated with holistic and preventive care, thus maximizing profit. The profit is increased, but the person does not experience wholeness and healing. Because reductionist and physicalist health does not address radically the causes, the patient becomes all the more dependent on costly medications and invasive procedures.

41. Chesterton, cited by Vanhoozer, "One Rule to Rule them All," 87.
42. Chesterton, cited by Vanhoozer, Ibid., 88.

The church as an exorcist of contemporary madness must risk being called insane or a fool if healing is to happen. It cannot continue toeing the dominant rationality that is maddening and sickening. In the face of the insanity and horrors that our society has experienced, what is direly needed is neither complicit silence nor apathy but a kind of "moral madness." Moral madness, in Rabbi Byron Sherwin's words, means registering our stubborn refusal not to let ourselves be "seduced by appearance and social conventions; to love where there is only indifference and hate; to try to live humanely in an inhumane world; to believe in humankind in spite of what we have done."[43] Moral madness is imaginative madness that refuses to be boxed in by the dominant conventions, that refuses to be boxed in by reductionist and mechanistic logic, and that refuses to be swallowed by the religion of the market and its logic of profit.

THE CHURCH: A COMMUNITY THAT DETOXIFIES ITSELF

Concern about health has been central to the church's identity, and the church has been involved in specific ministries of health. Unfortunately, its history is mixed. The church has also been a contributor in supporting a dualistic understanding of reality, which puts the priority on the spirit at the expense of the body. In several instances, many churches have counseled sacrifice of the body for the sake of the spirit. While this dualistic thinking has adversely affected everyone, it has been most destructive to the marginalized—the poor, women, and nature. The sacrificed body has turned out to be the body of the marginalized. The church has counseled oppressed communities to forget their bodies and expect spiritual reward. In other words, it has encouraged marginalized people not to transform the sick body politic that is responsible for their victimization.

Another toxin in the church's theological arsenal is its confusion of faith with superstition and fanaticism. In this kind of church, members are expected to crucify their intellect and inquiring spirit. These churches make faith in general and prayer in particular a substitute for a scientific approach to medicine. A story of a young man named Sig illumines this point. Sig was born with epilepsy that was not curable, but it was manageable by medication. He found a welcoming church and decided to join. This church preached that if he had enough faith

43. Stewart, *Jesus the Holy Fool*, 219.

he would be cured of his sickness. Wanting to prove the strength of his faith, Sig stopped taking medication. Not long after, he had a severe seizure and died. As his mother said, he "overdosed on religion."[44]

While some churches have confused faith with fanaticism and shun modern medicine, other churches have sold out to modern medicine; they have become an enemy of other alternatives. They have become agents of modern Western medicine and cannot think outside this framework. Even when they consider prayer, it is interpreted in terms of quantifiable and measurable bodily effects. These churches are avid prosecutors of those who explore other ways. A personal experience confirms this point. In pain after the sharp fins of a poisonous fish pierced my skin, I went to our community *tambalan* (medicine person) for help. The *tambalan* performed the ritual, and in a few minutes I could feel the pain coming out of my body. I was cured; I was healed. What is wrong with that? But another pastor said that I should not submit myself to this kind of healing practice for it is from the devil or of demonic source. How can something be of demonic source if it promotes healing? Shall we say that even the demonic is subordinate to God's power?

There are also other theological toxins that the church must rid itself because they aggravate the disease and ostracize the sick. Kathy Black has identified a few of these theological toxins: (1) the illness is a punishment for the persons sin or for the sin of the parents; (2) it is a test of faith and character; (3) it is an opportunity for personal development of the person with disability or of those who are related to persons with disabilities; (4) it presents an occasion for the power of God to become manifest; (5) suffering is redemptive; and (6) the mysterious power of God simply makes it impossible for people to know God's will.[45] I agree with Bruce Epperly: "The God who would hurt to cure, the God who would punish a child to reform a parent, the God who would kill a college student to strengthen the faith of others cannot be trusted with our destiny, either in this life or the next."[46]

---

44. Black, *A Healing Homiletic*, 11.

45. Ibid., 23.

46. Epperly, *God's Touch*, 79.

THE CHURCH: SIGN OF HOLISTIC WORLD (HEALTH) VIEW

More than exorcising epistemic modernist narrowness and detoxifying the church of toxic theologies, the church must seek to embody a worldview (health view) that overcomes dualism. It must articulate a worldview that sees persons holistically in the context of the web of relation: God, human beings, and the rest of creation. It must see health in the fullness of shalom: just and right relation, harmony, abundance, and sustainability. New understandings of the reality of our interconnections are moving in the direction of holistic care. Physicist David Bohm claims that the universe is a "holoverse" or undivided whole, in which the whole is present and reflected holographically in each part and the part shapes the character of the whole.[47] In this view, health cannot be understood apart from the whole. The health of the whole impacts the health of a part, and the health of a part mirrors overall health.

A holistic approach to health care must go beyond getting rid of the symptoms. Rather than simply addressing a specific problem area, it must engage in health care that takes the various interconnections of life at the social and ecological levels. A holistic approach must lead to exploring alternative cares and not allow itself to be imprisoned by conventional medicine: modern, orthodox, allopathic, reductionistic, biochemical, or physicalistic medicine.[48] This does not mean abandonment of conventional medicine; rather, it means being more open to other forms of delivering and administering health care. The power-knowledge regime of conventional medicine has been resistant even in the face of changes throughout history. A holistic approach cannot be what it seeks to be without being open to the participation of various professions: medical doctors (including naturopathic physicians), nurses, midwives, chaplains, pastors, theologians, bioethicists, epidemiologists, pharmaceutical laboratories, public health advocates, community health workers, police, communities, and so forth. We cannot address the health-care needs of the public in disciplinary isolation. We must integrate various disciplines and skills to respond effectively to our common challenge.

47. Ibid., 110.
48. O'Mathuna, "Emerging Alternative Therapies," 260.

THE CHURCH: EMPOWERED COMMUNITY
OF MENDING HEALERS

On several occasions I have noted that theology is too important to be left to experts (theologians). The same needs to be said of health and health care. They are too important to be left to the experts and professionals; they are too important to be left to the health insurance companies. When profits dictate health care, we must reclaim our agency and be proactive advocates. When our primary physicians become guardians or gatekeepers for HMOs, we should strongly advocate for our health. When food companies make products that do not list ingredients that may be harmful to health, we must raise our voices in protest. When industrial companies dump their toxic wastes in our neighborhood, we must voice our opposition and hold those companies accountable. When big health insurance companies lobby in the U.S. Congress to gain profit at the expense of health care, we need empowered people who will stand up to advocate for affordable health care. Everyone must be an advocate of his or her health and well-being as well as for all. Certainly, this should be the posture of the church—a follower of the radical healer.

When health care is denied to many, we need empowered communities to make it available to all in need, particularly to those who cannot pay the high cost of medical care. While there is a place for highly sophisticated and expensive health procedures, the basic and elementary health-care needs of the people must be the priority and must be adequately addressed. Primary health care is a measure of justice in society. Primary health care is a test of society and the church. It is a test of the church's solidarity with the poor and the marginalized; it is a barometer of the church's commitment to Christ through the downtrodden. Sadly, this continues to be denied to many as powerful forces block attempts to make universal health insurance and basic health care available to all. Thus, we need an empowered people to advocate for their health interest.

Empowered citizenry or members of the church, however, is not a solo approach. In his characteristic eloquence Saul Alinsky reminds us: "Solo is dodo."[49] We need to empower every individual, but an empowered individual is only as strong as the strength of community support. In other words, empowerment must be a community effort.

49. Cited in Rasmussen, "Power Analysis," 12.

In facing corporate interests, we need a coordinated work of empowered individuals and institutions. The church—a sign of holistic healing and follower of the radical healer—must be a community of empowered believers working in concert with others for the health of all. It is for this reason that organizing work is a crucial component.

THE CHURCH EMBODIES THE MENDING HEALER IN THE MINISTRY

The fundamental identity of the church as a follower of the radical healer and a sign of holistic healing must come to life in its ministry. If concern for health is an expression of the church's identity, it is essential that we make our language convey more clearly this identity and commitment. To arrive at this clarity, Mary Chase-Ziolek suggests that we distinguish "health ministry" from "ministries of health." The term "health ministry," she argues, "can imply that health is being brought to the church where it will be a ministry." On the other hand, talking about "ministries of health" means "we first and foremost understand this as a ministry."[50] It is not that we totally abandon the language of health ministry; rather, that it be articulated in such a manner as to combine both. Chase-Ziolek puts it this way: "Ministries of health, then, is the broader term, with health ministries referring to those activities in which a church intentionally engages for the explicit purpose of promoting health."[51]

Churches and church-related ecumenical bodies and programs have affirmed health-care ministry as a mandate. To cite a few examples, the Evangelical Lutheran Church in America affirms that, "The Christian Church is called to be an active participant in fashioning a just and effective health care system. Responding to those who were sick was integral to the life and ministry of Jesus and has been a central aspect of the Church's mission throughout its history."[52] For the Episcopal Church (USA), "Health ministry is a living witness of the healing activity of God through the local congregation, encouraging whole-person health through: integration of body, mind and spirit, increased self-knowledge, personal responsibility, interdependence

---

50. Chase-Ziolek, *Health, Healing and Wholeness*, 6.

51. Ibid., 8.

52. ELCA, "Health and Health Care."

among God's people."[53] The principles of the United Methodist Church's Comprehensive Community-based Primary Health Care (CCPHC), strike at the heart of health-care ministry: (1) equity, (2) integration, and (3) empowerment. Health care is a matter of justice or of equity in the context of unjust body politic. It is also a matter of integration. Throughout, I have lifted up holistic health care. It must not only be curative and preventive; it must be integrated with other factors that promote overall health, such as water supply, agriculture, sanitation, employment, education, and so on. It must lead to the empowerment of people. Only an empowered people can be active participants in promoting their own health and of the whole society.[54]

To these principles I add a fourth: sustainability. It is obviously related to the above three principles, but it occupies a distinctive and crucial place. Health care is about stewardship of health and resources. It is stewardship of our gifts and skills and material resources. It is about cultivating resources, managing rightly, and transparency in accounting. It is about leadership development and skills and walking lightly in the journey to healing. Cure is an endpoint, healing is a journey. Health care must be pursued with an eye to its sustainability.

With the above theological mandate and principles in mind, I propose that the focus of health ministry must be cast wider. Denomination-and congregation-based ministries are important areas. Nonetheless, we cannot be effective if ministries are only congregationally based, and if they remain focused on the health needs of congregations. As health is a concern of all, the importance of community health to congregationally based health ministry should not be overlooked. The full potential and impact of the integration of faith and health will not come to fruition if churches remain focused on the health needs of the individuals, families, and congregations. We must maximize the strength of congregations and build on their core commitments to improve the health of other communities as well.[55] Moving closer to this goal would, of course, require a variety of approaches, several agents, and coordinated action.

Basically, the health ministries of the church must include service, education, advocacy, organizing, and mobilization. Service remains a

53. ECUSA, "What is health ministry?"

54. UMC, "Comprehensive Community-based."

55. Chase-Ziolek, *Health, Healing and Wholeness*, 8.

vital expression of our health ministry, especially in response to immediate needs. Immediate needs demand immediate services. Service may include providing for basic health-care needs as well as interpreters (particularly important for migrants and new immigrants). Along with service is education. Education may include training volunteers for health-care ministries as well as general education for the wider public about health issues such as food safety and nutrition, sanitation, drug addiction, emotional crisis, and lifestyle changes. It must help people, particularly church members, articulate healthful theologies and critique theological toxins that contribute to the health crisis. Overall, the educational thrust must lead people to an understanding of the larger and systemic causes (body politic pathology) of their health situation.

Education for the sake of being informed is not enough. Education provides the opportunity to study and identify health issues that need advocacy and mobilization. These are some of the key issues for advocacy and mobilization: (1) to promote equity in our international economic system; (2) to ban or put restrictions on international trade of products that are designed or destined to kill, such as military armaments; (3) to make national governments responsible for the provision of health-care to all and resist privatization of health-care; (4) to demand and assure that basic needs (e.g., food, clean water) are seen as basic human rights and are protected from various forms of profiteering; (5) to design and enforce an international essential-drug policy so that basic medicine is available to all who need them; (6) to make sure that worker health and well-being are included in discussions on industrial production and trade; and (7) to demand ecological protection from toxic wastes and promote clean and efficient use of energy and similar measures.[56]

Churches must support, collaborate, and network with other faith-based organizations, nongovernmental organizations, and governmental agencies when needed. They need to link or work with organized communities in making basic and quality care accessible to all in need. Support for primary health care is very significant for communities that are often left out by the large corporate health-care industries. Churches need to network with local and global NGOs that promote and advocate health. When needed, churches must work with

56. Mercer, "Shall We Leave it to Experts?" 171.

governmental agencies to make them more accountable to the people and make them deliver much-needed health services. Networking and coalition building are crucial for the gargantuan task that the church is called to do.

SEEDS OF HOPE, SEEDS OF HEALTH

Health is a journey, a process—not a static state. The journey toward health is a continuing walk, continuing struggle, continual striving toward health and wholeness. The obstacles to the formation of healthy societies and individuals abound, but there are signs of hope in the global struggle for equitable and quality health care for all. Individuals, communities, churches, faith-based and nongovernmental organizations, and people's movements both local and global are sowing seeds of hope—seeds of health. One non-governmental, people-oriented program is the Visayas Primary Health Care based in Cebu City, Philippines. No amount of florid prose can describe what it has meant to the lives it has touched. Individuals and groups organized the Visayas Primary Health Care during the Martial Law years in response to the basic health needs of the poor and to advocate for change in the health-care system. Even with limited financial means, it has continued to offer its services to the poor of Cebu and neighboring islands of Bohol, Negros, and Leyte. I had the privilege of going with its health workers and volunteers on a medical mission and saw with my own eyes how they have touched the lives of the poor and the marginalized. The Visayas Primary Health Care and its committed health workers such as Dr. Erlinda Posadas, Dr. Mark Molina, Dr. Petty de Castro, and others are seeds of hope and seeds of health. These individuals embody in their lives what it means to care and heal in the face of various odds.

Another seed of hope is the Gonoshasthaya Kendra (GK) or the People's Health Center of Bengal, which was founded in 1972 to provide primary health-care services for rural communities. The center is involved in multiple efforts and programs: it has worked with various stakeholders in efforts to improve access to medicines, the empowerment and health of women, and community-based initiatives. With the support of paramedics and village health workers, the center provides comprehensive care to low-income people and runs programs in education, nutrition, agriculture, employment generation, and the production of basic medicines at its Gono Pharmaceuticals factory. The result is astonishing, outstanding, and encouraging: infant and maternal mortality in the area that GK is serving has fallen to about half of Bangladesh's national average.[57]

Seeds of hope and seeds of health are sprouting at the global level as well. Transborder coalition work helped to gain an important victory at the ministerial meeting in Doha, Qatar, in November 2001. At this meeting, the declaration on trade-related aspects of intellectual property rights (TRIPS) and public health was passed by the ministers representing various countries. The declaration made clear that "the TRIPS agreement should not prevent WTO members from protecting public health, and it emphasized the importance of access to medicines."[58] The declaration (though it suffered assault) ensured the right of countries from the global South to provide low-cost generics to their populations and reined in patent protection of much-needed drugs.

Likewise, our churches are sowing seeds of hope and seeds of health. They have been a succor to the marginalized and the forgotten. Separately, ecumenically, and in interfaith aspects, churches are responding to the matter of health from the global to local levels. Major church bodies or denominations are involved in health ministries of various sorts. As an interfaith aspect, one endeavor is the Interfaith Health Program (IHP) at Emory University in Atlanta, Georgia, which attempts to connect faith communities and public health agencies at the local level. Recognizing health disparity due to income, race, and environmental factors, IHP targets marginalized neighborhoods with the purpose of eliminating the disparities. In keeping with its purpose, IHP does not present itself to the marginalized communities as outside experts but works to empower the people who are already living and working in the communities.[59]

One expression of health ministry is the NetWorkers Malaria Prevention Program of the Presbyterian Church (USA), which is community-based and implemented by the women of PC (USA) partner churches overseas. This project may sound small, but it deserves highlighting because it is something that common people (and even children) can do, and it provides an entry point into the health min-

57. Cerón et al., "The Struggle for People's Health," 164.

58. Ibid., 166.

59. McNamara, Health and Wellness, 82.

istry. Led by Presbyterian women's groups, this program distributes mosquito nets and educational materials in countries where malaria is prevalent. Young people in the congregations can help based on what they are capable of giving through the "Nickels for Nets."[60] We should not underestimate the power of these nickels: they save lives; they are seeds of hope.

Seeds of hope and seeds of health are scattered everywhere. They are not only out there; they are deep in our hearts. These seeds are alive when we begin to recognize the health crisis of our times. These seeds sprout when we take concrete steps to challenge theological ideas and socio-political and economic structures that are destructive to the health of all. And these seeds of hope grow when we bond together to give birth to healthy churches and healthy communities. Our relentless work for health is already an indication that we are experiencing health. Let us continue our journey to health.

60. "Networkers Malaria Prevention," in PC(USA).

11

The Church as a Community
of Dialogians of Faith

Living in a Religiously Diverse World

THE SOCIAL ENVIRONMENT OF my younger years did not prepare me well for living with a hospitable heart in relation to people of other faiths. In many instances, the atmosphere nurtured prejudice against people of other faiths, particularly Muslims. A stage performance that I loved to watch as a young boy during barrio fiestas such as the *moro-moro*, I later realized, was a reenactment of the *Reconquista*, which represents the capture of the city by the Moors and the subsequent re-conquest by Christians. And often, though it may have been only a social device that parents used to prevent children from wandering far away, we were told not to get closer to the ocean because the *Moros* (identified as pirates) might snatch and kill us. Additionally, in some instances parents would say, "the *Moros* are coming," in an attempt to quiet a crying child. We grew up learning to distrust and fear Muslims.

Relationships among Christians, however, were not cordial either. Public debates on certain doctrines were common. Knowing how to debate was deemed important if a pastor was to defend his or her flock. I am glad I learned it, and it served its purpose. Fortunately, as my theological education progressed, I was exposed to a different and, I believe, better way of living together with people of other faiths. I was exposed to interfaith dialogue, which, as Yossi Klein Halevi puts it, is "the true spiritual adventure of our time."[1] I have chosen to participate

---

1. Halevi, "A Coming Together," cited in Smock, *Interfaith Dialogue*, 7.

in this spiritual adventure, and in this adventure I have learned to witness with passion to what God in Jesus the Christ has done in my life, and at the same time remain open to the claims of others. The pages that follow are my evolving thoughts on this spiritual adventure.

RELIGIONS ARE THRIVING: EXPOSING SECULARIST ASSUMPTIONS

If the Enlightenment thinkers expected that religion would wither away once reason replaced the infantile religious supernaturalism of the common people, many in the twentieth century were inclined to think that religion would become unnecessary once the market came to decide all critical questions of value and meaning. Like many of the Enlightenment thinkers, when Harvey Cox wrote *The Secular City* (1965) he was expecting the decline of religion.[2] Riding with the waves of modernist-secularist advance, Bishop John Shelby Spong articulates what it means to be a Christian in a postreligious and postChristian world in his best selling work, *Why Christianity Must Change or Die.*[3] Are we really heading toward a postreligious and postChristian world? Whose world is Bishop Spong talking about? And lastly, what does he mean by postreligious?

There are basic presuppositions to the postreligious claim that I would like to highlight, even if only in a cursory way. The claim presupposes a context that has faced the challenge of secularism and a people who have experienced disenchantment of their religious world. It also presupposes having gone through modernity and away from the mumbo jumbo of religious infantilism. While there are those who contend that secularism is not an inevitable outcome of modernity, secularism presupposes modernity.[4] In short, the postreligious discourse presupposes secularism and modernity.

Now let us ask the question, whose world are we talking about when speaking of a postreligious world? Are we speaking of the whole world? If we mean the global North, I concede to that claim while at the same time reminding us that the world of the global North is also uneven. I see the need to remind us again of our location because obliviousness to one's context is a common predilection among

2. Cox, *The Secular City.*

3. Spong, *Why Christianity Must Change.*

4. Schreiter, "Globalization, Postmodernity," 29.

those who have grown up believing that their local game is the World Series. Having this context in mind, I concede that the global North, generally speaking, has become postreligious. I cannot make the same claim for the global South, though I recognize that many individuals in the global South have arrived at a postreligious consciousness. The traditional theistic worldview no longer makes sense to many, especially in countries where secularization has taken hold. Great Britain offers a model of secularization in general and of de-Christianization in particular. According to a survey taken in 2000, 44 percent claim no religious affiliation. This is also true in France and, to a certain extent, Italy, both historically Catholic nations.[5] Countries of Eastern Europe share a similar situation, even if in varying degrees.[6]

A postreligious world is not, however, a world with which most of the people of the global South can identify with easily. In certain areas of the world, modernity is not the dominant reality, although they suffer from the incursions of modernity. In addition, although modernity has made an impact, these communities do not fully share the Western secular disenchantment of the religious world. Even in those countries that have achieved some degree of modern progress, secularism, and, consequently, religious disenchantment, it appears that religious disenchantment is not an inevitable outcome of modernity. This is the world in which religions are thriving and experiencing exponential growth. In this context, it would not make sense for postreligious discourse to presuppose the waning and dying of religion.

Thirty years later, in the preface to his *Fire from Heaven*, Harvey Cox admitted that he was mistaken about the decline of religion. Instead of religion being in decline, Cox said, "Today it is secularity that may be headed for extinction."[7] When I reviewed John A. T. Robinson's 40th anniversary edition of *Honest to God*, I noticed that Cox, forty years later, admitted the same point in his cover endorsement of the book: "I concede now that I seem to have been mistaken about the 'decline of religion'!"[8] Not only are religions not declining, they are thriving even in places where religious practices have been

---

5. Jenkins, *The Next Christendom*, 94–95.

6. Hünermann, "Evangelization of Europe?" 57–80.

7. Cox, *Fire from Heaven*.

8. See Cox's back cover endorsement to Robinson's *Honest to God*.

closely monitored by the state or have been under assault by a more secular culture. Moreover, not only are religions thriving, they are also spreading side-by-side with each other in places far away from their original homelands. For example, Buddhism, Islam, and Hinduism are experiencing tremendous growth in the more secular society of the global North. Simultaneously, there has been a shift in Christianity's center of vitality from the global North to the global South, such as Latin America, the Pacific Islands, Africa, and portions of Asia (e.g., the Philippines), although the Christianity of the global North remains the center of economic and political power.[9]

In spite of the efforts of modernist-secularism to ignore, suppress, and persecute religions, naming them as human "projection" or "alienation"(Feuerbach), "opium of the people" (Marx), and "regression" or psychological immaturity (Freud), they are very much alive and thriving.[10] The resurgence of religion not only disproves the modernist-secularist prediction, it also puts into question the thesis that religion belongs to the inchoate stage of humankind's evolution. Orthodox Marxist socialists and neoliberal capitalists' views on this subject are basically the same in spite of their mortal opposition. This is hardly surprising. After all, they are both children of modernity and positivistic science.

Ironically, the modernist-secularist mind that gave birth to religion as a special field of study has, from the very start, misunderstood religion. Its basic assumption regarding religion and its role in life is flawed. Not only does it err in relegating religion to the inchoate or infantile stage of humankind, the secularist mind also errs in the assumption that religion can be separated from the secular or, in the words of David Lochhead, "a matter of private preference, as relevant to public life as the brand of deodorant you happen to prefer."[11] The notion of the separation of church and state has not escaped from being wrongly interpreted to support this view. However, even as the secular state has pushed religion to the private, religion has maintained its presence in the public realm because religion, by its very nature, always

---

9. Barrett, cited by Douglas, in "Globalization and the Local Church," 203. See Escobar, *Changing Tides*, 84–87; Hünermann, "Evangelization of Europe?" 61–63; de Freitas, "Response to Peter Hünermann," 85; Tienou, "Christian Theology," 37–51.

10. Küng, *Global Responsibility*, 44.

11. Lochhead, *The Dialogical Imperative*, 2.

seeks expression in the complex web of social relations. There is no such thing as private religion, which should not be confused with the word personal. A private religion with no bearing on social life is only conceivable under a wrong anthropological presupposition: that one is first an individual before one becomes a social subject or a member of society. Even an individualistic account of the individual already points to a kind of society that promotes that way of thinking.

The modernist-secularist approach to religion is either manipulative or schizophrenic: it amputates religion by isolating it to the private but, oddly, puts almost everything negative on its doorstep. How can religion be blamed for almost everything bad if it is only one aspect of society and one that can be relegated to the private? The best way to understand religion is to see it in relation to the whole web of social interaction. Religion is certainly a distinct phenomenon, but it cannot be understood apart from the complex web of socio-political and economic relations. This is true with other issues related to diversity. Religious diversity should be viewed as one dimension of the broader question of how we treat those considered as the "other," the "different," and the strangers in our midst. To talk about religious diversity "without taking into account the larger context, where political and economic factors are probably as influential as the religious," argues Stanley Samartha, "would be to miss the depth and complexity of the phenomenon and its far-reaching effects on human relations in the global community."[12]

As long as the modernist-secularist assumption reigns over how society understands religion, we will forever misunderstand the place of religion in society. The modernist-secularist privatizing of religious faith has made us ignorant of the role of religion and, sadly, at our peril. While it is easily acknowledged that there is religious diversity, our secular and privatized world has made it possible for people to avoid engaging with people of different religions, partly because it is relatively easy for people to live with each other without reference to their religious identities. Because one's religious identity is a private affair, it requires a great deal of tact to ask about it. There is a quick way to confirm this point: we only need to ask people if they know someone who belongs to another religious tradition. I would not be surprised if a large majority were unable to name even one. The capitulation of the

12. Samartha, *One Christ*, 1.

historic mainline Christian churches to a modernist-secularist mind-set, following Lochhead, is partly responsible for Christianity's relative disengagement with people of other faiths, for its relative disinterest in interfaith dialogue and, moreover, for the general religious ignorance of its members.[13] Following the September 11, 2001 tragedy, there was euphoria of interest among Christian churches with regard to other religions, but the general euphoria did not last long. I agree with M. Douglas Meeks that our secularity (which is making us ignorant about religion) is "making us vulnerable. We don't know Islam. We don't know the faith, the daily discipline, the hopes and the fears of Muslims . . . Most [Islamic] fundamentalists are seeking to lead a religious life. But there is an extreme and violent fundamentalism of which we remain ignorant at our great peril."[14] I doubt, however, Meek's statement that "we are *learning* that our secularity is making us vulnerable."[15] I can only hope that I am wrong and Meeks is right for the sake of our imperiled world.

GLOBALIZATION AND THE NEW RELIGIOUS LANDSCAPE

Though not the only factor, globalization is an important one in the spread of various religions around the world. Along with the flow of goods and services is the flow of information and religious beliefs. Likewise, along with the diaspora of people is the diasporizing of various religious faiths, a trend that has transformed once religiously homogenous places into religiously diverse ones. This phenomenon is observable not only in the large urban areas or cities of the world but also in the rural areas, particularly where agribusiness factories are present. These agribusiness factories are drawing workers of varied ethnicity and religious beliefs from around the world. One such place, already mentioned in earlier chapters, is southwestern Minnesota. The demise of the family farm and the presence of agribusiness companies or, more particularly, food processing plants in this region of Minnesota, have drawn newcomers (migrants and immigrants, including Somalis, Hmong, Laotians, Cambodians, Vietnamese, and Mexicans).[16] The presence of these newcomers has changed the de-

13. Lochhead, *The Dialogical Imperative*, 2.

14. Meeks, "What Can We Hope for Now?" 258.

15. Meeks, Ibid. Emphasis added.

16. See Amato, *To Call It Home.*

mographics and socio-cultural-religious landscape of the place and, of course, has brought attendant challenges.

This changing socio-political and cultural-religious landscape is more common in large urban centers. Among the largest non-Christian religions in the U.S. today are Islam, Judaism, Buddhism, and Hinduism. The Council on American Islamic Relations (CAIR) reports that there are seven million Muslims in the U.S, a figure almost comparable to the Jewish population.[17] The city of Birmingham in the United Kingdom, which is one of the largest Muslim cities outside of the Middle East, has more than fifty mosques, including a central mosque claimed to be the largest in Europe outside Istanbul.[18]

Western secularism, the global market, and Christianity have each, in varying ways, engaged in homogenizing the world. Christianity's homogenizing project has been carried out in the name of Christianizing the whole pagan world. As pointed out in chapter 3, the popular magazine *The Christian Century* welcomed with excitement the twentieth century as a Christian century. Believing in the superiority of Christianity, Christians have simply assumed that people around the world would come into the fold of the church. The future that Christians have confidently anticipated or simply assumed, however, is not the future they are likely to get, or, are getting. True, there are places in the world in which Christianity is making headway. Yet, in spite of the Christian missionary zeal to homogenize the world for Christ, it has not been very successful in eliminating other rivals. On the contrary, other religions are growing and thriving, and their followers have become skillful evangelists themselves.

GLOBALIZATION, RELIGION, AND GLOBAL CONFLICTS

More than two hundred years ago, Voltaire expressed a huge sigh of relief that the era of the Wars of Religion—those "abominable monuments of fanaticism"—had finally, with the Peace of Westphalia, come to an end. Sadly, that is not the case. At the beginning of the twenty-first century, religion is once again in the news and in the thick of violent conflicts.[19] And when religions are intertwined, one can be

17. The numbers are contested. The estimates range between two million and as many as 11 million. See Haddad, *Not Quite Americans*, 1–2.

18. Thangaraj, *The Common Task*, 21.

19. Juergensmeyer, *Religion in Global Society*, 3.

sure, as Hans Küng rightly points out, that the "most fanatical and cruelest political struggles are those that have been colored, inspired, and legitimized by religion."[20]

It may be misleading to speak of "religious conflicts." After all, religion, contrary to the Western secular mindset that has given birth to religion as an academic discipline, cannot be separated from the totality of life. If I continue to speak of "religious conflicts," it is primarily to highlight the crucial role of religion in many global conflicts and not to isolate it from the complex web of social relations. It may be a critical triggering factor in some conflicts, but it is hardly the sole factor. "Rarely is religion the principal cause of conflict," argues David Smock, "even when the opposing groups, such as Protestants and Catholics in Northern Ireland, are differentiated by religious identities. But religion is nevertheless a contributing factor to conflict in places as widely scattered as Northern Ireland, the Middle East, the Balkans, Sudan, Indonesia, and Kashmir."[21]

Though violent conflicts with religious motivation are not new, globalization provides a new context and a new framework for understanding the many and most recent expressions of religious conflicts. Not only has globalization accelerated the encounters of various religious believers, it has generated tensions, reactions, and violent conflicts in which religion has played a crucial role as well.

It is significant to note that as homogenizing and predatory globalization spreads, movements of various motivations—ethnic, religious, nationalistic, cultural—are rising also.[22] The erosion of religiously-based traditional worldview by modernist, secularist, market-driven worldview and values, the collusion of Western-educated global South leaders with foreign powers, and the massive violation of people's rights have given birth to cynicism and other forms antiglobalist sentiments. These are often supported by religious motivations, the most desperate and disastrous expression of which is terrorism—a terrorism intertwined with (and often responding to) the terrorism of the global market and imperial project of some countries of the global North.[23] Within the past decade or so, religion has been associated

20. Küng, cited in Smock, *Interfaith Dialogue and Peacebuilding*, 3.
21. Smock, Ibid.
22. Lochhead, *Shifting Realities*, 100.
23. See Berquist, *Strike Terror No More*; Griffith, *The War on Terrorism*;

with the vociferous rhetoric of patriotic and xenophobic political leaders and parties, ethnic cleansing, tribal wars, imperialistic-militaristic
American exceptionalism, militant fundamentalism, and the devastating and vicious acts of terrorism and counter-terrorism.

Religious fundamentalism and religious militant extremism is
not a new social phenomenon, and it is not the monopoly of one religion. As noted in chapter 2, religious fundamentalism, which does
not necessarily lead to militant extremism, is a reaction to perceived
threats: Its basic impulse is reactive. In essence, it is a reaction to what
is perceived by adherents of a particular religious faith as a threat to
their cherished worldview and values or core convictions. In the context of the United States, the term fundamentalism is used to describe
conservative Protestant Christians who have rejected the modernist-
liberal trend of biblical hermeneutics and theological interpretation as
well as the progressive agenda of many mainline Christian denominations. In recent years, however, the term fundamentalism has acquired
a fatal twist: it has become closely linked to or is often identified with
violent extremism and terrorism.[24]

Fundamentalist Christians, such as those identified with the
Army of God, committed heinous crimes all in the name of obedience
to God and faithfulness to what they believe as absolute truth. We
also have examples in Judaism. Israeli Prime Minister Yitzhak Rabin's
effort to forge peace with Palestinians was welcomed by many, but
not all Jews. For some Jews, Rabin betrayed the Jewish cause; he was a
traitor. On November 4, 1995, Rabin was assassinated by Yigal Amir,
a student from Tel Aviv's conservative Bar-Ilan University. When interviewed regarding his action, Amir said that he had "no regrets" for
what he had done and that he "acted alone and on orders from God."
He may have acted alone in killing Rabin, but he was not alone in
his cause. Others could have carried out the assassination, says Yoel
Lerner, who believes in a form of Messianic Zionism. What surprised
him, continues Lerner, is that "no one had done it earlier."[25]

While religious militant extremism is present in various religions (especially evident in the Abrahamic faiths), it is Islamic mili-

---

Juergensmeyer, *Terror in the Mind of God*; Duchrow and Hinkelammert, *Property for
People*, particularly pages 109-39; Chomsky, *Pirates and Emperors*.

24. Ucko, *Changing the Present*, 137.

25. Juergensmeyer, *Terror in the Mind of God*, 46–47.

tant fundamentalism that has been the focus of the world's attention. The September 11, 2001 Islamic militants attack and the escalation of suicide bombings around the world only reinforced the existing stereotype that people have about Muslims. Rollin Armour Sr. makes the observation: "In the thirty-eight years I taught courses in world religions, the religion that consistently raised the greatest problems among students was Islam: not Hinduism, not Buddhism, not Shinto, or Sikhism."[26] Yet, Islam is the closest to Christianity because of its high regard for Jesus. Unlike Buddhism in which many Westerners are at home, either embracing it whole or putting it into "meditation-relaxation-technique-bottles," Islam has remained problematic for many. In spite of the disavowal by Muslims around the world (who, of course, received very little media coverage), the perception of the general public is that, indeed, Islam is a violent religion. Not only did the media fail to present the larger context and the history of Western, Christian, and Jewish encounters with Muslims, the media continued to reinforce the deeply embedded fears of the general public by its selective coverage. While I want to believe that the negative portrayal of Muslims is mainly due to ignorance, this is not the case. In addition to the right wing of the Republican Party, one powerful force that works behind the scenes to promote stereotypes and hostility against Muslims is the pro-Israel lobby group.[27] Despite occasional official statements from the Bush administration that "Islam and Muslims and Arabs are not enemies of the United States, everything else about the current situation argues the exact opposite," claims Edward Said.[28]

Following the September 11 attack, many Christian churches came to sympathize with Muslims and worked to prevent hate crimes committed against Muslim communities. Also, there has been a renewed interest in learning about Islam, and some Muslims have been invited to speak in Christian congregations. In general, however, Christian churches have continued to show a crusading mindset and have been dragging out the same old stereotype. Additionally, both fundamentalist as well as many liberal churches have danced to the drumbeat of war in recent years and identified Christianity with the interest of the state. The idea that we are witnessing a clash of civili-

26. Armour Sr., *Islam*, xiii.

27. Haddad, *Not Quite American*, 23, 47.

28. Said, "Thoughts about America," cited in *The Prophetic Call*, 70.

zation—that Islamic civilization is in a collision course with Western-Christian civilization—has only widened the divide, fanned fears, and reinforced deeply-etched stereotypes. Moreover, the notion of a clash of civilization has diverted the people's attention from what Tariq Ali calls a "clash of fundamentalisms."[29]

RECOVERING THE POSITIVE ROLE OF RELIGION
IN OUR GLOBAL SOCIETY

The involvement of religion in unimaginable atrocities of various kinds has led some to conclude that we need to rid ourselves of religion altogether: Religion is evil. This idea is, of course, not new. Secularism is a legitimate reaction to the heteronomous authority of the church and its opposition to science (though it also helped pave the way for science) as well as to its alliance with authoritarian politics. Secularism is a legitimate reaction to the wars of religion, but it is not, in my judgment, a viable option if secularism automatically means religionlessness. In the first place, it has been proven already that it is not acceptable to the world's majority. We will not see religion simply go away. Modernist-secularism of various stripes—atheistic humanism (à la Feuerbach), atheistic socialism (à la Marx), atheistic science (à la Freud or Russell)—have all failed in replacing religion.[30] First, it is becoming more and more fashionable to hear people speak of postideological or even postChristian denominationalism, but not of a post-religious era, even though many prefer to speak of being spiritual while not being religious. Second, fundamentalism or fanaticism is not limited to religions; in many disgusting ways, it is present as well in modernist-secularism. It has been fanatical in promoting its own homogenizing worldview and reductionistic logic and in banishing religion from the public realm (co-opting it when needed). In other words, modernist-secularism has become a form of fanatical religion even as it attacks religion. Third, as previously stated, modernist-secularism is based on an inadequate framework for understanding religion. Fourth, it is not helpful in dealing with the more violent expressions of religion. Finally, modernist-secularism does not offer ways of tapping the positive role that religion can play in our global civil society.

29. Ali, *The Clash of Fundamentalisms*.
30. Küng, *Global Responsibility*, 45.

The resurgence of religion, after years of trying to banish it from the face of the earth, demonstrates the significance of religion in human society, either for good or for ill. Religion plays a positive role, which is why human communities continue to thirst for it. Even those who say they are spiritual but not religious are not, in my understanding, denying religion itself or religious sensibilities. It is not a wholesale rejection of religious sensibilities; rather, it is a response to a context in which organized religion has been identified, if not actively involved, in harming humanity and creation.

The history of religion is, of course, mixed; thus, we cannot be a Pollyanna about its promise. Nonetheless, religion has something positive to offer that modernist-secularism does not; it has something to contribute to the peace and healing of our world that narrow and self-serving nationalism and wars have destroyed; and it has something to contribute to our quest for greater well-being which predatory globalization can destroy and has destroyed. Recognizing this crucial and positive role that religion can play, Richard Falk has this to say: "The prospects of creating some form of human global governance in the 21st century seem likely to depend on whether the religious resurgence is able to provide the basis for a more socially and politically responsible form of globalization than what currently exists."[31]

Paul Knitter has identified two vital, if not determinative, contributions that religions can offer to the building of our global civil society: vision and energy.[32] Primarily through symbols and narratives, religions offer their followers a vision of hope—a vision of a different world and a hope that the world they are currently in can be changed. This vision of a different world, along with the hope that another world is possible, is nourished and vitalized by the energy that religions instill in believers as they act on their conviction. And, when success is not visible on the immediate horizon or nonexistent, committed believers pursue and persevere even when stakes are high, such as threat to one's life, because of the empowering energy that religions provide to their followers.

We can elaborate on the two vital ingredients that Knitter has identified as well as explore or expound on other dimensions. Vital, indeed, is the vision of hope that religions offer to their followers. Out

---

31. Falk, cited in Raiser, *For a Culture of Life*, 38.
32. Knitter, *One Earth*, 71.

of this vision of hope, religious believers utter their prophetic "no" to what they perceive as wrong or not in consonance with the vision. It is in light of this vision that they seek to live differently, as if the not-yet were already a present reality. As they become committed to the vision, religious experience gives the fire (energy) of prophetic courage—a courage which is not a complete absence of fear, but which affirms that there is something greater than fear that is worth daring. Both vision and energy gives the followers the stamina to persevere and refuse to give up hope, a hope that is not simply based on optimistic signs but on the ultimate promise of a new life—a new tomorrow.

Crucial, indeed, is the role of religion in society and, much more so, in a time of global fragmentation. When the forces of predatory globalization crush communities, impoverish the populace, trample human dignity, push many into diaspora, distort priorities and values, commodify lives, destroy the ecosystem, leave families fragmented and alienated, drive the multitude into cynicism and despair, and consume the lives even of the winners, religion provides transcendent orientation and "antisystemic" force.[33] To be sure, religion can be easily co-opted by traditional and emerging political forces, such as what Juergensmeyer calls "guerrilla antiglobalism," but the crucial point is to channel the vision and energies of the various religious communities for the creation of the global common good.[34] This means that the "antisystemic" force of religion must be directed toward the creation of the common good and an ethics of global responsibility. All religious communities are called to the enormous and complex task of articulating and channeling the "antisystemic" force of religions so that it may become a midwife for the birthing of a new and better tomorrow. Obviously, this cannot be done by one religion. This is a challenge to all religions, and certainly to Christianity. To this I now give attention.

CLEANING THE CHRISTIAN HOUSEHOLD
AND OPENING ITS WINDOWS

Christianity cannot effectively respond to the challenge of working with people of other faiths to resist the predatory forces of globalization and build a new and better tomorrow until and unless it does

33. Beyer, cited by Schreiter, *The New Catholicity*, 16.
34. Juergensmeyer, "Religious Antiglobalism," 144–45.

some self-cleaning. This self-cleaning involves an examination of its attitude and relationship with other religions and a self-exorcism of its unholy alliance (wittingly and unwittingly) with the colonizing, imperializing, and globalizing power of the global North. Although I cannot be exhaustive, a short historical retrieval and deconstruction of Christianity's self-understanding is useful.

The formation of Christianity's self-understanding and attitude toward the world in general and of other religions in particular has been informed by historical circumstances and has changed throughout history. One approach that I have found useful in dealing with the long history and the vast material on this particular issue is by Raimundo Panikkar.[35] Panikkar proposes five categories in Christianity's self-understanding: (1) witness, (2) conversion, (3) crusade, (4) mission, and (5) dialogue. Although these five categories can be seen "chronologically," that is, they are more pronounced at certain points in history, all are present today, and they permeate each other. Hence, it is better, suggests Panikkar, to call these five historical-chronological periods "kairological moments."

Witness represents the most prevalent self-consciousness of Christians during the first centuries until the fall of Rome under the Alaric (410 CE), or the death of St. Augustine (430 CE). With Christ's *parousia* coming at any given moment, they could not have imagined forming a religion called Christianity. Their primary concern was to live faithfully and bear witness to what they had known of the transforming work of Jesus through testimonies, communal life, worship, acts of healing, and services. Under a hostile and idolatrous environment, they were aware of the high price they had to pay for their faithfulness: martyrdom. To be a martyr (witness) was the ultimate test of Christian faithfulness.

A shift from self-understanding construed as witness to a self-understanding as conversion occurred when the fortunes of Christianity changed: This is commonly called the Constantinization of Christianity. During this period, Christianity was wedded to the empire. All people within the reach and power of Christendom became Christians. Because membership in the Christian religion was no longer a sufficient badge of faithfulness, another test was employed: experience of conversion or change of lifestyle (*conversio morum*—a

---

35. Panikkar, "The Jordan, the Tiber, and the Ganges," 89–116.

monastic slogan). Conversion to Christ became the litmus test of being a true Christian. This category of self-understanding lasted until the Middle Ages when Christianity clashed with Islam. The clash with Islam triggered a new Christian self-understanding.

Crusade followed conversion as the next dominant Christian self-understanding. This new period of Christian self-understanding extends from the eighth century until well past the fall of Constantinople (1453 CE), or probably until the defeat of the Turks in Lepanto (1571 CE). Certainly, Christendom was inundated with internal conflicts and threats, but nothing was more defining than the Islamic threat. Christendom was threatened from multiple sides: Spain fell quickly into Islamic hands (713 CE), Vienna was under threat, south of France was under assault, and Jerusalem and many holy places were under Muslim dominion. As a consequence, the Christian empire asserted itself and defense of Christendom became a collective obsession. In this context, the true Christian was a soldier (militia Christi) and a crusader. It was also during this period that Christianity began to shift the notion of true religion (*vera religio*) understood as true religiousness to "the only true and salvific institutionalized religion."[36]

Mission followed crusade as the dominant self-understanding of Christianity. This self-understanding dominated throughout the modern period. Exploration, "discovery," conquest, and occupation of new territories needed new justification. Mission became the justification for the *conquista*. Wherever there was conquest and colonization there was Christian mission. Conquest and occupation of new lands were providential: they provided the opportune moment to carry out the mission to civilize and Christianize the heathens. Participation in Christian mission became the duty of the followers of Christ. To be a true Christian requires that one be a missionary. However, the independence of new nations after the Second World War, the continuing struggle of the people of the global South, and the irruption of the people of the non-Christian world made many Christians of the global North realize that they could no longer continue to "missionize" other peoples. Hence, a new self-understanding has emerged in the scene: dialogue.

Dialogue may not yet be the dominant and pervasive self-understanding of the general populace, but the current historical moment

36. Ibid., 94.

(*kairos*) points to dialogue. Today, arrogant exclusivism and unilateralism by religious bodies and nations respectively face a serious challenge. Crusading and missionizing attitudes and practices are called to give way to dialogue by a growing number of people. Dialogue is not simply a strategy but a way of living; it is the way to live if there is to be peace in our world. The survival of our planet demands dialogical relations. The true Christian must embody a dialogical spirit.

BIRTHING A DIALOGICAL
AND GLOBALLY RESPONSIBLE CHURCH

Indeed, the historical moment (*kairos*) is pointing toward dialogue as the shape of God's liberating presence in our polycentric, multicultural and multi-religious but socio-politically conflictive global context. As God's people, it is but natural to assume that the church exists wherever the spirit is. Unfortunately, reality tells us that this is not always the case. Calling the church to dialogical attitude and responsibility will not be easy. The church's track record on dialogue is dismal. Other religions are not better either, and are mostly suspicious—for good reasons—of Christian interest in dialogue. Calling religions to dialogue, as someone puts it, "is as hopeful a task as calling for conversation between fighting cocks."[37]

To be sure, leading the church to dialogue is difficult, nevertheless, the hard work that it calls for should not deter us. Part of this work, as stated earlier (regarding the retrieval and deconstructive work of Christian self-understanding), is to articulate a Christian theology of religion that is both faithful and open. Total agreement to what I will articulate as a Christian theology of religions is not necessary in order to respond to the dialogical call of our historical moment. Nonetheless, it is crucial that Christians examine and articulate their theology of religions, which can be understood analogously as a Christian foreign policy toward other religions. Why do Christians need to engage in dialogue with people of other faiths? What is the theological basis of our engagement? Again, I can offer the reader only the basic tenets of my theological motivations for dialogical engagement.

37. Knitter, in Cobb, *Transforming Christianity*, 49.

Historical, Mystical and Practical Reasons

First, from a historical and hermeneutical point of view, liberal Christianity affirms that as historical creatures we do not see reality from the point of view of eternity (*sub specie aeternitatis*), but only through our limited socio-historical and geographical location. Historical beings that we are, what we see is a part and not the totality of reality. If our perception is limited by our historicity and circumscribed by our relationship with the world around us, then we should not close ourselves to other dimensions of the total reality or to other expressions of truth that our neighbors may see and experience. We should not be threatened by what our neighbors affirm as true, because his or her truth affirmation does not necessarily negate what we deeply hold as true. The Nobel Prize physicist Niels Bohr puts it well: "The opposite of a true statement is a false statement, but the opposite of a profound truth can be another profound truth."[38]

When we apply this insight to Christianity and the question of revelation and salvation, what we know of God and God's revelatory and salvific acts in the world is limited to our historical window—the Christian window. This is not bad in and of itself. In fact, we see only because we see through a particular window. Not only is it impossible for a single human being to see through all windows, there is no way of seeing apart from our particular window. This Christian window, however, may become our Christian box—our prison cell—if we do not embrace it consciously and take account of it critically. When we are conscious and critical of our Christian window, we know that even our notion of salvation is set already within the Christian framework. In addition, we must acknowledge that believers from other religious traditions may not want to play our Christian game—the game of salvation.

Second, from the theological-mystical point of view, not only is our knowledge of God limited and historically conditioned, but God is also the Ultimate Mystery. Moreover, the Ultimate Mystery is not only ineluctably ineffable, at the heart of the Ultimate Mystery is plurality. We can discern the Ultimate Mystery's ontological plurality in the manifold particularities. To confine the Ultimate Mystery to one particular expression is to misunderstand what is at the heart of the Ultimate Mystery: the mystery of plurality—a plurality that at the

---

38. Bohr, cited in Palmer, *The Courage to Teach*, 62.

same time does not deny the mystery of unity.[39] I have underscored ontological plurality as central to the Ultimate Mystery to counter embedded habits of thinking that reduce, swallow, or melt the many into *one*.[40] In a society with a long history of devouring and melting the many into *one*, there is more reason to be suspicious that the discourse on *oneness* with regard to the Ultimate Mystery could be a religious projection of political hegemony. Instead of thinking in numbers and starting to count, we must see the other side of plurality. This is not simply "manyness," or oneness understood as mono, but plurality understood in a non-dualistic way—*the unity* and *the inextricable connection of the many*.[41] There is always a hidden connection between all things (*semper occulta quaedam est concatenatio*).[42]

Third, from an ethical and practical point of view, Christianity does more than affirm that our knowledge is limited and that plurality is at the heart of the Ultimate Reality. It also affirms that the building of a just, humane, and sustainable world demands openness to the claims of other religious believers and to what their religious praxis can contribute into our common life, particularly to our shared well-being. Openness to the truth-claims of others and testing them in light of their contribution to greater well-being is reminiscent of Aristotle's notion of *phronesis* (practical wisdom). Practical wisdom knows that something is "true" because of its "good" effects. If the "true" is the "good," then the true is discernible in the "good" that a person does or what a "good person" does.[43] In short, a particular religious expression that claims monopoly of the absolute truth violates that truth-claim when it undermines mutual respect and when it harms the other. Monopolistic claims and imposition of truth-claims are contrary to the nature of truth. Such actions devour people in the name of the sacred truth.

The Particularity of the Christian Experience

Where does our openness to the revelatory and salvific claims of other religions lead to? Does it relativize or water down the Christian claim?

39. Panikkar, "The Jordan, the Tiber, and the Ganges," 109.

40. Cf. Heim, *Salvations*; also see, Knitter, *Introducing Theologies*, 192–202.

41. Panikkar, "The Jordan, the Tiber, and the Ganges," 111.

42. Cited in Panikkar, *The Intra-Religious Dialogue*, xvi.

43. Knitter, One *Earth, Many Religions*, 82.

How does it take account of the particular and decisive claim of the Christian faith? What will it say about the mandate to evangelize the whole world of the good news of Jesus Christ? Are we destined to a wishy-washy or mushy kind of relativism and non-engaging niceness or tolerance that fits so very well into our individualistic-privatistic culture? My answer is a resounding *no*.

The best Christian theological position overcomes religious schizophrenia and integrates the insights of scientific, historical, cultural, and literary studies as well as the nature and language of religious commitment. A Christian does not crucify his or her intellect even as she or he continues to be a committed Christian. The de-absolutizing and relativizing perspective of historical studies and comparative religion is affirmed and valued by a liberal Christian. Relativity is the nature of all historical and religious institutions. One cannot escape from it. But an astute Christian interpreter of religious traditions does not confuse or equate historical relativity with relativism. In fact, relativism is a contradiction to the spirit of the tradition, because relativism is absolutism in disguise. In its subtle form, it is repressive tolerance.

What I affirm as a Christian is not relativism but relationality. Relativity does not mean being "limited" only, but also, as John Cobb Jr. puts it, of being "potentially *relatable* to other truth claims."[44] Relationality does not ask us to abdicate faith commitment through one religious medium, such as Christianity, but affirms it in the context of relationship with other claims. In fact, our day-to-day lives call us to make commitments in the context of seeing "only through a mirror dimly," which is to say, only through the relative and the particular and amidst competing claims. When the particular presents to us in the form of competing claims each demanding our wholehearted commitment, we know that we must make a choice that is beyond the trivial. It is not, for instance, a choice between different kinds of doughnuts (old fashioned, honey glazed, cream and strawberry doughnuts, etc.) but a serious one. I cannot deny that there are other claims, but committing myself to a particular claim demands my total commitment. This is particularly true of the claim of Christ in Jesus.

As a Christian, the Christ who calls and demands my total commitment has become fully particular in Jesus. It is through this partic-

44. Cobb, *Transforming Christianity*, 6.

ularity that Christ's saving work in Jesus has become a reality. If I may pair the word "only" with the word "salvation," I say that it is "only" through the particular that we are "saved." To use the syntax of the famous exclusivist dictum, "outside of the particular there is no salvation." God loves particularities, lots of them. Yes, God saves through the particularity of Christ in Jesus, but God's saving act in Christ is not limited to this particularity, and this particularity does not exhaust God's saving acts through other particularities. This is at the core of what we call the incarnation. Incarnation means that the Divine has assumed the fullness of humanity, not that a particular humanity has taken on the totality of the Divine.[45] To make a particular assume the totality of the Divine is not an expression of Christian faithfulness but an act of betrayal. It is to fall into what the Christian tradition calls idolatry. Idolatry makes God a prisoner of a particular. To limit God's saving act in Christ through Jesus is to imprison God, which is often done in the name of Christian faithfulness.

The Spirit/Christ in Jesus—a Breakthrough Figure

It may help us understand the creative tension between the particularity and decisiveness of the Christian claim in relation to Christian openness. I suggest that we see Christ in Jesus as a prototype (breakthrough figure) and not as an archetype figure. Unfortunately, the prevailing mindset of many well-intentioned Christians is that of Jesus as an archetype. If I may use a more mundane language, to construe Jesus as an archetype is to image Jesus like a cookie-cutter, which is to assume a cookie-cutter mentality. In the cookie-cutter mentality, the present as well as the future are strangulated and cut to fit the past. Similarly, threatened by the freedom of the Holy Spirit, the cookie-cutter mindset abducts and imprisons the Spirit. The guardians of the cookie-cutter mindset have the Spirit (Sophia) controlled and subordinated by the Son. The *filioque* controversy is an account of the history of the subordination of the Spirit. The subordination of the Spirit by the Son has been disastrous. The Church, through the Son, has imprisoned the Spirit and has limited its creative saving work by making the Christian container the only correct container of God's grace.

45. See Knitter, *Jesus and the Other Names*, 73; also Schillebeeckx, *The Church*, 164–68.

It is, however, a different matter when we think of Jesus as a prototype. While archetype thinking equates Christ's particularity in Jesus with exclusivity (a way of thinking among fundamentalist Christians), prototype thinking sees Christ's particularity in Jesus as openness to other particularities. While archetype thinking confuses Christian faithfulness with exclusivity, prototype thinking holds in creative balance faithfulness and openness. Jesus the prototype allows freedom of movement of the Spirit, and it does not call Christians to live in the past; rather, it calls Christians to live creatively in the present. Jesus the prototype—God's breakthrough figure—is not threatened by the freedom of the Spirit, but celebrates the novel and creative work of the Spirit to bring about salvation both within the confines of Christianity as well as beyond its walls and even beyond the work of Christ in Jesus. This does not mean that the Spirit contradicts the work of Christ in Jesus, but neither does Christ confine the Spirit. The Spirit's freedom is in line with the work of Christ in Jesus. Put differently, we are open to others and to the work of the Spirit in others because we are faithful to the work of Christ in Jesus. Cobb puts it this way: "We must show that we are open to the other because we are truly faithful to our heritage."[46]

Christian faithfulness is not a contradiction to Christian openness. Jesus construed as a prototype—God's breakthrough figure— offers that possibility for liberal Christians. Christians can and must affirm that Jesus is *the* way, *the* truth, and *the* life (Jn 14:6), but in affirming this they affirm *the way* who is *open to other ways*. Put differently, to affirm that Jesus is the way is to be led to the way that is open to other ways and other paths. The way of Jesus is the way that is open to the presence of the Spirit who is doing its creative and saving work even beyond the historical deeds of Jesus. The way of the open Jesus is the way of the one who is *truly but not the only* nor the *totality* of the incarnation of the Divine.

Christian faithfulness walks in light of this understanding. Wholehearted commitment to the way of Jesus does not require that he be the *only* and the *totality* but that he be *truly* and *fully* an embodiment of God's saving work. *Truly* is indispensable or essential to experiencing the saving work of Christ in Jesus and to faithful discipleship, but this is not the case with *solely* or *only*. Throughout the ages, faithful Christians have committed themselves to Jesus not because of

46. Cobb, *Transforming Christianity*, 60.

their belief that he is *the only* or the *exclusive* manifestation of God's saving grace, but because they have experienced him as the *true, indispensable, universal,* and *decisive* manifestation of the Divine.[47] Yes, true religious experience—an experience that strikes at the core of one's being—cannot be true only for me; it has to be true for others as well.[48] But the truth and universality of the Christian truth-claim does not demand the elimination of other truth-claims; neither does the recognition of other truth-claims require that one must water down the universal validity of the Christian truth-claim.

Christian Language of Commitment: Performative Language

Wholehearted commitment may be expressed in words that demand absolute devotion, but it should not be confused with arrogant exclusivism. The absolute language that comes from an experience of God's saving power and calls us to witness is not the language of comparison, but the language of commitment and devotion. Words and phrases such as "one and only" and "no other name" belong to the language of devotion (love language) and what scholars call performative or call to action language.[49] In the transformation of a common language to a language of devotion a slippage from *a* to *the* happens or that *a* has become *the.*[50] When something at stake is of ultimate significance, there is no other language short of the absolute language of commitment. No other language can make people leave what they have and make great sacrifices short of the absolute language of commitment. The absolute language of commitment and devotion is not, however, synonymous with exclusivism, which fundamentalist Christians confuse. Rather, it is a language of commitment in the face of other claims, and it is a language that finds a creative balance between faithfulness and openness.

Indeed, one can be both faithful as a Christian and open to the claims of others and to the saving work of God in other religious faiths. Rather than be sad, we should be feasting and dancing that God is at work not only in us and through us but also *beyond* us Christians. The

---

47. Borg, "Jesus and Buddhism," 80. Also, Knitter, *Jesus and the Other Names,* 72.

48. Polanyi cited in Maguire, *The Moral Core of Judaism,* 63.

49. Knitter, *Jesus and the Other Names,* 70.

50. Crossan, "Exclusivity and Particularity," 86.

central point of the Christian Story is not God's exclusivity but God's radical love and hospitality. Christians must proclaim God's radical saving hospitality whenever and wherever Christian exclusivism is present; Christians must witness to God's radical comma where exclusivism has put a period. Moreover, Christians must proclaim God's radical openness with the passion and excitement of an exclamation point!

THE CHURCH'S MISSION AND MINISTRY IN A RELIGIOUSLY DIVERSE AND SUFFERING WORLD

The challenge of our religiously diverse and suffering world demands a different articulation of ecclesiology, mission, and new ways of doing ministry. An ecclesiological model that fits our current context and challenges, without necessarily canceling out the best elements of other models, is one proposed by D. Preman Niles: "The people of God in the midst of people of God."[51] Consistent with this view of ecclesiology is mission understood as *missio Dei*. The primary agent of mission is God. The church has no mission of its own except as it participates with God in God's mission for the world. Not to be forgotten is that the church itself is an object of mission. Even as the church seeks to embody God's mission in its own life, the missionary God is already present and at work among God's people before the church arrives at the mission field. Thus, in its encounter with people of other religious faiths, the church must be open to God's surprise through the voices of other religious believers.

Consistent with this way of understanding God's missionary activity is the current articulation of mission as dialogue. The challenge of religious diversity demands such an understanding of mission. Mission must be understood as dialogue and must be carried out in the spirit of dialogue. Dialogue is not simply an approach or a method (understood as tool), or a means to an end but, following Konrad Raiser, "the expression of an attitude of life, which forms relationships while respecting differences, in a situation of religious and cultural pluralism."[52] This dialogical attitude to life finds expressions in actions or ways of relating that take seriously the claims of the other—particularly the religious others. A dialogical attitude to life leads to dialogical engagement and, conversely, dialogical engagement

51. Niles, *From East and West*.
52. Raiser, *Ecumenism in Transition*, 82.

nourishes dialogical attitude. Dialogical engagement, appropriating Eck's notion of pluralism, is not the mere recognition of religious diversity; neither does it mean the mere toleration of religious diversity. Rather, it is "energetic engagement with diversity," "active seeking of understanding across lines of difference," and an "encounter of commitments." It does not require that everyone at the "table" has to agree, but it does require a "commitment to being at the table—with one's commitments."[53]

What happens to the calling of Christians to proclaim the gospel of Jesus the Christ when mission becomes dialogical? And, what about the issue of conversion? This is a kind of question that is often raised in Christian circles and, no doubt, is legitimate, but it normally comes with the presupposition that dialogue is separate from proclamation. Knitter, in *Jesus and the Other Names*, is articulate on this: "'to proclaim' and 'to dialogue' are not two aspects of a broader, distinct activity; rather, dialogue is the broader activity that includes and is made up of proclaiming and listening. Both undertakings—witnessing and listening—have to be carried out in a 'dialogical manner.'"[54] In another essay, Knitter, in a metaphorical manner, speaks of "mission-as-dialogue" as consisting—like water—of the "hydrogen and oxygen of proclaiming and listening."[55] Mission-as-dialogue does not sacrifice proclamation and the possibility of conversion (believers of other religions being converted to Christianity and vice versa), but proclamation is done in the spirit of dialogue in which respect, sincerity, truthfulness and mutuality are present.

This mission-as-dialogue must be seen as "prophetic dialogue" (Bevans) or as dialogical global responsibility (Knitter and Küng).[56] I say this because the challenge of religious diversity cannot be separated from but is connected to the challenge of the suffering world. Put differently, the irruption of the Third World (global South) is connected to the irruption of the non-Christian world (Pieris).[57] In relation to the challenge of violence and the vision of peace, mission-as-dialogue

53. See The Pluralism Project at Harvard University.

54. Knitter, *Jesus and the Other Names*, 143.

55. Knitter, "The Transformation of Mission," 98.

56. Bevans and Schroeder, *Constants in Context*; Knitter, *Jesus and the Other Names*; Küng, *Global Responsibility*.

57. Pieris, *An Asian Theology of Liberation*.

must also be mission as reconciliation (Schreiter).[58] Dialogue must be broad enough to embrace the many dimensions of life in our global society (dialogue of action, theological exchange, dialogue of religious experience or spirituality), but there are pressing issues that globalization has brought or exacerbated that must be addressed ecumenically and dialogically with urgency.

Creating and Promoting a Culture of Dialogue

A culture of dialogue is crucial in a context when diversity is our present reality, but prejudices and conflicts are abundant. A culture of dialogue provides the structure and frame in which we relate with other beings. It is one in which the dominant way of thinking and acting is characterized by dialogical engagement, mutual trust and respect, and openness. A culture of dialogue is foundational for the health and well-being of our world. Our world cannot be built on the foundations of McDonald's and Walmart, profits, technology, competition and polarization, and mutual fear and suspicion. The foundations of our one world, asserts Diana Eck, are in the "stockpiling of trust through dialogue and the creation of relationships that can sustain both agreements and disagreements."[59] Furthermore, following Miroslav Volf, we must see our difficult dialogues not in the framework of exclusion but of true embrace: an embrace that makes room for otherness and differences and even in opposition to us. In a true dialogue we may oppose, but it is an opposition that does not exclude.[60]

Creating and promoting a culture of dialogue is a crucial ministry of the church for our times. No doubt there are a great number of obstacles—secularism, deeply-entrenched stereotypes and prejudices, massive disinformation, cynicism, and threats to security—to the creation and promotion of a culture of dialogue. The church itself is part of the problem as much as it is part of the solution. Education is certainly needed beyond the usual Sunday school to cure Christian ignorance. There is an example, perhaps apocryphal, of a U.S. ambassador (Christian) who is reported to have blurted out in a moment of frustration over the conflict in the Middle East, "If only Arabs and

---

58. Schreiter, *Reconciliation*.

59. Eck, *Minutes*, 20–30, cited by Smock in *Interfaith Dialogue and Peacebuildig*, 7.

60. Volf, "Exclusion and Embrace," 230–48, cited in Knitter, *One Earth*, 148.

Jews would learn to resolve their conflict like good Christians."[61] I like to believe that this is simple ignorance, but it is the ignorance of someone who thinks that Christian hands are clean in relation to the Middle East conflict. Moreover, this is an ignorance framed by prejudice. This means that the church must undertake the colossal task of educating itself, which includes both deconstructing deeply-held religious prejudices of members and learning alternative ways of relating to people of other faiths. Moreover, it also means working with other religious communities in educating the wider public.

Other religions certainly have some religious stereotypes and prejudices to unlearn, but my concern here is Christianity. From my readings and encounters, it appears that Christianity has the worse track record of religious bigotry, arrogance, superiority, and exclusivist and absolutistic claims. Its alliance with modernity and imperializing powers of the global North has made it also a missionizing and imperializing religion. A major educational project must be pursued. The seminary education of pastors and priests needs to include a critical assessment of Christian theologies of religions, a comparative study of religions, and an experience on interfaith dialogue at various levels. One form of exercise, for example, that I used for my theology of religions course was to require every student to relate to and engage in dialogue with a believer of another religious tradition. Likewise, churches need to create opportunities for its members to hear the views of other religious believers on pressing issues as well as create opportunities for interaction at both the personal and communal level.

Conspiring Interfaith Praxis for Eco-Human Well-being

I am not going to explore in detail the many dimensions of interfaith praxis but will subsume them under the subtopic of conspiracy for eco-human well-being. A conspiracy (con-spire or share breath) of various individuals and groups at various levels (local, national, international) is crucial in our highly globalized world. The magnitude and complexity of our world's pressing issues require the cooperation of all stakeholders, including religious communities. Though religious differences cannot be ignored, followers of all religious traditions share a common world and common threats: massive global suffering, marginalization and poverty, war, ecological catastrophe, fanatical

61. Young, "American Jews, Christians, and Muslims," 68.

secularism, the market religion, neoliberalism and imperialism, and so on. Deep in the heart of the world's major religious traditions is a prophetic vision: a vision of harmony, peace, just or right relation, and ecological balance. The major world religions have the gift of prophetic imagination and the tradition of prophetic criticism against various forms of idolatry, such as the idolatry of the global market and U.S. nationalism. In the Jewish tradition, Yahweh is a jealous God who has zero tolerance for idols. Similarly, no idols can stand before Allah. A Muslim (Islam means submission or surrender) will render submission only to Allah, never to the market-god.[62] Thich Nhat Hanh, a Buddhist monk, warns of absolutizing Buddha and his teachings, for to do so is like mistaking the finger pointing to the moon with the moon itself. Likewise, "the raft is not the shore. If we cling to the raft, if we cling to the finger, we miss everything."[63] A Sukuma proverb from Tanzania puts it this way: "I pointed out to you the stars and all you saw was the tip of my finger."[64]

Suffering caused by massive poverty is certainly a concern of major religions around the world. A central theme of major religions is care for the most vulnerable or those who are dying before their time. Poverty is pathological. Many physical diseases have their pathological basis in poverty. The cry of those who are dying before their time is growing louder and louder every day, and it is calling the various religious groups to respond both individually and collectively as well as locally and internationally. Additionally, it is calling the various religious traditions to employ various approaches—emergency assistance, community organizing, community empowerment projects of various sorts and policy advocacy. Various religious groups have resources, though often not recognized and maximized, such as vision, energy, communities and networks from the local to the global. The number of inter-religious faith based organizations are growing around the world in response to global poverty and other challenges.

Global conflicts are a distinct issue to which major religions must wake up and respond. Since religions are wedded in many of the global conflicts, they must be active participants in the solution as well. Like

62. The principal meaning of the word "Islam" is "surrender" or "submission." "Muslim," a cognate word to "Islam," means one who submits to God. See Ahmed, *Islam Today*, 17.

63. Hanh, "The Fourteen Mindfulness Trainings," 450.

64. Healy, *Once Upon a Time*, 95.

other global concerns, the search for peace in the midst of conflicts requires interfaith dialogue and cooperation at various levels—interfaith prophetic resolutions in denouncing war, education, mediation and conflict transformation, and interfaith community projects. Harmony, shalom, peace, and right relations are at the core teachings of major religions even as day-to-day practices betray them. Interfaith dialogue in various forms creates a space for followers of various religions to start the stockpiling of trust and the building of bridges of fractured relationships. What war and prejudices have separated, interfaith praxes have sought to overcome by building bridges for understanding interfaith differences. The base of the bridge, according to Jaco Cilliers, "should be built on the foundations of justice and reconciliation, while the pillars that support the 'paths of interfaith dialogue' should be constructed on deep understandings of truth, forgiveness, and mercy as well as peacebuilding and conflict transformation processes and initiatives."[65] Beyond interfaith pronouncements, important as they are, is the hard work of creating interfaith circles for peace at both the local and global level. These interfaith circles have the daunting task of transforming "zones of interfaith conflict into zones of interfaith peace."[66]

A global concern that is related but cannot be subsumed under other categories is the plight of our ecological system. Like the matter of massive poverty and global conflicts, the ecological crisis demands an interfaith praxis, and it appears to be a concern that is uniting various segments of our global civil society. Like the matter of peace, justice, and care for the marginalized, the major religions of the world have at their core teachings care for the ecosystem, and they all can learn from each other. Though the world's major religions have different ways of thinking about ecology, they have as part of their foundational worldview and core convictions such notions as living in cosmic harmony, ecological reverence, walking lightly, ecological justice, and sustainable living. Both in theory and practice, Buddhism has been at the forefront of ecological concerns. Islam (a monotheistic religion) views ecology in light of the *Tawhid* or the absolute oneness of God who stands in dual relationship with the created. All creatures

65. Cilliers, "Building Bridges," 50.

66. Gibbs, "The United Religious Initiative," Ibid, 116.

are equal and they are sacred but only in relation to God and in fulfilling God's purpose for creation.[67]

A final area for conspiring interfaith praxis is spirituality. The number is growing of those who have embraced the wisdom and spirituality of various religious traditions. More than a strategic move for effective action, interfaith conspiracy (breathing together) is necessary if we are to endure in the long and arduous struggle. Without the life-giving and nourishing breath (spirit) of our companions, we easily fall into compassion fatigue and cynicism. Detached from the company of breath-sharers, we easily dry-up and wither under the scorching heat of the noon-day sun. In the words of Thich Nhat Hanh, "If we are a drop of water and we try to get to the ocean as only an individual drop we will surely evaporate along the way. To arrive at the ocean, [we] must go as a river."[68] The interfaith community is our river if we are to arrive at the ocean. Furthermore, the wisdom and spiritual practices of religious traditions will nurture us in the journey and prevent us from becoming what we are against or that which we are opposed. When asked why he did not hate the Chinese for what they have done to Tibet, the Dalai Lama said, "They have taken so much else from me, I will not give them my peace of mind."[69]

SEEDS OF HOPE:
SEEDS OF INTERFAITH CONSPIRATORIAL PRAXIS

The seeds of hope of a church whose primary identity is that of dialogians of faith have been scattered by the Spirit; they are sprouting everywhere. As the work of the Spirit, I have the confidence of faith that they will continue to grow and bear fruits: men and women who embody the dialogical spirit in all that they care and do. In like manner, this dialogical spirit is growing and bearing fruits not only among Christians, but also followers of other religions. Instead of a clash of civilizations or a clash of fundamentalisms, we have dialogue of life. Instead of a clash of religions, we have a dialogue of religions. Instead of a clash of convictions, we have a dialogue of convictions. The indwelling of the spirit of dialogue is now felt everywhere and in places where it is needed the most. Instead of meeting each other in

---

67. Ammar, "Islam and Deep Ecology," 552.

68. Hanh, *Creating True Peace*, 176.

69. Cited in Gottlieb, "Saving the World," 508.

the battlefield, followers of various religious traditions are now meeting at the dialogue table. Instead of drawing their firearms to kill each other, they are drawing their spiritual resources to promote life-giving and empowering projects. We need to hear some of the stories of seeds of hope to nourish us in the journey of interfaith relations.

Somewhere in Dinas, a town in Zamboanga del Sur on the island of Mindanao (Philippines), a story of a seed of hope grows. It is the story of two persons of different faiths, Ver Albarico (Christian) and Toto Anig (Muslim), and the story of the Dinas Interfaith Movement. At the height of war between the Philippine government and the Moro National Liberation Front (MNLF), Ver and Toto (MNLF fighter), still at the threshold of their manhood, met. On the day they met, Toto was on the run trying to evade government soldiers. Toto found himself on Ver's family farm. When Ver saw him, he begged, "Please don't squeal on me." Without delay, Ver hid Toto in the ceiling of their house. Soon the soldiers arrived and asked Ver if he had seen a young man fleeing in the direction of their house. Ver denied seeing the man the soldiers described. After the soldiers had eaten their meals and left, he asked Toto to come down from the ceiling and took him to a place where it was difficult for the military to find him. This was a momentous and unforgettable incident in the life of Ver and Toto. For Toto it was the day that Ver "saved his life" and for it, he was eternally grateful. They now relate to each other as brothers. Today Ver and Toto are peacemakers and members of the Dinas Interfaith Movement, a movement composed of three ethnic-religious communities, namely, Bisaya-Christians, Maguindanaon-Muslims, and Subanen (indigenous tribe).[70]

In southern Asia (Sri Lanka), the Christian Workers Fellowship (CWF) offers other seeds of hope.[71] Although Christian in its origin (formed in 1958), CWF was designed as an ecumenical project to help bring justice to the working poor and to heal the animosity between the Buddhist Sinhala majority and Hindu Tamil minority. CWF members met in groups to study the Bible in relation to the social issues of their context, particularly the plight of the working class. Soon they realized that they could not continue to talk about the issues of the working class simply as Christians. Convinced of the relevance

70. Gaspar, "Bringing Christians and Muslims Together," 96–97.
71. Knitter, *One Earth*, 173–76.

of the CWF, Buddhist workers wanted to join the Christian fellowship but remain Buddhists. This was an opportune moment (*kairos*) in the fellowship's transformation. The Christian fellowship moved beyond its Christian origins: it became an interfaith workers fellowship. In this shared praxis of addressing basic social needs, Buddhist and Christians soon came to an understanding that the Dharma of Buddha and the gospel of Christ were calling them to work together for a just and equitable system.

Without doubt, these few examples are fragile embodiments, but they are seeds of hope for our global village. We must help build the foundations of a dialogical global society out of our fragile embodiments. We cannot predict with certainty how our project will evolve in the future, but we must start our walk because it is only in the walking that we will know the path (*solvitur ambulando*—we know the path by walking it) or, to put it differently, "the road is made by walking."[72]

---

72. Gill, *Borderlinks,* Also, Tracy, cited in Knitter, *One Earth*, 133.

12

The Church as a Community of Hope

Facing Global Cynicism and Despair

I<small>T WAS A GREAT</small> winter day in Minnesota. The clear sky and bright sun made the snow to sparkle its enchanting whiteness. It was on this day that I had an uplifting experience after delivering what I felt was a well-received homily. After worship, people expressed deep appreciation for my homily, especially in that it challenged them to live differently as Christians. That afternoon I cherished the delightful feeling that I had made a contribution, no matter how small, in the work of helping people live differently. As the sun faded into the distant horizon and the mantle of darkness covered its radiant light, however, the delightful feeling faded as well, and the darkness of doubt and a sense of powerlessness gripped my soul. It seemed as if doubt and powerlessness were telling me that I had been basking in the radiant light of a tiny accomplishment; as if both doubt and a sense of powerlessness wanted me to come to terms with the stark and brutal reality of our globalized world.

I am writing this chapter as part of my own wrestling. I cannot deny that there have been times in my life when I have felt discouraged by the turn of events, especially following the September 11, 2001 tragedy and the war on terror that followed. To make matters worse, not long after, Senator Paul Wellstone died in a tragic plane crash in the fall of 2002. While I did not know him personally, I admired his courage and audacity to speak truth to power. Upon hearing the news of his untimely death in the late hours of that tragic day, I felt as if the whole sky had fallen on me. The longer nights of the approaching winter only added weight to the already heavy heart of this child of the tropics. It was with this heavy heart that I continued coming to class, and it shaped and informed my teaching. It certainly did with my decision to change the sequence of topics in my Constructive Theology course. Following my heart's leading, instead of dealing with eschatology and the matter of hope at the end of the semester, which I normally do, I decided to lecture on eschatology and hope that week. Certainly, it was difficult to speak with a grieving heart, but I was glad I had done so. It was then that I realized that I had named the pain that my students were carrying in their hearts as well but had kept it to themselves.

CYNICISM, FATALISM, AND DESPAIR: THE PERVASIVENESS AND THE DURABILITY OF THE FORCES OF DEATH

Already burdened with a heavy heart, more bad news arrived—this time from the country of my birth. A dear friend, the Rev. Edison Lapuz, became one of the victims in a recent spate of extrajudicial killings. Edison was added to the already-long list of martyrs, some close to my family—lawyer Alfonso Surigao and the Rev. Amando Añosa, who was my wife's uncle. After many years of struggle for a just and sustainable tomorrow, the forces of reaction are still pervasive and in control. The writer of the book of Malachi articulates this poignant cry not only for the Israelites of old, but also for me in our desperate times: "Now we count the arrogant happy; evildoers not only prosper, but when they put God to the test they escape" (3:15). They get away with their evil deeds.

The seeming silence of God adds poignancy to the already precarious situation. Compounding to the poignancy of the situation, particularly for church members, is that the church I care about and have thought of as God's light and a harbinger of hope seems to offer less hope. It has become generally at home in the world or has become a church of the establishment. We can see expressions of this way of being a church among congregations that have confused their core values with the world. We find such examples among congregations that preach the gospel of prosperity, promise more material blessings to those who already have more while encouraging others who are economically marginalized to be faithful to the god of prosperity. In more subtle and sophisticated ways, this establishment mindset is present in churches that do nice things but refuse to question the dominant cultural, economic, and political structures. The continuing silence of many churches or congregations on human rights violations, ecological destruction, and corporate assault on people's health is appalling and does not offer much hope. Instead, the dominant gospel that we often hear is the exhortation to be nice and to expect more of the same.

Fatalism, cynicism, and despair seem to be a more natural response to what is going on around the world, particularly to the pervasiveness and the durability of the forces of death. I have seen enough of fatalism in my work in the Philippines, especially among marginalized people in rural communities. Undergirded by a religious-naturalistic worldview, the fatalist is one who has accepted his or her plight as a kind of destiny or *pagbuot sa Dios* (will of God). While there is a positive spin to the concept of *gulong ng palad* (wheel of fortune) or *kapalaran* (literally, the line on one's palm), in general this concept has worked to stifle self-agency. Reinforcing this fatalism are churches that preach passivity and subservience to the power wielders or, what we call in my native Cebuano language *dako'g tai* (people with huge manure).

Cynicism, like fatalism, is becoming pervasive as well, perhaps made possible by highfalutin rhetoric without substance, rampant corruption, and callous disregard for the common good. Interestingly, the word cynic comes from the Greek word *kunikos* (adjective, meaning "doglike"; *kuōn* means dog). Diogenes of Sinope, the prototypical cynic, is said to have barked in public and urinated on the leg of a table.[1] A cynic is one who barks in public and pees everywhere but exercises no responsibility. There are certainly thousands of reasons for us to pee and poop everywhere, particularly in the halls of power that continue to trample people's lives, but cynicism is not an adequate response to our sickly body politic. There are certainly thousands of reasons to bark as loud as we can, but cynicism is not an effective response against those who have known how to play deaf to the cry of the people.

If fatalism and cynicism are common but ineffective responses to our current malady, so is despair. When dreams are constantly betrayed and hope dashed, a ground is prepared for despair. The Latin root of despair (*de+esperare*) suggests loss (*de*) of spirit. Despair suggests

1. See *The American Heritage College Dictionary*, Third Edition.

absence of the Spirit or abandonment of the Spirit. When the Spirit is absent, life withers away. Following the writer of Ezekiel: When we are "cut-off" from the Spirit "our bones are dried-up, and our hope is lost" (37:11). Bones dry up when the life-giving breath is absent. When there is a drought of the life-giving breath, individual and social lives dry up and the forces of death dominate the social landscape. Bones dry up when the universal culture of death prevails; they dry up when people are covenanting with the idols of death. "Dried-up bones" and being "cut off" speak of a situation in which people's zest for life has dried up and is replaced by chilly apathy. Dried-up bones, chilly apathy, and psychic numbing are but a few of the metaphors we can use to refer to the drought of this life-giving breath.

Are we consigned to fatalism, cynicism, and despair or to the hell of hopelessness? Living without hope is living in hell; it is to ex- perience death long before one's physical cessation. It is no accident that when Dante, in his *Inferno*, wanted his readers to understand the depths of evil, he pictured the gates of hell with these words writ- ten over them: "Abandon hope, all ye who enter here."[2] Long ago the church father Chrysostom said: "What plunges us into disaster is not so much our sins as our despair."[3] Without hope, we can only be swal- lowed by despair. Alternatively, as Piers Paul Reed expressed it, "Sins become more subtle as [we] grow older: [we] commit sins of despair rather than lust."[4]

LEARNING HOPE: OPTIMISM, PESSIMISM, REALISM, AND HOPE

How can we continue to live in hope when signs of hope are few and far between? How can we continue to live in hope when old certain- ties have been undermined to their core and quixotic jousting with windmills seems the way things are? It is difficult to live in hope when our day-to-day lives are saturated by events that continue to make a mockery of hope. Our experience in life may make us wise, but not necessarily hopeful. We may even become so wise that we know how to masquerade our growing status quo conservatism in the form of piecemeal pragmatism and more-calculated-do-not-rock-the-boat-

2. Dante's *Inferno*, cited in Hall, *Why Christian?*, 103.

3. Chrysostom, cited in Moltmann, *The Source of Life*, 39.

4. Chittister, *Living Well*, 142.

realism. We may become wise in hiding the death of our youthful and daring idealism in the form of ludic or playful intellectualism. Likewise, we may become wise so as to know how to hide our complicity through calculated silence, which can be complicit silence masquerading as prudence.

The temptation for cynicism is real and strong, but a spark inside me continues to resist the idea that the world has no rhyme or reason. There still is the voice of life that calls me to believe that life is greater than senselessness and death. How can I nourish or shelter this seed of hope so it does not whither under the scorching heat of the summer sun or freeze to death in the long and severe cold winter? "[B]ecause we don't bring this true hope with us from birth, and because our experiences of life may perhaps make us wise but not necessarily hopeful," says Jürgen Moltmann, "we have to *go out* to learn hope. We learn to love when we say yes to life. So we learn to hope when we say yes to the future."[5]

Indeed, we must learn to hope and say "yes" to the future. As we mature in years the likelihood of losing hope increases. We may become bitter. Yet, while we cannot prevent wrinkles from writing upon our brows, hope prevents them from being written upon our hearts. How can we learn to hope? Crucial in learning hope is to understand clearly the heart of hope and what constitutes hope. To do this, it is necessary to clarify it in light of other related concepts, the first being optimism. Hearing someone say "I am an optimist" is not unusual; further, it is normally uttered to distinguish oneself from others whom he or she labels pessimist. In general, society favors the optimist and frowns upon the pessimist. In addition, it typically lumps the pessimist with the despairing ones. At worse, pessimism is classified as an enemy of hope. Before we let optimism off the hook, let us examine it seriously. Maybe it does more harm than we have assumed, perhaps even more than the much-despised pessimism.

Optimism, more than what we have often recognized, is a more deceptive enemy of hope than pessimism, because it wears a false smile. In the Filipino idiomatic street language, the smile of optimism is like the "grin of a mad dog" (Cebuano language, *ngisi sa irong buang*) that is ready to bite at the slightest, or even without, provocation. Optimism is dangerous because it does not take seriously the

5. Moltmann, *The Source of Life*, 39.

pervasiveness and the magnitude of the world's problems, the pain of those who have been crushed, and it makes a mockery of those who are pessimistically critical of the status quo. Optimism is dangerously deceptive and most often espoused by people who have gotten their way in life. Like the doglike cynic, it pees in public places while masquerading and parading responsible citizenship. Anyone who sells optimism, promises quick change, and speaks of something new has to be suspected.

We must maintain a critical eye on the optimists. The optimists, writes Walter Wink, still would like us to believe that "reason will save us," as if our world has not suffered from the reason and logic of the optimists. Moreover, the optimists would want to prevent us "from becoming *really afraid*" when there is enormous reason to be afraid, and that we should be afraid. The problem, he continues, is not fear but "our capacity to fear that is too small and that does not correspond to the magnitude of the present danger." Therefore, following the philosopher Günter Anders, Wink calls us to muster the "courage to be frightened" (Anders). Finding courage to be frightened is a "fearless fear" because it dares to face the real magnitude of the present danger, and it is a "loving fear" because "it embraces fear in order to save the generations to come."[6] We must embrace fear—this fearless fear—because the magnitude of the danger and our love for life demands it. Only then can fear be a blessing. This is William Stafford's advice: "What you fear will not go away: it will take you into yourself and bless you and keep you. That's the world, and we all live there."[7]

The magnitude of the real danger calls for a response beyond easy and lousy optimism. Optimism is not an alternative to fatalism, cynicism, and despair. There is no easy way out of the crisis. We must bite the bitter pill of the durability of the forces of reaction, following Derrick Bell, not as a "sign of submission" but as an "act of ultimate defiance."[8] Certainly, there is the risk that overexposure to the magnitude of our current crisis may kill whatever hope we have, but the naming and exposing of the durability of the forces of death should not be avoided. I worry less about pessimism than optimism. Pessimism has a place in a context of continuing betrayal of people's dreams. We

6. Wink, "The Wrong Apocalypse," 49. Emphasis supplied.

7. Stafford, *The Darkness Around Us*, 118.

8. Bell, *Faces at the Bottom*, 12.

need a certain dose of pessimism, not naive optimism. In the context of a perpetual cycle of violence, John Paul Lederach rightly contends that "pessimism is a gift of survival." Marginalized communities and victims of violence must not quickly let their guards down, for abusive power is cunning and brutal. Pessimism is a way that disenfranchised communities shelter whatever tiny zest for life has remained; it is a way of safeguarding themselves from another debilitating blow. Pessimism is not indifference to life, like an indifference born of apathy. Beyond being a "gift of survival," to paraphrase Lederach, pessimism serves as a gauge for measuring or testing the authenticity of any promised change within an "expansive view of time" and an "intuitive sense of complexity."[9]

Scholars and activists who have taken the durability of the forces of reaction seriously in their theorizing have always sought to maintain a delicate balance between embracing the stark reality and maintaining openness to the possibility of the new. Michel Foucault calls for a stance of "hyper-and pessimistic activism." Antonio Gramsci speaks of the "pessimism of the intellect and optimism of the will."[10] Lederach calls for "grounded realism" or "constructive pessimism."[11] Lederach's "grounded realism" or "constructive pessimism" brings to mind Reinhold Niebuhr's "Christian realism." Supporters of Niebuhr have used his idea to critique, I believe wrongly, what they have perceived of liberation theologies' utopian naiveté (naive hope) or failure to grasp "genuine limit-situations." Given this pitfall, they argue that liberation theology is doomed to fail politically and doomed to produce cynicism, apathy, and despair.[12]

Niebuhr's stance of Christian realism is important in helping us grapple with the hard reality, but I am concerned lest we sacrifice Christian hope to realism. We certainly need to be realistic, but we need to see reality from the horizon of hope and on account of love. In distinction from Niebuhr's Christian realism, I call this stance "hopeful realism" or "eschatological realism." Hope takes reality seriously but does not let reality make hope a hostage. Hope works in and through socio-political reality, but it is not imprisoned by any

9. Lederach, *The Moral Imagination*, 54.

10. See Gramsci, *Letters from Prison*.

11. Lederach, *The Moral Imagination*, 58.

12. Welch, *A Feminist Ethic*, 109.

given reality because it obeys the boundlessness of love. While rigid realism narrows hope, hopeful realism embraces the stark reality so that it conforms to the demands of love. The starting point then of action, following Sharon Welch's interpretation of liberation theologies' view of hope in response to the criticism of Christian realism, "is not a particular view of what is possible in history but is rather a perspective from which one determines the current boundaries of human hope."[13] When we love ourselves and the world, especially those who are dying before their time, our hopes for our lives are expanded—not simply confined to what is possible in a given context. When we truly care and truly love, it is not that we ignore the genuine limits but that we engage in political praxis that explodes the imposed boundaries that have been accorded sacred status. To adopt William Lee Miller's lines, "high politics is *not* the art of the possible; it is the art of enlarging what is possible and making what has heretofore been impossible come in the range of what can be considered" [possible].[14] This is what it means to be embraced and empowered by "unbounded hope" and to act in hope.

Hope does not simply extrapolate from the given; it anticipates the not-yet in the present. In other words, hope has a transcendent basis, though I say it must be understood immanently. Using this transcendent lens, I say that hope is beyond the predictable, calculable, and quantifiable. It is that which is hidden from sight. The Apostle Paul is clear on this: "Now hope that is seen is not hope. For who hopes for what is seen?"(Rom 8:24). Not that there are no "signs of hope," but they remain invisible until we receive the gift of sight. These are "signs" beyond what technical reason can see, measure, and calculate. These are signs that only hope grounded in faith and motivated by love has the eyes to see.

Because of its transcendent basis, hope, like joy (in contrast to happiness), does not rise or fall based on outside circumstances or on the limits imposed by the circumstances. Authentic hope cannot be swallowed by despair because it does not stand or fall based on optimistic signs around us. Regardless of any measurable positive outcomes, we must wager in hope because we love and truly care for life—our own and the wider web of life-giving relations. Because we truly care for life, we cannot and must not give up hope and the courage to act on that hope.

13. Ibid., 110.

14. Miller, cited in Hessel, *Social Ministry*, 163.

LOVING LIFE: WAGING AND FINDING COURAGE
TO RISK IN HOPE

When we love life, we cannot but choose to take risk for the sake of life. When we love life, especially when our lives are touched by those who want to simply live but are denied life, we cannot help but continue waging in hope and taking risk even when the odds are great—even when our best efforts do not show immediate results, or when our best efforts are defeated. This is difficult to accept. But, as Welch puts it, "Love provides the resiliency of commitment, vision, and hope when efforts for change either are defeated repeatedly or are shown to be insufficient."[15]

Jesus loved life, and so he took the risk of ushering the reign of God—the reign of life. Jesus loved life, and so he took, to use Paul Tillich's words, "the strange work of love to destroy what is against love" but which does "not destroy him who acts against love."[16] The reign of life and of love was, of course, a threat to the reign of death. We know what happened next. The powers that were did everything within their might to stop Jesus. Jesus was aware of the threat, yet he chose to go on, but not because he was unafraid of dying. He was afraid of death, but he cared for life even more; so he acted in hope. He cared for life, so he mustered courage in the face of threats to his life.

New generations of martyrs embodied in their distinct ways the cost of loving life. Archbishop Oscar Romero loved the Salvadoran people, and so he mustered prophetic courage to denounce death-dealing systems. He paid dearly for it. Nelson Mandela loved the oppressed people of South Africa, and so he summoned courage to help dismantle the apartheid system. Victims of extrajudicial killings in the Philippines took a similar stance. They took the risk not because they were unafraid to die, but because they loved life more. This is what it is like to find courage.

Courage is not the absence of fear; courage is founded on the belief that there is something greater than fear, something that even fear itself cannot hold us back from pursuing. Courage does not deny the danger but demands a full recognition of what is to be feared. But it is precisely at this point when, in the lines of Annie Dillard, "we start feeling the weight of the atmosphere and learn that there's death in the

15. Welch, *A Feminist Ethic*, 165.

16. Tillich, *Love, Power and Justice*, 49–50.

pot,"[17] that is, when we learn what really is to be feared, then the atmosphere is ripe for the birth of courage. Knowing what is to be feared can paralyze us, but courage refuses to let that happen. Courage comes from the often-neglected side of knowledge. In courage we know not only what is to be feared, but also what is to be dared. What is to be dared is human dignity in the face of its desecration and violation; what is to be dared is the just and democratic society in the face of corrosion to its very core; what is to be dared is the sanctity of life that is terrorized by the forces of death; what is to be dared is our earth habitat that is threatened with destruction. These are reasons to dare, and dare we must!

RESURRECTION: GOD'S "YES" TO LIFE AND "NO" TO DEATH

So we must dare for the sake of life. But how can we keep on daring in the face of continuing failures and globalized indifference? How can we keep on daring when the storms of life are relentless? How can we keep on daring for the sake of life when death is everywhere? How can we keep on daring for the sake of life when death seems to have the final word? The Christian tradition's answer to these questions is the doctrine of resurrection. Resurrection is the wellspring of Christian hope. Resurrection is God's "no" to death and "yes" to life. Even while in the midst of a death-laden situation, life claims the final word. History does not end with the triumph of death. Resurrection, following Dermot Lane, is "a protest against the premature closure of our understanding of the present and a plea for openness towards the future."[18] History is open. This openness of history is rooted in the fundamental belief that God is not finished yet with history. To use a religious idiom of the black church in North America: "God ain't finished with us yet!"[19] To say this is to say "no" to those who want to close history. It is an ontological belief that history is open because God's act of creation is continuing still.

Resurrection proclaims the belief that the fate of victims is not sealed in the graveyard, and those who have suffered have not suffered in vain. No one has died in vain for a noble cause. It is for this reason that the apocalyptist could write, "And I heard a voice from heaven

17. Dillard, *Pilgrim*, 92.
18. Lane, *Keeping Hope Alive*, 2.
19. Oglesby, *Born in the Fire*, viii.

saying, 'Write this: Blessed are the dead who from now on die in the Lord.' 'Yes,' says the Spirit, 'they will rest from their labors, for their deeds follow them'" (Rev 14:13). Deeds done in the name of life will last; they belong to eternity. By "eternity" I do not mean timelessness and endless time or simply somewhere outside of time and space, but that the divine ground is eternally present in every moment.

With an ecological sensibility, we cannot limit this resurrection to human beings. Resurrection is the resurrection of life, of the whole of creation. Humans cannot experience the reality of resurrection without a resurrected earth, for human beings are a part of the earth, and being earthly is inseparable from being human. The whole of creation, along with human beings, has been groaning, mourning, and is waiting for its resurrection—for its redemption. Even if it were possible to be resurrected without the earth, I do not want to have any part in that kind of resurrection. It is my joy to be resurrected with the earth—with the trees, streams, ocean, and rocks. I consider it my joy after I am gone from my current physical shape for my children and grandchildren to encounter my spirit in the verdant foliage, turquoise lagoon, and deep-blue ocean. It is there that I want to be resurrected.

Lest resurrection be construed as simply a future reality, I say, following Christine Smith, that resurrection "is that which happens to us on the other side of various kinds of death."[20] Christians hope for that grand resurrection beyond the daily crucifixions and deaths, but I speak of the resurrection that happens to us in our earthly existence: this resurrection happens to us, not outside or beyond in an imagined sweet paradise, but in the midst of a world threatened and tyrannized by death. *Aling* Panchang's story is a foretaste of this resurrection. She has lived in the North Cemetery (Manila) since 1955. In 1960, at the request of her son, who had acquired a small piece of land and house at a relocation site, she joined him. But the situation in the relocation site was so desperate that, in the words of *Aling* Panchang, "I couldn't stand it anymore. You know squatter areas are terrible! So much noise and so crowded. I came back to the cemetery after a month—and have not left since. I think I might stay here—forever."[21] Living in the cemetery where there was peace was, for *Aling* Panchang, a resurrection experience.

20. Smith, *Risking the Terror*, 2.
21. Gerlock, "The Living and the Dead," 75.

THE CHURCH: A COMMUNITY BIRTHED
BY THE CRUCIFIED AND RESURRECTED HOPE

Sheer courage failed. Jesus was killed, and his zealous disciples scurried for safety and denied any involvement with him. His once brave disciples abandoned him. Terror tyrannized them. It was only with their encounter of the resurrected Jesus that they regained their courage. It was only with their experience of the resurrection that they experienced new life and a resurrected hope. Resurrection blossomed into hope. It was out of this resurrection hope that the Christian community was born. Without the resurrection, says the apostle Paul, our hope is in vain (1 Cor 15:12–34). In short, the church is a community birthed by the resurrection. It is a child of hope. The church is an event of the resurrection; it is an event of hope.

It was through the experience of resurrection hope that the scattered followers of Jesus became a new people. It is through this resurrection experience that we need to interpret the life of early Christian communities, particularly their experience of crucifixions. It is through this resurrection hope that we need to see and interpret crucifixions in our times. Resurrection experience is not a relief or escape from crucifixions; indeed, it may lead to more crucifixions. Yes, *more* crucifixions, because to experience resurrection is to experience life, and to experience life is to defend life against death. And when we defend life, the experience of crucifixion is to be expected. Resurrection is not the end in this sense; it is a beginning. It is not a one-time event; it is also a journey. It is an experience of living life and birthing life, which, in a world terrorized by death, always includes confrontations with the powers of death. It is in this regard that we can say that there is no path to resurrection without crucifixion. We do not romanticize crucifixion or claim that crucifixion is a requirement (sequentially) for resurrection, but we do claim that the experience of crucifixion is already a life lived in the power of the resurrection. Crucifixion is not necessary for resurrection, but crucifixion is a common reality as well as a consequence of commitment to life. When we are committed to promote life, the forces of reaction will always be there to stop us.

It is in this context that we need to see the death of Jesus. His death was not salvific as such. It became salvific, however, because it was a death against death. Not even to save his life did he give himself up to the powers that be. His death was death against death. There is nothing salvific in the cross itself; there is nothing salvific in being put to a ghastly death. It is salvific only insofar as it is a death in confrontation with the powers of death. Yes, death against death!

It is also in this context in which we need to see the banality of crucifixions. It is in this context in which we need to see the power of resurrection. The healing and liberating power of Easter is real only when we have grasped the ugliness of the tomb and confronted the idols of death. No victory worth having is cheaply won. No real hope is born out of lousy optimism, for optimism is not the wellspring of hope. In the enduring words of Dietrich Bonhoeffer, there is no "cheap grace" on the way to resurrection— "grace without discipleship, grace without cross."[22] The road to our Easter celebration is littered with daily crucifixions. It is precisely this banality of daily crucifixions that makes a claim on the way we live as individuals and members of the body of Christ. It is precisely in the banality of daily crucifixions, when crucifixions are ordinary, when society is colonized by the culture of death, and when psychic numbing has engulfed the land that the power of the risen Jesus must be witnessed. It is here that the power of the resurrection must blossom.

THE CHURCH AS COMMUNITY OF MEMORY: A HOPE THAT REMEMBERS

It was through the experience of the resurrection that the early Christian communities became a new people—with a new memory. Yes, a new memory, because they interpreted the past crucifixions through the power of hope. With resurrection hope as the lens of reading, the past is not jettisoned as a whole but read and remembered differently. This is what I mean by the church as a community of memory. As in my account on forgiveness, the past is not forgotten. In fact, the past is remembered, though remembered differently. It is this kind of remembering that gives future to the past. By this I do not mean a simple continuation of the past but a new future for the past, which is the fulfillment of the longing of the past. This is similar to what Fumitaka Matsuoka describes as "visionary memory," a vision that remembers.[23]

---

22. Bonhoeffer, *The Cost of Discipleship*, 36.

23. Matsuoka, *Out of Silence*, 117.

At this point I am reminded of the 1937 debate between Walter Benjamin and Frank Horkheimer, both of the Frankfurt School of Philosophy. Horkheimer, out of his historical materialist position, claims that any notion of an unclosed past and an open future is idealistic. He argues that "[w]hat happened to those human beings who have perished does not have any part in the future. They will never be called forth to be blessed in eternity."[24] Horkheimer operates on the presupposition of a closed history.

In contrast, Benjamin strives to work out a notion of history that does not ignore our unity in history with past generations, especially those who were crucified by the idolatrous forces. Benjamin refuses to see history as closed and finished. For him the work of the past is not closed, not even to a historical materialist. He believes that we can keep past history open. Responding to Horkheimer, Benjamin claims that the corrective for the idea that history is closed "lies in the reflection that history is . . . a form of emphatic memory (*Eingedenken*). What science has 'settled,' emphatic memory can modify."[25] Furthermore, emphatic memory gives us an experience that "prohibits us from conceiving history completely non-theologically," or it "forbids us to regard history completely without theology."[26] Emphatic memory helps us to read history theologically.

While in agreement with the main direction of Benjamin's ideas, I propose that we reverse his order. Reading history theologically demands emphatic memory. One cannot do authentic theology without embracing the spirit of emphatic memory, especially if the sufferings of the victims are not to be in vain. Emphatic memory opens up the past and reconnects the living with the dead. The history of suffering is not closed; it is open to us through emphatic memory or through remembrance. Through our emphatic memories we open the past to establish our solidarity with those who have gone before us. This is what Christian Lenhardt calls "anamnestic solidarity."[27] When emphatic memory or remembrance opens up the past and our solidarity

24. For English readers see Peukert, *Science,* 206; also, Lane, *Keeping Hope Alive,* 119–23; 200–10.

25. Peukert, *Science,* 207.

26. Ibid, 207. Also, see Lane, *Keeping Hope Alive,* 202, quoting Rolf Tiedemann, 'Historical Materialism,' 79.

27. Lenhardt, "Anamnestic Solidarity," 133–55, cited by Peukert, *Science,* 208.

with the dead, it also opens up the future. The past is opened not only for its own sake but also in relation to the future. Those who have gone before us have a future, and this future is tied to our acts of remembrance and solidarity.

CHURCH: MIDWIFE OF MOVEMENTS OF RESURRECTED MEMORIES AND ANTICIPATED NEW TOMORROW

There is no visionary memory that forgets the pains of the past. To forgive and move forward is not to forget. After all, we can only forgive what we remember. Rather, to exhume is to re-member the dis-membered; it is to make whole those who have experienced brokenness. That which is buried is exhumed not simply for its own sake, for there is no joy in merely exhuming the unfinished dreams of previous generations. The buried is exhumed because it is necessary in the forging of a new and better tomorrow.

Retrieval of dangerous memories is, however, only a moment in the process of forging a new and better tomorrow. Painful moments and proud monuments of the past must find resurrection in our movements of today. We must be grateful to the monuments of the past, especially for those who have paved the way for us, but true gratitude is expressed when we transform the monuments of the past into movements of today—movements of transformation and movements that weave together our scattered voices and visions.

Turning past monuments into people's movements is our way of making the victims and the "dis-appeared" into martyrs or witnesses.[28] We proclaim liturgically the turning of the tortured bodies and the "dis-appeared" into martyrs in the eucharistic meal, but it is in the concreteness of people's movements that carry forward the memory of the "dis-appeared" that they are made bodily present—that they are resurrected among us. Archbishop Oscar Romero spoke about this kind of resurrection:

> My life has been threatened many times. I have to confess that, as a Christian, I don't believe in death without resurrection. If they kill me, *I will rise again in the Salvadoran people.* I'm not boasting, or saying this out of pride, but rather humbly as I can . . . Martyrdom is a grace of God that I do not feel worthy of. But if God accepts the sacrifice of my life, my hope is that my

28. See Cavanaugh, *Torture and Eucharist.*

blood will be like a seed of liberty and a sign that our hopes
will soon become a reality... A Bishop will die, but the church
of God, which is the people, will never perish.[29]

Oscar Romero believed in the resurrection. He believed that his
"blood will be like a seed of liberty and a sign that our hopes will soon
become a reality." Like a seed, he will "rise again," this time "in the
Salvadoran people." Indeed, Romero has risen, and in his new form he
has become a people. The one has become many. But I will claim what
Romero was too humble to claim. He has risen not only among the
Salvadoran people, but also among the people of the world who have
embodied his memory, dreams, and hopes. Romero's martyr-seed belongs to the world; it is a gift to the world. Romero is humanity breaking forth from the soil fertilized by blood and budding into new life.

Our challenge is to make Romero's life and the lives of martyrs
of every clime and place find resurrection in us—the still living. Our
challenge is to make their memory become a movement. Like Carlos
Bulosan who took the task of making the poor peasants of northern
Philippines "live in [his] words," it is our task to make the monuments
of the past live in our contemporary movements.

The story of Ligaya Domingo and her father Silme Domingo—
both labor organizers—illustrates true gratitude to the labors of the
past, the shift from anguish into anger, and the turning of monuments
into movements.[30] Ligaya Domingo was only five years old when
Ferdinand Marcos's henchmen shot and killed Silme and a fellow activist in Seattle on June 21, 1981. Silme had become the target of the
Marcos regime's ire for his responsibility in making the International
Longshoremen and Warehousemen's Union (ILWU) place an unprecedented international focus on the Philippines.

Twenty years after the incident, Ligaya is following in the steps
of her father. In an interview, Ligaya says that her father continues to
be a persistent presence in her life: "Sometimes I think about what
he would want me to do, and how he would see me in what I'm doing
... Sometimes I really get sad about it." Memory is very much alive
in Ligaya's life.

In speaking about her labor involvement, Ligaya said that her
father taught her an important lesson: "It's that you cannot simply give

29. Erdozaín, *Archbishop Romero*, 75–76.
30. Soriano, "Organizer's Daughter," 31–32.

up the fight." Not surprisingly, there were moments when her tone, as organizers can easily understand, revealed weariness and fatigue. "One thing that's frustrating for me," she said, "is that even when we see victories, they're small, they're really small." She went on with an example: "We had a strike at West Seattle Psychiatric Hospital last year, and after 138 days we got the contract that we wanted. But you know, that's just one victory in a cloud of a million other things to fight for."[31]

As Ligaya was speaking about the enormity of the things to fight for and how small a single victory is, her words came out "between laugh and sigh." "Between laugh and sigh" is an expression of a Filipina upbringing, perhaps part of the survival mechanisms of people who have to surmount hardships of various sorts. "Between laugh and sigh" also captures a deep moment in the life of a person who is committed to a better tomorrow in the face of the stubborn forces of reaction. What Ligaya has done is small when we think of the millions of issues to fight for, but she has done something significant. She has turned the monuments of her father's labor and sacrifice into a movement.

Another story of turning memory into a movement comes to us from Las Abejas (literally, "the bees"). In Acteal, Mexico, a community was caught in the middle of a violent conflict, primarily between the Zapatistas and the Priitas (PRI—Partido Revolucionario Institucional). Las Abejas refused to take sides in the conflict and called for a dialogue. On December 12, 1997, members of Las Abejas were gathered in a chapel in Acteal for their third day of fasting and praying for peace when military men surrounded them and began shooting. After the sound and smoke of guns cleared, forty-five members of Las Abejas were slaughtered. Some left the community, but many decided to remain in Acteal. Every year members of Las Abejas gather to commemorate the tragic event and renew their commitment to work for peace and transformation. They turned their painful memory into a movement.[32]

31. Ibid., 32.
32. Gaillardetz, *Ecclesiology for a Global Church*, 244–45.

A COMMUNITY THAT CELEBRATES
AND WORSHIPS IN HOPE

We would not be speaking of a church—community of resurrected memories and hope—without speaking of worship. What the church seeks to embody in its wider life finds expressions in its liturgy, worship, and celebrations. Liturgy, worship, and celebrations nurture the church in its journey of faithfulness and hope. Conversely, the church's hope-filled ministries find expressions in worship and liturgy. The church's liturgy and worship celebrate the hope that the community has known. The church embodies liturgically the hope that it has received from the resurrected Christ in and through the work of the Spirit in its invocations, hymns, confession and forgiveness, petitions, proclamation of the Word, offering of lives and fruits of labor, and sending forth. In the singing of hymns of praise, the church praises the God of life and hope; in the confession and offer of forgiveness, the church affirms the hope of a new beginning; in the preaching of the Word, the church proclaims the gospel of hope. When the congregation in worship calls the people to offer their lives and gifts, the congregation offers them for the realization of the coming reign of God. When the worshipping congregation sends forth the gathered community to go out into the world, the congregation is sent forth to live in hope.

The sacraments of the church are sacraments of hope. Baptism is a sacrament of hope. In the sacrament of baptism the gathered community affirms the crucified and risen Christ. Baptism is an affirmation of our membership and participation in the death and resurrection of Jesus. In baptism we have died to the old self and have risen to a new life, a life of hope. Similarly, the eucharist is a sacrament of memory and hope. In the eucharist the church remembers the suffering and death of Jesus. The broken bread is a symbol of his broken body, and the wine is a symbol of his blood. At the same time, the act of remembrance is an act of hope. The eucharist is not only a liturgy of remembrance of Jesus' passion; it is also a celebration of Jesus' resurrection. In fact, it is through the lens of the resurrection that we are re-membering the dis-membered and celebrating the hope of healing and wholeness.

MISSION AND MINISTRY: GROUNDING HOPE
AND IMAGINATION IN PRAXIS

What the church does in worship and in its liturgical expression cannot be separated from its ministry. Worship informs and enriches the
ministry. If worship is an expression of hope and worship informs
ministry, then a hope-filled worship finds expressions in a hope-filled
ministry. Ministry is a church's embodiment of hope. Ministry is an
expression of the church's living out its hope. Ministries are planned
and acted out not simply to survive in the present but with an eye to
the new tomorrow. A community that is embraced by the vision of a
new tomorrow cannot do otherwise but engage in hope-filled ministries. Whatever expression of ministry the church engages, it is a
ministry of planting seeds of hope.

The story of Pedrito and his Guanacaste seeds may help us
understand better this ministry of planting seeds of hope.[33] Pedrito
is a humble person from Nicaragua. Like many of the peasants of
Nicaragua, he struggles to eke out a living. On some days, he walks
with a sack of Guanacaste seeds on his back. Pedrito's sack of seeds
symbolizes the dreams of his people. Pedrito is a dreamer. He is a
dream-keeper. More than that, he walks the dream: He is a dream-
walker. His feet are grounded in the stark realities of his native place
even as his head is in the clouds. Day and night Pedrito is "living by a
dream that things can be different."[34]

People around the world share Lederach's story of Pedrito and his
Guanacaste seeds. I had a similar experience in my youth. As the el-
dest son, I had to do physical labor, such as taking care of our ricefield.
Walking around the ricefield requires having one's feet firmly grounded on the *pilapil* (a narrow walkway). This is all the more challenging
during planting and harvest seasons. When harvest time comes, carrying a sack of *palay* (unpolished rice) on one's head along the *pilapil*
to the nearest road is strenuous and difficult work. The challenge is not
over. In preparation for the next planting season, I had to carry again
on my head a sack of *palay*—this time of germinated seeds—back to
the ricefield as seedlings.

We need to carry our own sack of seeds—seeds of dreams. And,
we must have our feet grounded on the *pilapil*, that is, in the realities

---

33. Story cited from Lederach, *Journey Toward Reconciliation*, 196.
34. Ibid., 196.

of our globalized localities. In the lines of a Colombian saying, "You must be so close to the ground that you can hear the grass grow." We must stay close to the ground so we can feel the soil's life; yet we must also stay close to our dreams so we can feel the seeds longing and struggling to break forth from the ground to what they can be. Are our dreams closely connected to the ground on which we walk?

Planting seeds of hope is an appropriate imagery for thinking about church mission and ministry. The church is called to plant the seeds of the reign of God—the reign of new life. Its mission is not to plant churches but to plant the seeds of the reign of God. This is not to negate the importance of planting churches, but we do so only because we need churches to plant the seeds of the reign of God. In planting the seeds of the reign of God, the church is planting seeds of hope. Put differently, as the church participates with God in planting the seeds of the reign of God, it participates with God in planting seeds of hope.

The ministries of the church are its main avenue in planting seeds of hope. In its various caring ministries the church participates with God in planting seeds of hope. In its ministry of human rights advocacy, health care, ecological justice, and peace, it plants seeds of hope. In its education and nurture ministry the church helps its members take account of the hope that is in them as members of Christ's resurrected body. It nurtures the lives of members for seeds of hope to sprout. It provides opportunities for members to develop hopeful living by engaging in various forms of hope-filled practices or ministries. Without engaging in hope-filled ministries, hope will not grow and thrive. The hope that Carl Dudley has observed among churches with social ministries makes sense here. While discouragement, or even despondency, often mark congregations that see no other way out of our present crisis, "hope is more characteristic of congregations with social ministries, not because they believe they are winning, but because they offer members at least an opportunity to express their faith in action."[35]

In sum, the ministries of the church must lead to empowering people to hope. Church ministry is about empowering people to hope. Serving, educating, advocating, and worshipping must all contribute to the empowerment of people to hope and act on their hope. Empowered people are God's expressions of hope; they are God's miracle at work. It is only when they are empowered by hope can we

35. Dudley, *Community Ministry*, 50.

expect them to become active participants in the ministry of giving birth to a new and better tomorrow. Empowered by hope, they can truly embrace the words of Bishop José Maria Pires:

> I believe there'll be a better world
> When the littlest one who falls
> Believes in that little one-
> When the small can trust that all will be well for each,
> When we feel each other's needs:
> One in Jesus Christ, one with everyone.[36]

THE CHURCH: A COMMUNITY THAT WAITS IN HOPE

Without hope, one cannot truly wait. Only those who have learned hope can *truly wait*. I am not speaking about waiting in general, but about a waiting that is generated by hope or a hope-that-waits. Robert McAfee Brown differentiates between waiting in hope, waiting casually, waiting in doubt, and waiting in dread.[37] Those who wait in hope do more than simply expect something external to themselves to come; those who wait in hope are being grasped by its power as they wait. "[A]lthough waiting is *not* having," as Paul Tillich puts it, "it is also having." He argues:

> The fact that we wait for something shows that in some way we already possess it. Waiting anticipates that which is not yet real. If we wait in hope and patience, the power of that for which we wait is already effective within us. He who waits in ultimate sense is not far from that for which he waits. He who waits in absolute seriousness is already grasped by that for which he waits. He who waits in patience has already received the power of that for which he waits. He who waits passionately is already an active power himself, the greatest power of transformation in personal and historical life.[38]

Waiting in hope is not the kind of casual waiting we commonly think of, nor is it an aimless and idle waiting, much less a waiting in dread. The waiting that is generated by a deep sense of hope is an active waiting. Active waiting anticipates that for which one waits. It is a kind of waiting characterized by readiness and anticipation. The

---

36. Cited in Boff, *Ecclesiogenesis*, 43.
37. Brown, *Persuade Us to Rejoice*, 41–52.
38. Tillich, *The Shaking of the Foundations*, 151.

activity that is generated by waiting in hope does not kill time but redeems the in-between time or the time-being from being simply another time. Waiting in hope redeems and gives significance to the time being. For those who wait in hope, this time being is not to be written off or grimly avoided but embraced as an occasion for faithful living. The time being is our time, a precious and momentous time, a time to be reclaimed for creative and active living.

It amazes and humbles me to be in touch with the lives of people who, when there is no other choice but to wait, have responded to the situation creatively in order to transform it. Marginalized people have waited and have been told to wait for years. Instead of being reduced to cynicism, they have produced a waiting that is transformative. There is no denying that this waiting is forced upon them, with no choice except to wait in order to survive, but they have transformed this waiting into strength, a waiting that in turn creatively transforms the situation.

Around the time when South Africa had its first national election—after the collapse of the apartheid regime—a cartoon depicted a white person complaining that he had been waiting for thirty minutes in the polling place. Then a black South African said: "But I have been waiting for decades for this national election." I am aware that it is difficult to wait for a long time and stay awake. Like Jesus' disciples who could not stay awake in Gethsemane during his final hours (Mk 14:32-41), there is a temptation to sleep while waiting. Staying awake is a struggle; struggle is staying awake. Giving voice to unfinished dreams keeps us awake while we continue to wait.

As a young boy, I waited in wakefulness as I watched for the water from the main irrigation canal to flow to our ricefield from nightfall till dawn during drought seasons. It was a long and agonizing wait, especially in company with hungry mosquitoes, and I was tempted to sleep in our ricefield's small hut. But I had to stay awake or perform a *minanok* (rooster) *nga pagkatulog* (sleep)—rooster-like sleep, as we say it in my native Cebuano language—if our ricefield was to have water. I had to make sure that no one would steal or divert the water to another field. Waiting and watching for the water to flow to our field was crucial. Rice was our life; rice was our hope, as it was for others. It was worth waiting for; it was worth staying awake. Certainly, it was worth fighting for!

WALKING IN HOPE: A SPIRITUALITY OF HOPE

Deep inside I cry for the world I love so dearly yet often serve so poorly. I cry because I am afraid that I may lose hope. It is easy to lose hope when events that make a mockery of hope inundate us. So we must learn to cultivate hope; we must learn to shelter hope so it survives from prodigious storms. As it is true in all matters of spirituality, a spirituality of hope requires practices that kindle and nurture hope. These practices involve ways of thinking and seeing and relating and acting that nourish hope. I use the word "practice" because it carries the understanding that we cannot separate knowing from acting. Intentional reflection is constitutive in practicing the spirituality of hope. It is constitutive in developing a new set of eyes that sees hope.

In spite of hope's strong association with the future or the not-yet, hope is about living in the present. No vehicle can take us to our dreamed-for future or leap-frog over our precarious present, for the present matters when we are grasped by the power of hope. The present matters because the present is constitutive of the future. The journey matters because the journey is constitutive of the destination. Hope does not rob us of the joy of living in the present; it gifts us with a grateful and joyful heart. Rather than making us oblivious to the minute and common daily moments of living, hope gives us eyes to behold beauty along our path. Hope piques our senses in order that we may smell the fragrance of flowers and the aroma of delicious meals, hear the chirping bird and the cry of the starving people, feel the caress of our loved ones and the gentle breeze that comes our way, take delight in the radiant face that comes in the chuckle of a little child, laugh at ourselves when we discover our own ignorance, and marvel at serendipitous events.

Another way of speaking about hope's attentiveness to the present moment is conveyed by the practice of mindfulness. Hope calls us to live mindfully in the present. When we walk with mindfulness we walk lightly. When we walk with mindfulness we are attentive to precious encounters along the way. There is another aspect of mindfulness that I would like to highlight that is often neglected. When we are mindful we are more attentive to the cry and aspirations of those around us. When we are attentive we become porous, and this allows the pain and hopes of those who have died before their time as well as the future of those who are yet to come make a claim on how we live in the present. As we let the tears and hopes of others make a claim on us and speak through us, their tears and hopes will be like rivers that will carry us into the wide ocean of new possibilities.

We cannot be nourished in hope apart from our relationship with people who need our acts of hope. We maintain our hope and vision only in solidarity with those whose hopes have been dashed by the forces of death and only in concrete acts of righting the wrongs. As Welch puts it, "We move from critique to action and back to critique, maintaining our hope and our vision if our critique occurs in the context of working with others for justice." When separated from such practices critique becomes "all encompassing and enervating"; it becomes "despairing and cynical." The "cultured despair" and "middle class" numbness that are so pervasive in our society, continues Welch, are expressions of having the "luxury of being able to avoid direct interaction with victims."[39]

Hope cannot be sustained without solidarity with the victims, and it certainly cannot be sustained without practices that embody hope on a globalized scale vis-à-vis globalized despair. This globalized cynicism and despair finds expression in the following lines: "If everything is connected, then you can't change anything without changing everything. But you can't change everything, so that means that you can't change anything."[40] There is, however, a different, if not a hopeful, reading of our globalized interconnections. Rhizomatically spread and connected throughout the world, we have more and varied entry points to transform the global system and make a global difference. This is not to underestimate the power of the global imperial system; rather, it is to say that we also have greater opportunities.

Cultivating and nourishing a spirituality of hope is no doubt a tremendous challenge when the world seems to move in a different direction or when our determined actions seem to suffer setbacks. It is at this point in which hope takes us to its real depth: it helps us see and relate to the world differently. A moment in the life of Albert Camus is instructive of hope's way of seeing. When the Second World War had wasted Europe away, the young Camus returned from France to his native Algeria. "In the light cast by the flames," he wrote, "the world had suddenly shown its wrinkles and afflictions old and new. It had

39. Welch, *A Feminist Ethic*, 168.
40. Bigelow, "Defeating Despair," 329.

suddenly grown old, and we had too." Exhausted morally and spiritually, he returned to his village in the Mediterranean—Tipasa. There he wrote: "[Misery] taught me that all was not well under the sun, but the sun taught me that [misery] was not everything."[41] No doubt misery is everywhere, but hope helps us to see that misery is not everything. If I may use a different imagery, our days might be cloudy, but our ability to see the clouds is already an indication that the power of hope is at work in us. Hope gives us a different set of eyes.

Yes, a different set of eyes, a different way of seeing. It is always easy to feel small and insignificant. This was what I felt while teaching in Yaoundé, Cameroon, in January 2007. My limitation in communicating in French made the work tedious. I worked hard, but the learning seemed slow. It felt as if the French word for work (*travail*) was the equivalent of the English word "travail." Emotionally drained and physically exhausted, Christi Boyd (mission co-worker of Presbyterian Church, USA, in Cameroon) helped me to see things differently. She helped me to see my work not from my own measure of success but from the needs of my students in their own context. It was only then that I regained my bearing. What I considered small was already significant to them. The poet Jose Ortega y Gasset wrote, "For the person for whom small things do not exist, the great is not great."[42] This resonates with Joan Chittister's words: "Until we do what we ourselves are capable of doing for the world, we can never appreciate those who do even more."[43]

Seeds may be small, but in the seed there is a promise, which is often, as the lines of a hymn express it, "unrevealed until its season, something God alone can see."[44] There is the promise of a fully grown plant or a tree. There is the promise of a bulb turning into a flower, or a blossom into a fruit, and then into a seed and into another tree. Let us not underestimate the power of seeds, for seeds carry the promise of new life and new beginnings. In the seeds there is hope. We must nurture these precious seeds, to paraphrase Dawna Markova, by refusing to live an unlived life, by risking our own significance, and by turning

41. Cited in Leddy, *Radical Gratitude*. I substituted "poverty" with the word "misery."

42. Cited in Chittister, *Becoming Fully Human*, 121.

43. Chittister, Ibid.

44. "In the Bulb," *The New Century Hymnal*, 433.

our lives into a soil, a light, a wing, and a promise, so that what comes to us as seeds goes to the next generation as blossoms, and that which comes to us as blossoms goes on as fruits.[45]

Our challenge is to nurture these seeds so they may blossom and bear fruits—bearing fruits in our movements and daring acts of courage in the present. We are grateful and must be grateful for the lives of those who paid dearly for what we truly care about and what we truly believe is to be dared, but true gratitude must be expressed in transforming the dangerous monuments of the past into movements of today. So, citizens of the new tomorrow, let us stand and dare to transform the sacred gift of seeds into blossoms and the blossoms into fruits through prophetic acts of courage until the stones will cry out with us and justice will roll down like an ever-flowing stream, and the new day blossoms!

45. Markova, I Will not Die, 1.

Bibliography

Abelmann, N., and John Lie. *Blue Dreams: Korean Americans and the Los Angeles Riots.* Cambridge: Harvard University Press, 1995.

Achcar, Gilbert. *The Clash of Barbarisms: The Making of the New World Disorder.* Boulder: Paradigm. 2006.

Ahmed, Akbar S. *Islam Today: A Short Introduction to the Muslim World.* New York: I. B. Tauris, 1999.

Ali, Tariq. *The Clash of Fundamentalisms: Crusades, Jihads, and Modernity.* New York: Verso, 2002.

Almond, Gabriel, et al. *Strong Religion: The Rise of Fundamentalisms around the World.* Chicago: The University of Chicago Press, 2003.

Amato, Joseph. *To Call it Home: The New Immigrants of Southwestern Minnesota.* Marshall, Minnesota: Crossings, 1996.

The American Heritage College Dictionary, Third Edition. New York: Houghton Mifflin, 1993.

Ammar, Nawal. "Islam and Deep Ecology." In *Liberating Faith: Religious Voices for Justice, Peace, and Ecological Wisdom*, edited by Roger Gottlieb, 531–63. New York: Rowman & Littlefield, 2003.

Anderson, Gerald, ed. *Studies in Philippine Church History.* Ithaca: Cornell University Press, 1969.

Antoun, Richard. *Understanding Fundamentalism: Christian, Islamic, and Jewish Movements.* 2nd ed. New York: Rowman & Littlefield, 2008.

Aoanan, Melanio. "Teolohiya ng Bituka at Pagkain: Tungo sa Teolohiyang Pumipiglas." In *Explorations in Theology: Journal of the Union Theological Seminary*, Vol. 1, No. 1, 23–44. Dasmariñas, Cavite, Philippines: Union Theological Seminary, 1996.

Appadurai, Arjun. "Disjuncture and Difference in the Global Cultural Economy." In *Global Culture: Nationalism, Globalization and Modernity*, edited by M. Featherstone, 295–310. London: Sage, 1990.

Appleby, R. Scott. "Religion and Conflict Transformation." In *Liberating Faith: Religious Voices for Justice, Peace, and Ecological Wisdom*, edited by Roger Gottlieb, 435–40. New York: Rowman & Littlefield, 2003.

Arendt, Hannah. *Between Past and Future: Eight Exercises in Political Thought.* New York: Viking, 1968.

Arias, Mortimer. "Global and Local: A Critical View of Mission Models." In *Global Good News: Mission in a New Context*, edited by Howard Snyder, 55–65. Nashville: Abingdon, 2001.

Aristide, Jean-Bertrand. "Globalization: A View from Below." In *Rethinking Globalization: Teaching for Justice in an Unjust World*, edited by Bill Bigelow and Bob Peterson, 9–13. Milwaukee: Rethinking Schools, 2002.

Armour Sr., Rollin. *Islam, Christianity, and the West: A Troubled History.* New York: Orbis, 2002.

Arthur, Chris. *The Globalization of Communications: Some Religious Implications.* Geneva, Switzerland: WCC Publications; London: World Association for Christian Communication, 1998.

Avila, Charles. *Ownership: Early Christian Teaching.* New York: Orbis, 1983.

Bachelor, Stephen. "The Other Enlightenment Project: Buddhism, Agnosticism, and Postmodernity." In *Faith and Praxis in a Postmodern Age*, edited by Ursula King, 113–27. London: Cassell, 1998.

Bacon, David. "The Story of a Maquiladora Worker." In *Rethinking Globalization: Teaching for Justice in an Unjust World*, edited by Bill Bigelow and Bob Peterson, 146–48. Milwaukee: Rethinking School, 2002.

Baker-Fletcher, Karen, and Garth KASIMU Baker-Fletcher. *My Sister, My Brother: Womanist and Xodus God-Talk.* New York: Orbis, 1997.

Barstow, Anne Llewellyn, ed. *War's Dirty Secret: Rape, Prostitution, and Other Crimes against Women.* Cleveland: Pilgrim, 2000.

Baum, Gregory, and Harold Wells, eds. *The Reconciliation of Peoples: Challenge to the Churches.* Maryknoll, New York: Orbis; Switzerland: WCC Publications, 1997.

Beach, George Kimmich, ed. *The Essential James Luther Adams: Selected Essays and Addresses.* Boston: Skinner House, 1998.

Beidelman, T. O. *Colonial Evangelism: A Socio-Historical Study of an East African Mission at the Grassroots.* Bloomington: Indiana University Press, 1982.

Bell, Derrick. *Faces at the Bottom of the Well: The Permanence of Racism.* New York: Basic, 1992.

Bellagamba, Anthony. *Mission and Ministry in the Global Church.* Maryknoll, New York: Orbis, 1992.

Benner, Patricia. "When Health Care Becomes a Commodity: The Need for Compassionate Strangers." In *The Changing Face of Health Care: A Christian Appraisal of Managed Care, Resource Allocation, and Patient-Caregiver Relationships*, edited by John Kilner et al., 119–35. Grand Rapids: Wm. B. Eerdmans, 1998.

Berger, Teresa. "Fragments of a Vision in a September 11 World." In *Strike Terror No More: Theology, Ethics, and the New War*, edited by Jon Berquist, 110–15. St. Louis: Chalice, 2002.

Betcher, Sharon. *Spirit and the Politics of Disablement.* Minneapolis: Fortress, 2007.

Bevans, Stephen, and Roger Schroeder. *Constants in Context: A Theology of Mission for Today.* New York: Orbis, 2004.

Bezruchka, Stephen, and Mary Anne Mercer. "The Lethal Divide: How Economic Inequality Affects Health." In *Sickness and Wealth: The Corporate Assault on Global Health*, edited by Meredith Fort et al., 11–18. Cambridge: South End, 2004.

Bhabha, Homi. *The Location of Culture.* New York: Routledge, 1994.

Bianchi, Eugene, and Rosemary Ruether, eds. *A Democratic Church: The Reconstruction of Roman Catholicism.* New York: Crossroad, 1992.

Bigelow, Bill. "Defeating Despair." In *Rethinking Globalization: Teaching for Justice in an Unjust World,* edited by Bill Bigelow and Bob Peterson, 329–34. Milwaukee: Rethinking School, 2002.

Black, Kathy. *A Healing Homiletic: Preaching and Disability.* Nashville: Abingdon, 1996.

Boff, Leonardo. *Church: Charism and Power.* Translated by John W. Diercksmeier. New York: Crossroad, 1986.

———. *Ecclesiogenesis: The Base Communities Reinvent the Church.* Translated by Robert Barr. New York: Orbis, 1986.

———. *Cry of the Earth, Cry of the Poor. Translated by* Phillip Berryman. Maryknoll, New York: Orbis, 1997.

———. "It is Dark, But I Sing!" In *Witness Magazine,* February 7 2006. Online: http://www.thewitness.org.

Bonhoeffer, Dietrich. *The Cost of Discipleship.* Revised Edition. London: SCM Press, 1959.

Bonilla, Yosenia. "A Trade Unionist Must Leave Her Fear Behind." In *Rethinking Globalization: Teaching for Justice in an Unjust World,* edited by Bill Bigelow and Bob Peterson, 142–45. Milwaukee: Rethinking School, 2002.

Bookless, Dave. "To Strive to Safeguard the Integrity of Creation and Sustain and Renew the Life of the Earth." In *Mission in the 21st Century: Exploring the Five Marks of Global Mission,* edited by Andrew Walls and Cathy Ross, 94–104. New York: Orbis, 2008.

Borg, Marcus. *Jesus, A New Vision: Spirit, Culture, and the Life of Discipleship.* San Francisco: Harper & Row, 1987.

———. *The Heart of Christianity: Rediscovering a Life of Faith.* New York: Harper San Francisco, 2003.

———. "Jesus and Buddhism: A Christian View." In *Buddhist Talk about Jesus, Christians Talk about Buddha,* edited by Rita Gross and Terry Muck, 77–82. New York: Continuum, 2000.

Bosch, David. *Transforming Mission: Paradigm Shifts in Theology of Mission.* New York: Orbis, 1991.

Boulding, Elise. "Cultures of Peace and Communities of Faith." In *Transforming Violence: Linking Local and Global Peacemaking,* edited by Robert Herr and Judy Zimmerman, 95–104. Scottdale: Herald, 1998.

Bower, Bruce. "Deadly Aftermath for Vietnam Veterans-Higher Death Rate in First Five Years out of Service." *Science News,* February 21 1987. Online: http://www.findarticles.com/p/articles/mi_m1200/is_v131/ai_4702869.

Branfman, Fred. "The Need to De-Mystify the Presidency." In *Tikkun,* September/October, 2002, 37–38.

Brecher, Jeremy, and Tim Costello. *Global Village or Global Pillage: Economic Reconstruction from the Bottom Up.* Cambridge: South End, 1994.

Brecher, Jeremy, et al. *Globalization from Below: The Power of Solidarity.* 2nd ed. Cambridge: South End, 2002.

Brennan, Teresa. *Globalization and its Terrors: Daily Life in the West.* New York: Routledge, 2003.

Brennan, Denise. "Selling Sex for Visas: Sex Tourism as a Stepping-stone to International Migration." In *Global Woman: Nannies, Maids, and Sex Workers in the New Economy,* edited by Barbara Ehrenreich and Arlie Russell Hochschild, 154–68. New York: Metropolitan Books, 2002.

Brock, Rita Nakashima, and Susan Brooks Thistlethwaite. *Casting Stones: Prostitution and Liberation in Asia and the United States.* Minneapolis: Fortress, 1996.

Brock, Rita Nakashima. *Journeys by Heart: A Christology of Erotic Power.* New York: The Crossroad Publishing, 1988.

Brown, Rober McAfee. *Saying Yes and Saying No: On Rendering to God and Caesar.* Philadelphia: Westminster, 1986.

———. *Spirituality and Liberation: Overcoming the Great Fallacy.* Philadelphia: Westminster John Knox, 1988.

———. *Gustavo Gutiérrez: An Introduction to Liberation Theology.* New York: Orbis, 1990.

———. *Persuade Us to Rejoice: The Liberating Power of Fiction.* Louisville: Westminster John Knox, 1982.

Brubaker, Pamela. *Globalization at What Price? Economic Change and Daily Life.* Cleveland: Pilgrim, 2001.

Brubaker, Pamela, et al., eds. *Justice in a Global Economy: Strategies for Home, Community, and the World.* Louisville: Westminster John Knox, 2006.

Brueggemann, Walter. *Peace.* St. Louis: Chalice, 2001.

Budde, Michael. *The (Magic) Kingdom of God: Christianity and the Global Culture Industries.* Boulder: Westview, 1997.

———. "God is not Capitalist." In *God is no t . . . Religious, Nice, 'One of Us,' an American, a Capitalist,* edited by D. Brent Laytham, 77–95. Grand Rapids: Brazos, 2004.

Bula-at, Leticia. "The Kalinga Women against the Chico Dam." In *Rethinking Globalization: Teaching for Justice in an Unjust World,* edited by Bill Bigelow and Bob Peterson, 89–92. Milwaukee: Rethinking School, 2002.

Butler-Bass, Diana. *The Practicing Congregation: Imaging a New Old Church.* Herdon: The Alban Institute, 2004.

Carney, Scott. "Why a Kidney (Street Value: $3,000) Sells For," in *Wire,* May 8, 2007, 7. Online: http://www.http://www.wired.com/medtech/health/news/2007/05 /india_transplants_ prices

Caroll, Lewis. *Alice's Adventures in Wonderland.* New York: Sterling Publishing, 2004.

Casalis, Georges. *Correct Ideas Don't Fall from the Skies: Elements for an Inductive Theology.* New York: Orbis, 1984.

Castles, Stephen, and Mark Miller. *The Age of Migration: International Population Movements in the Modern World.* 4th ed. Revised and Updated. New York: Palgrave Macmillan, 2009.

Castles, Stephen. *Ethnicity and Globalization.* London: Sage, 2000.

Cavanaugh, William. *Torture and Eucharist.* Oxford, UK: Blackwell, 1998.

———. *Being Consumed: Economics and Christian Desire.* Grand Rapids: Wm. B. Eerdmans, 2008.

Center for Investigative Reporting and Bill Moyers. *Global Dumping Ground: The International Traffic in Hazardous Waste,* 96–100. Washington: Seven Locks, 1990.

Cerón, Alejandro, et al. "The Struggle for People's Health." In *Sickness and Wealth: The Corporate Assault on Global Health,* edited by Meredith Fort et al., 161–66. Cambridge: South End, 2004.

Chase-Ziolek, Mary. *Health, Healing and Wholeness: Engaging Congregations in Health Ministries.* Cleveland: Pilgrim, 2005.

Chittister, Joan. *Winds of Change: Women Challenge the Church.* Kansas City: Sheed and Ward, 1986.

———. *The Fire in These Ashes: A Spirituality of Contemporary Religious Life.* Kansas City: Sheed & Ward, 1995.

———. *Living Well: Scriptural Reflections for Everyday Life.* New York: Orbis, 2000.

———. *In the Heart of the Temple: My Spiritual Vision for Today's World.* New York: BlueBridge, 2004.

———. *Listen with the Heart: Sacred Moments in Everyday Life.* New York: Sheed & Ward, 2003.

—. *Becoming Fully Human: The Greatest Glory of God.* Lanham: Sheed & Ward, 2005.

Chomsky, Noam. *The Culture of Terrorism.* Boston: South End, 1988.

—. *Pirates and Emperors, Old and New: International Terrorism in the Real World,* Cambridge: South End, 2002.

Church, Forrest. "We Need More Patriots." In *The Magazine of the Universalist Association,* Vol. xvii. No. 1, January/February 2003, 12–13.

Cilliers, Jaco. "Building Bridges of Interfaith Dialogue." In *Interfaith Dialogue and Peace Building,* edited by David Smock, 47–60. Washington, D.C.: United States Institute of Peace, 2002.

Cobb Jr., John. *Reclaiming the Church: Where the Mainline Church Went Wrong and What to Do about It.* Louisville: Westminster John Knox, 1997.

—. *Transforming Christianity and the World: A Way beyond Absolutism and Relativism,* edited and introduced by Paul Knitter. New York: Orbis, 1999.

—. "Economism or Planetism: The Coming Choice." In *Earth Ethics 3.* Fall 1991.

—. "A War Against Terrorism." In *Strike Terror No More: Theology, Ethics, and the New War,* edited by Jon Berquist, 2–9. St. Louis: Chalice, 2002.

Cobb Jr., John, and Herman Daly. *For the Common Good: Redirecting the Economy toward Community, the Environment, and a Sustainable Future.* Boston: Beacon, 1994.

Community Resources for Responsible Living. Online: http://www.sanjoseuu.org /Responsibleliving/ clothing.htm.

Cone, James. "Whose Earth Is It, Anyway?" In *Earth Habitat: Eco-justice and the Church's Response,* edited by Dieter Hessel and Larry Rasmussen, 23–32. Minneapolis: Fortress, 2001.

Coop, William, ed. *Pacific People Sing Out Strong.* New York: Friendship, 1982.

Cox, Harvey. *The Secular City: Secularization and Urbanization in Theological Perspective.* New York: Macmillan, 1965.

—. *Fire from Heaven: The Rise of Pentecostal Spirituality and the Reshaping of Religion in the Twenty-first Century.* Reading, Massachusetts: Addison-Wesley, 1995.

—. "Mammon and the Culture of the Market: A Socio-Theological Critique." In *Liberating Faith: Religious Voices for Justice, Peace, and Ecological Wisdom,* edited by Roger Gottlieb, 274–83. New York: Rowman and Littlefield, 2003.

Crane, Richard. "Ecclesial Discipleship and the Unity of Spirituality and Justice." In *Vital Christianity: Spirituality, Justice, and Christian Practice,* edited by David Weaver-Zercher and William Willimon, 59–71. New York: T & T Clark, 2005.

Croatto, Severino. "A Reading of the Story of the Tower of Babel from the Perspective of Non-Identity." In *Teaching the Bible: The Discourse and Politics of Biblical Pedagogy,* edited by Fernando Segovia and Mary Ann Tolbert, 203–23. New York: Orbis, 1998.

Crossan, John Dominic. *Jesus: A Revolutionary Biography.* New York: HarperSanFrancisco, 1994.

de Freitas, María Carmelita. "Response to Peter Hünermann." In *Mission in the Third Millennium,* edited by Robert Schreiter, 81–87. New York: Orbis, 2001.

Delgado, Sharon. *Shaking the Gates of Hell: Faith-Led Resistance to Corporate Globalization.* Minneapolis: Fortress, 2007.

Deloria,Vine. "Indian Humor." In *Race, Class, and Gender: An Anthology*, edited by Patricia Hill Collins and Margaret Andersen, 341–46. Belmont: Wadsworth, 1992.

de Mello, Anthony. *The Song of the Bird*. New York: Doubleday, 1982.

DeWitt, Calvin. "To Strive to Safeguard the Integrity of Creation and Sustain and Renew the Life of the Earth." In *Mission in the 21ˢᵗ Century: Exploring the Five Marks of Global Mission,* edited by Andrew Walls and Cathy Ross, 84–93. New York: Orbis, 2008.

Dick, Dan R. *Revolutionizing Christian Stewardship for the 21st Century: Lessons from Copernicus*. Nashville: Discipleship Resources, 1997.

Dickens, Charles. *A Tale of Two Cities*, Vol.1. New York: Sheldon and Company, 1863.

Dillard, Annie. *Pilgrim at Tinker Creek: A Mystical Excursion into the Natural World*. New York: Bantam, 1974.

Docena, Herbert. "When Uncle Sam comes marching in." *Asia Times*, February 25 2006. Online: http://www.atimes.com/atimes/Southeast_Asia/HB25Ae04.htm

Douglas, Ian T. "Globalization and the Local Church." In *The Local Church in a Global Era: Reflections for a New Century*, edited by Max Stackhouse et al., 202–08. Grand Rapids: Wm. B. Eerdmans, 2000.

Drakulić, Slavenka. *The Balkan Express: Fragments from the Other Side of War*. New York: W. W. Norton, 1993.

Dryer, Elizabeth. "An Advent of the Spirit: Medieval Mystics and Saints." In *Advents of the Spirit: An Introduction to the Current Study of Pneumatology*, edited by Bradford Hinze and D. Lyle Dabney, 123–62. Marquette: Marquette University Press, 2001.

Duchrow, Ulrich, and Franz Hinkelammert. *Property for People, Not for Profit: Alternatives to the Global Tyranny of Capital*. Geneva: WCC Publications, 2004.

Dudley, Carl. *Community Ministry: New Challenges, Proven Steps to Faith-based Initiatives*. Bethesda: The Alban Institute, 2002.

Dulles, Avery. *The Catholicity of the Church*. Oxford: Clarendon, 1985.

Dussel, Enrique. "1492: The Apparition of the Other—Conquest and Prophetical Criticism in the Origin of Modernity." Cole Lectures, Vanderbilt University, February 5 1992.

Easum, Bill. *Put On Your Own Oxygen Mask First: Rediscovering Ministry*. Nashville: Abingdon, 2004.

Eck, Diana. *A New Religious America: How a "Christian Nation" Has Become the World's Most Religiously Diverse Nation*. New York: HarperSanFrancisco, 2001.

———. In *Minutes: Sixth Meeting of the Working Group Dialogue with People of Living Faiths*. Geneva: World Council of Churches, 1985.

Edwards, Dennis. *Jesus the Wisdom of God: An Ecological Theology*. New York: Orbis, 1995.

———. *Ecology at the Heart of Faith: The Change of Heart that Leads to a New Way of Living on Earth*. New York: Orbis, 2006.

Edwards,Tilden. "Living the Day from the Heart." In *The Weavings Reader: Living with God in the World*, edited by John S. Mogabgab, 55–61. Nashville: Upper Room, 1993.

Eisenstein, Zillah. *Hatreds: Racialized and Sexualized Conflicts in the 21st Century*. New York: Routledge, 1996.

Episcopal Church USA, "What is Health Ministry?" Online: http://www .episcopalhealthministries.org/ what_is_ health_ ministry.html

Epperly, Bruce *God's Touch: Faith, Wholeness, and the Healing Miracles of Jesus.* Louisville: Westminster John Knox, 2001.

Erdozaín, Plácido. *Archbishop Romero: Martyr of Salvador.* Translated by John McFadden and Ruth Warner. New York: Orbis, 1980.

Escobar, Samuel. *Changing Tides: Latin America and World Mission Today.* New York: Orbis, 2002.

Esposito, John. *Unholy War: Terror in the Name of Islam.* New York: Oxford University Press, 2002.

Evangelical Lutheran Church of America (ELCA), "Health and Health Care." Online: http://www.elca.org/what-we-believe/social-issues/socialstatements/ health-and -healthcare.aspx

Facing AIDS: The Challenge, the Churches' Response. Geneva: WCC Publications, 1997.

Farley, Edward. *Ecclesial Reflection: An Anatomy of Theological Method.* Philadelphia: Fortress, 1982.

Featherstone, Mike, ed. *Global Culture: Nationalism, Globalization and Modernity.* London: Sage, 1990.

———. *Undoing Culture: Globalization, Postmodernism and Identity.* London: Sage, 1995.

Fernandez, Eleazar. *Toward a Theology of Struggle.* New York: Orbis, 1994.

———. *Reimagining the Human: Theological Anthropology in Response to Systemic Evil.* St. Louis: Chalice, 2004.

———. "From Babel to Pentecost: Finding a Home in the Belly of the Empire." In *Semeia: The Bible in Asian America,* edited by Tat-siong Benny Liew, 29–50. Atlanta: Society of Biblical Literature, 2002.

———. "Filipino Popular Christianity." In *Twentieth Century Global Christianity: A People's History of Christianity,* Vol. 7, edited by Mary Farrell Bednarowski, 37–60. Minneapolis: Fortress, 2008.

———. "Colonial Legacies in the Pacific and Minnesota." In *Witness Magazine,* Vol. 86, No. 7/8, July/August 2003, 30–31.

Ferris, Elizabeth. *Uprooted: Refugees and Forced Migrants.* New York: Friendship, 1998.

Finger, Thomas. "A Mennonite Theology for Interfaith Relations." In *Grounds for Understanding: Ecumenical Resources for Responses to Religious Pluralism,* edited by S. Mark Heim, 69–92. Grand Rapids: Wm. B. Eerdmans, 1998.

Forrest, Jim. "A Dialogue on Reconciliation in Belgrade: The Report of a Participant." In *The Reconciliation of Peoples: Challenge to the Churches,* edited by Gregory Baum and Harold Wells, 110–17. New York: Orbis/Geneva: WCC Publications, 1997.

Forman, Charles. *The Island Churches of the South Pacific: Emergence in the Twentieth Century.* New York: Orbis, 1982.

Fort, Meredith. "Globalization and Health." In *Sickness and Wealth: The Corporate Assault on Global Health,* edited by Meredith Fort et al., 1–7. Cambridge: South End, 2004.

Foucault, Michel. *The Order of Things: An Archeology of the Human Sciences.* New York: Vintage, 1973.

———. *The Foucault Reader,* edited by Paul Rabinow. New York: Pantheon, 1984.

Franchetti, Mark. "Dozens Killed for Body Parts." Moscow. In *The Sunday Times*, July 29, 2001. Online: http://www.vachss.com/help_text/archive/body/_parts.htm.

Friedman, Thomas. *The Lexus and the Olive Tree*. New York: Farrar, Straus, Giroux, 1999.

———. "What the World Needs Today." *New York Times*. March 19, 1999.

Fuellenbach, John. *Church: Community for the Kingdom*. New York: Orbis, 2002.

Gaillardetz, Richard. *Ecclesiology for a Global Church: A People Called and Sent*. New York: Orbis, 2008.

Gandhi, Mohandas. "Selections from His Writings." In *Liberating Faith: Religious Voices for Justice, Peace, and Ecological Wisdom*, edited by Roger Gottlieb, 85–95. New York: Rowman & Littlefield, 2003.

Gaspar, Karl M. "Bringing Christians and Muslims Together in Peace." In *Artisans of Peace: Grassroots Peacemaking among Christian Communities*, edited by Mary Ann Cejka and Thomas Bamat, 96–131. New York: Orbis, 2003.

Gebara, Ivone. "A Cry for Life from Latin America." In *Spirituality of the Third World*, edited by K. C. Abraham and Bernadette Mbuy-Beya, 109–18. New York: Orbis, 1994.

Gerlock, Ed. "The Living and the Dead." In *Signs of Hope: Stories of Hope in the Philippines,* edited by Ed Gerlock, 73–75. Quezon City, Philippines: Claretian, 1990.

Gibbs, Charles. "The United Religious Initiative at Work." In *Interfaith Dialogue and Peace Building*, edited by David Smock, 115–26. Washington, D.C.: United States Institute of Peace, 2002.

Giddens, Anthony. *The Consequences of Modernity*. Stanford: Stanford University Press, 1990.

Gill, Jerry. *Borderlinks: The Road is Made by Walking*. Tucson: Borderlinks, 1999.

———.*Borderland Theology*. Washington, D.C.: EPICA, 2003.

Global Exchange, "The Free Trade Area of the Americas Places Corporate Rights above Human Rights," April 2, 2001. Online: http://www.globalexchange.org /campaigns/ftaa/statement040201.html

Globalizing Alternatives to Globalization. Dossier Prepared by the Justice, Peace and Creation Team of the World Council of Churches, October 2000.

Golson, Blair. *America's Eating Disorder*. Online: http://www.globalissues.org/ TradeRelated/consumption/obesity.asp

González, Justo. "The Changing Geography of Church History." In *Theology and the New Histories*. College Theology Society. Annual Volume, 44, 1998, edited by Gary Macy, 23–32. New York: Orbis, 1999.

———. *Mañana: Christian Theology from a Hispanic Perspective*. Nashville: Abingdon, 1990.

Gopin, Marc. "The Heart of the Stranger." In *Explorations in Reconciliation: New Directions in Theology*, edited by David Tombs and Joseph Liechty, 3–21. England: Ashgate, 2006.

Gottlieb, Roger. *A Spirituality of Resistance: Finding Peaceful Heart and Protecting the Earth*. New York: Crossroad, 1999.

———. "Saving the World: Religion and Politics in the Environmental Movement." In *Liberating Faith: Religious Voices for Justice, Peace, and Ecological Wisdom*, edited by Roger Gottlieb, 491–512. New York: Rowman & Littlefield, 2003.

Goudzwaard, Bob, and Harry de Lange. *Beyond Poverty and Affluence: Toward an Economy of Care.* Grand Rapids: Wm. B. Eerdmans, 1995; Geneva: WCC Publications, 1995.

Gramsci, Antonio. *Letters from Prison,* Vol.1. Edited by Frank Rosengarten and translated by Raymond Rosenthal. New York: Columbia University Press, 1993.

Gray, Elizabeth Dodson. *Green Paradise Lost.* Wellesley: Roundtable, 1981.

Griffin, David Ray. "The Moral Need for Global Democracy." In *Belonging Together: Faith and Politics in a Relational World,* edited by Douglas Sturm, 119–39. Claremont: P & F Press, 2003.

Griffith, Lee. *The War on Terrorism and the Terror of God.* Grand Rapids: Wm. B. Eerdmans, 2002.

Groome, Thomas. *What Makes Us Catholic: Eight Gifts for Life.* New York: HarperSanFrancisco, 2002.

Gushee, David. "New Frontiers in Ecological Theology." In *Creation Care: A Christian Environmental Quarterly,* No. 36, Summer 2008, 46.

———. "Opinion: Our Theology of Ecology Should Place Us within Creation." In *Associated Baptist Press,* April 23, 2008. Online: www.abpnews.com/index .php?optin=com_content&task=view&id=3256& Itemid=121&fontsyle=f- smaller

Hadaway, C. Kirk. *Behold I Do a New Thing: Transforming Communities of Faith.* Cleveland: Pilgrim, 2001.

Haddad, Yvonne Yazbeck. *Not Quite Americans: The Shaping of Arab and Muslim Identity in the United States.* Waco: Baylor University, 2004.

Hagedorn, Jessica. "The Exile Within/The Question of Identity." In *The State of Asian America: Activism and Resistance in the 1990s,* edited by Karen Aguilar-San Juan, 173–82. Boston: South End, 1994.

Hall, John Douglas. *The Future of the Church: Where are We Headed?* Canada: The United Church Publishing House, 1989.

———. *Why Christian? For Those on the Edge of Faith.* Minneapolis: Fortress, 1998.

Halverson, Delia. *The Gift of Hospitality: In the Church, In the Home, In All of Life.* St. Louis: Chalice, 1999.

Hamilton, Neill. *Recovery of the Protestant Adventure.* New York: Seabury, 1981.

Handy, Robert. *A Christian America: Protestant Hopes and Historical Realities.* New York: Oxford University Press, 1971.

Hanh, Thich Nhat. *Creating True Peace: Ending Violence in Yourself, Your Family, Your Community, and the World.* New York: Free Press, 2003.

———. "The Fourteen Mindfulness Trainings of the Order of Interbeing." In *Liberating Faith: Religious Voices for Justice, Peace, and Ecological Wisdom,* edited by Roger Gottlieb, 450–55. New York: Rowman & Littlefield, 2003).

Hardt, Michael, and Antonio Negri. *Empire.* Cambridge: Harvard University Press, 2000.

———. *Multitude: War and Democracy in the Age of Empire.* New York: Penguin Group (USA), 2004.

Hauerwas, Stanley, and William Willimon. *Resident Aliens: A Provocative Christian Assessment of Culture and Ministry for People who Know that Something is Wrong.* Nashville: Abingdon, 1989.

Healy, Joseph. *Once Upon a Time in Africa: Stories of Wisdom and Joy.* New York: Orbis, 2004.

Healey, Joseph, and Donald Sybertz. *Towards an African Narrative Theology.* New York: Orbis, 1997.

Heim, S. Mark. *Salvations: Truth and Difference in Religion.* New York: Orbis, 1995.

——— . "Elements of a Conversation." In *Grounds for Understanding: Ecumenical Resources for Responses to Religious Pluralism,* edited by S. Mark Heim, 208–23. Grand Rapids: Wm. B. Eerdmans, 1998.

Held, David. "Becoming Cosmopolitan: The Dimensions and Challenges of Globalization." In *Globalization and the Good,* edited by Peter Heslam, 3–15. Grand Rapids: Wm. B. Eerdmans, 2004.

Hertig, Young Lee. "The Korean Immigrant Church and Naked Public Square." In *Realizing the America of our Hearts: Theological Voices of Asian Americans,* edited by Fumitaka Matsuoka and Eleazar Fernandez, 131–46. St. Louis: Chalice, 2003.

Hessel, Dieter. *Social Ministry,* Revised Edition. Louisville: Westminster/John Knox, 1992.

——— . "The Church Ecologically Reformed." In *Earth Habitat: Eco-justice and the Church's Response,* edited by Dieter Hessel and Larry Rasmussen, 185–206. Minneapolis: Fortress, 2001.

Hick, John, and Paul Knitter. *The Myth of Christian Uniqueness: Toward a Pluralistic Theology of Religion.* New York: Orbis, 1987.

Hildegard of Bingen. *Scivias.* Translated by Mother Columbia Hart and Jane Bishop. New York: Paulist, 1990.

Hines, Mary. "Community for Liberation: Church." In *Freeing Theology: The Essentials of Theology in Feminist Perspective,* edited by Catherine Mowry LaCugna, 161–84. New York: HarperSanFrancisco, 1993.

Hinkelammert, Franz. "The Economic Roots of Idolatry: Entrepreneurial Metaphysics." In *The Idols of Death and the God of Life: A Theology,* edited by Pablo Richard et al., 165–93. New York: Orbis, 1983.

Hoedemaker, Bert. *Secularization and Mission: A Theological Essay.* Harrisburg: Trinity Press International, 1998.

Hodgson, Peter. *Winds of the Spirit: A Constructive Christian Theology.* Louisville: Westminster John Knox Press, 1994.

Holmes, Barbara. "The Spirit Holy, Hip, and Free." In *The Lord and Giver of Life: Perspectives on Constructive Pneumatology,* edited by David Jensen, 97–111. Louisville: Westminster John Knox, 2008.

Holtz, Timothy, and S. Patrick Kachur. "The Reglobalization of Malaria." In *Sickness and Wealth: The Corporate Assault on Global Health,* edited by Meredith Fort et al., 131–43. Cambridge: South End, 2004.

Hong, Evelyne. "The Primary Health Care Movement Meets the Free Market." In *Sickness and Wealth: The Corporate Assault on Global Health,* edited by Meredith Fort et al., 27–36. Cambridge: South End, 2004.

Horsley, Richard. *Paul and Empire: Religion and Power in Roman Imperial Society.* Harrisburg: Trinity Press International, 1997.

Hudnut-Beumler, James. *Generous Saints: Congregations Rethinking Ethics and Money.* Bethesda: The Alban Institute, 1999.

Hünermann, Peter. "Evangelization of Europe? Observations on a Church in Peril." In *Mission in the Third Millennium,* edited by Robert Schreiter, 57–58. New York: Orbis, 2001.

Hunger: 1995: Causes of Hunger, Fifth Annual Report on the State of World Hunger. Silver Spring, Maryland: Bread for the World, 1994.

Hunt, Charles. "Africa and AIDS: Dependent Development, Sexism and Racism." In *Monthly Review,* Vol. 30, No. 9. February 1988. Online: http://www.findarticles.com/p/articles/mi_m1132/is_n9_v39/ai_6445835/p_3

Hunter, Victor. *Desert Hearts and Healing Fountains: Gaining Pastoral Vocational Clarity.* St. Louis: Chalice, 2003.

Huntington, Samuel. *The Clash of Civilizations and the Remaking of World Order.* New York: Simon & Schuster, 1996.

Hussain, Amir. *Oil and Water: Two Faiths: One God.* Kelowna, BC: Copper House, 2006.

Jarl, Ann-Cathrin. *In Justice: Women and Global Economics.* Minneapolis: Fortress, 2003.

Jenkins, Philip. *The Next Christendom: The Coming of Global Christianity.* New York: Oxford University Press, 2002.

Jensen, David. *The Lord and Giver of Life: Perspectives on Constructive Pneumatology.* Louisville: Westminster John Knox, 2008.

Jesudasan, Usha "Entertaining Violence." In *Echoes: Justice, Peace and Creation News,* 18. Geneva: World Council of Churches, 2000, 28–29.

Johnson, Ben Campbell, and Andrew Dreitcer. *Beyond the Ordinary: Spirituality for Church Leaders.* Grand Rapids: Wm. B. Eerdmans, 2001.

Jones, Laurie Beth. *Jesus CEO: Using Ancient Wisdom for Visionary Leadership.* New York: Hyperion, 1995.

Jordans, Frank. "WHO: Global Death Toll from Swine Flu Now Over 700." In *Associated Press,* July 21, 2009. Online: http://www.google.com/ hostednews/ap/article/ALeqM5hG6zmXnY6v5La-llZ8qbQIrdE-WAD99IU0980.

Juergensmeyer, Mark. *Terror in the Mind of God: The Global Rise of Religious Violence,* updated edition with a new preface. Berkeley: University of California Press, 2000.

———. "Religious Antiglobalism." In *Religion in Global Civil Society,* edited by Mark Juergensmeyer, 135–48. New York: Oxford University Press, 2005.

Jung, Shannon, et al. *Rural Ministry: The Shape of the Renewal to Come.* Nashville: Abingdon, 1998.

Kaminer, Wendy. "Freedom…and Preserving our Liberties." In *Fear Versus Freedom: Living by our Faith and Preserving Our Liberties, The Magazine of the Unitarian Universalist Association,* Vol. xvii, No. 1, January/February 2003, 21–25.

Kammer III, Charles L. *Ethics and Liberation: An Introduction.* New York: Orbis, 1988.

Keller, Catherine. "The Love of Postcolonialism: Theology in the Interstices of Empire." In *Postcolonial Theologies: Divinity and Empire,* edited by Catherine Keller et al., 221–42. St. Louis: Chalice, 2004.

Kimball, Charles. *When Religion Becomes Evil.* New York: HarperSanFrancisco, 2002.

Kinnamon, Michael. *The Vision of the Ecumenical Movement and How It Has Been Impoverished by its Friends.* St. Louis: Chalice, 2003.

King, Ursula, ed. *Faith and Praxis in a Postmodern Age.* London: Cassell, 1998.

King, Paul, and David Woodyard. *Liberating Nature: Theology and Economics in a New Order.* Cleveland: Pilgrim, 1999.

Kirk-Duggan, Cheryl. "Civil War, Civil Rights, World Trade Center." In *Strike Terror No More: Theology, Ethics, and the New War*, edited by Jon Berquist, 30–46. St. Louis: Chalice, 2002.

Knight, Douglas. "Cosmogony and Order in the Hebrew Tradition." In *Cosmogony and Ethical Order: New Studies in Comparative Ethics*, edited by Robin Lovin and Frank Reynolds, 133–57. Chicago: The University of Chicago, 1985.

Knitter, Paul. *One Earth, Many Religions: Multifaith Dialogue and Global Responsibility.* New York: Orbis, 1995.

———. *Jesus and the Other Names: Christian Mission and Global Responsibility.* New York: Orbis, 1999.

———. *Introducing Theologies of Religions.* New York: Orbis, 2002.

———. "The Transformation of Mission in the Pluralist Paradigm." In *Pluralist Theology: The Emerging Paradigm*, edited by Andrés Torres Queiruga et al., 93–101. London: SCM Press, 2007.

Kobia, Samuel. "Violence in Africa." In *Echoes: Justice, Peace and Creation News*, 18/2000. Geneva: World Council of Churches, 2000, 9–12.

Korten, David C. *The Great Turning: From Empire to Earth Community.* San Francisco: Berrett-Koehler; Bloomfield: Kumarian, 2006.

Küng, Hans. *Global Responsibility: In Search of a New World Ethic.* New York: Crossroad, 1991.

Kurtz, Lester. *Gods in the Global Village: The World's Religions in Sociological Perspective.* Thousand Oaks: Pine Forge, 1995.

LaDuke, Winona. "Traditional Ecological Knowledge and Environmental Futures." In *Liberating Faith: Religious Voices for Justice, Peace, and Ecological Wisdom*, edited by Roger Gottlieb, 513–18. New York: Rowman & Littlefied, 2003.

Lakeland, Paul. *Theology and Critical Theory: Discourse of the Church.* Nashville: Abingdon, 1990.

Lane, Dermot. *Keeping Hope Alive: Stirrings in Christian Theology.* Mahwah: Paulist, 1996.

Law, Eric H. F. *The Wolf Shall Dwell with the Lamb: A Spirituality for Leadership in a Multicultural Community.* St. Louis: Chalice, 1993.

———. *Sacred Acts, Holy Change: Faithful Diversity and Practical Transformation.* St. Louis: Chalice, 2002.

Lechner, Frank. "Religious Rejections of Globalization." In *Religion in Global Civil Society*, edited by Mark Juergensmeyer, 115–33. New York: Oxford University Press, 2005.

Lederach, John Paul. *The Journey Toward Reconciliation.* Scottdale: Herald, 1999.

———. *The Moral Imagination: The Art and Soul of Building Peace.* New York: Oxford University Press, 2005.

———. "The Mystery of Transformative Times and Spaces: Exploring a Theology of Grassroots Peacebuilding." In *Artisans of Peace: Grassroot Peacemaking among Christian Communities*, edited by Mary Ann Cejka and Thomas Bamat, 256–67. New York: Orbis, 2003.

Leddy, Mary Jo. *Radical Gratitude.* New York: Orbis, 2002.

Lee, Charles. "The Integrity of Justice: Evidence of Environmental Racism," *Sojourner* 19, February-March 1990, 23–25.

Lee, Helen. "Hospitable Household: Evangelism." In *Growing Healthy Asian American Churches: Ministry Insights from Groundbreaking Congregations*, edited by Peter Cha et al., 122–44. Downers Grove: InterVarsity, 2006.

Leffel, Gregory. "Churches in the Mode of Mission: Toward a Missional Model of the Church." In *Global Good News: Mission in a New Context*, edited by Howard A. Snyder, 65–95. Nashville: Abingdon, 2001.

Lemonick, Michael D, and Alice Park. "The Truth about SARS." In *Time Magazine*, May 5, 2003, 48–53.

Lenhardt, Christian. "Anamnestic Solidarity: The Proletariat and its Manes." *Telos* 25, 1975.

Liechty, Joseph. "Putting Forgiveness in its Place: The Dynamics of Reconciliation." In *Explorations in Reconciliation: New Directions in Theology*, edited by David Tombs and Joseph Liechty, 59–68. Vermont: Ashgate, 2006.

Linden, Ian. "The Church and Genocide: Lessons from the Rwandan Tragedy." In *The Reconciliation of Peoples: Challenge to the Churches*, edited by Gregory Baum and Harold Wells, 43–55. New York: Orbis/Geneva: WCC Publications, 1997.

Lintner, Jay. "Building a Peacemaking Church." In *The Prophetic Call: Celebrating Community, Earth, Justice, and Peace*, edited by Hugh Sanborn, 165–78. St. Louis: Chalice, 2004.

Lochhead, David. *The Dialogical Imperative: A Christian Reflection on Interfaith Encounter*. New York: Orbis, 1988.

———. *Shifting Realities: Information Technology and the Church*. Geneva: WCC Publications, 1997.

Long Jr., Edward LeRoy. *Facing Terrorism: Responding as Christians*. Louisville: Westminster John Knox, 2004.

Long, D. Stephen. "God is Not Nice." In *God is not...Religious, Nice, 'One of Us', an American, a Capitalist*, edited by D. Brent Laytham, 39–54. Grand Rapids: Brazos, 2004.

Lujan, Nereo C. "Boracay on the Brink." In *Filipinas Magazine*, April 2003, 34–35.

Maguire, Daniel. *The Moral Core of Judaism and Christianity: Reclaiming the Revolution*. Minneapolis: Fortress, 1993.

Markova, Dawna. *I Will not Die an Unlived Life: Reclaiming Purpose and Passion*. Berkeley: Conari, 2000.

Marshall, Joretta . "When Listening Is Not Enough: Pastoral Theology and Care in Turbulent Times." In *Strike Terror No More: Theology, Ethics, and the New War*, edited by Jon Berquist, 164–71. St. Louis: Chalice, 2002.

Marty, Martin. *The Fire We Can Light*. Garden City: Doubleday, 1975.

Mather, Clive. "Combining Principle with Profit: A Business Response to the Challenges of Globalization." In *Globalization and the Good*, edited by Peter Heslam, 29–38. Grand Rapids: Wm. B. Eerdmans, 2004.

Matsuoka, Fumitaka. *Out of Silence: Emerging Themes in Asian American Churches*. Cleveland: United Church Press, 1995.

McDaniel, Jay B. *Of God and Pelicans: A Theology of Reverence for Life*. Louisville: Westminster/John Knox, 1989.

———.*With Roots and Wings: Christianity in an Age of Ecology and Dialogue*. New York: Orbis, 1995.

———. *Living from the Center: Spirituality in an Age of Consumerism*. St. Louis: Chalice, 2000.

———. In the Beginning is Listening." In *Theology that Matters: Ecology, Economy, and God*, edited by Darby Kathleen Ray, 26–41. Minneapolis: Fortress, 2006.

McFague, Sallie. *Models of God: Theology for an Ecological, Nuclear Age*. Minneapolis: Fortress, 1987.

———. *The Body of God: An Ecological Theology.* Minneapolis: Fortress, 1993.

———. McFague, Sallie. *Super, Natural Christians: How We Should Love Nature.* Minneapolis: Fortress, 1997.

———. *Life Abundant: Rethinking Theology and Economy for a Planet in Peril.* Minneapolis: Fortress, 2001.

McGinnis, Kathleen and James. *Parenting for Peace and Justice.* New York: Orbis, 1981.

McGovern, George, et al., eds. *Ending Hunger Now: A Challenge to Persons of Faith.* Minneapolis: Fortress, 2005.

McKinney, William, and Wade Clark Roof. *American Mainline Religion: Its Changing Shape and Future.* New Brunswick: Rutgers University Press, 1987.

McLaren, Peter, and Kris Gutierrez, "Global Politics and Local Antagonisms: Research and Practice as Dissent and Possibility." In *Revolutionary Multiculturalism: Pedagogies of Dissent for the New Millennium,* edited by Peter McLaren, 192–222. Boulder: Westview, 1997.

McLaren, Peter, and Zeus Leonardo, "Jean Baudrillard's Chamber of Horrors: From Marxism to Terrorist Pedagogy." In *Revolutionary Multiculturalism: Pedagogies of Dissent for the New Millennium,* edited by Peter McLaren, 114–49. Boulder: Westview, 1997.

McNamara, Jill Westberg. *Health and Wellness: What Your Faith Community Can Do.* Cleveland: Pilgrim, 2006.

Meeks, M. Douglas. *God the Economist: The Doctrine of God and Political Economy.* Minneapolis: Fortress, 1989.

———. "What Can We Hope for Now." In *Strike Terror No More: Theology, Ethics, and the New War,* edited by Jon Berquist, 253–63. St. Louis: Chalice, 2002.

Mercer, Mary Ann. "Shall We Leave it to Experts?" In *Sickness and Wealth: The Corporate Assault on Global Health,* edited by Meredith Fort et al., 167–72. Cambridge: South End, 2004.

Merton, Thomas. *Conjectures of a Guilty Bystander.* Garden City: Doubleday, 1966.

Messer, Donald. *Contemporary Images of Christian Ministry.* Nashville: Abingdon, 1989.

———. *A Conspiracy of Goodness: Contemporary Images of Mission.* Nashville: Abingdon, 1992.

———. Messer, Donald. *Calling Church and Seminary into the 21st Century.* Nashville: Abingdon, 1995.

———. *Breaking the Conspiracy of Silence: Christian Churches and the Global AIDS Crisis.* Minneapolis: Fortress, 2004.

———. "More than Random Acts of Kindness." In *Ending Hunger Now: A Challenge to Persons of Faith,* edited by George McGovern et al., 87–107. Minneapolis: Fortress, 2005.

Messenger, Troy. "These Stones Shall Be God's House: Tools for Earth Liturgy. " In *Earth Habitat: Eco-justice and the Church's Response,* edited by Dieter Hessel and Larry Rasmussen, 173–83. Minneapolis: Fortress, 2001.

Meyer, Art, and Jocele Meyer. *Earth-Keepers: Environmental Perspectives on Hunger, Poverty, and Injustice.* Waterloo, Ontario: Herald, 1991.

Mihalic, Frank. *1000 Stories You Can Use,* Vol. 2. Manila: Divine Word, 1989.

Mirikitani, Janice. *Shedding Silence: Poetry and Prose.* Berkeley: Celestial Arts, 1987.

Moltmann, Jürgen. *The Source of Life: The Holy Spirit and the Theology of Life.* Minneapolis: Fortress, 1997.

A Moment to Choose: Risking to be with Uprooted People: A Resource Book. Geneva: World Council of Churches, 1996.

Moore, Mary Elizabeth. *Ministering with the Earth.* St. Louis: Chalice, 1998.

Moore, Mary Elizabeth Mullino. "Wounds of Hurt, Words of Faith." In *Strike Terror No More: Theology, Ethics, and the New War,* edited by Jon Berquist, 316–25. St. Louis: Chalice, 2002.

Moore, Michael. *Downsize This!* New York: Crown, 1996.

Moore, Stephen. "Mark and Empire: 'Zealot' and 'Postcolonial' Readings." In *Postcolonial Theologies: Divinity and Empire,* edited by Catherine Keller et al., 134–48. St. Louis: Chalice, 2004.

Müller-Fahrenholz, Geiko. *God's Spirit: Transforming a World in Crisis.* New York: Continuum; Geneva: World Council of Churches, 1995.

Nandy, Ashis. *The Intimate Enemy: Loss and Recovery of Self under Colonialism.* Delhi: Oxford University Press, 1983.

Naylor, Thomas H. and William H. Willimon. *Downsizing the U.S.A.* Grand Rapids: Wm. B. Eerdmans, 1997.

Netland, Harold. "Globalization and Theology Today." In *Globalizing Theology: Belief and Practice in the Era of World Christianity,* edited by Craig Ott and Harold Netland, 14–34. Grand Rapids: Baker Academics, 2006.

The New Century Hymnal. Cleveland: Pilgrim, 1995.

Niles, D. Priman. *From East and West: Rethinking Christian Mission.* St. Louis: Chalice, 2004.

Nissen, Johannes. "Mission and Globalization in a New Testament Perspective." In *For All People: Global Theologies in Context,* edited by Else Marie Wiberg Pedersen et al., 32–51. Grand Rapids: Wm. B. Eerdmans, 2002.

Nomora, Yushi. *The Desert Wisdom.* New York: Doubleday, 1982.

Nouwen, Henri. *The Wounded Healer: Ministry in Contemporary Society.* Garden City: Doubleday, 1972.

———. *Reaching Out: Three Movements of the Spiritual Life.* New York: Image, 1975.

Oglesby, Enoch. *Born in the Fire: Case Studies in Christian Ethics and Globalization.* New York: Pilgrim, 1990.

O'Gorman, Thomas, ed. *An Advent Sourcebook.* Chicago: Diocese of Chicago, Liturgy Training Publications, 1988.

Okamura, Jonathan. *Imagining the Filipino American Diaspora: Transnational Relations, Identities, and Communities.* New York: Garland, 1998.

O'Mathuna, Donal. "Emerging Alternative Therapies." In *The Changing Face of Health Care: A Christian Appraisal of Managed Care, Resource Allocation, and Patient-Caregiver Relationships,* edited by John Kilner et al., 258–79. Grand Rapids: Wm. B Eerdmans, 1998.

Ottati, Douglas. "What it Means to Stand in a Living Tradition." In *From Christ to the World: Introductory Readings in Christian Ethics,* edited by Wayne Boulton et al., 79–87. Grand Rapids: Wm. B. Eerdmans, 1984.

Owens, Marcia Allen. "Consuming Responsibly." In *Justice in a Global Economy: Strategies for Home, Community, and the World,* edited by Pamela Brubaker et al., 40–49. Louisville: Westminster John Knox, 2006.

Palmer, Parker. *The Courage to Teach: Exploring the Inner Landscape of a Teacher's Life.* San Francisco: Jossey-Bass, 1998.

Panikkar, Raimundo. *Cultural Disarmament: The Way to Peace,* translated by Robert Barr. Louisville: Westminster John Knox, 1995.

———. *The Intra-Religious Dialogue*, revised edition. New York: Paulist, 1999.

———. "The Jordan, the Tiber, and the Ganges: Three Kairological Moments of Christic Self-Consciousness." In *The Myth of Christian Uniqueness: Toward a Pluralistic Theology of Religion*, edited by John Hick and Paul Knitter, 89–116. New York: Orbis, 1987.

Parreñas, Rhacel Salazar. "The Care Crisis in the Philippines: Children and Transnational Families in the New Global Economy." In *Global Woman: Nannies, Maids, and Sex Workers in the New Economy,* edited by Barbara Ehrenreich and Arlie Russell Hochschild, 39–54. New York: Metropolitan Books, 2002.

Pearson, Clive "Criss-Crossing Cultures." In *Faith in a Hyphen: Cross-Cultural Theologies Down Under*, edited by Clive Pearson, 5–22. Adelaide, Australia: Openbook, 2004.

Peck, Catherine. "The Palestinian Center for Rapproachment between People." In *The Reconciliation of Peoples: Challenge to the Churches*, edited by Gregory Baum and Harold Wells, 96–109. NewYork: Orbis/Geneva: WCC Publications, 1997.

Peters, Ted. *Sin: Radical Evil in Soul and Society*. Grand Rapids: Wm. B. Eerdmans, 1994.

Peterson, Bob. "Sweatshop Fact Sheet." In *Rethinking Globalization: Teaching for Justice in an Unjust World*, edited by Bill Bigelow and Bob Peterson, 158–59. Milwaukee: Rethinking School, 2002.

Peukert, H. *Science, Action, and Fundamental Theology: Towards a Theology of Communicative Action*. Boston: MIT Press, 1984.

Phan, Peter C. *Christianity with an Asian Face: Asian American Theology in the Making*. New York: Orbis, 2003.

Pieris, Aloysius. *An Asian Theology of Liberation*. New York: Orbis, 1998.

The Pluralism Project at Harvard University, Massachusetts. Online: http://www .pluralism.org/pluralism/what_is_pluralism.php

Pogue, Carolyn. *Treasury of Celebrations: Create Celebrations that Reflect Your Values and Don't Cost the Earth*. Canada: Northstone, 1996.

Postman, David. "'Battle in Seattle' brings memories of WTO Riots." In *Seattle Times*, September 18, 2008. Online: http://seattletimes.nwsource.com/html /localnews/2008187167_battle18m0.html

Premdas, Ralph R. "The Church and Reconciliation in Ethnic Conflicts: The Case of Fiji." In *The Reconciliation of Peoples: Challenge to the Churches*, edited by Gregory Baum and Harold Wells, 79–95. New York: Orbis/Geneva: WCC Publications, 1997.

Presbyterian Church (USA), "Networkers Malaria Prevention Program." Online: http://gamc.pcusa.org/ministries/internationalhealth/networkers/

Prichard, Rebecca Button. *Sensing the Spirit: The Holy Spirit in Feminist Perspective*. St. Louis: Chalice, 1999.

Project Ploughshares, Institute of Peace and Conflict Studies, Conrad Grebel College, Ontario, Canada. Cited in *Echoes: Justice, Peace and Creation News*, 18. Geneva: World Council of Churches, 2000, 14–15.

Project Ploughshares, Press Release, September 18, 2008. Online: http://www .ploughshares.ca/libraries/ACRTEXT/ACRPressrelease08.pdf

Queiruga, Andrés Torres, et al., eds. *Pluralist Theology: The Emerging Paradigm*. London: SCM Press, 2007.

Raiser, Konrad. *Ecumenism in Transition: A Paradigm Shift in the Ecumenical Movement*. Geneva: World Council of Churches, 1991.

———. *For a Culture of Life: Transforming Globalization and Violence.* Geneva: World Council of Churches, 2002.

Rasmussen, Larry. "Power Analysis: A Neglected Agenda in Christian Ethics." In *The Annual of the Society of Christian Ethic* (1991): 3–17.

Rayan, Samuel. "Theological Perspectives on the Environmental Crisis." In *Frontiers in Asian Theology: Emerging Trends*, edited by R. S. Sugirtharajah, 221–35. New York: Orbis, 1994.

Reich, Robert. *The Next American Frontier.* New York: Penguin, 1983.

Rice, Howard. *The Pastor as Spiritual Guide.* Nashville: Upper Room, 1998.

Richmond, Anthony H. *Global Apartheid: Refugees, Racism, and the New World Order.* New York: Oxford University Press, 1994.

Rieger, Joerg. *Christ and Empire: From Paul to Postcolonial Times.* Minneapolis: Fortress, 2007.

———. "Theology and Mission between Colonialism and Postcolonialism." In *Mission Studies: Journal for the International Association for Mission Studies* 21.2 (2004): 201–27.

Robertson, Roland . "Globalization and the Future of 'Traditional Religion.'" In *God and Globalization: Religion and the Powers of the Common Life,* Vol. 1, edited by Max Stackhouse with Peter Paris, 53–68. Harrisburg: Trinity Press International, 2000.

Robinson, Anthony. *What's Theology got to do with it? Convictions, Vitality, and the Church.* Herndon: The Alban Institute, 2006.

Robinson, John A. T. *Honest to God*, 40th Anniversary Edition. Louisville: Westminster John Knox, 2002.

Rock, Jay. "Resources in the Reformed Tradition for Responding to Religious Plurality." In *Grounds for Understanding: Ecumenical Resources for Responses to Religious Pluralism*, edited by S. Mark Heim, 46–68. Grand Rapids: Wm. B. Eerdmans, 1998.

Roy, Arundhati. *War Talk.* Cambridge: South End, 2003.

———. Arundhati. "Come September." In *Peacework*, November 2002, 1.

Rudolph, Susanne Hoeber. "Religious Transnationalism." In *Religion in Global Civil Society*, edited by Mark Juergensmeyer, 189–200. New York: Oxford University Press, 2005.

Ruiz, Lester Edwin J. "Diaspora, Empire, Solidarity: Hope and the (Marginalized) Subaltern as rupture(s) and repetition(s)." In *CTC Bulletin* 23, No. 1 (Summer 2007): 39–59.

———. "Cultures of Peace: The Other Side of War." In *The Peace Chronicle: The Newsletter of the Peace and Justice Studies Association*, Vol. 2. No. 2 (Summer 2003). Online: http://www.peacejusticestudies.org/documents/ summer2003 /pdf

Russell, Keith. *In Search of the Church: New Testament Images for Tomorrow's Congregations.* Bethesda, Maryland: The Alban Institute, 1994.

Russell, Letty. *Church in the Round: Feminist Interpretation of the Church.* Louisville: Westminster/John Knox, 1993.

Ryan, Chris, and C. Michael Hall. *Sex Tourism: Marginal People and Liminalities.* New York: Routledge, 2001.

Said, Edward. *Culture and Imperialism.* London: Chatto & Windus, 1993.

———. "Thoughts about America," *Al-Ahram Weekly* 28, February, 2002.

Samartha, Stanley. *One Christ-Many Religions: Toward a Revised Christology.* New York: Orbis, 1991.

Sanborn, Hugh. *The Prophetic Call: Celebrating Community, Earth, Justice, and Peace.* St. Louis: Chalice, 2004.

San Juan Jr, E. "Postcolonial Dialogics: Between Edward Said and Antonio Gramsci." In *Journal of Commonwealth and Postcolonial Studies*, Vol. 11, No. 1 & 2. (Spring and Fall, 2004): 56–76.

Sanneh, Lamin. *Whose Religion is Christianity? The Gospel Beyond the West.* Grand Rapids: Wm. B. Eerdmans, 2003.

Schieler, Robert D. *Revive Your Mainline Congregation: Prescriptions for Vital Church Life.* Cleveland: Pilgrim, 2003.

Schillebeckx, Edward. *The Church: The Human Story of God.* New York: Crossroad, 1990.

Schirch, Lisa. *Strategic Peacebuilding: A Vision and Framework for Peace with Justice.* Intercourse, Pennsylvania: Good Books, 2004.

Schreiter, Robert. *Reconciliation: Mission and Ministry in a Changing Social Order.* New York: Orbis, 1992.

———. *The New Catholicity: Theology between the Global and the Local.* New York: Orbis, 1997.

———. ed. *Mission in the Third Millennium.* New York: Orbis, 2001.

———. "Contextualization from a World Perspective." In *ATS Theological Education 1993*, Supplement 1, Vol. xxx. (Autumn 1993): 63–86.

———. "Globalization, Postmodernity, and the New Catholicity." In *For All People: Global Theologies in Contexts*, edited by Else Marie Wiberg Pedersen et al., 13–31. Grand Rapids: Wm. B. Eerdmans, 2002.

Segovia, Fernando. "Aliens in the Promised Land: The Manifest Destiny of U.S. Hispanic Theology." In *Hispanic/Latino Theology: Challenges and Promise*, edited by Ada Mariá Isasi-Diaz and Fernando Segovia, 15–42. Minneapolis: Fortress, 1996.

Segovia, Fernando, and Mary Ann Tolbert, eds. *Teaching the Bible: The Discourse and Politics of Biblical Pedagogy.* New York: Orbis, 1998.

Shaffer, Ellen, and Joseph Brenner. "Trade and Health Care: Corporatizing Vital Human Services." In *Sickness and Wealth: The Corporate Assault on Global Health*, edited by Meredith Fort et al., 79–89. Cambridge: South End, 2004.

Shelly, Judith Allen. "Nursing: Remaining Faithful in the Era of Change." In *The Changing Face of Health Care: A Christian Appraisal of Managed Care, Resource Allocation, and Patient-Caregiver Relationships*, edited by John Kilner et al., 45–62. Grand Rapids: Wm. B Eerdmans, 1998.

Selmanovic, Samir. *It's Really All About God: Reflections of a Muslim, Atheist, Jewish, Christian.* San Francisco: Jossey-Bass, 2009.

Sernau, Scott. *Bound: Living in the Globalized World.* Bloomfield: Kumarian, 2000.

Shiva, Vandana. *Stolen Harvest: The Hijacking of the Global Food Supply.* Cambridge: South End, 2000.

———. "Stealing Nature's Harvest." In *Rethinking Globalization: Teaching for Justice in an Unjust World*, edited by Bill Bigelow and Bob Peterson, 224–27. Milwaukee: Rethinking School, 2002.

Shriver Jr., Donald. *An Ethic for Enemies: Forgiveness in Politics.* New York: Oxford University Press, 1995.

———. "Is There Forgiveness in Politics? Germany, Vietnam, and America." In *Exploring Forgiveness*, edited by Robert Enright and Joanna North, 131–49. Madison: The University of Wisconsin Press, 1998.

Sine, Tom. *Mustard Seed versus McWorld: Reinventing Life and Faith for the Future.* Grand Rapids: Baker Book, 1999.

Sivaraksa, Sulak. "Alternatives to Consumerism." In *Liberating Faith: Religious Voices for Justice, Peace, and Ecological Wisdom,* edited by Roger Gottlieb, 287–91. New York: Rowman & Littlefied, 2003.

Slaughter, Jane. "An Interview with Michael Klare." In *The Witness Magazine,* Vol. 85, No. 10, October 2002, 18–23.

Smith, Sidonie, and Julian Watson. *De/Colonizing the Subject: The Politics of Gender in Women's Autobiography.* Minneapolis: University of Minnesota Press, 1992.

Smith, Christine. *Risking the Terror: Resurrection in this Life.* Cleveland: Pilgrim, 2001.

Sobrino, Jon. *The Principle of Mercy: Taking the Crucified People from the Cross.* New York: Orbis, 1994.

Sölle, Dorothee. *Thinking About God: An Introduction to Theology.* London: SCM Press; Philadelphia: Trinity Press International, 1990.

Song, C.S. *Jesus, The Crucified People.* Minneapolis: Fortress, 1990.

———. *Jesus and the Reign of God.* Minneapolis: Fortress, 1993.

Soriano, Jennifer. "Organizer's Daughter: Labor Organizer Ligaya Domingo." In *Filipinas,* March 2000, 28–29; 31–32.

*SPATS Profile: Toward the New Millennium, 1997-2000.*Suva, Fiji: South Pacific Association of Theological Schools, 1998.

"Special Article: Migrant Health and Migration Medicine: Expanding the Scope of Activities of the ISTM." In *Travel Medicine Newshare,* 3rd Quarter 1999, 1–2.

Spong, John Shelby. *Why Christianity Must Change or Die.* New York: HarperSanFrancisco, 1998.

Spurr, David. *The Rhetoric of Empire: Colonial Discourse in Journalism, Travel Writing, and Imperial Administration.* Durham: Duke University Press, 1993.

Stafford, William. *Darkness around Us Is Deep: Selected Poems of William Stafford.* Edited and with introduction by Robert Bly. New York: HarperCollins, 1993.

Standish, N. Graham. *Becoming a Blessed Church: Forming a Church of Spiritual Purpose, Presence, and Power.* Herndon: The Alban Institute, 2005.

Steere, Douglas. *Mutual Irradiation.* Pendle Hill, Pennsylvania: Sowers, 1971.

Stepick, Alex. "God is Apparently Not Dead: The Obvious, the Emergent, and the Still Unknown in Immigration and Religion" In *Immigrant Faiths: Transforming Religious Life in America,* edited by Karen Leonard et al., 11–37. Walnut Creek: Alta Mira, 2005.

Stepping Up: One Strong United Voice for Minnesota Workers, Vol. 3, No. 3. May/June 2008.

Stewart, Elizabeth-Anne. *Jesus the Holy Fool.* Franklin, Wisconsin: Sheed and Ward, 1999.

Stewart III, Carlyle Fielding. *The Empowerment Church: Speaking a New Language for Church Growth.* Nashville: Abingdon, 2001.

Stockwell, Clinton. "Cathedrals of Power: Engaging the Powers in Urban North America." In *Confident Witness—Changing World: Rediscovering the Gospel in North America,* edited by Craig Van Gelder, 80–93. Grand Rapids: Wm. B. Eerdmans, 1999.

Sugirtharajah, R. S. *Postcolonial Criticism and Biblical Interpretation.* Oxford, UK: Oxford University Press, 2002.

Suchocki, Marjorie Hewitt. *The Fall to Violence: Original Sin in Relational Theology.* New York: Continuum, 1995.

"Suicide bomb kills 20, injures over 100 in Russia." *The Associated Press*. Online: http://www.news.yahoo.com/s/ap/20090817/ap on re eu/eu russia caucasus violence.

Surendra, Lawrence. "Global Solidarity for the Future: Where Do We Go from Here in South-North Relations?" In *Spirituality of the Third World*, edited by K.C Abraham and Bernadette Mbuy-Beya, 20–35. New York: Orbis, 1994.

Sutherland, Arthur. *I was a Stranger: A Christian Theology of Hospitality*. Nashville: Abingdon, 2006.

Sweet, Leonard, ed. *The Church in Emerging Culture: Five Perspectives*. Grand Rapids: Zondervan, 2003.

Tandon, Yash. "The Violence of Globalization." In *Echoes: Justice, Peace and Creation News*, 18 Geneva, Switzerland: World Council of Churches, 2000, 22–27.

Taylor, Mark Lewis. "Spirit and Liberation: Achieving Postcolonial Theology in the United States." In *Postcolonial Theologies: Divinity and Empire*, edited by Catherine Keller et al., 39–55. St. Louis: Chalice, 2004.

Tebtebba Foundation and the International Forum on Globalization, "The Philippine Mining Act of 1995." In *Paradigm Wars: Indigenous Peoples' Resistance to Globalization*, edited by Jerry Mander and Victoria Tauli-Corpuz, 159–60. San Francisco: Sierra Club, 2006.

Thangaraj, Thomas. *The Common Task: A Theology of Christian Mission*. Nashville: Abingdon, 1999.

Thistlethwaite, Susan Brooks. "New Wars, Old Wineskin" in *Strike Terror No More: Theology, Ethics, and the New War*, edited by Jon Berquist, 264–77. St. Louis: Chalice, 2002.

Thomas, Janet. "The Battle in Seattle: The Story Behind and Beyond the WTO Demonstrations." Online: http://www.battleinseattlebook.com/index.html

Thompson Jr., George B. *Treasures in Clay Jars: New Ways to Understand Your Church*. Cleveland: Pilgrim, 2003.

Thompson, Marjorie. *Soul Feast: An Invitation to the Christian Spiritual Life*. Louisville: Westminster John Knox, 2005.

Thorpe, Grace. "Our Homes are Not Dumps: Creating Nuclear-Free Zones." In *Defending Mother Earth: Native American Perspectives on Environment Justice*, edited by Jace Weaver, 47–58. New York: Orbis, 1996.

Tiedemann, Rolf. 'Historical Materialism...' In *The Philosophical Forum*. XV. Fall-Winter 1983–1984.

Tienou, Tite. "Christian Theology in an Era of World Christianity." In *Globalization of Theology: Belief and Practice in an Era of World Christianity*, edited by Craig Ott and Harold Netland, 37–51. Michigan: Baker Academics, 2006.

Tillich, Paul. *The Shaking of the Foundations*. New York: Charles Scribner's Sons, 1948.

———. *Love, Power and Justice*. New York: Oxford University Press, 1954.

Todres, Vladimer. "Chevron pipeline to boost Kazakhstan's exports." In *San Francisco Chronicle*, November 28 2001, B3.

Tomlinson, John. *Globalization and Culture*. Chicago: University of Chicago Press, 1999.

Toxic Wastes and Race in the United States: A National Report on the Racial and Socio-Economic Characteristics of Communities with Hazardous Waste Sites. Commission for Racial Justice. United Church of Christ.1987.

Tucker, Frank. *The White Conscience*. New York: Frederick Ungar, 1968.

Twain, Mark. *The Adventures of Huckleberry Finn*. New York: Washington Square, 1950.

Ucko, Hans, ed. *Changing the Present, Dreaming the Future: A Critical Moment in Interreligious Dialogue*. Geneva: World Council of Churches, 2006.

United Methodist Church, "Comprehensive Community-based Primary Health Care." Online: http://www.new.gbgmumc.org/umcor/work/health/community health

United Nations Human Development Report. 1994.

Unnatural Causes . . . Is Inequality Making Us Sick? California Newsreel, 2008.

Uregei,Yan Celené. "The Kanak Struggle for Independence." In *Pacific People Sing Out Strong*, edited by William Coop, 66–69. New York: Friendship, 1982.

"U.S. Heads for Record Overseas Arms Sales in 2009." Reuters. *The Epoch Times*. July 25, 2010. Online: http://www.theepochtimes.com/n2/content /view/22312.htm

Van Engen, Charles. "The Glocal Church: Locality and Catholicity in a Globalizing World." In *Globalizing Theology Globalizing Theology: Belief and Practice in the Era of World Christianity*, edited by Craig Ott and Harold Netland, 157–79. Grand Rapids: Baker Academics, 2006.

Vanhoozer, Kevin. "One Rule to Rule them All: Theological Method in an Era of World Christianity." In *Globalizing Theology: Belief and Practice in an Era of World Christianity*, edited by Craig Ott and Harold Netland, 85–126. Grand Rapids: Baker Academic, 2006.

Verán, Cristina. "Resisting Exploitation in the Solomon Islands: An Interview with Ian Aujare." In *Witness Magazine*, Vol. 85, No. 10, October 2002, 24–26.

Victorin-Vangerud, Nancy. "From Metaphors and Models to Maps: Thinking Theology with an Archipelagic Imagination." In *Theology that Matters: Ecology, Economy, and God*, edited by Darby Kathleen Ray, 79–90. Minneapolis: Fortress, 2006.

Volf, Miroslav. *Exclusion and Embrace: A Theological Exploration of Identity, Otherness and Reconciliation*. Nashville: Abingdon, 1996.

———. "A Theology of Embrace for a World of Exclusion." In *Explorations in Reconciliation: New Directions in Theology*, edited by David Tombs and Joseph Liechty, 22–33. Vermont: Ashgate, 2006.

———. "Exclusion and Embrace: Theological Reflections in the Wake of 'Ethnic Cleansing,'" *Journal of Ecumenical Studies*, Vol. 29, No. 2 (Spring 1992): 230–48.

Walker, Randi Jones. "Lessons for a New America: An Anglo American Reflection on Korean American Christian History." In *Realizing the America of our Hearts: Theological Voices of Asian Americans*, edited by Fumitaka Matsuoka and Eleazar S. Fernandez, 180–99. St. Louis: Chalice, 2003.

Wallace, Mark *Finding God in the Singing River: Christianity, Spirituality, Nature*. Minneapolis: Fortress, 2005.

———. "Crum Creek Spirituality: Earth as a Living Sacrament" In *Theology that Matters: Ecology, Economy, and God*, edited by Darby Kathleen Ray, 121–37. Minneapolis: Fortress, 2006.

Wallis, Jim. "Changing the Wind: The Role of Prophetic Witness and Faith-Based Initiatives in Tackling Inequality." In *Globalization and the Good*, edited by Peter Heslam, 116–26. Grand Rapids: Wm. B. Eerdmans, 2004.

Warren, Karen. "Feminism and Ecology: Making Connections." In *Environmental Ethic* 9:3–20. 1987.

Warner, Stephen. "Coming to America." In *The Christian Century*. February 10, 2004.

Watt-Cloutier, Sheila. "Climate Change in the Arctic." In *Paradigm Wars: Indigenous Peoples' Resistance to Globalization*, edited by Jerry Mander and Victoria Tauli-Corpuz, 97–99. San Francisco: Sierra Club, 2006.

Wei, Deborah, and Rachel Kamel. *Resistance in Paradise: Rethinking 100 Years of U.S. Involvement in the Caribbean and the Pacific.* Philadelphia, Pennsylvania: American Friends Service Committee in cooperation with Office of Curriculum Support, School District of Philadelphia, 1998.

Welch, Sharon. *A Feminist Ethic of Risk.* Minneapolis: Fortress, 1990.

———. *Sweet Dreams in America: Making Ethics and Spirituality Work.* New York: Routledge, 1999.

Wells, Harold. "Theology for Reconciliation: Biblical Perspectives on Forgiveness and Grace." In *The Reconciliation of Peoples: Challenge to the Churches*, edited by Gregory Baum and Harold Wells, 1–15. New York: Orbis/Geneva: WCC Publications, 1997.

Wessels, Cletus. *The Holy Web: Church and the Universe Story.* New York: Orbis, 2000.

Westhelle, Vitor. "Is Europe Christian? A Challenge to A Viking." In *For All People: Global Theologies in Contexts*, edited by Else Marie Wiberg Pedersen et al., 75–85. Grand Rapids: Wm. B. Eerdmans, 2002.

Whitman, Walt. "There Was a Child Went Forth." In *Leaves of Grass*. Philadelphia: Sherman, 1900.

Wiley, Tatha. "Paul and Early Christianity." In *Empire: The Christian Tradition: New Readings of Classical Theologians*, edited by Kwok Pui-Lan et al., 47–61. Minneapolis: Fortress, 2007.

Williamson, Clark. *Way of Blessing, Way of Life: A Christian Theology.* St. Louis: Chalice, 1999.

Williamson, Clark, and Ronald Allen. *The Vital Church: Teaching, Worship, Community, Service.* St. Louis: Chalice, 1998.

Willimon, William. "What September 11 taught me about preaching." In *In the Aftermath: What September 11 is Teaching Us About our World, our Faith, and Ourselves*, edited by James Taylor, 103–13. British Columbia: Northstone, 2002.

Wink, Walter. *The Powers that Be: Theology for a New Millennium.* New York: Galilee Doubleday, 1998.

———. "The Wrong Apocalypse." In *In the Aftermath: What September 11 is Teaching Us about Our World, Our Faith, and Ourselves*, edited by James Taylor, 47–53. British Columbia: Northstone, 2002.

Woods, C. Jeff. *Congregational Megatrends.* Bethesda: The Alban Institute, 1996.

Wuthnow, Robert. *Acts of Compassion: Caring for Others and Helping Ourselves.* Princeton: Princeton University Press, 1991.

———. *After Heaven: Spirituality in America since the 1950.* Berkeley: University of California Press, 1998.

Yoder, Carolyn. *The Little Book of Trauma Healing: When Violence Strikes and Community Security is Threatened.* Intercourse, Pennsylvania: Good Books, 2005.

Young, Ronald. "American Jews, Christians, and Muslims: Working Together for Peace in the Middle East." In *Interfaith Dialogue and Peace Building*, edited by David Smock, 63–71. Washington, D.C.: United States Institute of Peace, 2002.